ARCHAEOLOGY FOR EVERYONE

ARCHAEOLOGY FOR EVERYONE

Mark Feldman

A Demeter Press Book

Quadrangle/The New York Times Book Co.

Book design: Beth Tondreau

Library of Congress Cataloging in Publication Data

Feldman, Mark, 1946-
  Archaeology for everyone.

  "A Demeter Press book."
  Bibliography: p.
  Includes index.
  1. Archaeology—Methodology. 2. Archaeology.
I. Title.
CC75.5.F44   1977   930'.1   76-9703
ISBN 0-8129-0661-6

Dedicated to the memory of
Stacey Messina

Contents

CONTENTS

List of Illustrations

List of Forms

Acknowledgments

I must take this opportunity to thank a number of individuals and organizations for their assistance as I put together the material for this book.

I am indebted to the American Anthropological Association, the Society for American Archaeology, the Archaeological Institute of America, the New England Antiquities Research Association, the National Park Service and U.S. Department of the Interior, and the Forest Service and U.S. Department of Agriculture for supplying me with current information and data.

My thanks also to the many state archaeologists, university anthropologists, museum directors, archaeological and historical societies, and individuals around the country who informed me of their activities.

I am particularly indebted to Robert E. Stone of Derry, New Hampshire, who kept in constant touch with me, allowed me to pick his brain and search through his extensive files, and informed me of numerous archaeological activities that had come to his attention. My appreciation to Sheryl Gaudrean, for her quick response to my cry for a typist; to Byron Dix, for sending copies of his manuscripts and research reports prior to publication and for keeping me informed of his important work; to Osborn Stone, for taking the time to update me on his research; to Dr. Manuel Da Silva, for his time and hospitality; and to Geof Gray-Cobb, for his special effort.

I must especially thank my editor, Edward Gruson, president of Demeter Press, for his ideas in formulating this book and for his genuine interest in the project.

Finally, and most importantly, I am forever grateful and indebted to that very special person without whose patience and understanding this book would never have become a reality. Thank you, Judy.

Mark Feldman
Litchfield, New Hampshire
June 1976

PART I
What Is Archaeology?

CHAPTER 1

Overview and Definition

Archaeology. The word means many things to many people. To some it conjures up visions of incredible excitement as they imagine finding the treasures of a long-lost empire. To others it means the careful and studious examination of the past with the hope of obtaining information or establishing some important factor or detail about the customs of an ancient people. And to still others it brings thoughts of digging for hours in the dirt under the hot sun, combing through hundreds of pieces of apparently worthless pottery, and finally retiring exhausted to a tent with nothing more than bags full of junk and pockets full of sand to show for the laborious effort.

Archaeology can be all of this, but it is probably best represented by the last two examples, or somewhere in between. It is a discipline that is both exciting and exhausting, challenging and discouraging. But it is a discipline with an immensely important purpose, a purpose that cannot be ignored or treated lightly, for the objects of archaeological inquiry will not remain intact forever. It is a discipline, therefore, that in a very real sense is fighting time and all that the passage of time brings with it.

Archaeology has become a broad discipline, the origins and growth of which will be discussed in other chapters. At this point it is important that we establish just what archaeology is and what archaeologists do. This is not as easy as it sounds, for even among professional archaeologists there are misconceptions and differences of opinion as to the formal and proper functions of those involved in this field, though there is, of course, general agreement as to what archaeology represents.

The reasons for the confusion and differences of opinion are various. Archaeology did not begin as a serious study in England, Europe, Asia, the Far East, and America all at the same time, nor did it begin for the same reasons or with the same goals. Added to this is the fact that archaeological research in different countries requires different—sometimes vastly different—skills and backgrounds. Also, the parent disciplines from which archaeology arose differ depending on where you are and whom you ask. And finally, the type of archaeological research one does depends not only on the country, but also on the region of the country, under investigation.

Many professional archaeologists over the years have devoted no small amount of time and effort toward establishing a cohesive, all-encompassing definition of their field. This has been done not so much for the benefit of their colleagues as for the education of professionals in other fields of scientific inquiry. The attempt has failed, for the very simple reason that archaeology is not a cohesive, singular discipline. On the contrary, with the exception of one factor—that of the archaeological method of excavation—archaeology is a composite of numerous other subjects and their knowledge.

The situation is such that a university graduate may do archaeological research even if he has never taken a formal course in the subject; on the other hand, those with graduate degrees specializing in one aspect of archaeology may not be proficient enough to be allowed on an excavation project.

DEFINITION

In its broadest sense, archaeology is the study of man. This is obviously the definition for quite a number of other disciplines too, from biogenetics to social psychology. As a result of the numerous specialties within the scope of organized science, we have today dozens of subspecialties which concentrate on a specific realm of inquiry or offer a particular approach to obtaining information or assessing data. Archaeology is one of these.

In the strictest sense, archaeology is devoted to the study of "things" that men have made. That is, it is specifically involved with material items, as opposed to political systems or religious philosophies. It is the only system that is supposed to obtain and analyze objects created by the hand of man. All other systems involved with the study of man do not come on the scene until later, for without the archaeologist there is nothing to study or evaluate.

As such, archaeology offers a particular *manner*, or *method*, for studying the human species. This method is known as excavation. The absence of the archaeological method of excavation means the absence of archaeology as a specific discipline.

Archaeology offers the world a method, or system, that is both systematic and descriptive. As the only discipline devoted to obtaining, studying, and interpreting the remains that civilizations have left in the ground, it offers a completely objective analysis of what it finds. Archaeologists are not interested in art for art's sake, or in the aesthetic value of a particular statue or figurine. They are instead interested initially in the preservation of the object for further research, and generally are hopeful that it will prove to be an important historical document. Archaeologists are not collectors.

PURPOSE

The purpose of archaeology is to bring to our attention factors that would otherwise be unavailable. In that it deals with material property, we can learn things that other disciplines do not get involved with. By properly obtaining and evaluating various materials, archaeology affords us the opportunity of increasing our knowledge of a people in many outstanding ways.

If we examine, for example, all the extant writings about an ancient culture in Asia, we will learn quite a bit about the hierarchy of their religious and political system. The reason for this is simply that ancient leaders, priests, and kings wrote about themselves to the exclusion of the common man. And most of the commoners did not have enough training to write down their side of the story. An important point to consider in such extant writings is that of exaggeration: when a priest or prince told his scribes to take down the history of his empire, he naturally expected the account to be favorable. Hence, we may not get a true picture of what really went on.

The archaeologist, however, can fill in many gaps, even if there is no written account. If the archaeologist finds that men and animals of a given society were buried in proper graves, but women and children were buried in the local dump, he can quickly deduce who directed the roles of the sexes. We would not expect a prince to preserve for posterity the fact that men and animals rated higher than women and children. Furthermore, we would hardly expect a lengthy narrative on the day-to-day life-style of the peasant stock; but the archaeologist once again can step in and attempt to offer a pretty clear explanation of how the common man lived his life.

Some archaeologists say they almost prefer no written accounts of a culture's past so as not to be biased. They would rather move right in and start from scratch. Assuming there is something left of a culture that is suitable for excavation, the archaeologist can offer a great deal of insight which no other discipline has the means to do.

Archaeology is concerned with the whole way of life of a people, and therefore wants to find everything it can of their remains. Slowly and painstakingly it tries to piece together any and all possible parts that make up the whole puzzle that describes what was once a culture. Archaeologists are interested as much in the slave as in the ruler, and we all know there have always been many more slaves around than rulers. This discipline, therefore, concentrates more on what people *did* than on what they *say* they did, and it is not unusual for an archaeologist to prove that the written proclamation of a given king is so much nonsense. If a king proclaimed that his people all led happy lives and that there was plenty of food and no disease, the archaeologist can determine to some extent, through the excavation and examination of grave sites, the truth of this claim. If he finds that there appears to have been a particular period when many deaths occurred, or when a great number of children died very young, he can attribute the fact to either starvation or an epidemic. If the deaths were the result of war, the human remains would show evidence of brutal killing. Such information may be available from no other source whatsoever.

The prime duty of the archaeologist is to bring forth as much material as possible through his particular method. When the fieldwork is completed, the research really only begins; the archaeologist never has the last word. If he does his job right and is strict in his objectivity, experts in other fields will be able to begin a systematic interpretation of the data.

I do not mean to suggest that the archaeologist is involved *only* with the excavation to the exclusion of the ensuing analysis of material. Rather, it is a matter of expertise; some archaeologists, for example, are well equipped for excavation but unsophisticated in terms of their ability to synthesize the findings.

SCOPE

To what extent can archaeology be useful? Wherever man has been on this planet for the last two million years, archaeology can be of use. Needless to say, there is much for archaeologists to do, and while some are involved with the megalithic cultures of ancient Iberia, others are working on sites inhabited by American Indians and colonists.

Archaeology adapts itself to the needs of the particular situation or circumstance, and hence covers a very wide sphere in time, space, and subject matter. The scope of archaeology is expanded as necessary: if there are written records, fine; if not, the archaeologist begins with an overall examination of the environment during the period under consideration. This includes the general climate as well as the ability of inhabitants to hunt, farm, and domesticate animals. Determination of any one of these factors can be extremely helpful, for we know that some animals thrived on certain types of agriculture. If the people were hunters, we realize they may have moved more often than if they had been farmers. If the remains of pigs are found, then there must have been forest land about; if sheep, then open grazing fields were plentiful.

If the archaeologist locates more than one specific type of artifact or tool, he can surmise that there was either cultural infusion at one point or else at least an active trade between two or more separate groups. This can also account for the variety of animals or even of architecture.

Another important thing the archaeologist looks for is the remains of domiciles. These can be helpful in establishing the type of social structure within a culture, for if in the center of a primitive "town" there is a single large hut (or the remains of such a structure) surrounded by smaller huts, then obviously there was some form of aristocracy—perhaps a chief or a priest.

In virtually every instance, it is the archaeologist who puts these factors together as he surveys and contemplates a site. The exploration and excavation method of archaeology is therefore of paramount importance. In some cases it is not even necessary—or desirable—to excavate, and here the discriminating archaeologist will refrain from doing so. Whatever is necessary, however, to put together a fully informative picture of the past, to reconstruct as much of the remains as is advisable in order to better come to terms with the people who inhabited a particular area, the archaeologist must do. There is simply no one else to take his place.

The material items with which archaeologists are involved have been referred to as "unconscious evidence." The people who used the material did not purposely bury it for some researcher to dig up a thousand years later; no one in ancient Egypt broke a pot into little pieces just to give an archaeologist a hard time in 1976. The material was not considered by the original owners to be "important historical evidence," hence they gave no thought to how they handled or disposed of it—except, sometimes, in the case of burials.

The archaeologist, therefore, is trying to put together a picture of a people who certainly gave no thought to him, and this does not make his job any easier. When he zeroes in on a particular artifact or implement, its character changes from a piece of junk to a piece of evidence.

CHAPTER 2

Archaeology and Other Disciplines

One of modern man's most fascinating pastimes is the study of himself. We are the only species on earth which considers the past, analyzes the present, and contemplates the future. We look back in time to see where we have come from and what we have been, with the hope that we can establish and control where we will go and what we will become.

Both biologically through our genes and socially through our cultures, we are today the sum total of all that man has even been. We represent yesterday's posterity, the future of the past. Through no control or fault on our part, we are—like all other species—totally influenced by the evolution of our ancestors.

When we stop to consider for a moment that elusive entity known as time, we begin to realize that the existence of man occurred only very recently. We are comparatively sophisticated, for no other animal records its own growth and passing; other beings are concerned with survival in the present. Man alone questions the past.

How do we do this? We must first *establish* a past by *recognizing* one. We must come to terms with the *idea* of a past, present, and future. For only by first realizing that there is a former and a future aspect to the present can we relate to the past. The past is the past because we have established such an idea in the present. We consider the past out of curiosity, for a better understanding of ourselves, for a key to our existence, and in order to find a purpose in the course of past events which have led to the present. This we do through history.

We have established the discipline of history in order to come to terms with time. We can do this only by correlating events, or series of events, and labeling them with dates or periods in time. In this manner we take the concept of time, divide it into ages or periods or years, and place therein those events that have come to our attention. Through history, therefore, we *account* for both the passage of time and the occurrence of past events.

History is a general term we use to reflect the passage of time in an overall sense as we recognize it. We use the term loosely, as we employ phrases like "the history of the universe" or "the history of the earth," along with "the history of science," "the history of publishing," or "the history of the airplane."

In its broadest sense, the term covers all inquiry into the past, from the earliest times to the present. A five-year diary is in effect a history of someone's life during a specific period, just as a detailed study of the automobile can be considered a history of that industry. The word is from the Latin (and Greek) *historia*, meaning "a learning by inquiry or knowledge." History is simply an account, or narrative, of an event.

But to the historian, history is something else. The term has a particular use and a specific meaning to the professional in this field, and the involved amateur should make a point of employing the term correctly. When a historian says history, he means two things: first, he means the history *of man*; and second, he means the history of man *from the time he began keeping records*. In other words, history goes back only to when man learned to write and account for his activities by putting down in words what he picked up in experience. Everything before that is *prehistory*. These two terms, therefore, are employed to divide the past into two specific periods.

We know of course that man's past extends far beyond the point at which he invented writing, and that history prior to that event certainly occurred. Indeed, fully 99 percent of the history of man occurred before he learned to write, but we have no historical documents to prove it. Further, writing was not established throughout the globe all at once. While we know it was widely developed in Mesopotamia and Egypt in the third millennium B.C., we also know it was probably not in use in Britain before the Roman invasion of the first century A.D. Even the earliest systems of writing are only five to six thousand years old, whereas the emergence of man as a species apart from the ape was in full swing over half a million years ago.

Historians are, and have been, primarily concerned with written records. Over the last two hundred years, American historians have published accounts of history *based on written records*. Only within the last hundred years or so has there been any material available about man during the period before he began to write. This phenomenon was a major breakthrough for two reasons. First, modern man had finally realized that his ancestry existed before 3000 B.C.; and second, there was a discipline which began investigating these ancient people. For the first time, we were actually examining cultures that had left no records of their existence. The discipline responsible for this was archaeology, the study of ancient man from the things he left behind, from the way he buried his dead, from the foundations of his shelters, and from the carvings on his monuments.

As a result of the idea of prehistory, archaeology came under the discipline of history. And in Europe to this day, those archaeologists involved with the study of man before written records are known as prehistorians. In the United States, however, archaeology falls under a different discipline, that of anthropology. Of all the disciplines that purport to study man, anthropology is probably the broadest and most involved. Anthropology differs from history in the sense that the former studies man while the latter accounts for man's existence through time.

The field of anthropology is so vast that it covers the physical, cultural, and psychological aspects of man; it even goes one step further by formulating the interrelationships of these three fields of inquiry. Archaeology has been referred to as the anthropology of extinct peoples; it represents a *method* whereby anthropological research is conducted. The counterpart of the European prehistorian is the American palaeoanthropologist, the anthropologist specifically interested in very old ways of life. Prehistory, prehistoric archaeology, and palaeoanthropology are virtually the same field, but with different origins and parent disciplines.

ARCHAEOLOGY AND PREHISTORY

By saying that history begins at the time man learned to write, and that prehistory covers everything prior to that event, we are obviously relegating to the prehistoric era a great deal of time.

The historic period begins approximately five to seven thousand years ago, but this can change if and when new observations are made regarding the onset of writing. A problem of nomenclature, or the labeling of periods in time, arose as a result of the incredible length of time with which archaeologists and historians were involved. Up until a few decades ago, scholars had neatly divided the course of human history into four great phases: prehistory, ancient history, medieval history, and modern history. This caused a number of problems for scholars around the world, which are still under discussion. When translated into different languages, terms like *prehistory* (*la préhistoire*) take on different meanings. In French, the definition is very close to that of English, although it more strictly refers to the Stone Ages. In German, there are different words for "prehistory" and "early history," but confusion over when one ends and the other begins. An added problem is the fact that the prehistory of one region or even country is not contiguous with that of another: some countries established writing earlier than others, hence their prehistory begins earlier. Another problem involves the existence of two different kinds or uses of such terminology: there is the common, mundane, or layman's use and meaning, and then there is the learned, scientific, or scholar's use and meaning. Laymen may begin to use such terms as *prehistoric* as though they were universally accepted, when they are not.

We must also keep in mind that prehistory did not all of a sudden end one day, thereby introducing the era of modern history. In order to break down the long span of prehistoric time into more usable and cogent periods, archaeologists and prehistorians have divided it in terms of its length of time before the beginning of recorded history.

Within the scope of prehistory, the term *protohistory* has been applied as that period just prior to formal history, or just "beginning to become" history. Immediately prior to that period is penehistory, or "almost at" the historic era. Moving further back in time within the scope of prehistory is parahistory, meaning "alongside history." These three subdivisions of prehistoric time are meant to express the period during which man was at the brink of inventing writing, a period that may be referred to as recent prehistory. Prehistory prior to this has been broken down into two major periods: the era of telehistory, which is the Neolithic Age and the beginning of the Early Metal Ages (literally "far off from history"); and antehistory, which represents the beginning or primary Neolithic Age, and goes back to include the Mesolithic and Paleolithic ages (literally, "before all history").

All of this represents the major scope of archaeology, and it is due to archaeology that we are aware of such divisions in prehistory at all.

FRAMEWORK IN PREHISTORY

Without written records, how did archaeology establish the existence of prehistoric man? More to the point, how did archaeology come to terms with the passage of time to the extent of dividing it into periods? Although prehistoric man did not leave daily, annual, or generational diaries for us to pick up and peruse, he did leave behind evidence that he existed, and this evidence represents the framework of archaeological research within prehistory.

It is first necessary to realize that man progressed in certain *stages*, both general and well defined. As man progressed and developed, he improved the manner in which he conducted activities; the type of tools he formed and utilized became more sophisticated; and his ability to survive became more pronounced. All of this is obvious to someone who has excavated or studied ancient remains of a village or campsite. The stages of man's development, therefore, had to be divided. The great divisions, or periods, of man's prehistoric progress are known as the Paleolithic, Mesolithic, Neolithic, Bronze and Iron ages.

These are not arbitrary terms, but are based specifically on the principal materials utilized by *Homo sapiens* during those periods. The first three labels—Paleolithic, Mesolithic, and Neolithic—represent collectively the great Stone Age; the last two—Bronze and Iron—make up the age of metals.

These great divisions are of interest not only to the archaeologist or archaeological researcher. They have not been established merely so that one scholar will be able to determine immediately the period with which another is dealing. More importantly, the divisions are based on physical evidence; and when possible the psychological behavior, sociocultural traditions, and even the biological constitution of these early men are considered. At the time when man utilized only stone, obviously he was not far removed from the animal kingdom; whereas the use of various metals usually leads to cross-cultural infusion—trade, travel, and additional activities. The more sophisticated a being becomes, the more likely he is to enlarge the scope of his geographic knowledge. Hence, the progress of man's growth is of immense value to a number of disciplines in addition to archaeology. Prehistoric study is not solely the province of the archaeologist.

Paleolithic. This first very ancient period lasted anywhere from tens to hundreds of thousands of years. It is the first, primary era in which modern researchers include the onset of human ancestry. This period is so far back in terms of man's evolution that we can hardly differentiate between him and other animals. The early Paleolithic period saw man as virtually another animal, with the same day-to-day pursuits. He was dependent for his food on nature and other animals, though wild vegetables were his most plentiful source. As the Paleolithic period progresses, man learns how to form stone into tools, and here he begins to slowly separate himself from other animals: he can hunt better, challenge adversaries, and become more diversified in his activities. Culturally, he lives like an animal, in a cave, in small family groups. Biologically, he is developing into a more versatile creature, and his mental capabilities undergo a constant growth. Physically, he need not expend so much effort to hunt, for his weapons now make that job a little easier. His chances of survival are enhanced, not only for the reasons noted above, but because he now knows that by making clothes he can stay warmer, and this allows him to travel more extensively. It is the archaeologist who, by his techniques, gave us the evidence to establish or deduce such facts. But it is owing to the cooperation of many other scientific fields that such information is now available.

Throughout the Paleolithic Age, the earth went through many vast changes; the landscape today does not in any way resemble what it looked like as man slowly progressed to his *Homo sapiens* status. Fortunately, however, stone remains were unaffected by such geological alterations, and we therefore have quite a bit of evidence to work with. The archaeologist instinctively begins to look for such evidence in caves, for obvious reasons, and follows up with an investigation of ancient river terraces, hoping to find stone implements in the gravel. As the Paleolithic period slowly came to an end, man slowly widened the gap between himself and other animals for all time. His use of stone accounted principally for his development. If it were not for the archaeologist's method of extracting evidence from the earth, we would never have known when or how the Stone Age began.

Mesolithic.   Man's ability to progress far beyond what any other animal has accomplished brought with it particular problems, and these problems first presented themselves as the Mesolithic Age came into being. Man's growing sophistication at the end of the Paleolithic period meant that he was able to survive under conditions that other animals could not tolerate. The result was that while man staved off destruction, a major source of his food didn't. The cause of this was the movement of the ice cap. The ability to adapt to the then new temperate climate was a feat most successfully accomplished by man. So the Mesolithic Age, or postglacial period, saw man altering his food source from large animals and wild vegetables to fish, birds, and small forest mammals. It was a difficult period, but one in which the struggle for survival brought with it new methods and modes of dealing with problems. The end of the Mesolithic Age was the beginning of a new man, a man who was extroverted and active in his pursuits as opposed to the passive creature he had once been. This alteration began to occur between ten and twelve thousand years ago, and in fact represents the foundation of all future civilization.

Neolithic. The Neolithic Age established once and for all that man ruled the earth. A number of momentous changes occurred, which archaeologists were quick to note. The first of these was that man began to grind and polish tools from stone, instead of just crudely chipping them out. His tools, therefore, had additional uses and were more effective. But possibly the most outstanding change was the one whereby man became a food *producer* instead of merely a food *gatherer*. He had invented agriculture. Another major alteration had to do with man's association with animals: he began to domesticate, rather than merely hunt, them. Thanks to researchers in the fields of geology and climatology, we know exactly why these alterations occurred. Much of the desert area of the earth was established during the Neolithic Age; hence more and more people were forced to inhabit less and less area. There is no vegetation or livestock in the desert, so animals also began moving to those areas more suitable to survival. In this way, both hunters of game and gatherers of vegetation found themselves in the same place with the same problem, and the food supply itself was threatened. In order for man to survive, he had to pool his efforts and resources and this marked the beginning of a cultural society as defined by anthropology. Cultural anthropologists are particularly interested in this period, for it represents social order, interaction between various groups, and differing life-styles. It is owing to the work of anthropologists that we today have so much information about the Neolithic Age.

Bronze Age. As the Neolithic Age drew to a close, the use of stone was common and widespread. The Bronze Age got its name, obviously, from the fact that the use of this metal was discovered. One other factor, however, occurred during this changeover with everlasting effects: the primitive, closely knit villages were becoming towns; these towns were expanding into cities and city-states; and finally, the idea of empires was brought to the fore. The expansion of small villages to towns or cities came about for two reasons. First, the population was steadily growing, and both space and food had to be acquired to handle the increase; and second, the concept of *organization* came about because various groups had to combine their efforts to dig canals, control flooding, set up irrigation, etc.—all of which could be handled much more easily and efficiently through cooperative effort, and all of which would of course benefit all concerned. This cooperative effort brought with it the need for a leader, and here we have the first official hierarchy, or class distinction. The results of organizational efforts was a stockpile of food; hence less time was necessary for the procurement of food, and efforts could be directed toward other pursuits. It was at this point in prehistory that bronze, followed by tin and copper, was used. The quality of tools improved dramatically, particularly as people realized that the three metals could be mixed together to create new standards of durability. The desire and need for more copper and tin brought about trade, and this saw the "specialist" establish his forte: he could do something that most members of the population were not trained to do. Craftsmanship began to spread, and craftsmen were paid in food because they had no time to grow their own. Commerce and agricultural trade expanded, and towns became less sedentary and more active in pursuits beyond their borders. This change was gradual, but it signaled the end of the self-sufficient and self-sustaining character of Neolithic villages. The change was never to reverse itself, and continues to this day. Man had experienced his first social revolution.

This is the beginning of the end of prehistory, as man slowly and painfully reaches what we today refer to as the historical era. As empires enlarged, rulers found themselves with vast lands and numerous people under their control. Their empires had become too unwieldy to govern solely by means of day-to-day discourse with advisors, and the need for written records was evident. Wealth had to be accounted for, and a practical arithmetic was developed. Legal systems arose, calendrical dating came into being, and man began to recognize a past, present, and future. Government planning became a necessity. Iron was developed as an important replacement for bronze, tin, and copper. This made tools cheaper, for iron was readily available.

We have reached the historic era, but the account of the journey through prehistory is nothing less than a major detective story. The further back we go, the more difficult the task for archaeologists. This is due not only to the ravages of time, but also as a result of man using fewer material objects. We therefore know much less about Paleolithic man than about Bronze Age man. Archaeology is principally responsible for *obtaining* all the evidence we have of these prehistoric peoples, but the interpretation of the data comes from many other disciplines. What we read in standard history books is the *result* of all that research and all that interpretation. The historian is the commentator on man's past. The archaeologist brings the past into the laboratory.

ARCHAEOLOGY AND HISTORY

Archaeology has enlarged its scope and framework to include investigation of all peoples, from the Paleolithic to the recent generation. I have concentrated thus far on prehistory mainly because archaeology began as a discipline by looking into the past, and because the uniqueness of this field is best illustrated by showing the challenges it faces as it moves further back in time.

It is safe to say, however, that archaeology can be and is useful whenever there is something to be "dug up," even if it was placed there only a year ago. This may surprise some people, but those who have seen an archaeologist play the Sherlock Holmes role will know what I mean. A proficient archaeologist can determine a number of details regarding an object just by the manner in which he obtains it from the ground. If you were to bury an old dish in your backyard, for example, and then ask an archaeologist to dig it up, he would know whether—despite the object's age—it was buried a week, six months, or two years ago. He can determine this by the depth in the ground at which it was found, the texture of the soil, the size and shape of stones or gravel, and the color, quantity, type, and condition of any growth around the object and on the ground's surface. He may then proceed to tell you that the dish was probably first purchased by your grandmother and handed down through succeeding generations. He knows this by the weight and style of the object, and can determine, if any design was painted on it, whether the background of the owner was Indian, Colonial, French, German, or English. He does this, obviously, through his knowledge of the subject.

In America, the idea of history—much less that of prehistory—is something more recent than in Europe. This is due, of course, to the fact that we always look to Europe, Asia, and the Far East as founding modern civilization. It is not surprising that to Americans the idea of "old" means 1850 or so, especially when we realize that writing was not utilized in California until that year. An old house in some parts of the United States might be one that was built around 1900, whereas an old house in Europe goes back to the Renaissance, and an old house in Egypt goes back two thousand years. As a result of this, most American archaeologists deal with what is "old" in this country or on this continent: the colonists and the Indians—to the exclusion, unfortunately, of much older remains.

The early Colonial settlers, and to a much greater extent the Indians who preceded them, did not make a great effort to record their activities. The Indians did not do so because they did not suspect their way of life was about to be threatened by either the Spanish or the Americans, and hence saw no reason to preserve their historical traditions; and the colonists because they were too busy surviving. Writing was not a popular pastime anyway: it was too laborious, too expensive, and too time-consuming; and many people couldn't read.

This did change, of course, and colonists began keeping track of their activities, though mostly this was done by those who could afford such leisurely pursuits and who were in a position to see the course of history through silver-lined glasses. They did not tell us of many day-to-day activities of the common farmer, cattleman, or tradesman; nor did they bother with details about the building and repairing of structures. Much of what we know today about Colonial America is not from historical documents—though there are of course many—but from archaeological research conducted in the twentieth century.

One may suspect that there is no great hurry to get involved with Colonial archaeology, since it deals with a recent period. But the exact opposite is true. It is more likely that the remains of Colonial America will disappear and that the remains of Egyptian kingdoms will continue, for we are dealing here with the menace of progress, and the bulldozer may not wait. The colonists built their structures mostly out of wood, hence decay sets in quickly if restoration is not immediate. This is not as much a problem with regard to the marble and granite, gold and stone structures in the Eastern Hemisphere.

We have obtained a pretty clear picture of Colonial life and customs, thanks mainly to archaeology rather than history. When Colonial Williamsburg (Virginia) was being rebuilt, it was done so under the auspices of archaeology—not history. It was the archaeologist who determined that in Colonial taverns the main dining area was separate from the kitchen for fear of fire; and it was the archaeologist who established the fact that the dairy and smokehouse are always separate from the main house, with the latter always containing a stove in the ground in the center of the structure. It was the archaeologist also who realized how colonists got rid of their garbage: they tossed it out the back window into the yard and allowed family members and animals to trod upon it and push it into the ground. When a well had lost its usefulness, they filled it up with garbage.

Written records of Colonial days do not bother to offer such interesting details. We do know from historical documents when Plymouth Colony was founded, the name of the first ship bringing settlers, how the British land grants were divided, and the names of the first governors. But we do not know from these documents the main sources of food, how animals were treated, what animals were raised, when or where or how the first building materials—such as bricks—were produced, how or when they began making glass, or what dishes were used in the home. All of these questions have been answered because the archaeologist moved in and offered his particular method of research.

So we see that archaeology can be useful wherever it is possible to gain additional information and data about a particular people, period, or event.

ARCHAEOLOGY AND ART

Some archaeologists might prefer to entitle this subsection "Classical Archaeology," which invokes more an idea or attitude about this subject then it does a methodology. The important thing about art, like writing, in archaeology is that we do not really know how it began. Each time we think we have zeroed in on the original art, an archaeologist comes along and finds something earlier. But this is not really the point of classical archaeology—a field which some do not regard as archaeology at all—as it is really part of the field that deals with the history of art.

When archaeology began during the Renaissance, it was not the type of archaeology that I have been discussing so far in this book. Renaissance archaeology came about when the movement of humanism erupted, and devoted itself to the works of art, buildings, and sculpture of ancient Greece and Rome (hence the term *classical*). Furthermore, this field may be divorced from archaeology in general because its adherents were primarily interested in the aesthetic value of such objects. To the humanists, archaeology was synonymous with art history and the history of the classical movement. To some, archaeology did not even deserve such prestige, and they relegated this discipline to a subspecialty within philology (the study of words, literature, and general scholarship) as merely an additional commentary on the text or painting under consideration.

It is incorrect, therefore, for classical archaeologists to refer to themselves as such. They are, rather, art historians or specialists in the history of the classical period. To apply the term *archaeology* is to suggest that they use the scientific method, which they do not. Archaeology is interested in art, of course, but only if it aids in producing additional evidence about a past civilization. In addition, archaeology as a formal discipline never considers an object for its aesthetic value.

ARCHAEOLOGY AND GEOLOGY

If one had to choose a single discipline within science which is most closely related to archaeology, that discipline would have to be geology.

Geology (from the Greek *geo-logos*, "description of the earth") is that discipline concerned specifically with the structure, formation, and development of the earth's crust and its layers. Specialists within geology may concentrate on individual rock types, movements of rivers, early forms of life found as fossils in rocks, or vegetative growth. Offshoots of geology, therefore, include petrology, mineralogy, paleontology, historical geology, economic geology, and physical geology.

These specialties have been of immense assistance to the archaeologist. Indeed, geology actually created—as we shall see in Part III—the formation of an archaeological method, and was a sufficiently exact science by 1860. A healthy respect for and knowledge of what geology is and what geologists do is necessary for the amateur today. Geology deals with terrestrial time on a much larger scale than any other field of inquiry. Its scope covers a range of over two billion years—the age of certain rocks.

Experts in this field contend that there are "no traces of a beginning, no prospect of an end." Hence, the parameters of the geologist's inquiry have no bounds. Geology attempts to explain how the earth came to be the way it is, and it does this—as do archaeology and history—by stages. Geology describes its stages in terms of eras, of which there are five; epochs, of which there are twenty-two; and ages, of which there are seven. Archaeology is concerned with only the most recent geological era: the Cenozoic, or Modern, Era, which extends back one million years; the three most recent epochs: the Recent, the Pleistocene (or Glacial), and the Pliocene, during which occurred mental dominance by man, periodic glaciations, development of Stone Age cultures of man, the extinction of large mammals, the change of ape-man into man, and the cooling of climate; and the most recent age: the Age of Man.

The geologist can tell the archaeologist about changes that have occurred on the earth's surface during a particular point in prehistory. He can offer information regarding the movement of the ice cap, the changing course of rivers and streams, alteration in the land surface, and data on rock formations. All of this is of course very important to the prehistorian, particularly the researcher involved in the Paleolithic and Mesolithic ages.

We learn also from the geologist that rocks will in time crumble into loose material, called mantle rock, when exposed to the weather. In this process, known simply as weathering, huge blocks of stone disintegrate until little is left but mud and sand. Different climates produce different results. In moist climates, where plant decay supplies acids to ground water and chemical decomposition predominates, mantle rock and soil are formed so rapidly that little rock is exposed. In very dry climates, on the other hand, rock breaking by mechanical processes goes on slowly, and desert plains are built up of rock particles insufficiently weathered to form a true soil.

All of this is of interest to the archaeologist as well as to specialists in other fields. As the study of the earth, geology as a discipline offers at the very least a context in which the archaeologist places his spade.

ARCHAEOLOGY AND CULTURE

Culture, first and foremost, is a form of nonbiological, social heritage that flows from the past and continues through one generation after another. Every human being has lived within some form of cultural matrix. Man depends upon his culture for the development of his human qualities, one of the most important of which is social organization. Culture dictates relationships and social arrangements; it establishes survival needs; it protects and educates the young. Culture is a means of coping with the world.

Differences in culture originate in the geographic and historic factors unique to a society. A culture is influenced by climate, weather, natural resources, and relationships with neighboring societies. The archaeologist is not only interested in what we know about past cultures, but is able to initiate new ideas in the form of evidence for cultural changes.

In the United States, the study of culture under the wing of anthropology is particularly prominent. The palaeoanthropologist has established a number of important factors necessary for a more steadfast understanding of man. We know, for example, that there is a certain influence received by people that is extrasomatic: apart from the body. Culture is *learned* behavior; it is everything a person would *not* do if he were born and raised completely isolated from all people and society. Cultural habits and traditions are learned, and they are passed on from generation to generation or from society to society by means of interaction or cultural infusion. A particular artifact or monument represents some kind of relationship between the person who utilized the artifact or built the monument and the parent culture. The job of the archaeologist is to connect an artifact with the culture that spawned it.

We know that as an adaptive behavior, and as a means of coping with the environment, culture is uniquely human. Man reacts to environmental pressures, like cold weather, by performing tasks to protect himself as dictated by his culture. Culture, therefore, can be perishable, for we cannot excavate the dictates of a culture; nor can we dig up a system of beliefs or a social organization or a political process or a set of ideas, ideals, and attitudes. But we can excavate the material *remains* of a system or organization, and in that culture is *patterned* we can perceive a reflection of that pattern and produce a picture of the culture involved. The archaeologist deals with the products of a culture, rather than with culture itself. His job is to find and systematically evaluate such products, and then discover characteristics of the culture represented in them.

CHAPTER 3

The Training of Archaeologists

Having seen what archaeology is, how it deals with and contributes to our knowledge of man's past and history, and how it is associated with other disciplines, we should now look at the training of an archaeologist.

This chapter will deal with the educating of archaeologists today, the various emphases within that training, and the different kinds of archaeological research that may be undertaken. The beginning amateur in this field will thus get a good idea of what is necessary in order to specialize in a certain aspect of prehistory.

Probably no two archaeologists living today have had precisely the same training and background. A student going for his degree in medicine will major in biology or biochemistry in college, attend a recognized medical school, serve an internship at an accredited hospital where he may begin to specialize in say, orthopedics, fulfill his residency requirements, and then decide the manner in which he will begin to practice. In archaeology, it is not so easy to establish the necessary requirements in order to "set up practice."

There are a number of reasons for what may appear to many readers as a haphazard situation. Archaeology, particularly in the United States, is a very young discipline, and for many years there were no formal courses in the subject available at universities. But there were still archaeologists who came out of universities and whose training was diverse. That is, they studied different subjects *of interest* to archaeology and then went out to perform the tasks that archaeologists do. Archaeology is still flexing its muscles, still trying to establish itself as a specific field of inquiry, rather than as an offshoot of one or more sciences.

There are many archaeologists today whose formal training is in geology, but who, as they conducted their fieldwork, became familiar with the archaeological method of excavation. After additional training in this method, plus perhaps a study of anthropology, they crossed the street and are known now as archaeologists. Although a young field, archaeology has acquired a massive accumulation of knowledge and experience, and anyone desiring to become a part of this field must familiarize himself with it.

Archaeology has also grown very complex and has subdivided itself as have other sciences. It is difficult, therefore, for a university to make available specific courses whereby a student will become an archaeologist, for much depends on the period in history in which the student is interested as well as the area of the world where he may work. A solid background in megalithic archaeology will not be of much help in studying the Pueblo, just as a profound knowledge of classical archaeology will not be of much use in Colonial Williamsburg. But the single most important prerequisite in archaeology is both an intrinsic appreciation for and practical knowledge of history, the growth and movements of peoples, the great empires, and the unfolding of time on earth and man's part in it.

Many archaeologists today devoted undergraduate years to history as well as geology, but this is only the beginning. A well-rounded background in archaeology includes some knowledge of physical anthropology, which is the study of physical types and races. It is closely associated with biology, only on a larger scale, and is related to zoology. The physical anthropologist compares ancient and modern man, studies the effects of food and environment on the human organism, and seeks to find out what physical types are produced by the mixing of races. An understanding of cultural anthropology is also important; it is the study of human ways of living, and is therefore related to the social sciences. The cultural anthropologist tries to find out what particular customs and beliefs a people developed, how they procured and prepared food, how they clothed themselves, how they made shelters, and what tools, weapons, and utensils they used. He contrasts and compares cultures, to see how one has influenced another. A further field of importance to the archaeologist is linguistics, the study of the relationships between languages. It deals with the growth and change of language systems.

In that archaeology is yet another branch of anthropology in the United States, most archaeologists here do have some background in these other subjects. American archaeologists are primarily anthropologists who have chosen to study ancient peoples, as opposed to ethnologists who study living peoples. Obviously, it is impossible for any one archaeologist to become an expert in half a dozen fields, and it is unnecessary. What is wanted, however, is an overall comprehension of the knowledge available from these other subjects. The more an archaeologist knows, the more he can accomplish with regard to interpreting what he has found.

In a world used to the specialist, the archaeologist must also zero in on a particular framework. Although he may have a broad knowledge of many fields, he will undoubtedly specialize. This is advisable for two reasons. First, he owes it to the past to devote all his mental and physical efforts to the particular period he has chosen to study and work in; and second, he will specialize in an area where he expects to find employment and where he expects to be useful. There are not many full-time archaeologists around, and it is highly unlikely that there will ever be any vacant posts available on a large scale.

I have been dealing thus far with archaeology as a branch of anthropology in the United States, but there is another kind of archaeologist whose training—or rather the *emphasis* of whose training—is different. He is the classical or classical-biblical archaeologist, whose primary interest is in fine arts and history. He is an archaeologist only in the sense that he deals with material remains of a people. He is not trained in the university department of anthropology; rather, he receives his training from either the fine arts or classics department, or both. The difference is that he may wish to specialize in biblical history as opposed to the early history of Western man based on his art.

The classical-biblical archaeologist concentrates on learning a number of ancient languages and their history. This will lead him into the field of epigraphy (the deciphering and translating of ancient inscriptions), where he will learn to decipher ancient texts. He must next become completely familiar with the history of art and all manner of sculpture, and become a specialist in ancient painting. Finally, an immensely important part of his training is in architecture. When new discoveries are made that require an expert in early architecture, the classical archaeologist is called in. Some classical-biblical archaeologists are very experienced and knowledgeable in archaeological excavation, and handle the survey work, the excavation itself, plus all the postexcavation research and interpretation required. Many get nervous when they hear that a palaeoanthropologist is digging up a site that may produce valuable paintings, sculpture, or similar relics from the Greek or Roman Empire. On the other side of the coin is the classical-biblical archaeologist who has never been out of a museum, and who doesn't know the difference between a spade and a spoon. He is the in-house researcher, the interpreter of what has been found. While others are digging, he is poring over ancient scrolls or carefully analyzing the remains of a painting or seeking to determine when a bust could have been made. He is trained as art historian rather than as archaeological anthropologist, which means that he is interested in the aesthetic value of his objects of study.

THE AMATEUR ARCHAEOLOGIST

It is now time to discuss the amateur in this field, and what is available for him or her in terms of training. First, however, it is necessary to explain just what an amateur archaeologist is.

Anyone interested or involved in archaeological research who does not hold a full-time post as an archaeologist or who is not solely dependent on archaeology for his income is an amateur archaeologist. The distinction is *not* based on competence; it is made only to establish the difference between those actively employed full-time and those whose activities preclude such an arrangement. Part of this distinction does, of course, involve the fact that the professional, full-time archaeologist is more elaborately trained with a more formal background; but this, in and of itself, has little if anything to do with competence. The term *amateur*, therefore, is not a description of one's abilities or usefulness.

Amateur archaeologists come from all different backgrounds. Their common thread is simply a desire to study history, prehistory, or culture, and the method they have chosen to do this is the archaeological one. Some have learned to do this by following around professionals on excavations; others have studied with more advanced amateurs; some have devoted many years to reading anything and everything available on the subject; while still others have spent previous years during their spare time in museums quizzing curators and concentrating on collections of art, pottery, bones, clay, and arrowheads.

The different levels of amateur archaeology, the opportunities available, and the contributions of amateurs in this field will all be discussed in later chapters. Suffice it to say at this point that there is a great need for serious, competent amateur archaeologists, and they come in all sizes and shapes. A friend of mine who is an M.D. specializing in internal medicine in Rhode Island has devoted over twenty years to a single archaeological project; a technical librarian for a major defense contractor is also one of the most esteemed members of the amateur archaeological community; a mechanical engineer with a telephone manufacturing firm will be remembered as one of the outstanding and most active amateurs of his day; an attorney in Connecticut devotes all his spare time to Indian culture; a housewife in Oklahoma is known throughout the world for her discoveries and research; a marine biologist in Massachusetts has virtually altered the course of America's prehistory by his knowledge of linguistics and epigraphy. All of these people and thousands more like them are amateur archaeologists. They have their own professions and careers in everything from science writing to selling shoes and from repairing automobiles to rewiring houses.

Their education, background, and life-styles are different, but they all have one thing in common: they all are seriously interested in the course of man's activity through the passage of time. As was the case with the growth of archaeology, the amateur (see chapter 6) represents the future of archaeology to a much, much greater degree than does the professional in this field.

It is important, therefore, that as archaeology grows and becomes more complex, the amateur be prepared. "There is no substitute for experience," the axiom goes, and amateur archaeologists are classic examples of the truth of this statement. Many of them have a great deal more field experience than most professionals, experience accumulated over years of devoted activity on weekends and during vacations. Other amateurs have spent a lot of time reading and studying about a particular era of history or prehistory, but have refrained from actively participating in excavation work.

There are four main ways in which one may become familiar with this subject: attending lectures or meetings, reading as much as possible, helping on excavation work to the degree that one is competent to do so, and attending school. The second way, reading comprehensively and exhaustively, is completely up to the individual. How to get to attend meetings and how to arrange to help on expeditions will be discussed in detail further along in this book. But it is the fourth way, formal schooling, that concerns us in this chapter, for it involves the formal training of amateur archaeologists under the auspices of a university. This can involve attending a class or two a week in the evenings or a summer course for two months; it may include on-the-spot excavation work or just classroom instruction; it may be open to literally anyone interested, or to high school graduates and college undergraduates; it may result in academic credits or a certificate of proficiency; or it may be only an informal introduction to fieldwork.

An amateur must first decide on his own the extent to which he is able to contribute his time. If he is satisfied with working along with others in the field in order to be the recipient of valuable experience, then perhaps the classroom is not for him; indeed, he may be way ahead of an introductory course. On the other hand, an amateur may feel uncomfortable tagging along on an excavation project without benefit of some formal training. Theoretical training in the classroom can offer a firm foundation for the amateur, and will probably afford him more opportunity to express his ideas and capabilities when working alongside a professional archaeologist or with a group of fellow amateurs.

FIELD SCHOOLS

A number of universities in the United States offer a special summer course for those interested in archaeology. These are known as field schools and are usually active as soon as the formal semester ends. I have listed at the end of this chapter those schools which actively involve the student in excavation work as part of his training, and have included all relevant information.

The majority of these universities and educational institutions welcome not only college undergraduates but also high school graduates, high school students, and anyone else interested enough to attend. Two purposes are served: the beginning amateur has the opportunity to both observe and participate in active excavation work; and the professionals who direct such operations have at their disposal many willing hands to assist in the project. There is no reason whatsoever, therefore, for anyone interested in archaeology but involved in another career or other pursuits to assume there is no room for his interest or potential services. Anyone who really wants to can make himself useful, and the extent of that usefulness has only to do with the amount of time the individual can offer.

SPECIALTIES WITHIN ARCHAEOLOGY

It will not be too long before the amateur in this field begins to realize the extraordinary diversity of the subject. From Indian and Colonial archaeology to classical and Eastern archaeology, the amateur comes across numerous specialties and subspecialties. Just as it is both impossible and self-defeating to study and specialize in *all* fields of medicine, so is it unwise to try and become fluent in all branches of archaeology. The amateur, like the professional, should attempt to concentrate on one or perhaps two aspects of this field—particularly if he wants to be recognized as one who is proficient in his work and dependable in his results.

The easiest, initial way to break down and categorize the complexity of archaeological inquiry is geographically. The amateur should first become familiar with who studies what where. If he wishes to specialize in Chinese archaeology, he will have little opportunity to do so in the Rocky Mountain region of the North American continent. The geographical divisions are America, Europe, the Mediterranean, Africa, Asia-Australia, and the Near, Middle, and Far East. These divisions are obviously very general. In America alone we have such separate and diverse cultures as the Vikings, Indians, Colonists, Spaniards, and even the Iberians! In Europe the problem is still more complicated.

It is far better to study archaeology in terms of time, or the flow of man's culture historically, than by continent or even country. Some archaeologists specialize in a certain culture, at a particular point in history, in a specific region of a country. The idea of a whole country coming under the archaeologist's gaze is like suggesting that someone zero in on a study of all the species of all animals that ever existed on the earth. When we consider the fact that more species have died out than exist today, and that the Age of Man began about a million years ago, the idea of specializing seems a bit more palatable to all but the most expansive mind.

TYPES AND KINDS OF SPECIALTIES

A better way to categorize archaeological inquiry than the geographic break-down is to combine certain regions, or even continents and countries, of the world with points in time. That is, instead of dealing with the Paleolithic era or the prehistory of Europe, we combine them to form European Paleolithic archaeology. Each division requires additional training in certain subjects and particular proficiency in others. If one is planning to be active in archaeological research devoted to analyzing man during the paleolithic period in Europe, then a full and working knowledge of Roman pottery will be of little use, unless one has his own ideas about rewriting the course of cultural evolution.

The following divisions amply illustrate, I trust, the different kinds of archaeology involved.

European Paleolithic Archaeology. The Paleolithic period, as noted in chapter 2, extends back from tens of thousands to hundreds of thousands of years. It is as far back as we go in terms of relating to man.

Obviously, therefore, archaeology works very closely with geology, for two reasons: geology is familiar with such vast expanses of time (geologists deal in tens of millions of years); and the archaeologist usually obtains his material from geological deposits. We learn from geology the significance of terrestrial structure and how it has changed since Paleolithic man viewed it, and we learn about glacial movement and river beds. Assuming the archaeologist obtains animal bones, for example, he must be able to identify them as having come from the Paleolithic period. Formal excavation is rarely conducted here, because objects are by now too deeply buried and because they undoubtedly are far from their original position. A knowledge of stone implements is mandatory, for these represent virtually all we have left of Paleolithic man. Little else has survived, little else was used, and little else is obtainable. So the three subjects of interest to the archaeologist here are geology, zoology, and the typology of stone implements.

European Mesolithic Archaeology. This period in Europe was similar to the previous, Paleolithic, except that it is now more conducive to archaeological research. We know from geology that the Mesolithic period came after the end of the Ice Age, hence excavation becomes a more productive pursuit. We can not only determine *where* Mesolithic man was by finding his material remains pretty much where he left them, but we can also determine more about how and where he lived. The weather conditions underwent a change during this era, and man moved to protect himself. Climatology, therefore, has influenced archaeological thinking here. The use of fish and shellfish as well as vegetation came into play as a necessary source of food, so special knowledge of these subjects from within the scope of science is important. Climatology, botany, and marine biology should be studied by the student of archaeology working in this particular period.

European Neolithic Archaeology. Added to the knowledge necessary in studying Mesolithic man is the need now for the archaeologist to study the typology of pot forms. As more material from Neolithic man may now be excavated, the archaeologist's job actually becomes more difficult and involved, because he must deal with more *types* of objects. Because agriculture was developed during this period, an understanding of agronomy along with botany is paramount. Also, Neolithic man in

Europe brought with him the idea of burial mounds, most of which today are hardly recognizable; therefore a knowledge of *structural* typology becomes necessary.

Bronze Age Europe.   This era obviously brings with it a greater diversity of tools, weapons, and utensils, so the student here must understand the principles of distribution through various contiguous societies. A knowledge of culture, or cultural anthropology, becomes necessary now, for man has become more mobile as a result of his newly gained efficiency. The study of burial mounds continues, and since as man entered the Iron Age in Europe the idea of trade expanded greatly, other cultures are entering and leaving a certain area on a regular basis. With the introduction of metals, a whole new specialty is opened up to the archaeological researcher, and a whole new typology must be mastered. The end of the Iron Age in Europe introduces yet another major subject: art. A working knowledge of art history then becomes essential for the student.

The reader can easily deduce that a knowledge of certain subjects is beneficial depending on the kind of archaeology involved, and that a careful study of post–Iron Age European metal flints will not aid the team trying to analyze the movements of Mesolithic man. This is not to suggest that such knowledge is a waste of time; on the contrary, only as a result of such knowledge will an archaeologist realize that he is indeed digging up Iron Age man at all. I mean only to suggest that if one begins in this field with the intention of working with, and in a locale necessary for, Mesolithic man, he should devote his energy to studying applicable branches of science *first*, and then perhaps expand his outlook and sphere of knowledge.

Europe during the Roman Empire.   This period marks the first time that archaeology comes across recorded history in Europe, and must therefore determine the extent to which such records are accurate. Written documents during this time were, to be kind, scanty, and we must rely to a very great degree on the archaeologist and his spade. Since Britain was controlled by Rome, her history was put down in Rome by Romans; the conqueror always explains what happens. Similarly, the prevailing history of World War II was written by the Americans, not the Germans. The first step a student takes here is to familiarize himself not only with Roman history, but with Roman organization and culture, as well as social philosophy to include political systems. Architecture also becomes an important subject, as do the history of construction of roads and the typology of coins. A knowledge of military science helps the student of archaeology perceive what made Romans tick. Since many English towns were established during the Roman period, an appreciation of Roman town planning is desired. Structural analysis becomes paramount to the archaeologist here, for there are a great numbers of different *kinds* of buildings, and a good researcher must determine if he has located the basement of a farmhouse, the foundation of a villa, or the remains of a town hall. A familiarity with engineering, mosaics, and linguistics will be put to good use by the student of archaeology working in Roman Britain.

Europe and the Dark Ages.   When Roman control ceased to exist in Britain, so did the continuity of written history—scant though it was. The archaeologist must again work from scratch, so to speak, and keep things in their proper chronological frame until at least some kind of documentation begins again. The archaeologist knows now that various cultures moved across Britain, so a need to recognize derivatives of language arises. It was during this period that what we know today as England was established, and we come face to face with Anglo-Saxons. Linguistics, particularly that branch dealing with place-names, affords the researcher a chance to separate the numerous groups, sects, and cultures that made their way across Britain during the Dark Ages. Cultural infusion occurred to a marked degree, and dialects were formed for the benefit of all concerned.

Medieval Europe.   As stated earlier in this book, an understanding of history is immensely important to the student of archaeology. The various stages of progress in man's evolution did not occur all at once throughout the world. While writing was in use in Egypt a few thousand years before Christ, it did not show up in California until just over a hundred years ago. When man was in the throes of the Mesolithic era in Britain, he was well into the Neolithic stage in the Near East. And the Medieval period in Europe was not only much slower in coming from the Dark Ages, the Dark Ages never even happened in the Mediterranean; that area moved right into the Middle Ages. Specific periods in history, therefore, are not contiguous with one another on every continent. It was because of the onset of the Medieval era that history becomes the parent discipline of archaeology in Europe; there are written records galore about and from this period, and the historian assumes that archaeology can add very little. This attitude also marks a difference between the historical and archaeological examination of a people, for the former concentrates on the national activities of a political and social system whereas the archaeologist examines and attempts to put together a picture of life on a more mundane, ordinary level. Further, there is less need for excavation, because many of the remains are above ground and visible. There are exceptions, of course, and the archaeologist is quick to note them. A knowledge of both engineering architecture and architectural history are mandatory here, followed by a practical familiarity with sculpture, coins, jewelry, the history of armor, ceramics, and other similar subjects.

Mediterranean Archaeology.   The study of Mediterranean archaeology, perhaps more than anything else, illustrates profoundly the importance of the archaeological method, for we are dependent almost entirely on excavation for the information we have gathered and the results we have obtained. I am referring specifically to the preclassical period of Crete, Greece, Malta, Sicily, Cyprus, and areas surrounding the Mediterranean. The student of archaeology is now confronted with the study of the typology of styles in painting, designing, and pottery, as well as what is generally referred to as stylistic analysis. In addition to this, a precise knowledge and experience in the excavation technique is mandatory, as is a broad knowledge of Eastern history. Those who do make such an effort will immediately realize that the cultural center of the world made its way from the East to the West during this period, for the Greek civilization was about to take hold.

Classical Archaeology.   This type of archaeology has already been sufficiently covered in this chapter, but I will add that the classically oriented archaeologist is primarily interested in the products and objects of Greece, the Hellenists, and Rome. A major advantage here is the fact that students of this specialty usually work with prime and easily identifiable material and are secure in the knowledge that they pretty much know what will be excavated in a certain area.

Prehistoric Near Eastern Archaeology. The excavation itself is alone of great importance here, for anything turned up in the process can be regarded as gravy; that is, any little bit of information gleaned from the ground can only add to our attempt at formulating a theory about ancient man in the Near East. Geographically, this area of the world probably represents the foundation of civilization even as we know it today, hence it is of particular interest and even fascination to many students of archaeology. An understanding, if not a solid knowledge, of the culture and social functions of this part of the world is absolutely essential, for we cannot transplant our American or European ideas and ideals in the Near East and thereby make value judgments on what they "probably" did or "should" have done as they progressed through prehistory to founding a way of life. We must be able to identify with the importance of *their* social organization, *their* economic and political system, *their* philosophy and life and religious affinity, and *their* attitudes about friends and foes. Some Western students of archaeology, as they move into the active study of a completely foreign type of culture, are unable to divorce themselves from the effects of their own cultural heritage; hence their ability to synthesize data is weak.

Historic Near Eastern Archaeology. This period marks the beginning of written records for the first time in the history of the world, about 5,000 years ago. The archaeologist's job here becomes increasingly complicated, for as man progresses he becomes more complex and more diversified. It is now necessary, without exception, for the student of archaeology to specialize. Every archaeologist involved with the Historic Near Eastern period concentrates on specific things, with the assumption that someone else is concentrating on other aspects. Even within the Near East geographically, researchers must specialize in a certain country or region, for while the Egyptian Empire was leading man to new heights of sophistication up to the Pyramid Age, the areas in and around Palestine and Syria were just barely moving into the Bronze and Iron ages. Those archaeologists who study linguistics and have experience in epigraphy will find plenty to do, for there is a wealth of material needing attention; indeed, there are vaults in museums containing hundreds of manuscripts that have never been translated because there just aren't enough accomplished epigraphers to go around. This branch of archaeology has become so broad that a new discipline, Egyptology, was established to identify those whose education, background, and experience deals almost solely with the history of Egypt.

Prehistoric Indian Archaeology. This kind of archaeology also represents a huge basis for research, principally because Asian Indian prehistory goes back 5,000 years. In addition, many cultures, subcultures, and societal organizations make up the era that brought India into the Historic period. Therefore, once again the student of archaeology must specialize or get bogged down in the immense amount of information and data produced by research. Prehistoric archaeology here is devoted mostly to the Indus Valley, and it is because of archaeology that we became aware of the magnificent cities of Mohenjo-Daro and Harappa. The sophistication of this area is matched only by the cultures that dwelt along the Nile, Tigris, and Euphrates rivers, and we now know that trade probably existed between the two in spite of a lack of written documentation.

Historic Indian Archaeology. The student of archaeology may wish to move into the Historic period in India, which is little related to the Prehistoric. Here attention is focused mainly on art and literature and on the Hindu, Buddhist, and Muslim cultures, which continue today. An understanding and appreciation of social, religious, and political systems of this region is therefore of major importance to the archaeologist who hopes to procure and interpret data. The main problem for the researcher in this field involves the numerous cultural and subcultural groups, a majority of which were not in contact with one another, preferring geographically and socially isolated existences. Chronologies need to be established, infusion theories must be backed up with more evidence, and excavations need to be conducted, all of which offers the student an immense opportunity and promise.

American Archaeology. This kind of archaeology has perhaps been more correctly termed New World archaeology, and it also covers a broad spectrum. Students of archaeology on this continent may specialize in Mayan, Inca, Aztec, or Olmec civilizations; the Vikings; Colonial or Historical archaeology; or Indian—known more specifically as Amerindian archaeology. The amateur need not assume, therefore, that he or she must journey to Cairo or Bahawalpur to find something to do. As opposed to other kinds of archaeology, American archaeology is conducted almost solely by Americans, and very little has been done compared to the wealth of opportunity available. The amateur archaeologist is more needed in North America than anywhere else on earth, and he is needed now. Most professional archaeologists in the United States specialize in either Historical (Colonial) or Amerindian research, for which there is a vast store of material awaiting attention. Almost everyone who has ever tried has located some remnant of Indian occupation, and evidence of the Colonial period can be found by walking down the street almost anywhere in the eastern United States.

ARCHAEOLOGISTS AND TREASURE HUNTERS

If a student of archaeology has what may be nicely described as itchy fingers, he will certainly be of no help to his cause or the history of his culture in the long run. The difference between the archaeologist and the treasure hunter is that the former has a built-in respect for the objects he retrieves and studies, while the latter looks only for either material gain or something to add to his personal collection.

Although the archaeologist deals with *things*, he is in effect digging up the remains of human beings—the results of man's thoughts and activities. As such, excavated remains belong to everyone; they are not the personal province of the excavator.

The history of archaeology is filled with horror stories of people hiding ancient relics until they got the right price from the researcher, of professional archaeologists building private collections that make many museums pale by comparison, and of amateur archaeologists trading important finds with one another to enhance the attractiveness of their mantelpieces. This sort of thing rarely happens today, if only because both professionals and amateurs won't stand for it, and because it is against the law.

FIELD SCHOOLS

ALABAMA

University of Alabama
Department of Anthropology Field School
P.O. Box 6135
University, Alabama 35486
205-348-5947
Location: Black Warrior River, 14 miles south of the Tuscaloosa campus.
Excavation Site: Major Mississippi ceremonial center at Moundville.
Tuition & Fees: Regular summer school tuition plus $60 for housing and equipment.
Credits: 12 hours per course for undergraduates.

ARIZONA

University of Arizona
Department of Anthropology Field School
Tucson, Arizona 85721
Location: Grasshopper, Fort Apache Indian Reservation, east central Arizona.
Excavation Site: 500-room Pueblo-occupied site, from 1275 to 1400 A.D.
Tuition & Fees: All provided, plus room and board, to worthy undergraduate students and advanced students.

ARKANSAS

University of Arkansas
Archaeological Field School
University Museum
Fayetteville, Arkansas 72701
501-575-3555
Location: Ouachita Mountains of west central Arkansas.
Excavation Site: Caddo Gap, Upper Caddo River Valley.
Tuition & Fees: Instate students, $105; out-of-state students, $225; living expenses, if necessary, $120.
Credits: 6 hours to undergraduates.

CALIFORNIA

California State University
Anthropology Department
Sacramento, California 95819
Location: Flagstaff, Arizona
Site: The Kahorsho Site, 12–13th century Sinagua.
Tuition & Fees: $300 to $600
Credits: 9 semester units.

California Polytechnic University
Extension Division
San Luis Obispo, California 93407
805-546-2053
Location: Mission San Antonio De Padua, Jolon.
Excavation Site: Same as location.
Tuition & Fees: $275
Credits: 6

COLORADO

Colorado State University
Department of Anthropology Field School
Fort Collins, Colorado 80523
Location: Near Fort Collins area.
Excavation Site: In foothills near Livermore.
Tuition & Fees: $160 to $410
Credits: 3 to 5

Trinidad State Junior College
Department of Anthropology
Trinidad, Colorado 81082
Location: Just outside Trinidad.
Excavation Site: Trinidad Reservoir Projects, cosponsored by the U.S. Army Corps of Engineers.
Credits: 1 to 9

University of Northern Colorado
Department of Anthropology
Greeley, Colorado 80639
Location: East of Greeley, in the Colorado High Plains.
Tuition & Fees: $102 to $432

CONNECTICUT

University of Connecticut
Department of Biocultural Anthropology
Storrs, Connecticut 06268
Location: (1) Cyprus; (2) Connecticut
Excavation Site: Cyprus, the city-state of Idalion, a survey of the Dhali region, and excavation in the vicinity of Lythrodonda.
Tuition & Fees: $45 per credit plus transportation and other essential costs.
Credits: 6 to 9

Western Connecticut State University
Same as the University of Connecticut

WASHINGTON, D.C.

Catholic University of America
Department of Anthropology
Washington, D.C. 20064
Location: 8 miles south of Front Royal, Virginia.
Site: "Thunderbird Site," Paleo-Indian culture.
Tuition & Fees: $150 to $260
Credits: Variable or none.

George Washington University
Department of Anthropology
American Studies Program
Washington, D.C. 20052
Location: Five locales in central Mexico and eight in Yucatán.
Excavation Sites: Major sites under Location.
Tuition & Fees: $1,275
Credits: 6

International Council of Monuments and Sites
Bicentennial Projects
Suite 1030
1522 K Street, N.W.
Washington, D.C. 20005
Location: France.
Excavation Site: Estaing (Midi-Pyrenees), Vissac and St. Romain (in the Auvergne, burial place of Marquis de la Fayette), and Chapelle de Port St. Maria (burial place of Marshal de la Fayette).
Tuition: $12; all other costs paid by student.

FLORIDA

University of South Florida
Department of Anthropology
Tampa, Florida 33620
Location: Tampa, Florida.
Site: Undetermined.
Tuition & Fees: $225 to $705

IDAHO

Idaho State University
Box 8183
Pocatello, Idaho 83209
Location: Approximately 80 miles northwest of Pocatello.
Excavation Site: Little Lost River Basin.
Tuition & Fees: $120 to $145

University of Idaho
Department of Sociology/Anthropology
Moscow, Idaho 83843
Location: San Juan Islands, Washington.
Excavation Site: San Juan National Historical Park on San Juan Island in Puget Sound.
Tuition & Fees: $80 to $180
Credits: 4 to 8

ILLINOIS

Loyola University
Department of Anthropology
6525 N. Sheridan Road
Chicago, Illinois 60626
312-274-3000/422 or 745
Location: The Crawfish River Valley, north of Aztalan, Wisconsin.
Site: Aztalan.
Tuition & Fees: $360 plus lodging.
Credits: 6

Northwestern University
Field School Archaeological Program
200 Sheridan Road
Evanston, Illinois 60201
Location: Kampsville, Illinois.
Sites: The Koster Site, the Audrey Site, and the Helton Cemetery.
Tuition & Fees: $960 for excavation program (three courses), and $640 for laboratory program (two courses), plus $15 health fee.
Credits: 8 to 24

*Upper Mississippi Valley Archaeological
Research Foundation*
2216 W. 112th Street
Chicago, Illinois 60643
Location: Near Peoria, Illinois.
Excavation Site: Orendorf Village.
Tuition & Fees: $350 or less.
Credits: Variable.

INDIANA

Ball State University
Department of Anthropology Field
School
Muncie, Indiana 47306
Location: Upper Mississinewa River,
Grant and Wabash counties.
Excavation Sites: Mississinewa Battlefield
(War of 1812) and associated Miami
Indian villages.
Tuition & Fees: $140 to $280
Credits: Variable, to 8.

Indiana State University
Anthropology Laboratory
Terre Haute, Indiana 47809
Location: Vigo County, Indiana.
Excavation Site: The Clark Site, multi-
component Late Archaic, Middle
Woodland and Mississippian.
Tuition & Fees: $84 to $288
Credits: Undecided.

KANSAS

University of Kansas
Museum of Anthropology
Lawrence, Kansas 66045
and
Kansas State University
Department of Sociology and Anthro-
pology
Manhattan, Kansas 66502
Location Site: General fieldwork at the
University of Kansas and field and lab
techniques at Kansas State University.
Tuition & Fees: $112 to $320, plus lodg-
ing.
Credits: 8

MARYLAND

University of Maryland
Department of Anthropology
College Park, Maryland 20742

or
University of Houston
School of Education
Victoria Center
Victoria, Texas
Locations: (1) British Virgin Islands and
in St. Lucia in the West Indies; (2)
College Park and Oldtown, Maryland,
for Shawnee in that region.
Tuition & Fees: (1) $1,300; (2) $34 to
$85 per credit hour.
Credits: 6 each.

MASSACHUSETTS

University of Massachusetts
Department of Anthropology
Machmer Hall
Amherst, Massachusetts 01002
Location Site: Undetermined.
Credits: 6

MISSISSIPPI

Mississippi State University
Department of Anthropology
P.O. Drawer GN
Mississippi State, Mississippi 39762
Location: Near Starkville, Mississippi.
Tuition & Fees: $56
Credits: 6

MISSOURI

University of Missouri–Columbia
Department of Archaeology Field School
Switzler Hall
Columbia, Missouri 65201
Location: Oneota Village.
Site: Utz Site.
Tuition & Fees: $135 to $655
Credits: 3 to 8

NEW MEXICO

Eastern New Mexico University
Student Archaeological Program
233 Chama, N.E.
Albuquerque, New Mexico 87106
Locations: (1) Puerco River, northwest-
ern New Mexico; (2) San Juan Valley,
Chacoan Salmon Ruin.
Tuition & Fees: None.
Credits: 1 to 9

Fort Burgwin Research Center
P.O. Box 314
Ranchos de Taos, New Mexico 87557
or
SMU, Box 739
Dallas, Texas 75275
Location: Undetermined.
Tuition & Fees: None.
Credits: 6

New Mexico State University
Box 3BV
Las Cruces, New Mexico 88003
Location: Near the H Bar Reservoir between Luna, New Mexico, and Springville, Arizona.
Sites: Mogollon sites, near junction of the Cibola, Black River, and Mimbres Branches.
Tuition & Fees: $160 plus accommodations.
Credits: Variable.

NEW YORK

State University College
Department of Anthropology
Archaeological Field School
New Paltz, New York 12561
Location: Ulster County.
Site: Archaic-Woodland.
Tuition and Fees: $21.50 to $50.00 per credit hour.
Credits: 6 to 9

Hartwick College
Curator of the Yager Museum
Oneonta, New York 13820
Location: Undetermined.
Tuition & Fees: $115 per credit hour maximum.
Credits: 6

State University of New York
Summer Sessions Office—AD 241
Albany, New York 12222
Locations: (1) Lake George; (2) Grand Teton; (3) State Museum, Oneonta.
Tuition & Fees: $21.50 per credit hour to $50 per credit hour.
Credits: 3 to 6
and
State University of New York
Department of Anthropology
Albany, New York 12222
518-457-1140

Location: National Museum of Anthropology, New Mexico.
Tuition & Fees: Same as above.
Credits: 9 maximum.

York College of the City University of New York
Archaeological Field School
107 Science Building
Jamaica, New York 11451
Location Site: Historical, urban, 19th-century site in Jamaica, New York, and Queens County, New York City.
Tuition & Fees: $108 to $270
Credits: 6

Rensselaer Polytechnic Institute
Office of Continuing Studies
Troy, New York 12181
Location: Hudson and Mohawk rivers, Troy, New York.
Site: Poestenkill Gorge Industrial Complex, Troy.
Tuition & Fees: $690 maximum.

New York University
Department of Anthropology
201 Smith Hall
25 Waverly Place
New York, New York 10003
Location: Undetermined.
Tuition & Fees: $150

NORTH CAROLINA

Wake Forest University
Museum of Man
Department of Sociology/Anthropology
Winston-Salem, North Carolina 27109
Location: Near Ramah, a small village 40 miles north of Gallup.
Excavation Site: Pettit Site.
Tuition & Fees: $200 to $430

OHIO

Case Western Reserve University
Department of Anthropology
Cleveland, Ohio 44106
Locations: (1) Kelley's Island, Lake Erie; (2) Scioto River Valley.
Sites: An enclosed seasonal village from the late Woodland period; a harness mound—major Hopewell mortuary complex.
Tuition & Fees: $125 per credit hour.
Credits: 3 to 6

University of Cincinnati
Summer Course in Archaeology
Department of Anthropology
Cincinnati, Ohio 45221
513-475-2772
Location: University of Cincinnati.
Course: Archaeological Laboratory methods.
Tuition & Fees: $22 to $58
Credits: 8

The Ohio State University
Department of Anthropology
1810 College Road
Columbus, Ohio 43210
Location: Columbus, Ohio.
Site: Galbreath Mound, an Adena burial mound.
Tuition & Fees: $270 to $680

OREGON

Oregon State University
Department of Anthropology Field School
Corvallis, Oregon 97331
Locations: (1) Western foothills of Willamette Valley; (2) Oregon coast.
Sites: (1) Fort Hoskins; (2) Shell midden.
Tuition & Fees: $150 to $320

University of Oregon
Department of Anthropology
Eugene, Oregon 97403
Location: Near Eugene, Oregon.
Site: Southern Willamette Valley.
Tuition & Fees: $219 to $330.

PENNSYLVANIA

Clarion State College
Archaeological Laboratory
Clarion, Pennsylvania 16241
Locations: (1) Near a ford on the Clarion River; (2) Allegheny River; (3) Local workshops in Field Archaeology.
Sites: (1) State Road Ripple Site; (2) Allegheny River; (3) campus laboratory.
Tuition & Fees: $33 to $60

University of Pennsylvania
Department of American Civilization
Philadelphia, Pennsylvania 19174

Location: East of Bryn Mawr, near Philadelphia.
Site: Harriton Plantation and Mill Creek.
Tuition & Fees: $270+

California State College
Center for Prehistoric and Historic Site Archaeology
California, Pennsylvania 15419
Location: Southwestern Pennsylvania.
Site: Fort Burd, English military fort of 1759, and a Late Woodland "Monongahela" village which the fort overlays.
Tuition & Fees: $378 to $540
Credits: 6

Alliance College
Archaeological Field School
Cambridge Springs, Pennsylvania 16403
Location: Northwestern Pennsylvania.
Site: French Creek Valley, the Crowe Site, and the O'Connor Site.
Tuition & Fees: $490

West Chester State College
Anthropology Section
West Chester, Pennsylvania 19380
Location: Southeastern Pennsylvania.
Sites: Taylor Burying Ground Site, Hunters' Hill Site, and the Okehocking Tract Indian Village.
Tuition & Fees: $90 to $150

University of Pittsburgh
Department of Anthropology
Pittsburgh, Pennsylvania 15260
Location: Southwestern Pennsylvania.
Site: Cross Creek drainage area.
Tuition & Fees: $240 to $630

SOUTH CAROLINA

University of South Carolina/Coastal Carolina College
Department of Archaeology and Anthropology
Conway, South Carolina 29526
Location: South Carolina.
Site: Undetermined.

SOUTH DAKOTA

Black Hills Natural Sciences Field Station
Augustana College
Sioux Falls, South Dakota 57102

or
South Dakota School of Mines and Technology
Department of Biology
Rapid City, South Dakota 57701
Location: Black Hills.

TENNESSEE

Memphis State University
Office of International Studies
Memphis, Tennessee 38152
901-454-2690
or
Department of Anthropology
901-454-2618
or
Chucalissa Museum
1987 Indian Village Drive
Memphis, Tennessee 38109
901-785-3160
Locations: (1) Mexico, Guanajuato center, (2) Sprink Creek, 125 miles east of Memphis; (3) Chucalissa Site, located on Mississippi River bluff in southwest Memphis; (4) Fort Pillow State Park, southwest of Ripley, Tennessee.
Tuition & Fees: $16 to $52 per semester hour.

Vanderbilt University
Archaeological Field School
Department of Sociology/Anthropology
Box 1532, Station B
Nashville, Tennessee 37235
Locations: (1) Near Vonore, Tennessee, Fort Loudoun Site; (2) Nashville, basement of First American Bank.
Tuition & Fees: $480 to $1,038
Credits: 6

TEXAS

University of Texas at San Antonio
Division of Social Sciences
San Antonio, Texas 78285
Location: South Central Texas
Tuition & Fees: $35 to $250
Credits: 4 to 6

Texas Tech University
Department of Anthropology
Lubbock, Texas 79409
Location: Near Junction, Texas.

Site: Prehistoric stratified Archaic and Neo-American.
Tuition & Fees: $106 to $300
Credits: 6

Museum of Texas Tech University
Lubbock Lake Project Director
Lubbock, Texas 79409
806-742-5151
Location: Lubbock Lake.
Site: Paleoindian.
Tuition & Fees: None.

S. F. Austin State University
Department of Sociology
Nacogdoches, Texas 75961
Location: Nacogdoches area.
Site: Early historic Caddo Indian village.
Credits: 6

UTAH

Brigham Young University
Department of Anthropology and Archaeology
Provo, Utah 84602
Location: Southeastern Utah.
Site: Montezuma Canyon.
Tuition & Fees: $170 to $270

VIRGINIA

Virginia Commonwealth University
Department of Sociology and Anthropology
Richmond, Virginia 23284
Location: Pamunkey Research Center.
Site: Pamunkey Indian Reservation.
Tuition & Fees: $168 to $198

WASHINGTON, State of

Washington State University
Archaeological Field School
Department of Anthropology
Pullman, Washington 99163
Locations: (1) Ozette Project, Northwest Coast Indian village; (2) Winchester Wasteway Clovis Project, near Quincy, Washington, in the Columbia basin; (3) The Owyhee Project, Castle Creek drainage of southwestern Idaho, between the Owyhee Mountains and the Snake River; (4) The Fort Walla

Walla Project, a way station in the development of the Pacific Northwest; and (5) The Lahav Research Project.
Tuition and Fees: $20 per credit hour.

University of Washington
Archaeological Field School
Department of Anthropology
Seattle, Washington 98195
Location: Lower Columbia River, Washington State.
Site: A pithouse village.
Tuition & Fees: $188 maximum.

Western Washington State College
Department of Sociology/Anthropology
Bellingham, Washington 98225
Location: Pacific Northwest.

WISCONSIN

University of Wisconsin
Department of Sociology and Anthropology
Stevens Point, Wisconsin 54481
715-346-2887
Location: Central Wisconsin.
Tuition & Fees: $114 to $350
Credits: 4

University of Wisconsin–Whitewater
Continuing Education and Outreach Program
Whitewater, Wisconsin 53190
414-472-1100
Location: Fulton County.
Site: Prehistoric Orendorf Site.

PART II

How Archaeology Began

CHAPTER 4

Three Beginnings

Before I get into a discussion of the foundations of archaeological thought, how they came about, and who was responsible, let me first say that there were three different "beginnings" of archaeology.

The fact that many professional archaeologists in many parts of the world cannot agree as to the who, when, where, and—most important—the why behind these different beginnings serves to illustrate the problems in the field today. European archaeologists have told me that, in their opinion, American archaeologists are the worst in the world. What they really mean is that American archaeologists have seen fit to alter certain dogmatic positions accepted by historians in Europe. American historians, on the other hand, tend to question the attitudes and "scientific open-mindedness" of their counterparts in England and on the Continent. The origins of such argument have to do with the fact that America is so very young compared with the panorama enjoyed by European researchers, and that American archaeologists—as "new boys on the block"—have little to offer. There are two factors, however, which historians in Europe fail to realize or choose to ignore: American archaeologists are the best trained in the world; and they deal, in America, with a series of cultures different from those which have inhabited Europe. As a result of their training, American researchers have accomplished more in the last twenty-five years then have Europeans in the last century.

There is no question that Europe is the cradle of archaeology—both the first and second beginning; hence, Europeans feel, anything that does not conform to the standards or archaeological "laws" established there must represent something other than scientific archaeological methodology and systematic historical truth.

The reader undoubtedly assumes that I, as an American, am biased; and the reader is correct. But my background in this field originated in Europe, and Europeans really do think that Columbus was the first to discover America; that the Amerindians are a young culture; and that the Celts never ventured beyond the Iberian Peninsula. It is as though the North American continent had suddenly appeared two or three hundred years ago between two oceans—despite the fact that traces of an American Indian language have been found in Africa, and Viking and Iberian inscriptions are at the point of being almost commonplace in New England.

Back to the beginning.

THE FIRST ARCHAEOLOGY

The Renaissance is described as one of the revolutionary eras in the history of the Western world. Its birth was an epoch for man, for it introduced a new kind of energy, a lasting excitement, and a splendor of achievement; it freed the bonds of human intellectual thought and gave us the system known as humanism, which survives today in such diverse places as America and India. The Renaissance brought with it explosions of creativity in art, music, literature, science, economics, religion, and politics. And the Renaissance gave us the first system by which a culture examined the remains of its predecessors: classical archaeology.

The Renaissance was to the medieval era preceding it what democracy was to the aristocracy. The changeover was slow and the length of its effects cannot be clearly defined; most will agree, however, that the Renaissance began sometime during the fourteenth century and lasted officially until sometime in the seventeenth century. The Renaissance was virtually a new kind of civilization that grew up in Italy and spread across Europe; and it was efficient. Latin and Greek literature were rediscovered and revived, having been lost since the fall of Rome in the fifth century; classicism became a major quality of the time as admirers began to relate to the sheer beauty of objects surviving from the Greeks and Romans. The minds of Michelangelo, Leonardo da Vinci, Shakespeare, Copernicus, Galileo, and Columbus came forth and found an era in which they could create.

All of this nurtured the founding of the archaeological attitude; the idea that we should attempt to appreciate, understand, and learn from the creations of those peoples and cultures that died out before we were even born. Renaissance man began to realize that history itself has a history.

The Renaissance sought to replace the variety of languages in use—

French, Italian, Spanish, English, and German—with an official tongue, Latin; hence, classical literature was studied and analyzed. Nineteenth-century social historians described this period as a rebirth (the term *renaissance,* from the Latin *renascentia,* means "new birth"), a period in which the past was revived. Rediscovered Roman and Greek literature became the guiding principle for a new classicism, first in Ciceronian Latin, then in the modern languages.

This interest in classical thought led Italians of the Renaissance to conduct "excavations"—for lack of a better term. Their methodology would cause an accomplished amateur archaeologist today to bury his head in his hands and cry, but the result was obtained. Amid the foundations of Rome and other ancient cities were numerous statues and other objects, left untouched for centuries, which were dug up and studied, and which left a heavy, lasting influence on Italian sculpture and painting.

The importance of architecture in archaeology was first brought forth during the Renaissance, as surviving monuments from antiquity were studied, analyzed, and rebuilt. The principles of architecture learned in this process allowed engineers to equal or surpass the original work. All of this came about through a passionate sympathy and empathy for the classical past, a passion still evident today in those who specialize in classical history and archaeology.

Obviously, classical archaeology was the province of the rich and/or the intellectual; the common man was busy trying to cope with his own problems of survival. Rich patrons would buy, sell, and trade objets d'art with one another, and attempt to apply as much of a scholastic attitude towards such activity as they could muster. The education of their children (especially their sons) included classical literature, art, and history to no small degree, and this was usually followed with a visit to those sites from antiquity with which their studies dealt.

In that there was no shortage of historical documentation about the cultures with which people in the Renaissance were interested, and in that an understanding of chronological history was fairly common, the classical researchers were thus interested in art, objects, and buildings *for their own sake.* Classical archaeology was thus comparatively unscientific in its genesis, concentrating more on *stylistic* studies. Those artifacts recovered during the Renaissance which did not belong within the realm of classical archaeology were simply tossed aside, reburied, or thrown out.

Classical archaeology, or the idea behind it, was not confined to Italy or even the continent of Europe. When travelers from Britain ventured into Renaissance Italy in the 1500s and 1600s, they immediately soaked up the practice of collecting and discussing objets d'art from previous cultures, and brought the idea back home with them. They even founded an organization to promote this practice in Britain, the Society of Dilettanti.

The major disadvantage of classical archaeology as practiced during the Renaissance was that, considering it was something less than scientific, proponents got carried away with collecting objects and interpreting their importance. These classicists began to glorify classical antiquity; they accumulated the objects, attempted to understand their importance historically, and then went the next step of imitating the civilization that spawned them. Their objectivity steadily declined, but nevertheless to these first archaeologists, the historians of classical history, we owe a great debt.

THE SECOND ARCHAEOLOGY

By the time the Renaissance came to a close, archaeology other than that of the classical vein was only beginning to take root. It was still a completely unscientific system interested only in the finds themselves rather than in the context in which they were found; hence, it can only vaguely be labeled archaeology at all.

There was during this post-Renaissance period, however, a growing realization that some kind of system had to be inaugurated in order to account for antiquity in a more systematic manner. The man who brought this realization to reality was Johann Winckelmann, considered by some to be the father of archaeology.

Born in 1717, Winckelmann devoted much of his life to studying art history in Rome, specializing in sculpture. In terms of scientific methodology, he, like others of his time, was a monumental blunderer; but he did know the difference between research and treasure hunting at a time when most people failed to recognize it.

Winckelmann had always been interested in digging up old urns and artifacts, first as a boy in Prussia and then in Germany. He ran a grammar school for a while, became a librarian, and eventually managed to locate himself amidst Europe's greatest collectors of antiquities. This along with his great love of old things and the influence of classical archaeology was all he needed to aim his sights towards Italy, and in 1758 he became the librarian to Cardinal Albani and keeper of his antiquities collection. This post led five years later to an appointment as chief supervisor of antiquities in Rome.

Excavations during this period were at best sloppy and haphazard, and Winckelmann sought to establish at least a simple, basic format to follow. His idea was not particularly popular among the collectors, for their greed precluded the following of any format established by some German who had converted to Catholicism just to work in Rome. Further, there was a great deal of politics, bribery, and theft conducted on a regular basis, so the attitudes that Winckelmann encountered were not exactly supportive of scholarly pursuits. Nevertheless, through some politics and bribery of his own, Winckelmann managed to accomplish quite a lot. He was the first to realize that *the context in which an object is found* can yield important information on its origin which would otherwise be unobtainable from the object itself.

In 1764 he published his massive *History of the Art of Antiquity*. It was an epoch-making treatise, the first of its kind in history. The past had been opened up. For the first time, a field of history had been approached from a *developmental* standpoint. With no previous model by which to guide him in such an endeavor, Winckelmann was himself the model. He demonstrated that a culture could be understood by what it had left behind. His was a particular kind of genius, for his manner of thinking was necessarily unlike that of any of his peers or predecessors.

Winckelmann made numerous—though certainly understandable—errors in both his theories and conclusions, and a student of classical archaeology today would probably have a good laugh perusing his writings. But Winckelmann represented a major alteration in the course of archaeological thought. He was the Copernicus of his field.

So the world had been granted a new system; order could begin to replace chaos, and conclusions could take the place of conjecture. By now Winckelmann had become very famous and was regarded as a scholar. On the evening of June 8, 1768, he was murdered by a known criminal. (If you happen to be in either Athens or Rome on any December 9, stop in at one of the national archaeological institutes. You will witness a short ceremony commemorating the birthday of Johann Winckelmann.)

We move now a bit closer to the founding of our second archaeology.

Those well read in the history of science will note that the most difficult thing to do is effect change. Regardless of one's purported evidence, change in academic thinking occurs only when there is absolutely no way around it. This phenomenon is based on authoritarianism, arrogance, and the assumption that dogmatism is permissible when the dogmatists say it is. The most supreme science of all, physics, underwent such a circumstance with regard to Newtonian physics and new ideas on the structure of the universe, about which the memorable Max Planck commented: "Change will occur when the old generation, now in control, dies off; the new generation will bring about change." Such incidents in science are by no means new. When Galileo was questioned about his theories by the scientific authorities of the day, he felt compelled to ask: "Are you indeed interested in science—or in authority?"

Changes in our thinking towards history and prehistory did not escape such circumstances. Even to this day, professional archaeologists and historians probably are the most narrow-minded members of academia. They are overcautious to a fault, and I have seen talented, even brilliant amateur researchers walk away in disgust from professionals who demand more proof from them than they would dare ask of a peer. They have failed to realize the lessons of history they teach.

When a major change in our thinking is in the wind, it usually means that a belief system is about to be forthrightly challenged. The "scientific authority" in the time of Galileo was the Church; and it was the Church that archaeology had to challenge in its genesis. A belief system had been developed by which all of man's history was scrupulously accounted for: the Bible. The battle began to take form over a period of some two centuries, having been initiated by classical researchers in Italy and systematized to an extent by Winckelmann. People in Europe and England began digging around in their backyards for anything that appeared old; more thought was given to finding out about unusual artifacts discovered by road crews; and serious thinkers began to wonder just how old this or that tool implement could be. It was a silent revolution, not particularly deliberate, and certainly no one at the time would have guessed at the result.

Up until the 1800s, the great source, the history book with all the answers, was the Bible. Historians of the day commented upon events described therein, and, as Geoffrey Bibby wrote, "Every school boy knew that at the time of the Roman invasions Britain was inhabited by naked blue-painted savages." Questions as to the age of man and his world are not spelled out in the Bible, but fear not, for a clergyman had that all figured out. The Irish Archbishop Ussher had informed the masses in 1636 that the world had been created in 4004 B.C. If that was not specific enough for some, the problem was further clarified a few years later by a Dr. Lightfoot, who fixed the *exact* time at 9 A.M. on October 23, 4004 B.C. Thus the entire world had existed during only biblical and classical times. Period.

This was very comforting, of course, to those who may be described in hindsight as less than imaginative and whose educational pursuits stopped at the age of nine. But perhaps they should not be derided, for we are dealing, again, with a belief system, the power of which controlled even the educated. We today find it hard to imagine that if, according to the Bible, Abraham was in Hebron, what was happening meanwhile in Britain and Europe did not occur to sophisticated thinkers to question up to the beginning of the *nineteenth century!*

And then something happened.

Actually, two important things happened. The first group of thinkers who could no longer accept the biblical thesis were those involved in the study of the earth, the geologists. Geology was far from becoming a recognized field of scientific inquiry, but researchers began to realize that the earth was much, much older than anything suggested in the Bible, and that it had to be studied and interpreted in terms of a slow evolutionary process of change rather than in terms of catastrophic events covering a mere 6,000 years or so. The second important thing to happen was the realization by collectors of artifacts that the stone implements had not been formed by the thunderbolts of an angry God, but that they had been fashioned by the hand of man—ancient man.

The archaeology of prehistory was born.

It was not really until the middle of the nineteenth century that archaeology became a firmly rooted discipline, due principally to the effect of the publication of *The Origin of Species* by Charles Darwin in 1859. This was followed by Sir Charles Lyell's *Antiquity of Man* in 1863. The biological revolution in the natural sciences was matched with a social revolution in prehistory. The growth in importance of the natural sciences was immensely helpful to researchers in archaeology in the 1800s, and today, according to Kurt W. Marek (who wrote under the name of C. W. Ceram), fifty-three sciences are handmaidens to archaeology.

The activities that led up to the realization by nineteenth-century students of history that man was much older than had ever been considered will be discussed in the next chapter, followed by a step-by-step analysis of archaeology's growing pains and contributions by amateurs.

But first—

THE THIRD ARCHAEOLOGY

Students of history, and of the history of science and archaeology, may choose not to recognize this final segment as important in the establishment of archaeology as a discipline of science. The third archaeology began in America.

Archaeology in the United States is very young indeed. When we discuss prehistory as history before written records, we are talking about a period that ends with Columbus in North America (for the Indians had no written records) only five hundred years ago, but which ended at least three *thousand* years ago in Egypt! While writing began at least five thousand years ago in the Near East, and much later than that in Britain, certain regions in America saw writing for the first time less than three generations ago! Hence we have somewhat of a paradox involving the correct use of the term prehistoric, or palaeoanthropologic, in the United States. It is a paradox that infuriates European historians. With the exception of portions of historical archaeology, students of this field in America deal solely with prehistory.

The reason archaeology falls under the wing of anthropology in the United States is because this continent witnessed no classical period, no great temple building, no scribes filling sheets of parchment. Americans had to be content with the study of man in general and *cultural* anthropology in particular. The confusion both in and about American archaeology comes as a result of too much growth too fast. While there are well over a hundred universities offering courses in archaeology today, one needs patience and the mind of a detective to find out what department sponsors such courses. These range from archaeology being taught along with sociology and geology to modern history and, yes, religion.

When the University of Kentucky decided to establish a department of anthropology and archaeology in 1927, it hired two hobbyists who dabbled in excavations on weekends—a zoologist and a physicist. This is an unsual case, of course, but it illustrates clearly how in America archaeology is younger than genetics.

A different attitude reigns in America regarding the concept of history. Most historians here are interested only in irrefutable fact; no conjecture, no philosophy, no grand cultural theme, no overriding conceptual thinking. It is a different, specialty-oriented outlook. Archaeology is a *method*; archaeologists in America *are not* archaeologists by title. They are anthropologists or geologists, perhaps, who happen to implement the archaeological system. One of the reasons why amateur archaeologists are so sorely needed here is that American archaeologists are always tied to other fields.

CHAPTER 5

The Antiquarians

By the beginning of the eighteenth century there were many collectors of old things in Europe and England. People spent Sunday afternoons digging here and there for any unusual object that was obviously not of their generation. They had no idea what these objects represented or who, if anyone, could have made use of them. The common attitude was to deny any possible ignorance regarding the people who had previously inhabited a region, and about whom nothing was known. This only perpetuated the idea that all British relics, for example, were simply the remains of Britons from prior generations, including the mysterious and mystical Druids. To this day, many people still believe that the Druids built Stonehenge, notwithstanding the fact that Gerald Hawkins established Stonehenge as probably older than the Druidic presence in Britain.

Slowly and cautiously, collectors allowed their thoughts to expand and carefully considered the possibility that man had been around— in their country!—for many more years than the experts insisted on. These were the antiquarians (from the Latin *antiquarius*), the first thinkers about the idea of a history before recorded history, the first pre-historians. It took over a century for this idea to become accepted, or even considered, popularly. The antiquarians clumsily groped their way toward archaeology. Working alone or in small groups, they were scattered throughout England and Europe, most plentifully in France, Britain, and Scandinavia. Many were inspired by travelers returning from Italy, where classical archaeology was well established. The local antiquarians were usually comparatively well educated and well heeled, though often poor farmers would devote precious spare time to contemplating and adding to their little collections of strange stone tools.

The study of antiquities was always a second vocation, a hobby, a pastime, or at best a serious pursuit of the rich. The first full-time researcher in this whole field would not be seen until the middle of the next century. But these antiquarians were busy and resourceful. After traveling the length and breadth of Britain, a schoolteacher named William Camden produced in 1586 the first general guide to antiquities in his country, *Britannia*. This was quite an accomplishment and of tremendous help to succeeding generations of antiquarians, for it was the first catalogue of its kind and it reinforced the feeling in the minds of individual collectors that what they were doing was important. Camden was way ahead of his time.

In 1660, John Aubrey had studied Stonehenge and other stone monuments long enough to be convinced that they were the work, at the very least, of very ancient Britons. His writings—one manuscript of which, the *Monumenta Britannica*, has never been published—brought into focus for the first time the idea that stone structures should be studied in terms of their origins in prehistory, and that a special discipline should be established for such study. He was formulating in his mind the idea of prehistoric archaeological research specializing in megalithic studies, a concept never before put forth.

By now there were many museums of antiquities in Scandinavia, Britain, and Europe, established as a result of the discovery of so many, many "old things." They differed from museums of today only in the sense that they could not adequately explain what it was they were exhibiting. The year 1707 saw the first publication dealing with fossils, the *Archaeologia Britannica* by Edward Lhwyd, who gleaned the information for it by viewing hundreds and hundreds of private and public collections and by an exhaustive study of languages, customs, and natural history. His approach was something less than scientific, but he planted a few more seeds from which the tree of archaeological thought would grow.

According to Glyn Daniel, one of England's leading archaeologists today, the shining example of professional antiquarianism in the 1700s was William Stukeley, who thought in terms of an archaeological methodology long before systematic excavation techniques were established. Stukeley began to divide prehistory according to the movements of peoples; he considered cultural influences in terms of immigration and emigration; and he examined old structures for their *design* in order to establish a relationship and, hence, a relative age.

A majority of these and other antiquarians were not closely associated with formal science in their day. By this I do not mean that they were uneducated, though some certainly did not hold university degrees, but rather that they worked outside the official influence of the academic world. This they did out of necessity, for the experts, the historians, would have little or nothing to do with such new and radical ideas. Prehistory? Ancient man? Nonsense! Those antiquarians who were involved in scientific pursuits were tolerated by authority, but those who were far removed from the halls of higher learning—the farmers, shopkeepers, and tradesmen—were completely ignored, if not actively condemned. They were often not allowed to voice their opinions in public meetings, were stopped from entering seminars sponsored by scientific organizations, and were certainly not allowed to publish anything in reputable journals.

This attitude continues to an extent today, but was most outstanding when archaeology began taking roots as a serious discipline. Had it not been for the incomparable dedication and stamina of nonauthoritative researchers, we would still be living under the assumption that the Britons of the time of the Roman invasions were naked, blue-painted savages.

CHAPTER 6
The First Archaeologists

Amateur archaeologists will be pleased to learn that it was their counterparts in the nineteenth century who founded this field. They were fought every step of the way by the academic authorities who refused to alter a lifetime of sedentary thinking.

I have always been struck by the fact that books on and about the history of archaeology rarely mention this. Historians will, of course, refer to *some* of the amateurs responsible for outstanding contributions, but they will not mention the fact that much more could have been accomplished much faster if the so-called experts had not exercised their arrogance and complacency. It was much safer, and certainly more comforting, to assume that all of history was intact and known; that breaking the barrier into such a thing as prehistory was absurd; and that those who sought to do so, well, the poor disenchanted fools knew not what they did.

Since most antiquarians up to the beginning of the nineteenth century were members of the leisure class—the wealthy landed gentry—they were in no particular hurry to add substance to considerations about prehistory. This may sound unfair, and probably is; nevertheless, those who did most of the work did *not* look upon this field as a hobby, or Sunday afternoon pastime, or something to discuss with leading citizens over dinner in order to impress them with one's collection of artifacts. In case there is any doubt in the reader's mind, it should be clear that the academic field of archaeology today was inherited from amateur researchers, with little or no help from professional historians. And a majority of the work today is still done by amateur archaeologists.

As the nineteenth century dawned it signaled the end of a dogmatic historical attitude. I will now set forth what the first archaeologists, the founders of this field, went through to get their voices heard. It is a story that represents a classic example of scientific authority working against outsiders—outsiders who happen to be right. It would be impractical to list the contributions of everyone involved in the growth of archaeology, so I have chosen to discuss this growth chronologically by presenting an overview of some of the more outstanding amateurs. Such a project cannot be expected to be forthcoming from the professional archaeological community, for historians today write books for and about one another; with a few exceptions, little attention has been given to the amateur in archaeology, and it's about time this situation was corrected.

We begin with the fact that at the end of the eighteenth century, the scholars and experts had pretty much everyone convinced—with the help of the Church—that there was recent history and perhaps an early history. And that was it. Then in Copenhagen, in the year 1788, Christian Jürgensen Thomsen, the son of a middle-class merchant, was born. Although trained to follow in his father's footsteps, the young man had a penchant for collecting and for listening to collectors of paintings, coins, and other objets d'art. He devoted all of his spare time learning everything he could about these objects and their history, and was known in his area as a sincere and accomplished student. In 1807, when half of Copenhagen was on fire during the Napoleonic Wars, Thomsen helped relocate the valuable collection of coins being stored for eventual display in the Danish National Museum. This increased his contacts, and he joined a small circle of important people who were devoted to studies in prehistory.

This group finally convinced the government to establish the Royal Commission for the Preservation of Danish Antiquities, directed by a bishop, five university professors, and a government representative. Its first secretary was Rasmus Nyerup, the royal librarian in Copenhagen. Enthusiasm for the new commission abounded, and collectors from around the country offered and forwarded their own collections for inclusion. So much material began to arrive, in fact, that it was all Nyerup could do to record its arrival and put it in a back room, which soon began to look like an attic filled with countless pieces of junk.

By the time Nyerup retired, there were hundreds of objects to be accounted for and catalogued—a job that appealed to no one. But the commission remembered young Thomsen and his training as a businessman under his father and offered him the nonpaying, nonvoting post. Thomsen was twenty-seven years old and accepted the assignment of putting everything into working order. Although without a university degree, he was considered very bright; besides, the commision had in him someone to clean the place up for free. Thomsen was given the title of secretary, whch really meant he also had to take care of the commission's correspondence, reports, minutes, and business affairs.

He worked a full day each week for three years at his thankless, though fascinating, job, and set out to bring some order to the more than one thousand objects received by the commission. He had neither experience in such things nor any money to work with, but then *no one* had experience in such things because the idea of putting objects of antiquity into any kind of order was unknown; there was simply no system for accounting, either by date, culture, type, or similarity. Because Thomsen had no model and was also unfamiliar, fortunately, with the incorrect systems put forth by historians of the day, he had to create, on the spot, as Winckelmann had, his own model. It was a unique problem he faced. How was he to properly exhibit all the material? How should it be arranged: by size, shape, area in which found, color, weight? No one had given any thought to a systematic arrangement, but to Thomsen this was a necessity; and we today know that a post-Neolithic copper utensil from the Near East does not belong with a pre-Mesolithic stone tool from Britain in a museum, any more than Pueblo pottery belongs on the same shelf as Egyptian cups. But in Thomsen's time there was no knowledge of Neolithic or Mesolithic eras, or of the activities of specific cultures in various parts of the world in antiquity.

The first thing Thomsen did was to borrow the idea from his father of dividing things into types. He set about separating objects of stone from those of metal, and then separating the pottery. He next subdivided these into apparent uses of the objects—tools, eating utensils, weapons, ornaments—and still further into shapes. As he performed this mundane activity, he began to think about the possible differences in age of the objects. If man had become sophisticated enough to utilize bronze or copper, would he still take the time to shape stone? Thomsen decided that stone must have been used by man before copper, although he decided this for the wrong reason, thinking that copper was expensive in antiquity and therefore man had been forced to rely on stone for his tools and weapons. In less than two years he had outlined in his own mind a chronology of prehistory.

When the museum finally opened to the public in 1819, Thomsen had everything arranged by material, use, and shape. He was not to realize for many years that his homemade system of classification did in fact represent authentic chronology. The idea of the three ages of man, Stone, Bronze, and Iron, originated with this unpaid volunteer whose background was that of a businessman without a university education.

And the opposition was fierce.

Both in Denmark and elsewhere, the experts remarked sarcastically that there should also be a Pottery Age, a Bone Age, a Painting Age, a Coin Age, and a Glass Age. It was only many years later that the three-age system became universally accepted. Thomsen ignored the derisive remarks and continued at the museum until 1833, when he was forced to take over the family business upon the death of his father. When his mother died in 1840, he sold the business and returned full-time to the museum, where he was given a budget and the title of director. He traveled widely—paying all his own expenses—and devoted all his time, being unmarried, to his work. Although uneducated, he was self-taught in a number of fields and expressed himself well. By the time he reached old age, his museum was considered among the best in all of Europe.

More than anything else, Thomsen gave us the idea of time unfolding over many millennia and introduced a way to account for the progress of man in prehistory. Having asked the right questions, he came forth with theories that produced the right answers. When he died in 1865, the world had lost the father of European prehistory.

When Thomsen was about thirty years old and at the point of bringing order out of chaos in his work, a young man in France was making his way up the ladder of achievement as a customs official. In 1825, Jacques Boucher de Crèvecoeur de Perthes became a director of a customs post, and at the age of thirty-seven was content to continue his career and eventually retire with an acceptable pension. Little did he know that he would make a mark on the world in a far different capacity.

Always interested in natural history, he began studying the basics of environmental principles and absorbed as much about geology as was available. As he studiously went around in his spare time examining the layout of the land, he found pieces of flint similar to those that had been described as the remains of the Flood in the Bible. De Perthes immediately thought this strange, for he found it difficult to believe that these flints were not formed by the hand of man instead of by acts of nature as decreed by the experts.

He continued his excursions until he found what he thought was objective proof of his theory. He had located a hand ax, in 1832, that could not possibly have been designed and cut by nature. This led him to devote more and more time to locating and collecting additional specimens, and by 1838 he had in his possession a massive collection of implements. Convinced beyond any doubt that his theory was correct, he formally presented it—along with his collection—to the French Société d'Émulation. The reception was cool and, to be kind, skeptical. A year later he went before the prestigious Paris Institute, where he was treated to unanimous skepticism and neglect. He was told that his theory was irrefutably incorrect, without substantiation, and quite impossible.

He published a five-volume work, *On the Creation*, which was passionately ignored. Nevertheless he went out to establish more evidence, but was referred to as a foolish crank wasting everybody's time with his ridiculous ideas. The authorities of the day employed the most horrendous weapon to stop him: they ignored him.

Within nine years he was back again with more material evidence, and again published his theory in a new, three-volume work on prehistory. In it he stated that the evidence he had compiled proved that man had been making stone implements thousands of years earlier, "unthinkably earlier," than ever thought possible by scholars. By now Thomsen's work had become well known, and some antiquarians in France were beginning to think that de Perthes might be right in principle, though he was certainly exaggerating when he talked about "thousands of years" into the past. The authorities either continued to ignore him or publicly damned his ideas outright.

Shortly after de Perthes's second work was released, a historian by the name of Dr. Rigollet decided once and for all to put a stop to all this nonsense by conducting his own excavations in order to prove to the world that de Perthes was in total error. The historian dug at a number of sites and began to realize that something was funny. He excavated specimen after specimen just as de Perthes had said he would, and could not bring himself to say that they had been formed by nature or that they had been formed only recently. After much contemplation, he issued a report that backed up de Perthes in every way. The barrier had been broken; the authorities were ready to listen.

In 1859 de Perthes was officially vindicated when his work was read before the British Association (of scientists) and the Royal Society. This was followed by an announcement at the Académie des Sciences in Paris that his theories deserved recognition. De Perthes continued his work, in light of his official vindication (a favorite term employed by authorities, as though their word were law), but was eventually harassed again for his methodology. He finally retired from active research, having lost a little faith in his fellow man and in the honesty of the so-called experts.

It had taken him thirty years to convince these experts that he had been right all along.

With few exceptions, archaeology of any kind was still a rich man's hobby. The exceptions involved only those who were willing to work into the night and conduct research as best they could. Many did not have collections of their own and thus spent much time in museums; they could not finance excavations, such as they were, and were forced either to follow others around or do a little digging whenever an opportunity presented itself. Archaeology, or the study of antiquities, was anything but a profession. If someone said he wanted to pursue this field as a career, he would immediately be asked, "Fine, but what will you do for a living? How will you support yourself and your career?" When European antiquarians saw what the Danes had accomplished with Thomsen, and without ever paying him a working salary, it became common practice to *expect* someone to devote his time, effort, and energy towards advancing the interesting pastime of working with ancient materials. It is interesting to note that the idea of people working in this field without remuneration has continued actively to this day. Professional archaeologists do, of course, get paid; but the amateurs, who do most of the work, do not—with a few rare exceptions.

During the mid-nineteenth century, the study of antiquities was of course open to anyone interested, and many people did show an interest. One of these was Jens Jacob Asmussen Worsaae, who presented himself to the Danish Society of Antiquaries in 1841 and asked to be a member. The acceptance of his application for membership by the crown prince of Denmark, who happened to be a tireless antiquarian and president of the society, marked the beginning of an important career and a change in the way amateur antiquarians conducted themselves. Worsaae was a struggling law student who had collected bronze tools and pottery as a boy and wanted now to enlarge his activities.

A few years earlier, Worsaae had worked under Thomsen in the museum as an unpaid clerk (along with everybody else) solely in order to gain experience and familiarity with the various, numerous collections. Before that, he had devoted all his spare time—evenings, weekends, vacations—to digging here and there in his neighborhood, an activity which absolutely fascinated him. The same year he joined the Society of Antiquaries, his father died, and Worsaae found that he and his family were broke.

In order to support himself, Worsaae could have taken some kind of job, but he refused, never considering anything but archaeological research. He asked Thomsen, therefore, to pay him a salary for his work at the museum, but was refused outright. Thomsen's refusal was both expected and understandable (except by Worsaae) for the idea of getting paid for this kind of activity was simply unheard of. Do people get paid for collecting butterflies? Worsaae explained that if he did not receive some support, he would have to leave the museum altogether, but there was nothing Thomsen could do. As the son of a respected officer of the state, Worsaae requested and was granted an audience with King Christian VIII.

With all the passion at his command, Worsaae pleaded for the opportunity to study prehistory. His first major work, *Prehistory of Denmark*, had just been released, and the king was so impressed with the young man's enthusiasm that he allowed a small grant to be furnished Worsaae for his efforts. *Prehistory of Denmark* was of an importance second only to the work published by Thomsen himself, for Worsaae had actually zeroed in on his country's history prior to the onset of writing. This led eventually to his being appointed inspector of ancient monuments, a far cry from the days when he was on the verge of starvation.

Worsaae traveled throughout Europe and conducted dozens of excavations, always reporting the results in a most meticulous manner. He was regarded as his country's most esteemed antiquarian after Thomsen. When Thomsen died and Worsaae replaced him at the National Museum, an era had come to an end. Whereas Thomsen had witnessed the growth of antiquity studies to the status of an important discipline, Worsaae became the first full-time, paid archaeologist in history. Hundreds of discoveries had been made all over the Continent, and the concept of prehistory was no longer considered absurd. The next few years were devoted to expanding the work that Thomsen had begun and trying to keep track of everything happening elsewhere in Europe in this field. It became obvious that all of European archaeology had to be coordinated, and the former law student who had collected pottery as a boy went forth to do the job.

He traveled again throughout Europe discussing prehistory with other researchers, and was invited to make a presentation at the Exposition Universelle in Paris. He then journeyed to Russia and was shown remarkable pieces of antiquity, but he saw that no thought was given to any system of their arrangement. Russia was thirty years behind Europe with regard to understanding its prehistory. It was now 1869, ten years after the scientific community had formally and officially accepted the doctrine of the antiquity of man. Geology had been recognized as a sufficiently exact science only nine years earlier, and it had been less than twenty years since several branches of science—archaeology, geology, and zoology—had pooled their efforts and knowledge for the first time to conduct an excavation.

Archaeology had just come of age, and the efforts of the antiquarians were finally being realized, understood, and appreciated by the public. For the first time, the official use of the term *prehistoric* was employed. But archaeology still had a long way to go.

As we move closer to the end of the nineteenth century, certain attitudes about social education began to change. In the strict and proper eighteenth-century tradition, well-to-do families sent their sons to the university because it was the thing to do, rather than out of a particular desire to have them obtain knowledge. Gentlemen were usually labeled such as a result of the quality and quantity of their schooling. Society demanded that sophisticated families continue the educational process, thereby further distinguishing among classes. Indeed, a prospective student to a university was forced to wait until his *family* passed muster; until the trustees agreed that they wanted their institution to include a member of a certain family among its potential graduates. In this sense, many of the esteemed antiquarians discussed above were actually undereducated, for they did not represent this gentlemanly attitude about learning. They were a bit too practical for the cultured gentry and took academic research too seriously.

The self-educated individualists first showed their colors during the latter half of the 1800s. One of these was William Pengelly. A poor cabin boy, he was forced to leave his little village school at the age of twelve, but a burning desire to learn persisted. If he couldn't obtain an education by way of family influence, then he would get it another way; he would educate himself. This he did, and by the age of twenty-four became involved in establishing a number of the small schools specializing in adult education for the working man which were springing up all over England. He lectured at many of these schools on a variety of subjects and became particularly interested in the field of geology as did many of his students.

He expanded his education by studying natural science in general, and eventually became a private tutor while devoting all his spare time to collecting fossils and concentrating on geological research. He was instrumental in founding a natural historical society, and while looking for a suitable project to undertake he came across a cavern in which two geologists had previously found flint implements. When these amateur geologists went to work, they had no model by which to instruct themselves, for the scientific methodology in excavation had not yet been established. Nevertheless, Pengelly and his group did come up with some interesting finds, and because of the location of these finds within the cavern, Pengelly began to think that everything he had studied about the antiquity of man was wrong; that the age of man was a great deal older than anyone had ever dreamed.

It was to be a repeat performance of what de Perthes experienced; the established authorities wanted nothing to do with Pengelly or his thoughts. But eventually he was allowed to excavate a site under the watchful eyes of some recognized geologists, and after digging through to a level containing what were obviously the remains of ancient animals,

Pengelly dug *further down* and excavated flint tools fashioned by the hand of man. There was now no possible argument against the idea that man had lived across Europe for tens of thousands of years.

Pengelly continued his research in geology and conducted many more excavation projects. In 1863, this former cabin boy whose formal education had ended at the age of twelve was elected a fellow of the Royal Society.

The natural sciences had exploded with new theories of their own just as Pengelly was finalizing his ideas on the age of man. Neanderthal man—the extinct missing link between the ape and *Homo sapiens*—had been discovered, and the theory of natural selection had been put forth. Darwin's *Origin of Species* had been received by a fascinated public. Everything fit, as the discoveries of different disciplines began to complement one another.

The year the theory of natural selection became popular, a twenty-nine-year-old farm laborer was busy conducting research that would result in spectacular specimens for prehistorians. Jakob Messikommer was like Pengelly. Forced to stop school at the age of fifteen in order to help support his family, he was a voracious reader. Too poor to buy books or even a newspaper, he was constantly borrowing everything in print he could find.

One of his jobs on the farm was to collect peat for fuel. Having read that peat was an excellent preserver of such materials as bone and wood, he was always on the lookout for anything unusual. When a prehistoric grave was located in Robenhausen, the town near where Messikommer lived in Switzerland, he raced down to acquire the objects and sent them off with a very proficient letter of explanation to an archaeologist in Zurich. The archaeologist suggested that more such finds might be available on the shores of Lake Pfäffikon, and Messikommer began to spend as much time there as possible examining the shoreline. Before long, he had located flint implements and other objects, and in order to preserve the area from any outside interference, he scraped together every bit of money he could get his hands on and purchased the land. Fortunately, the land was of no use or importance to anyone, so the price was relatively low. But it was all the money Messikommer had in the world.

He devoted the next fifty years of his life to carefully excavating the land, and produced an immense amount of material from what was a previously unknown buried primitive village. He was so careful and so meticulous in his work that even today his site reports, many written by his son, must be admired. People came from all over the world to view this massive and impressive project, and in 1867 the poor farm boy was awarded an honorary doctorate by the University of Zurich for his dedicated research.

A new type of research came into being thanks mainly to Messikommer: lake villages. Students all over Switzerland were quick to react to the success in Robenhausen by claiming lakefronts for excavation, and a great deal was accomplished, for the remains of primitive tribes were turned up with great regularity. We learned how small communities developed, how they handled population growth, and why they followed the lakes. We learned also that one of their main enemies was fire, and that they were not hunters. Finally, we learned that they were a people not indigenous to the area in which they were found. They were immigrants, travelers who had moved into Europe over 5,000 years earlier—Neolithic man.

Excavations in other parts of the world continued unabated on all kinds of sites. When a young lawyer named Édouard Lartet began studying geology in his spare time, he wondered why so little attention—other than Darwin's work—had been given to the physical evolution of man. He continued active in his profession for many years, but finally walked away from the practice of law to devote all his energy to finding the remains of the ape-man Darwin spoke of. Long before Darwin published his epoch-making work, Lartet had privately thought that man was little more than a super-ape. He was proved correct by showing that a being known as Cro-Magnon man once existed, and that he resembled modern man—not the ape. The anthropologists of the day had to completely reexamine their theses, thanks to a lawyer who eventually became a professor of paleontology in Paris.

As the evidence for prehistory grew at an incredible rate, more and more individuals became interested and involved in research and excavation work. The scientific authorities of the day represented a new generation, a new century, a new era, of thinkers regarding man's antiquity. There was still a lot of debate between the new and old schools of thought, between young students and recognized authorities, and between "specialists" in geology and "outsiders" who saw no reason not to offer their impressions and opinions. Numerous amateur organizations and societies sprang up to continue important work, and because of them a mountain of material accumulated to provide a solid basis with which to establish a new science. Although authoritarianism was reduced to a simmer, it had not been extinguished, and remains alive and well and hiding behind university walls today. A classic example of rampant arrogance by the experts occurred towards the end of the 1800s, the victim of which was a Spanish nobleman named Don de Sautuola.

De Sautuola was a nobleman in the strictest sense of the word. Educated, rich, and cultured, he was known as a kind, thoughtful man involved in many intellectual and business pursuits. His particular love was for anything ancient; he understood and had great respect for history and was regarded as somewhat of an expert in Spanish geology and monuments.

One day, quite by chance, he noticed his dog disappear into some kind of cavern on his estate in Spain. After a bit of a struggle, he managed to enter the cave himself to free his dog. Seven years later, in 1875, he returned with workmen, widened the entrance, and slowly worked his way down into the cavern. He noticed as he went along large quantities of bone remains of animals. He had them analyzed by Don Piera, professor of geology at Madrid University, and was told that they were the bones of at least two extinct mammals, and that they had been worked on by man.

Thinking he might have a prehistoric site on his property, de Sautuola returned four years later after exhaustive studies on other caves in Spain and elsewhere in Europe. Carefully clearing his way back into the cave, he noticed other organic remains and markings on walls further inside. He dug for several days and located specific evidence that man had once occupied the cave for a considerable length of time.

One day he returned to continue his work with his young daughter along for company, and as de Sautuola busied himself collecting material objects, his daughter wandered around with a torch. She suddenly gasped. The walls of the cave were covered with paintings of prehistoric animals! De Sautuola was overwhelmed as he marveled at the style and skill of these beautiful three-dimensional pictures made by some primitive people whose very existence was hardly even realized. When he told his friend Piera about the discovery, the latter thought de Sautuola was exaggerating, but upon examination Piera realized that, if anything, the nobleman had underplayed his discovery. Further, the visible art was not the first, for it had been superimposed on earlier pictures. The geologist was convinced that the people responsible for this work had inhabited the area at least 10,000 years ago. Paleolithic man in Spain. The evidence was overwhelming.

And then the experts heard about it.

De Sautuola prepared and published a full report of what had transpired, and included sketches of the pictures in the cave drawn for him by a French artist. The result was a precise scientific presentation, including comments on its authenticity by the geologist Piera.

The first reaction by the scientific community was one of surprise. But this did not last long, and was quickly followed by irate statements of ridicule and scorn. The authorities were downright angry that anyone would go to such lengths to perpetrate an obvious hoax. They labeled de Sautuola a fraud and charlatan. After all, they said, we already know that ancient man was a primitive savage incapable of such artistic feats.

The most outspoken authority and adamant opponent was one Dr. Cartailhac, well-known authority and professor of prehistory at the University of Toulouse. Cartailhac saw no reason even to bother to travel a mere three hundred miles to see the cave. He was so convinced, without seeing the evidence, that it was a hoax that he denounced it outright. None of it fit in with his view of prehistory, so therefore, it *must* be a hoax! (This attitude, by the way, is common today, and will be discussed in chapters 7 and 10.)

De Sautuola was stunned. He could not believe that his word was being challenged. To such a man honor was everything, and here he was being treated like a criminal who had purposely performed some despicable act against society. Although the opposition was fierce and vocal, de Sautuola did not respond. Gentlemen, he felt, did not have to prove that they were honorable.

But Professor Piera was not so conciliatory. His professional judgment had been rudely attacked, and when the International Congress of Archaeologists met in Lisbon in 1880, he delivered a scathing address to these the world's most prominent prehistorians, an address the likes of which has not been heard since. Piera made it perfectly clear that the evidence was there for anyone to view, and that those who chose not to had no recourse but to keep their mouths shut. The scientists backed off. Some visited the cave and saw the paintings, and a few agreed that there was something here worthy of further investigation. But Cartailhac would have none of it, and published his own report showing the impossibility of the whole situation.

Still de Sautuola did not respond. The unmerciful attacks continued; his honor was ridiculed regularly. He finally shook his head for the last time and died in 1888. His old friend Piera followed him five years later. This whole event, moreover, was not an isolated case in two respects. First, other researchers were excavating their way into caverns all over Europe and, pushed ever on by the success of Lartet, were discovering Cro-Magnon man and other remains. Second, researchers were beginning to examine the walls of caves more carefully, and sure enough, were finding paintings, drawings, sketches, engravings. Something had to be done.

One researcher from France who was about to present *his* evidence of ancient cave painting to the Prehistoric Society of France was prevented by Cartailhac, who was by then president of the society. The

researcher, however, bypassed Cartailhac and went directly to the immensely prestigious Academy of Science in Paris, where his evidence
was received, analyzed, studied, and pronounced sufficient to warrant
a public statement.

It still took a few more years for the scientific community to accept de
Sautuola's proposition. Finally, however, in 1902, Cartailhac publicly
announced that he was now prepared to agree that the Spanish nobleman had been right. It had been almost thirty years since de Sautuola
first discovered the cave with his dog, and fifteen years since his
death. Cartailhac, aware of this, traveled to pay a call on the person who
was actually the first to see the paintings, de Sautuola's daughter. He
humbly offered a formal apology for his attacks on her father. "I made a
mistake." Indeed.

It turned out that the cave paintings were among the most elaborate
in all of Europe, a testament to the skills of prehistoric man. There is
today above the entrance to the cave a tribute in stone to Don de
Sautuola.

But let us continue with our discussion of some of the important contributors to the founding of archaeology.

I stated a few pages earlier that by the beginning of the 1870s
archaeology was on its way to becoming a recognized field of inquiry,
but that it still had a long way to go. That is because it still had no
scientific methodology. Anyone who wanted to could simply dig up a site
in any manner he chose, though the more serious antiquarians took
great care in the process to account for as much as they could. The most
significant contribution of archaeology is the *manner* in which excavation
is conducted, as discussed in Part V, and this had not yet been systematized. Then a British general came along.

The British general was of a classic type—arrogant, strict, cultured.
He would today be referred to as a snob. A bright and accomplished
soldier, Augustus Henry Lane Fox, who later changed his name to
A. H. L. F. Pitt-Rivers in order to receive an inheritance, was the force
behind the eventual serious attention paid to the scientific classification
of firearms. Everything was broken down by typology, specific uses were
analyzed, and the developmental stages by which firearms steadily
improved were established. Pitt-Rivers's work led to the founding of the
well-known Hythe School of Musketry, where his ideas on specificity
were taught; these included the dicta that everything must be considered,
and that nothing can be left to chance in any kind of investigation.

Always having been interested in history and prehistory, he brought
his ideas of classification to these fields and became a lecturer at the
Anthropological Institute of England. Eventually he was elected a

fellow of the Royal Society. After receiving his inheritance, he continued studying and applying his methods of typology, classification, and sequence to other subjects. Archaeologists today, though aware of his background, will not remember him for his school of musketry or for his knowledge of the history of firearms. He is remembered instead as the greatest digger of them all, the man who first applied a systematic scientific methodology to the excavation technique—something the experts had never thought of or tried.

Pitt-Rivers's system was so refined and so meticulous that his published works can still be utilized as guides by the student of archaeology. His books represent the bible of excavation; little could be added to improve the system; everything else is commentary.

He was the first digger to recognize the single most outstanding principle in excavation: all excavation is destruction, and the more thorough the excavation the more complete the destruction. He recorded and illustrated for future diggers every single move in his own excavation work, and even left an account of what had transpired at a site *in the ground itself*, so that future excavators would know exactly what he had done before them. Antiquarians had often complained that "if only we had known who dug what here" or "if only he had been more careful," important material evidence might have a different meaning. Yet no one had given serious thought to a systematic approach until Pitt-Rivers came along and implemented sound logic, respect, patience, and a strict scientific pursuit. The garden party, Sunday afternoon excavation atmosphere had come to an end. The methodology of the treasure hunter had been replaced irrevocably by that of the scientist, and the excavator, a new specialty within a new field, was created.

The founder of modern excavation techniques died in 1900, a year in which two other important events also occurred. The world of professional scientists officially replaced the term *antiquarian* with that of *archaeologist,* and a very poor German electrician by the name of Alfred Rust was born.

Archaeology had just become a settled and disciplined science. Universities took it upon themselves to accord official recognition to this new field of inquiry by establishing a course of study. It was a difficult and arduous course of study, but upon completion the graduate was awarded the degree of master of arts in archaeology and ethnology, the first formal certification of its kind. But along with recognition, archaeology began to acquire an attitude of arrogance. Professionalism was demanded, and this was taken to mean that only university graduates were capable of contributions. The field had become rampant with authoritarianism over a jealously guarded discipline. The new archaeologists got a little carried away with their new-found importance; their professional status had gone to their heads, and amateurs were astounded that they were playing the same game the expert historians had played years earlier, when antiquarians were pushing man back to his prehistory. Many professional archaeologists of the day insisted that the self-trained, amateur researcher no longer held a place in the study of prehistory.

And so it would appear.

No examination of the history of amateur archaeology would be complete without a look at a man who represents what a dedicated amateur can accomplish, however, and we bring this chapter to a close with the story of Alfred Rust.

This unusual young man, for whom higher education was completely out of the question, attended lectures on anthropology, geology, and history at one of the workingmen's adult education evening programs. He was always attracted to anything that smacked of mystery and the unknown, and as he listened to lectures on prehistory he had an incredible urge to go out and find evidence that ancient man had lived in Germany. And that's exactly what he did.

With only a few dollars in his pocket, he quit his job as an apprentice electrician and began excavating in the Hamburg area. Not satisfied with the results, he decided to go to Syria after hearing that important research was under way there and that he might be able to gain some valuable experience. He financed the journey by performing assorted tasks as an electrician en route, and managed to cover the nearly three thousand miles—by *bicycle*—in about three months.. He returned to his native Hamburg after the winter season, and repeated the trip three more times to Syria and back. He was so busy excavating and studying Stone Age deposits that he fell ill more than once, and his budget allowed only twenty-five cents' worth of food a day. In exchange for the artifacts he found in Syria, he received $200 a year, and from this he in turn had to pay workers to assist him in the digging.

Adamant about making a career out of archaeology, which was in itself a recent conception in the professional world, he turned his sights back again on his native Germany when he was told that a few implements had been found *right near Hamburg* which suggested a far earlier *Homo sapiens* than anyone had considered. This was all Rust needed. Again with virtually no funds for excavation, he began digging for any hint of ancient habitation. He lived on two dollars a week and cycled fifty miles every day from his home to the site and back. Eventually, after weeks of difficult work, he began finding animal bones from the period just after the glacial ice cap began retreating! Further, he found evidence of man, for some antlers had obviously been fashioned, cut, and scraped for use in various human enterprises. When he turned his material over to a museum, it included nearly six hundred specimens.

The following year, after another trip to Syria, Rust returned to his Hamburg site to find that the German Archaeological Institute was funding an excavation program for continued research, a program that included a professional geologist and a pollen analyst. They wanted Rust to direct the project, because he had exposed the most important site then under excavation in all of Germany, a prehistoric lake village. The results were nothing short of fantastic. Rust located and identified remains of human activity that allowed researchers to put together a virtually complete picture of these early men's movements, habits, customs, and even religious attitudes.

Rust eventually identified forty-five successive stratified levels of occupation by ancient man, from the last Ice Age to the beginning of agriculture in prehistoric Germany. He was at first ignored, of course, by the establishment for his views about prehistory, and described as "a mere amateur." His attempt to publish the results of his work was thwarted by the editors of archaeological journals. Archaeology and its literature were a jealously guarded realm of the professional community, but it was obvious that Rust could not be ignored. It was eventually proven that Rust had been correct in every detail, and in 1940 he was given an honorary degree of doctor of arts by a grateful Kiel University.

In ten years of almost completely independent work, he revealed 15,000 years of prehistory.

I have been dealing thus far with the growth of archaeology in Europe from the standpoint of antiquarians of the nineteenth century trying to establish the idea of *prehistory,* for it was with them that such fields as palaeoanthropology in America and prehistoric archaeology in Europe began. There was much more going on in archaeology at its founding than has been alluded to here: the California gold-hunter named Schliemann found the city of Troy, the schoolteacher Grotefend deciphered cuneiform, and the genius Champollion opened a whole new world of knowledge by translating hieroglyphics. All of these men were important to the growth of archaeology for different reasons but none underwent such trials and tribulations as some of the amateur archaeologists described above, whose efforts and accomplishments required willpower, stamina, and the ability to ignore all opposition when they knew they were right. There are amateur archaeologists today who have experienced, or still are experiencing, the wrath of the professional community.

Before we get to them, however, let's move into the next phase of the growth of archaeology, which had indeed by now come of age throughout the world. It was moving fast and furiously to establish itself as an independent discipline, and was working its way up to becoming a specific branch of the new religion of the Western world: Science.

CHAPTER 7

Archaeology and Science

The growth of science over the last fifty years in the Western world has been nothing short of phenomenal. In the decade following the publishing of Einstein's general and specific theories of relativity, our knowledge of physics doubled, and is continuing to double every ten years, though there are signs that this is beginning to slow. The field of modern genetics was born in the year 1900, thirty-four years after the monk Mendel had published the results of his research on heredity based on experiments with garden peas. The field of psychology now has thirty-one subdisciplines, from Jungian to humanistic. Each year, no less than ninety thousand new research projects are initiated by scientists around the world; and we are continuously witness to new specialties and subspecialties being established within academic science, from cosmobiology and space genetics to archaeoastronomy and plasma physics. More scientific knowledge has been acquired in the last fifty years than in the entire history of mankind.

MODERN GROWTH

Archaeology has certainly not stood still in the twentieth century, but many of the factors involved in its growth came about through other fields of science.

The general system of three ages of man—Stone, Bronze, and Iron— had been improved and advanced to five ages in order to further isolate the growth and movement of *Homo sapiens*. It was eventually realized by anthropologists and geographers, however, that even this improved classificatory system could not of itself be reliable, for man's ancient progress and advancement did not occur in simultaneous stages everywhere on earth. It became necessary to study the people themselves, and thus the idea of *culture* came into being. The five ages themselves were further divided, and researchers found themselves dealing with an Early, Middle, and Late Bronze Age and the Neolithic I, II, III, and IV Period; moreover, these ages or periods differed depending on the geographical location with which one was involved!

As a result of assistance from many other fields of inquiry, archaeologists looked upon man's evolution not only in terms of ages, or divisions of time, but eventually from the standpoint of race, culture, economics, religion, trade, and function. This led to interpreting artifacts from a different standpoint and brought the idea of typology, or taxonomy, to a much sounder footing and expression. Rather than describing an artifact as "a tool from the Bronze Age," archaeology moved towards a much more specific and identifiable description which included the location, type of artifact, context, date, and historical stage.

In addition to a more descriptive typology, archaeology needed a better system of dating. Although it was relatively easy to date something based on historical reference, much of the research in this field dealt with prehistory, and the system of relative chronology—a major nineteenth-century advance though it was—was not absolute, as will be explained in Part V. Archaeology had reached a point of sophistication where a system was needed in which objects could be dated in and of themselves, without relative reference to other materials and without the hazards of cross-dating. In 1911, just eleven years after Pitt-Rivers died, a man by the name of V. F. Hess discovered cosmic radiation, and this was eventually to supply archaeology with its most impressive system of dating.

Willard F. Libby was three years old when Hess was born. Intending to pursue a career in engineering, he studied the necessary physics and mathematics, and became fascinated with chemistry. His particular interest was in radioactivity, and after conducting research on the atom bomb as part of the Manhattan Project, he became a professor at the University of Chicago.

Concluding that all matter was radioactive, he sought to find a way to measure this radioactivity, and in 1946 formulated a system to account for the consistent pattern by which radioactive substances decayed. This was his carbon-14 method, and the archaeological community was as excited about its potential as Libby was. The two fundamentally different sciences of archaeology and atomic physics enacted an immediate marriage, for not only did archaeology need such a system, but Libby realized that only archaeology could supply him with objects of antiquity already dated by other means with which he could establish the validity of his new system of measurement.

In 1948 the American Anthropological Association appointed a special committee to assist Libby in testing his method. Objects from all over the United States and the world were sent by researchers who hoped to settle once and for all the date of certain artifacts they had been mulling over for years. Although a majority of the specimens were from America, it was decided that something of Egyptian origin would be most easily referenced with regard to a date previously established by other means. The first item, which an historian said was dated to circa 2700 B.C., showed up at 2000 B.C. by the C-14 method. This was too large a difference, and although it did not prove Libby's method incorrect—for everyone agreed that the date of 2700 B.C. *could* be off—it certainly did not establish it as valid. So another specimen was called for out of Egypt, and the world's authority on Egyptology himself, J. H. Breasted, gave Libby bits of wood from a pharaoh's sarcophagus and told the chemist that it was quite old. But Libby measured it as being quite recent! Breasted reexamined the object and was forced to conclude that, expert though he was, he had been fooled by a forgery.

The machinery necessary to conduct radiocarbon dating is enormous and involved, because the measuring system itself is highly involved. What bothered archaeologists most was the fact that a specimen was destroyed in the process of testing, though the quantity necessary was not large.

The C-14 method has been constantly improved, and when Libby received the Nobel Prize in 1960, it was the first time any scientist connected with archaeology—though he was a chemist and atomic physicist—had been so honored.

In 1929, when Willard Libby was still a college student, another American, an astronomer and physicist named Andrew E. Douglass, put forth his principles for a dating system that could measure time to the *year*. After studying the influence of sunspots on terrestrial weather and thinking about Leonardo da Vinci's comment in his journals that an area's type of weather—wet or dry—could be traced in tree rings, Douglass established the system of dendrochronology (from the Greek *dendron*, "tree"), or tree-ring dating.

The idea of counting the rings on a tree, each one of which represents the full cycle of the seasons, or a year, had been contemplated by many people since da Vinci. But what Douglass noticed was that the rings are not all identical: some are thick, some thin; some seem to follow other rings in a pattern, some don't; and they differ in color. After determining that there is a correlation between the eleven-year sunspot activity cycle and its effect on the behavior of tree rings, Douglass was able to identify the weather patterns of specific years in the past solely by examining trees which had been felled. Douglass also offered evidence that *all* living things are profoundly affected by solar activity.

As Douglass perfected his system, it turned out that people did not have to chop down trees to tell how old they were. With a few slices from old trees already felled, pieces from beams, and even partially charred remains, a careful examination of the tree rings could determine to the year when the wood had been taken from the tree. Douglass further advanced this system by developing a rod with a hollow center by means of which a sample of the tree's core could be extracted and dated.

Dendrochronology and radiocarbon dating opened a whole new era to archaeologists in absolute dating of the past. More than anything else since the days of Thomsen, Worsaae, and Pitt-Rivers, these two new methods of dating made archaeology an important scientific discipline. Other dating methods have been developed and are in use by researchers, as noted in chapter 23, but none has had the impact of radiocarbon dating and dendrochronology.

A word now about how a system was developed for *locating* sites, a system described as the largest single source of new discoveries in archaeology—aerial photography. Just prior to World War II, after a lot of fooling around with hanging cameras on weather balloons, the Germans and then the English noticed that indentations in the land which could not be seen on the ground stood out when viewed from the air. Whole communities from the past were first noticed by aerial photographers. Particularly in the Near East, sites were found which had never been noticed even by those who walked through them day after day. More than that, the camera could show specific roads and prior alterations in the earth, and this of course gave researchers a much better idea of what was located where at a site. By the 1930s, aerial photography was well on its way to becoming a regular feature of archaeological work, and is in use today as an incomparable method for locating and outlining ancient sites.

These new systems are sufficient, I think, to illustrate the steady growth and "scientification" of archaeology since Pitt-Rivers gave us the method of the excavation technique and Alfred Rust showed the importance of ancient lake villages. Technology has played no small part in this growth. Some archaeologists now utilize a soil resistance measuring meter designed for archaeological reconnaissance and a mechanical sifting device to aid in—but not totally replace, yet—the task of recovering specimens by hand.

The scope of archaeological research and what archaeologists do has been enlarged until we now have specialists in underwater research, known as nautical or marine archaeology. The American Institute of Nautical Archaeology was founded in 1973 after years of pioneering work in this type of exploration. Many amateurs have conducted underwater research.

One underwater archaeologist, George Bass, an associate professor of classical archaeology, has devoted years to probing the Mediterranean Sea. It is a long, costly, involved process, requiring specialists in a number of areas and a lot of expensive equipment. Professor Bass has shown, however, that in spite of the incredible number of problems one encounters and the fact that "dusty diggers" on land have it easy logistically by comparison, it is nonetheless a worthwhile pursuit to locate numerous artifacts which help fill in some of the blank pages of both recent and ancient history. Another underwater researcher, ocean-ographer-engineer Willard Bascom, is convinced that a much greater quantity of ancient relics still lies in deep water than has ever been recovered.

A party of twenty-five divers who found and excavated an "under-water Pompeii" near Jamaica are inclined to agree with Bascom. After three years, the group brought up 26,000 bottles, 12,000 clay pipes, and the remains of eight taverns, a pottery shop, and a synagogue. They also found petrified butter, pots filled with cornmeal, 200 skeletons, wigs of human hair, clothing, and tobacco. The research on this material is only just beginning.

Another water digger, Sidney Wignall, formed the Atlantic Charter Maritime Archaeological Foundation and has interested 150 people in marine archaeology. The director of the Undersea Naval Museum in Newport, Rhode Island, Jackson Jenks, spotted stone towers some years ago in a hundred feet of water (but he has hesitated to elaborate for fear that souvenir hunters would pick them apart).

A rather recent addition to the scope of modern archaeology is a new field termed archaeoastronomy or astroarchaeology, which involves the examination of ancient terrestrial structures by their applicable astronomical alignments. This procedure was systematized by the English engineer-mathematician Alexander Thom and is being worked on in North America by Anthony Aveni, an astronomer and physicist at Colgate University. Another astronomer-physicist who has been involved in this type of research is Lyle B. Borst of the State University of New York at Buffalo. Dr. Borst has determined, for example, that London's two cathedrals are aligned with a major celestial object, thus suggesting that the terrestrial sites were once pagan places of worship in antiquity. The axes of the two cathedrals are in direct line with one another, and both align astronomically with the star Aldebaran as it rose above the horizon between 1600 and 1500 B.C. Since the aligning of special sites with stars was common during this period, Dr. Borst suggests that the churches today may sit atop ancient religious centers. This is a new field of research in archaeology, and a number of amateurs with good backgrounds in astronomy—like Byron Dix of Vermont— are adding to this field every day. Archaeoastronomy is another example of disciplines in science adding to the methodology of archaeological research. More will be discussed about this field in the next section.

ARCHAEOLOGICAL ACTIVITY

The various developments noted above have helped archaeology gain recognition in academic science. This has allowed professional archaeologists to become involved in a number of pursuits. Although the public usually hears only about those pursuits by professionals which lend themselves to eye-catching headlines, a great deal of activity goes on behind the scenes which rarely gets reported. The professional archaeologist has a habit of keeping things to himself in order to insure full and complete credit when he's ready, and the amateur archaeologist is often ignored by the press because he has no academic credentials.

In order that the reader, particularly the beginner to this field, be aware of the general scope of archaeological activity today, it is appropriate to report on some of it. While some professional archaeologists are involved in the United States with Indian cultures and Colonial settlements, others are examining infusion of man from Europe, Asia, Africa, and the Near East. As researchers grow more confident in their methodology, they are able to determine more readily the authenticity and origins of their finds—or at least that's the idea.

One area that many disciplines of science, including archaeology, are constantly analyzing deals with the age of man. Just how old *is* our earliest recognizable ancestor? Around 1960, it was pretty well established by science that man's greatest-grandparent goes back no more than 500,000 years. In 1975, however, all this changed, when discoveries in Africa extended man's roots to 3 million years and tentatively established that the tremendously significant cultural advance of the use of fire occurred a million years earlier than had been previously supposed. Fortunately, four major finds of early man occurred on two continents; hence the possibility that a freak being had been located could be ruled out. The laws of evolution according to anthropology are now being rewritten from scratch.

A question that has been tossed around in the United States for decades by archaeologists and that has been answered with a surety that reeks of intellectual arrogance deals with the age of *American* man. The traditional conception was that man had existed for thousands of millennia before ever appearing in the New World, and that the possibility of his having crossed the Bering Strait (once a large land bridge) could not have occurred more than 12,000 years ago. Part of the problem is the fact that Columbus didn't arrive until A.D. 1492, and that the Indians were not considered to be a prehistoric culture. Columbus did, of course, arrive in 1492, but by any possible standard at all he was a latecomer. As for the Indians, American archaeologists are apparently too close to the situation to think in broader terms with regard to evolution and time. A 250,000-year-old hand tool was recently discovered in Mexico, and this has led open-minded thinkers like anthropologist Bruce Raemsch of Hartwick College to insist that archaeologists reassess the early North American man. Dr. Raemsch now believes that the New World is not that new; that man may very well have existed here for half a million years or more. He backs up his statements with evidence of hand tools found in New York State that go back 70,000 years, and the ideas he is propagating conform with typical evolutionary patterns found in other parts of the world. Other sites in New Mexico and California have produced artifacts dating back 50,000, 100,000, and 300,000 years and more. In Wyoming, pebble tools have been tentatively dated to half a million years ago.

These and other discoveries have caused archaeologists to think twice about their tables of chronology—something they usually take care not to disturb. In Maine, as I write this chapter, archaeologists from the University of Maine are searching in the Upper St. John River Valley for evidence of early human habitation, which they expect to find. In England, a research team has turned up a Stone Age man about eighty miles north of London at that country's most important prehistoric site. The find forces experts to alter their conception of history and prehistory in ancient Britain.

Back in the New World, researchers have come a little closer to understanding the evolution of marine life, having found America's oldest fossil, dated at between 620 and 650 million years, in North Carolina. And Utah's oldest culture has recently been determined to be that of Indians who once flourished there as early as 8000 B.C. (not prehistoric indeed!).

There is today in many parts of the United States a massive amount

of research going on, principally by amateur archaeologists, in the area
of cultural diffusion. That is, there is a growing mountain of evidence
that entire cultures from Europe and the Mediterranean flourished in
various regions of this continent, and that many peoples populated this
land before Columbus arrived. Indeed, some of these cultures can be
found today by tracing their movements to other existing peoples, mainly
the Amerindians. By the same token, traces of the American Indian have
been found in Africa. There is an African language known as Vai which
is so similar to Cherokee that there is little doubt about a direct exchange. All the evidence points to the Cherokee language having
reached Africa, and not the other way around.

These broad examples illustrate the new horizons that beckon archaeologists—a long way from the days less than a century ago when antiquarians wondered if man was possibly more than five or six thousand
years old. The many fields of science involved in the study of man since
the turn of the century have assisted the professional archaeological community to reach new heights which would scarcely have been conceivable
just a few decades ago. But the professionals have not been alone in
their endeavors.

The amateur archaeologists in this country have made both a qualitative and a quantitative contribution. Some of the more outstanding of
them will be profiled later, but for the purposes of this chapter I should
like to mention some of their work in order that the unfamiliar reader
may obtain a more well-rounded idea of archaeological activity today.

Anthropologists and prehistorians are today working assiduously in
Florida as a result of some finds of great importance turned up there a
few years ago. The oldest human remains ever found in the Western
Hemisphere come from Venice, Florida, where a unique spear thrower
hook was also found. The hook is unique because, although it is known
that such hooks were used in Asia over 8,000 years ago, never before has
there been any evidence that they were also in use in the Western Hemisphere so far in the past. An amateur archaeologist was responsible for
these finds, and he learned a little about the way things are when one
becomes involved with professional archaeologists on their level. His
story smacks of the de Sautuola affair and makes one wonder if any
lessons have been learned by the experts since the 1880s.

Bill Royal, an amateur archaeologist and skin diver who had traveled
extensively around the world with the U.S. Air Force, finally decided to
settle down in Warm Mineral Springs in Florida. After casual investigation of the various submerged caves, Royal began digging in some sediment and procured several human skeletons and a large number of
animal bones known to be extinct since the last Ice Age. He turned his

specimens over to an anthropologist and never heard from him or saw the bones again.

Determined to start anew, and convinced that he was on the track of prehistoric man, Royal found more bones plus implements, and was told by an archaeologist from the University of Florida who took a quick glance at the material that it was somewhere around 500 years ago. After additional investigation, this time with marine biologist Eugenie Clark, Royal discovered another human skeleton whose skull contained a brain! This remarkable preservation was caused by the particular temperature and anaerobic condition of the spring water. Subsequent carbon-14 dating declared it the oldest extant human brain: 10,000 years, or a good 8,000 years older than any previous find. The scientific community was excited, but not in the way one might expect.

Royal was accused outright of committing a hoax. How? In Royal's travels all over the world, it was agreed, he must have found the remains at some prehistoric site and transported them to Florida for the publicity such a discovery would ensure. Completely stunned, Royal could not understand how the experts could choose to ignore sound evidence that man was in Florida as far back as 8000 B.C. He was aware, however, that it was their opinion that counted, not his or that of his friends. Back to work.

This amateur archaeologist devoted 5,000 hours of his time and spent no small amount of his savings to convince the scientific authorities that his evidence was authentic. In the process, he almost drowned twice and was bitten by an alligator. As he found more specimens, he did not remove them, but left them in place in the hope that he could keep the tourists and skin divers away long enough to lure another professional to the site for investigation. In 1971, public pressure brought the underwater archaeologist for the state of Florida to the site, who immediately stated that he was highly skeptical and suspicious of the whole situation. The archaeologist devoted a week to investigating on his own and came up with human remains subsequently dated at 10,300 years old.

Instead of joining Royal in a public statement about the find's authenticity and importance, however, the archaeologist suggested that it be kept quiet, and said he would return after arranging for additional crews to undertake a broader series of excavations. He did return, after several months, and told Royal that he and his crew would concentrate on Little Salt Springs. When Royal explained that he had already investigated that area thoroughly and that the oldest remains went back only 5,000 years, the archaeologist would hear none of it, and proceeded to waste two months and a lot of public money accomplishing precisely what Royal had already done on his own time with his own money.

It was not for another year and a half that the situation improved. Then the new underwater archaeologist for the state of Florida visited Royal, and this time it was a man particularly interested in early habitation in North America by *Homo sapiens*. The scientific community still labeled Royal a charlatan and a crackpot, so in order not to be involved in that mess, the new archaeologist decided to gather the sediment and pollen samples surrounding the area where the artifacts and specimens had been found. It was conceivable that Royal could have planted a smuggled skeleton of a prehistoric man in the springs, he thought, but there was no way he could have done the same with hundreds of tons of sediment and deep layers of extinct vegetation. The results of examination showed the samples to be between 10,000 and 12,000 years old. The archaeologist, now convinced that Royal was right, saw for *himself* a great opportunity, and the opportunity became a reality shortly thereafter.

In 1973, two archaeologists and a geologist found a 12,000-year-old human skeleton, skull, and brain just as Royal said they would. Additional excavations were to be carried out as soon as more funding could be obtained—something Royal never had a chance even to think about. The work continues today, and thanks to a determined, and smarter, amateur archaeologist, the history of early man in the Western Hemisphere is being revised.

When two scuba divers in California who were interested in underwater artifacts found large rocks with holes chipped in them, their first thought was that they had been fashioned by the hand of man. As it turned out, the divers may very well have found proof that Japanese or Chinese sailors visited the west coast of America over a thousand years ago.

Wayne Baldwin and Bob Meistrell had found rocks, all right, but they were rocks once utilized as ships' anchors, and they may corroborate Indian and Asian legends of transpacific commerce long before Europeans first journeyed to North America. Of the thirty stone anchors weighing 150 to 700 pounds each that were located by the pair in fifteen to thirty feet of water, six were retrieved. Archaeologists are virtually convinced that these items represent ocean crossings by Asians, and there is no question that the rocks were fashioned by men for a specific purpose. Researchers are now attempting to obtain some kind of confirmation and follow-up from the Japanese and Chinese governments.

Meanwhile, on the opposite coast, archaeologists are examining the remains of a massive ancient burial site that has yielded more than 5,000 artifacts. When James Griffin of Connecticut attempted to enlarge his basement, he unearthed some of the nineteen graves found thus far. It was determined by amateur researchers that the sudden dark soil meant the charred remains of a massive cremation. It was also realized that the culture responsible was not native or indigenous to the area, and that these people must have lived simultaneously with the Indians about 4,000 years ago. Some artifacts, such as a pegged molar, were noted to be commonly associated with the early Eskimos and natives of the Aleutian Islands.

In Arizona, a competent researcher whose experience matches that of Bill Royal has built a solid case in establishing that Roman Christians must have fled to the Americas, most likely to escape religious persecution. Thomas Bent owns some crudely made leaden crosses, short ceremonial swords, and roughly made lance heads. Inscribed on the crosses are messages in a confusing and jumbled Latin. Scientists who saw them immediately agreed that "it just couldn't be," that the whole thing was a hoax. Another hoax. The problem, however, rests in the fact that the artifacts are heavily encrusted and surrounded by caliche, a hard mineral deposit peculiar to desert regions and similar to concrete that forms only after water has percolated through mineral-rich soil for centuries. Amateur researcher Bent, who is in furious and adamant disagreement with the experts, has been able to refute every one of their arguments. The scientific community will probably not accept the validity of Bent's points until a couple dozen more such artifacts are found in some scientist's backyard.

Many other amateurs have located and studied less spectacular artifacts and specimens. One has devoted sixteen years to amassing documentary and archaeological evidence indicating that the Phoenicians made transatlantic crossings to the New World long before the Europeans. Many scholars, it seems, are almost totally ignorant of ancient shipping and the nautical capabilities of early mariners, and are of the opinion that the Phoenicians, for example, had neither the vessels nor the knowledge to undertake oceanic voyages. Fortunately, this attitude is just beginning to change, thanks mainly to the efforts of amateur archaeologists who did not wait around for someone to fund their endeavors.

Another amateur, a stockbroker, spends his vacations searching for artifacts in Israel. After locating an untold number of sardine and beer cans, bottle caps, and shell casings, he found what authorities said did not exist—a statue of the Roman Emperor Hadrian, who ruled from A.D. 117 to 138. It had long been thought that only one statue of the ruler had ever been constructed, but authorities are now reinvestigating many sites and have asked the amateur's assistance.

These short reports have been included here only to illustrate in part the new challenges facing archaeology today. The new discoveries, the new theories necessary to account for them, the wide scope of research and activity—all give witness to not only how far archaeology has come but also how far it has to go. By "archaeology today" I mean specifically to include both the professional and amateur segments, for it has become quite obvious to this writer after long and careful evaluation and assessment that the professional community cannot and will not handle the existing challenge adequately, and that the public will not even be aware of it until it's too late.

ACADEMIC ARCHAEOLOGY

The first course taught for credit in anthropology at a college or university in the United States was at the University of Vermont in 1885. Taught by a geologist, the junior-level course dealt with prehistory in Britain, the history of cultures, and the evolution of language. In 1895 a similar course was offered at Harvard University.

Much has happened since geology was the principal field of science involved with anything old; too much has happened, actually, and too fast. We can say that anthropology began with the material assembled by the Spanish conquistadors. Their efforts were followed by those of general travelers who haphazardly collected information as they went and kept diaries of what they saw. Anthropology in Europe was devoted almost exclusively to what Americans know as physical anthropology. When the study of ethnology made its way to the New World, researchers picked up where the Spanish and various travelers left off, and began to collect and correlate data on historic peoples. Anthropology then grew fast and furiously, spawning a host of other fields and subdisciplines which resulted in a considerable degree of confusion. One of those disciplines was cultural anthropology, the parent of archaeology in America.

As a result of very rapid growth in anthropology in general and archaeology in particular, no one is quite sure just exactly where the latter fits in. Some suggest archaeology should be no more than a tool of cultural anthropology, whereas others—archaeologists themselves, of course—adamantly insist that this field should be a separate, well-defined discipline with its own structure within science. The problem is that as a result of the many other fields of science that have formed the basis of and contributed regularly to archaeology, there can be no well-defined structure. Added to this is the fact that archaeologists in America today, though extremely well trained and versatile, are perhaps *too* versatile and are trying to cover too much ground at once, though not the ground they should cover.

A critical study was made of this situation recently by Robert Ascher of Cornell University. Writing in *Archaeology* magazine, October 1968, Ascher could only come to the conclusion that "archaeology in the university is anachronistic. It reflects the origins and earlier history of the subject, but not archaeology today." Because of its parent discipline and its basis as a system for examining culture, archaeology has gotten itself caught up in the intellectual argument of just what culture is. The situation is so diverse that a book has been written solely to *define the definitions* of culture.

There is a need now to determine first the most useful way in which archaeology can be and should be described as a functional discipline within science. This will not be easy, for even within the community of anthropologists there is major disagreement about these very points. But the first question that must be considered is, Is archaeology a science?

SCIENCE AND SOCIAL SCIENCE

The term *science* is a loose one, and includes under its umbrella physical science, behavioral science, and social science. In general, we can say without hesitation that any organized system of knowledge is a science. But this obviously includes anything from cooking to crockery making and from dowsing to desert photography. Is archaeology a science? It depends on whom you ask, for a sociologist would say yes while a physicist would loudly proclaim no. Further, in order to establish whether archaeology is a science one must first state specifically just what archaeology is and what it is not, and this can hardly be done without argument. Some may consider it irrelevant even to consider the question at hand. It should be stated here and now, however, that, no, archaeology is not a science.

There are two factors to consider: first, archaeology as a system of knowledge and as a discipline involved with *interpreting* data; second, archaeology as a method for *obtaining* data. With these two factors in mind, we must determine what makes *any* discipline a science by establishing criteria, and then seek to determine whether archaeology satisfies these criteria.

When I speak of science, I mean formal science; observable, experimental, testable, repeatable science: that which is scientific in the *scientific* sense of the word, and not as defined by a social studies teacher. Without getting into a long, drawn-out discussion, I will simply offer the observation that the three aspects of science which account for a discipline being labeled a science are the *goals* of science, the *phenomena* studied by science, and the *methods* of scientific study.

The *goals* of science are twofold: description and explanation; that is, a desire both to obtain knowledge of the way the world is and to understand why it is so. Because of the many variables involved in it, palaeo-anthropology cannot satisfactorily determine the way the world is to any degree of certainty, and it most assuredly cannot explain why it is so. In terms of scientific explanation, archaeology cannot *explain* that which it describes; it can only account for it.

The *phenomena* studied by archaeology represent scientific inquiry *only until* something more absolute is found. In that sense, the 12,000-year-old man found in Florida is indeed the oldest American, but only because we have yet to locate anything older. When the oldest man was set at a mere 2,000 years, we had no idea he would turn out to be so young—and we had no idea he *wouldn't* turn out to be comparatively recent. So the problem is that we cannot determine the importance of the phenomena we study, because the nature of those phenomena is under constant alteration as research marches on. Today's ancient man is tomorrow's recent newcomer.

Finally, the *methods* of scientific study. Does archaeology have a specific methodology? Yes! That which is *scientific* is *science*, and it is here that archaeology with its rather precise excavation technique measures up. But it is here also that archaeology brings in the second of two factors offered for consideration above. In terms of archaeology as a discipline involved with interpreting data, it is not a science; but in terms of archaeological *methodology*, it is.

Of all the systems of science, archaeology falls into the category of the social disciplines, under anthropology, and these fields *are not* sciences. Sociology and all its offshoots are no more to be considered scientific than are psychology and psychiatry, the behavioral disciplines. Consequently, archaeology deserves the high points it desires only in terms of its ability to procure data by a special procedure known as excavation.

Now that I have forever incurred the wrath of the archaeological establishment (and only them, for scientists of other fields would not argue with my assessment), it should be noted that archaeologists do consider themselves scientists and will settle for nothing less. My main argument with this is that it brings with it a feeling that no amateur archaeologist, no nonscientist, could *or should* attempt to contribute to this field, and that is so much nonsense in addition to being a blatant untruth. Because of the association of archaeology with other sciences which have contributed their technology to it, and because archaeology is a discipline which falls under anthropology and is therefore a social science, one could say, as Froelich Rainey of the University of Pennsylvania Museum suggested, that archaeology bridges a gap, or forms a connection, between science and the humanities.

One final note on this. Sir Mortimer Wheeler has described archaeology in *Archaeology from the Earth* (New York: G. P. Putnam, 1962) as primarily "a fact-finding discipline." His definition is rather lengthy, actually, and he gets a little carried away by bringing in the idea of humanism and philosophy as part of the archaeological attitude, which it is not, and most certainly is not in the United States. His primary definition of this field is accurate, however, and fits in well with the completely objective and clear-cut definition of an American archaeologist, W. W. Taylor, who stated: "Archaeology *per se* is no more than a method and a set of specialized techniques for the gathering of cultural information. The archaeologist, *as archaeologist* [emphasis added] is a technician."

ARCHAEOLOGY TODAY

So where does archaeology fit into the scheme of things? Although it has not stood still, it has fallen short of its desire to be raised to the level of a formal, independent science—the reasons for which will be discussed as we go along.

Archaeology today is whatever professional archaeologists say it is. A great deal of effort has been expended on the part of academic archaeologists to gain recognition for themselves within the scientific establishment, and this effort has pushed aside the primary function of their positions: to excavate, and then to work with other specialists in the interpretation of data.

Professionals in this field enjoy labeling themselves scientists in order to enhance their importance in the eyes of the public. Too much time has been spent *talking* about what archaeologists are supposed to do, and too little in actually doing it. All their talk has apparently done some good, however, for I notice that *Science Digest* magazine—the best publication of its kind for laymen—specifically separates the categories of archaeology and anthropology. Fine.

Because professionals have studiously welded themselves to the academic community and thus built a wall between themselves and the public that supports them, they have arrogantly gone the way of all academic flesh by refusing to do anything "unless I can get funding." Funding? What's funding? The word hardly exists in the amateur archaeologist's vocabulary, but to the professional it means everything. The professionals have reached the point where their personal careers are the only outstanding things on their minds, for in order to get funding one must be somewhat accomplished; and if funding is refused, well . . .

The difference between an amateur and a professional archaeologist is that while the latter is applying for and waiting around for funding the amateur is long gone, busy working, for free. The fall 1972 issue of *Man in the Northeast*, an excellent archaeological publication, contains an editorial by archaeologist Howard Sargent, who states that one of the primary problems in archaeology today is "the difficulty in obtaining funds for research." It would, of course, be ideal for every archaeologist to get all the funding he wanted, but *a lack of funding never stopped serious and involved amateur archaeologists from conducting research.* I know of some amateurs who put aside a certain percentage of their salaries each week for expenses involved in their archaeological work. No one funded Bill Royal in Florida or Thomas Bent in Arizona, but the archaeologists at the University of Maine did not move to examine a wilderness area selected as the spot for a power station until the U.S. Army Corps of Engineers gave them $75,000. Funding is necessary in situations that require a lot of special equipment and also where researchers are forced to work continuously for lengthy periods of time. But the amateur researchers who spend their own money on gas, food, and lodging—not to mention the giving of their time—do so because they are very much interested and because they know it has to be done. Weekend after weekend, plus vacations and holidays, amateur archaeologists are out doing what they can, and nobody ever offered them any funding. As amateur archaeologist James Whittall, director of archaeology for the Early Sites Research Society, said recently, "It is probably better that the 'establishment' leaves all this research to 'amateurs.' We go out and research rather than sit back and cry for funding. If this research was to wait for funding with today's destruction of sites there would be nothing to research."

The process whereby professionals obtain research grants is really a superb arrangement. They not only get all their expenses paid plus a crew to work for them, but they also receive a salary. When the colleges and universities finish their last semester each year, one can always see the archaeologists on their way to dig at a site—*if* they have funding. Again, funding is great for those who can get it, but the problem—and it is a major problem—is that funding is difficult for anyone to obtain, and therefore professionals refuse to budge. Enter the amateur.

ARCHAEOLOGY AND THE CITIZENRY

Some archaeologists, like Howard Sargent, quoted earlier, are concerned about the image of archaeology in the eyes of the public. Such a concern is of course natural, but Sargent fails to go to the root of the problem in his discourse. Stating that "the public concept of archaeology has not kept pace with recent growth in the discipline," he seems to infer that he's unsure why this is so, though he chalks it up to "ineffectiveness of communication." This is precisely the problem, and the blame for it rests squarely on the professional archaeological community. While these professionals are crying for funding, complaining that the public (which will pay for the funding) doesn't know what's going on, and writing editorials in their journals that no layman will ever see, the amateurs are looking for sites, studying sites, requesting permission from landowners to visit and photograph sites, reporting about sites, and trying to find a professional who will pay attention to the fact that "there is more out there than meets the eye." In the northeastern United States, many landowners who happen to have either recent or ancient Indian, Colonial, or other types of sites on their property have dealt only with amateurs, because (a) they have seen only amateurs, and are curious to know what a professional archaeologist looks like; (b) the amateurs have taken the time to fill these people in on precisely what they plan to do; (c) the amateurs keep the landowners updated on a regular basis; (d) the amateurs never publish anything in the popular press unless the landowner approves it; and (e) there is no problem with communication between the amateur and the landowner.

The importance of the amateur archaeologist today has slowly pervaded the consciousness of the professional community. Some archaeologists are "pleased to note" the contributions of amateurs and amateur societies, many of which experienced "unsteady beginnings." This patronizing type of attitude is a bit ironic, considering the source, for the amateur archaeologist has no choice but to move on his own since he is "displeased to note" the lack of activity among professionals. An accomplished amateur in this field recently put the whole matter rather succinctly when he remarked to this writer, "If it has to be done, do it; don't wait for funding and don't wait for professionals."

One professional who has a clear picture of what's been going on and who is striving to correct the situation is Robert Stephenson of the Institute of Archaeology and Anthropology at the University of South Carolina. Stephenson notes that many professionals turn against amateurs because they have seen some who were no more than pot hunters looking for valuables to add to collections or to sell. He also notes, however, that "there are many, many others who can, and do, contribute much to the science of archaeology." The problem is that because many professionals give no credit to amateurs, the amateurs in turn ignore the professionals for they are tired of being put down. "The professional archaeologist," Stephenson adds, "has a duty to his profession to help the sincere amateur." It is important to say that *not all* professional archaeologists are to be condemned. Some give of their valuable time to a host of activities, but these are so few they stand out and are easily recognized.

In closing this chapter, I trust the reader is aware of some of the problems within archaeology today. My purpose is not to attack the professional community so much as it is to awaken—by anger, if necessary—the public to the realization that archaeology needs all the help it can get. Many will think that the situation is really quite bad; actually, it's much worse. The biggest single problem in archaeology today is the destruction of sites—both intentional and accidental. The professional community has not moved nearly fast enough to reckon with this situation; it has spent too much time awaiting legislation and funding. The amateur community, however, seeing the problem and moving forcefully to cope with it, has made a significant contribution. There are some amateur organizations that have recorded the existence of hundreds and hundreds of sites throughout the country, sites which the professional community is unaware of and seems little interested in. As James Whittall commented, "In the end the 'establishment' will turn to the 'amateurs'' research to back up their long delayed involvement in the problem."

"The problem" cannot be solved, as it stands today, by either the professional or the amateur communities in archaeology. There is too much to do and too little time. The need for the interested layman to come forth has never been greater. As we shall see.

PART III
The Need for the Amateur Today

CHAPTER 8

A Plea for
Public Archaeology

There is a crisis in archaeology today: the rate of destruction and uncontrolled loss of historical sites.

A spokesman at a meeting of the New Hampshire Archaeological Society stated that we can save maybe fifty percent of existing sites. In Arizona, at least twenty-five percent of the known sites have been destroyed within the last ten years. In California, it was noticed that a series of ancient sites was being systematically destroyed by traffic. In New York State, a dozen sites were destroyed before anyone knew what had happened.

The list is endless.

In many states, the leveling of land continues unabated and without consideration for the location of historically important sites and antiquities. In some states, the crisis is so bad that all the land which is subject to being leveled may in fact *be* leveled within twenty years. The problem is staggering, and causes both professional and amateur archaeologists to shudder in disbelief and dismay, for if it continues the future will present no new material for researchers to investigate. Once a site is destroyed, or even tampered with, its potential value can never be regained. The loss is irreparable.

When I say historical sites, I refer to any type of structure that can offer information or data about the past. This includes everything from ancient Indian burial mounds to "recent" buildings of Colonial origin, and from primitive cave paintings to stone structures suggesting pre-Columbian contact. And anything—*anything*—in between. These sites represent America's link to its past: who was here, and when; where they came from, and why; what they did here, and why they left; and how they influenced existing cultures.

There are not merely a few such sites involved, or the remains of a handful of artifacts and implements from some past civilization whose passing is hardly even known. I am talking about *thousands* of sites, from the heavily wooded wilderness in Maine to the California desert. Sites are being destroyed every day, consciously or not—and it doesn't really matter which—by the building of dams, seaways, shopping centers, roads, and homes; by the clearing of land for agriculture; and by private citizens who are mostly unaware of the meaning of potentially valuable sites, structures, or materials on their property.

Whose fault is this? It is *everyone's* fault. It is the fault of the government for not reacting to the problem quickly enough; of the municipalities too interested in growth to care; of the professional archaeologists for not demanding more insistently that something be done; of the amateur archaeologists for not establishing a coalition of active supporters to bombard the legislators with proof of what has already gone on; and of the public for sitting back and waiting for someone else to do it.

Archaeology is everyone's business, for the activities that archaeology undertakes deal with everyone's past. It is a public activity, supported by the public, engaged in by the public, and it exists in order to show the public who and what preceded it. There is no such thing as private archaeology. All archaeology is public archaeology. There can and should be no other way to consider this discipline; but it is a discipline which may find itself with nothing new to evaluate by the time the next generation of Americans reaches maturity. Once an archaeologically important site is destroyed, it is destroyed forever, and the information it could have produced may be obtainable from no other location on the face of the earth.

Scientific publications devoted to the subject of archaeology continue to proclaim the concern of the professional archaeologist, and most will agree that the initial blame rests with them. Observers of this whole problem place responsibility for alleviating the crisis at the doorstep of the professional workers in each region. When we consider all the complaining they do with regard to lack of funds, we begin to assume—as they wish us to—that nothing can possibly be done without a total funding effort.

There are three separate segments within our society which can begin to overcome the problem by becoming more actively involved. The principal question here is whether these separate segments will become involved fast enough and whether they will form a united front against those who feel the situation is either not critical or else unimportant in general. These segments are (1) the professional archaeologists; (2) the amateur archaeologists; and (3) the public.

THE PROFESSIONAL ARCHAEOLOGISTS

Whether the blame for destruction of sites should rest initially with the professional community is irrelevant at this point. What is of concern now is the extent to which the situation can be improved. Professional archaeologists are usually involved or associated with a university system, a museum, or a scientific research organization. As such, their principal activity is teaching, or perhaps evaluating existing evidence and establishing its importance within the framework of current knowledge, or both. A university professor obviously cannot carry a full teaching load and at the same time be personally involved with directing activity at numerous sites all over his state. Although many institutions welcome reports of newly discovered sites and maintain some kind of a master file and listing, there are just enough archaeologists to go around investigating—much less excavating—them.

Archaeologists are by nature and by training accustomed to proceeding slowly and deliberately, and are often inclined to be unaware of the many activities in their field. With regard to potential sites, many are aware (though some are not) of the fact that such sites are being destroyed, but they insist that there is too much to do—too many sites, too little time, and not enough public funding. Many professional archaeologists also insist that they are the only ones who should be involved in such activity, for it represents their training and background.

The professional archaeologist is, of course, of great importance in this matter. He is highly trained, he is an expert in his field, and he certainly is more qualified to judge the importance of sites and materials than those trained in other fields.

Within the professional community, certain guidelines have been set up by archaeologists trying to activate their colleagues to a more systematic approach to this problem, an approach which, if implemented by all concerned, could certainly slow down, if not temporarily halt, the spreading crisis. The first step in this approach is for the professional archaeologist to assess the status of all known and all suspected sites in his region. This information could be obtained from active organizations and all known persons interested in or involved with archaeology. This should be followed by a complete listing of all site destruction, with particulars, which should be forwarded to those capable of impressing legislators.

The professional archaeologist must next determine what he is able to do to defer further destruction plus what he could do if given more assistance and funding. He must also actively engage the interest of colleagues, students, and friends in this effort. As part of a university system, the professional should at least be able to institute a survey project to determine the scope of existing and potential sites.

Finally, the professional should actively engage the interest and enlist the support of the public through announcements, speeches, public lectures, discussions, educational programs, and site tours.

This outline would be excellent if implemented, but the problem is that it is not implemented. It is too idealistic. The professional archaeologist, despite his occasional articles in scientific journals protesting the destruction of sites, is primarily interested in evaluating data and not in locating sites or informing the public of the problem. The articles published in *Science* magazine, *American Antiquity* magazine, the *Newsletter* of the American Anthropological Association, and other such professional journals are not seen by the public, nor are they published for the perusal of those without backgrounds in science. The archaeologists are to a large extent telling *each other* about the problem, but rarely are they so prolific in carefully and conscientiously informing the public that supports them.

I have spoken about the problem of destruction of sites with many people who can certainly be classified as being aware of what goes on around them in this world. Yet none of these persons had any idea of the extent of this particular problem, although most of them are involved with higher education! A few had "vaguely heard" that some sites were inadvertently destroyed by a building contractor clearing land, but they assumed that that sort of thing is uncommon. None had ever been approached, directly or indirectly, by anyone soliciting support for preservation of sites.

It can only be deduced that, for a number of reasons, the professional archaeological community does not represent the single, cohesive unit by which this crisis can be solved. As a result, active participation must also emanate from other quarters.

THE AMATEUR ARCHAEOLOGISTS

The largest single unit of individuals involved in the field of archaeology today is the amateur archaeologists. Where in New Hampshire, for example, there are only a handful of professionals—a rather small number compared to most other states, actually—there are scores of amateurs. In Arkansas, a call for help by professionals brings dozens of amateurs out of the woodwork and onto the site immediately.

The importance of the amateur in archaeology today has steadily increased. Carl H. Chapman of the University of Missouri does not hesitate to remind his professional colleagues that "without the serious interest in archaeology and history generated by amateur societies, both archaeological and historical, there would possibly be no historic sites acts. It is the organized amateur that makes for the preservation of sites." Amateur archaeologists are not employed by a university system or any organization. They may best be described as "public archaeologists," for their efforts are expended on public and other sites, and it is recognized that all sites and potential sites belong to the public. Another professional archaeologist, Charles McGimsey of the University of Arkansas, wrote in *Public Archaeology* (Seminar Press, 1972): "There is ample evidence today that interested and concerned amateur archaeologists are the professional's greatest source of assistance and support." The amateur archaeologist is certainly that, but he is more accurately the *public's* greatest advocate for archaeological preservation.

A lack of funding or the pursuit of their own careers has never interrupted the activity of amateur archaeologists. Where professionals have full teaching loads, amateurs have full-time jobs and other activities, yet many exercise a maximum effort towards locating, reporting, and preserving sites. There are, of course, different kinds of amateurs with varying degrees of ability in certain functions, and these will be discussed further on in this chapter. An amateur archaeologist is such that his activities in archaeology are conducted when possible and feasible, on his own time.

There are a number of procedures which amateurs should employ with regard to locating and preserving sites. If an existing site is threatened, the first thing to do is to contact local authorities—police, selectmen, mayors—and explain precisely what is occurring. If the site is on publicly owned land, all but a few states are bound by law to act immediately with preserving measures. If the site is on private land, the owner should be told of the situation and impressed to act immediately to defer any destruction. The amateur should next inform the public agency responsible for such matters—be it a state historical society or state museum—and then contact a professional archaeologist associated with a state university (who may also be on the staff of the museum or an advisor to the historical society). If there is a state archaeologist, he should be informed. As for sites on private land, there is little anyone can do if the owner is unconcerned with such matters. A few states rigorously implore property owners to protect such sites, and a few even stipulate a legal right to protect sites themselves if necessary.

There are instances of both states and amateurs purchasing pieces of land from private individuals solely to preserve and protect an historical site.

Some professional archaeologists suggest that an amateur archaeologist should no more be allowed to function in the field then an amateur brain surgeon should be allowed in the operating room. The similarities between an archaeologist and a brain surgeon are obvious, with regard to the formal education and training of each, but the comparison ends there. While it would be absurd to enlist an amateur brain surgeon to practice on someone's head, a competent amateur archaeologist may certainly have enough training and experience to excavate in the field. As Dr. McGimsey has pointed out to his professional colleagues: "There seems little reason to belabor the point that an advanced degree in archaeology, even one gained in an excellent department, does not alone provide absolute assurance that an individual will perform with complete competence or that the absence of such a degree precludes such competence." In addition, some amateurs may have devoted a good part of their lives to privately studying a particular aspect of archaeological research or specializing in a certain field—a people or culture—of archaeological inquiry. Hence, he or she may be more familiar with a given subject than a professional archaeologist whose specialty is in one or more other areas. Both must endeavor to function together. It should come as no surprise to anyone that there are few amateur archaeologists competent to direct entire field excavations on their own, though exceptions include people like Maurice Robbins of Massachusetts and Ben McCary of William and Mary College. But amateur archaeologists are probably more useful in other respects anyway, for it is they who locate a majority of the sites and move to preserve them; it is they who keep track of the status of various sites and their disposition; and it is they who record and account for the numerous materials and objects which those with less training would either ignore or throw out.

THE PUBLIC

Archaeology is the study of what man has left behind, and the objects of archaeological inquiry belong to the public. The public should be concerned mainly that important sites and materials be properly cared for and investigated, and that the results of such investigations be made available for all to see. The public should be assured that competent individuals are involved in such endeavors, that these individuals have proper support in order systematically to pursue their tasks, and that the disposition of finds is handled with the public interest in mind.

The public, obviously, represents the prime impetus behind archaeological work, and the public's attitude about what archaeologists do is not difficult to ascertain at any given time. If the public consistently shows that it is not concerned when local officials mention that some archaeologically or historically important site may have been destroyed during a road building or that a developer must level some land previously determined vital as an excavation project, then both the professional and amateur communities will wonder why they have been expending so much time and effort to save such sites.

These possibilities are rare, actually. It is not so much a matter of the public's not caring as it is a matter of its not *knowing* about the crisis, and this must be corrected. The only real hope of obtaining significant data from undamaged sites is through total public involvement. The tremendous increase in land development over the last two decades has obliterated and lost forever an untold number of important features, and a major move to recover anything left must be undertaken with the public's knowledge and involvement.

By total public involvement I neither mean nor expect *everyone* to become an involved amateur archaeologist, any more than "total employment" means that *everyone* is actively employed. Public involvement can be anything from keeping a watchful eye on potentially important sites slated for destruction to forming a public interest group with the purpose of impressing upon local officials and other citizens the need to move slowly when it comes to allowing land to be cleared; from supporting archaeological societies to demanding that students be introduced to this subject prior to the college level; and from urging state-level politicians to increase funding for research to helping with some of the simple tasks usually assigned to volunteers on excavation projects. Most states have antiquities legislation, but few enforce it to any degree of meaning or purpose; law-enforcement officials simply have too much to do with regard to controlling common crime. Most states also have at least one historical society or similar type of organization devoted to preserving, at least, those structures of obvious historical value and importance.

Some private citizens have set the rules for others to follow when a site or structure is threatened, and represent the very best examples of persons interested in and involved with such endeavors. An example was told to me by Mr. Robert Sincerbeaux of Vermont, an attorney closely involved with preservation of historic sites and president of the Eva Gebhard-Gourgaud Foundation. A Colonial building had been slated for destruction in order to make way for a new structure, and all efforts to save the building had failed. The day the bulldozer arrived, a citizen phoned Mr. Sincerbeaux, who had been busily trying to save the building, and asked if there was any possibility of a last-minute reprieve. "The only way to stop the bulldozer at this point," Mr. Sincerbeaux remarked to the caller, "is to lie down in front of it." And that is precisely what the person did. The bulldozer stopped, discussion ensued, negotiations were undertaken, and the building was subsequently purchased by a local bank much impressed with the sincerity of the citizens. The building is safe and well today.

Some professional archaeologists become nervous when they perceive that the public wants to learn more about what archaeology is, what archaeologists do, and how they can become involved. This attitude comes about usually for one of two reasons. Either certain private individuals have caused more harm than good in their attempts to assist professionals, or else the professionals feel that their science is diluted when nonprofessionals can and do accomplish more then they themselves would care to admit. Any such attitude is misplaced, however, for again, the *public* is the keeper of historical sites and archaeological data, and if the public wants to become involved they should be welcomed with open arms. Any instances of individuals causing more problems than they solve are just that—instances of individuals. Archaeology represents an outstanding example of nonprofessionals or nonscientists becoming actively involved in science today, whether as amateur archaeologists or simply interested citizens offering moral and political support.

The title for this book, *Archaeology for Everyone*, was not arrived at quickly and without thoughtful deliberation by a number of persons. It is meant not only to express the need for as much support as possible by as many people as is feasible for involvement in archaeology, but also to portray that anyone who is sincere and conscientious may make a worthy contribution which posterity will long remember. In this regard, any objective citizen may join the ranks of the amateur archaeologists and answer the call for public archaeology.

WHO IS AN AMATEUR ARCHAEOLOGIST?

Nonprofessional archaeologists have been given a number of titles, from volunteer, citizen, and public archaeologists to lay, amateur, and enthusiast archaeologists.

The proper practice of archaeology, professional or amateur, is mostly a matter of attitude. As with everything else in this world, there are good and bad practitioners. Some amateurs go way beyond their level of competence in attempting to excavate, while others will always insist that a professional either direct or at least be nearby any such project. Some amateurs do excellent excavation work but fail to adequately record and publish their activities. Other amateurs may, after careful excavation and recording, remove all materials and objects for display in their celler den. And still other amateurs, after superficial investigation of an unusual site, may immediately conclude that visitors from outer space arrived there a few thousand years ago and attempt to foster such a story on a headline-hungry reporter and an unsuspecting public.

The title "amateur archaeologist" has become one that accomplished workers are proud of. The realization that such practitioners have contributed tremendously to the cause of archaeology means that the title is no longer thrown around carelessly. To the hard-working amateur archaeologist, those who are out to make headlines or to collect antiquities for their mantelpiece do not deserve the title, and will not receive it.

As a part of his attitude, the amateur archaeologist knows his capabilities and his limits, and an inexperienced though sincere volunteer worker at a site is just as important as both the accomplished amateur and the professional in the field. One amateur, Edward Lenik of New Jersey, has a solid background and education in business administration, yet teaches archaeology on the college level and may be aptly referred to as a "professional amateur." Most amateurs, however, are not so accomplished, though they may be as involved with the subject. These are the people from all walks of life who are well read in one or more aspects of archaeology and can be counted upon to perform almost any task assigned by a professional. They can excavate, with proper direction; notice artifacts immediately which the untrained observer or digger would pass by, and usually make a quick determination as to the importance of the object; and they can be counted on to prepare precise reports which any professional would be able to make use of in an overall, final analysis of the excavation. Much of the work in archaeology—particularly excavation work—is often taxing and boring, yet without enough persons available to handle all the chores involved there could be no proper excavation at all, for everything must be done right the first time; you can't return a week later and try again.

When a number of relatively inexperienced volunteer archaeologists are needed at a site, they are usually needed badly. While some amateurs devote thirty or fifty hours a week to archaeology, others are able to squeeze in only perhaps a couple of weekends in the summer. There is of course a great difference between the professional amateur and the weekend volunteer, but there is a great need for both. The excavation represents the most advanced aspect of archaeological activity and is not to be undertaken lightly. But volunteer archaeologists and amateurs of all levels and with all manner of experience can spend time at home, at libraries, or in museums doing research on a particular segment of history with which they may be involved in excavation or in determining the proper classification of materials found during an excavation. This type of research is extremely important, and it is no secret that for every hour in the field there is anywhere from six to ten hours' worth of research necessary in the laboratory. So amateurs can contribute quite a bit even if they don't become involved in excavation work.

In an interview published in *Popular Archaeology* magazine, Massachusetts State Archaeologist Maurice Robbins contemplated the difference between a professional and an amateur archaeologist. "I started off as a rank amateur. Gradually over the years I picked up the experience, took courses and finally became state archaeologist. Now, where does that leave me? Am I professional or am I not?" The line must not be drawn based solely on one's title, for professionalism is a matter of both ability and attitude. But the proper attitude is mandatory.

ARCHAEOLOGY IN EDUCATION

The importance of archaeology is generally not realized until students reach college, for it is rarely taught in high school, much less in the lower grades.

One reason for this is that public education attempts to familiarize students with more "useful" information than archaeology may be considered to provide. Another reason is that it would require a high school teacher familiar enough with the subject to offer a desirable and substantive course. And finally, if such a course were offered, it would have to be as an elective, in that the standard scholastic program would disallow replacement of any subject.

The importance of history in general as a subject in high school has apparently not pervaded the public consciousness, if recent surveys are to be believed. The *New York Times* recently sponsored an American History Knowledge and Attitude Survey which involved the testing of students who had just completed high school. The results amply illustrated that the students admittedly knew less history than even they thought they should, and that "high schools are giving lower priority to teaching U.S. History."

History has apparently become one of those boring subjects that everyone has to take, rather than a discipline that reveals the growth of man, the movements of cultures, and the founding of countries. History and geology are the two subjects that could include courses in archaeology. The lack of such courses probably adds to the fact that the public is generally unaware not only of what archaeologists do ("Archaeologists go around digging in the ground for funny-looking and broken pots") but of the present crisis. As one professional archaeologist remarked, the public—through a lack of a proper educational introduction to this field—is totally unfamiliar with the importance of archaeology today.

Yet there is no question that people are fascinated with archaeology. I am somewhat amazed to hear people in all manner of careers tell me things like "If I had to do it all over again, I'd become an archaeologist" or "I'd change my college major to archaeology if I could go back twenty years." By the same token, an undergraduate student from Harvard University who was studying archaeology and needed some data from my files on pre-Columbian contacts for a paper told me unequivocally that he would be changing his major in order to exclude archaeology, because he found it less intriguing than he had thought it would be. He went on to say that "there was too much book work and not enough field experience shared with students."

Getting back to public education, however, it is gratifying to note that some high school teachers and instructors in lower grades deem it important to acquaint students with the subject of archaeology. In Bainbridge Island, Washington, for example, Ms. Anne Johansson includes as part of her seventh-grade humanities course a minicourse in archaeology, which includes an annual dig. An amateur archaeologist for many years, Ms. Johansson instructs students in the use of simple field tools and impresses upon them how archaeology has consistently unraveled the past. The program has been carefully designed to allow children firsthand experience in this manner of research, and all agree that the locating of an artifact gives the student another way of understanding historical information.

In Illinois, numerous high school students conducted a bona fide archaeological excavation on a number of sites slated to be leveled with the building of an electric power station. Most of the sites were pre-Columbian habitats going back four to five thousand years, and a quick survey had located forty of them. Under the direction of professional excavators and thanks to the efforts of Robert Stelton, a social studies teacher at Morgan Park Academy in Chicago, the students rigidly adhered to proper excavation techniques and conducted superb anthropological research.

Near San Francisco, students were given an opportunity to excavate when it was determined that a series of archaeological sites were about to be destroyed in the path of a new roads project. Just as the destruction began, the students moved in and closed off the area to bulldozers—something that the law empowered citizens to do—and the prescribed sixty days were spent in frantic excavation. Burial sites and innumerable artifacts were uncovered by high school students who were also members of the Novato High School Archaeology Club. These young volunteers, working under the direction of Dr. David Fredrickson, even followed the bulldozers around to see if anything they may have missed in the hectic excavation work would turn up. But nothing did. The students had done a thorough job.

One final example involves a group of children in England, and is offered here because of its uniqueness. An imaginative headmaster decided to let his students experience Stone Age life, which he had lectured about. The students built a mud hut utilizing only stone tools, sticks, straw, and mud. They then fashioned their own utensils, fired pottery, and prepared food, just as primitive man had done. Observers all felt that the project was noteworthy and that it put life into dull history books.

All these examples can only set the stage for further interest in archaeology as schoolchildren reach adulthood. At the very least, such activity can impress upon today's youth the importance and necessity of locating and preserving archaeological sites and data before it's too late. Students today represent the next generation of archaeologists—professional and amateur—and it is important that they become aware of the vital situation before they have little or nothing left to excavate.

HISTORIC SITES

Many archaeological sites—that is to say, prehistoric sites—cannot and should not be restored, but are best left alone and protected.

A great number of what are referred to as historical sites are amenable to both preservation and restoration, though in an archaeological sense it is unwise to restore certain structures because it necessarily causes alteration. Nevertheless, the federal government has established the National Trust for Historic Preservation to assist citizens in preserving and restoring important and valuable structures. Each state has its own historic preservation officer responsible for assisting communities in these matters. A list of these can be found at the end of this chapter.

In 1966 Congress passed the National Historic Preservation Act, declaring it necessary for the federal government to give maximum encouragement to agencies and individuals undertaking to preserve historic properties by public and private means. This act can be of great assistance to those involved in the preservation of sites which may not be considered important enough for national recognition.

Prior to 1966, historic preservation programs under the auspices of the federal government were limited to the acquisition or recognition of only the most significant properties, which left thousands of remaining important sites in the hands of bewildered states and private individuals. Now, however, the Department of Interior has expanded its framework by including any sites, buildings, structures, and even objects significant in American history, architecture, archaeology, and culture. Once it has been substantiated that a property is indeed of historical value, the government may offer a grant-in-aid to the state, which in turn usually obtains advice from individuals and organizations.

Individuals working hard to preserve sites should be sure that their state makes full use of the federal program. Matching grants-in-aid of up to fifty percent are available for this kind of work, and may be used for preparation of comprehensive statewide historic preservation surveys and plans and for acquiring property to be designated historic monuments. The funds from these grants may be transferred to individual communities, historic societies, or individuals. It is imperative that each state take advantage of this legislation, and that individual citizens impress upon their representatives the need and importance of such a program being implemented.

So the individual (or society) is not completely on his own, but he may have to bring to the public's attention the desirability of historic preservation and restoration. The need for the amateur-citizen-public-volunteer archaeologist has never been greater, and public officials are not going to go out of their way to spend money on such matters unless it is painfully obvious that the public wants it done.

It remains to be seen the extent to which the public is willing to demand that its history be preserved.

STATE HISTORIC PRESERVATION OFFICERS

Following is a list of officials primarily responsible for National Historic Preservation Act programs in each state.

ALABAMA

Director, Alabama Department of Archives and History
Chairman, Alabama Historical Commission
Archives and History Building
Montgomery, Alabama 36104

ALASKA

Director, Division of Parks
323 E. 4th Avenue
Anchorage, Alaska 99501

ARIZONA

Director, State Parks Board
1688 W. Adams
Phoenix, Arizona 85007

ARKANSAS

Director, Arkansas Department of Parks and Tourism
State Capitol, Room 149
Little Rock, Arkansas 72201

CALIFORNIA

Director, Department of Parks and Recreation
State Resources Agency, Box 2390
Sacramento, California 95811

COLORADO

Chairman, State Historical Society
Colorado State Museum
200 14th Avenue
Denver, Colorado 80203

CONNECTICUT

Director, Connecticut Historical Commission
59 South Prospect Street
Hartford, Connecticut 06106

DELAWARE

Secretary of State of Delaware
Acting Director, Division of Historical and Cultural Affairs
Hall of Records
Dover, Delaware 19901

FLORIDA

Director, Division of Archives, History and Records Management
Department of State
401 East Gaines Street
Tallahassee, Florida 32304

GEORGIA

Chief, Historic Preservation Section
Department of Natural Resources
710 Trinity-Washington Building
270 Washington Street Southwest
Atlanta, Georgia 30334

HAWAII

Chairman, Department of Land and Natural Resources
Box 621
Honolulu, Hawaii 96809

IDAHO

Director, Idaho Historical Society
610 North Julia Davis Drive
Boise, Idaho 83706

ILLINOIS

Director, Department of Conservation
602 State Office Building
400 South Spring Street
Springfield, Illinois 62706

INDIANA

Director, Department of Natural Resources
608 State Office Building
Indianapolis, Indiana 46204

IOWA

Director, State Historical Department
B-13
MacLean Hall
Iowa City, Iowa 52242

KANSAS

Executive Director, Kansas State Historical Society
120 West 10th Street
Topeka, Kansas 66612

KENTUCKY

Director, Kentucky Heritage Commission
401 Wapping Street
Frankfort, Kentucky 40601

LOUISIANA

Director, Department of Art, Historical and Cultural Preservation
Old State Capitol
Baton Rouge, Louisiana 70801

MAINE

Director, Maine Historical Preservation Commission
31 Western Avenue
Augusta, Maine 04330

MARYLAND

Director, Maryland Historical Trust
2525 Riva Road
Annapolis, Maryland 21401

MASSACHUSETTS

Executive Director, Massachusetts Historical Commission
40 Beacon Street
Boston, Massachusetts 02108

MICHIGAN

Director, Michigan History Division
Department of State
Lansing, Michigan 48918

MINNESOTA

Director, Minnesota Historical Society
690 Cedar Street
St. Paul, Minnesota 55101

MISSISSIPPI

Director, State of Mississippi Department of Archives and History
Box 571
Jackson, Mississippi 39205

MISSOURI

Director, Missouri Department of Natural Resources
P.O. Box 176
1204 Jefferson Building
Jefferson City, Missouri 65101

MONTANA

Administrator, Recreation and Parks Division
Department of Fish and Game
Mitchell Building
Helena, Montana 59601

NEBRASKA

Director, Nebraska State Historical Society
1500 R Street
Lincoln, Nebraska 68508

NEVADA

Administrator, Division of State Parks
201 South Fall Street
Carson City, Nevada 89701

NEW HAMPSHIRE

Commissioner, Department of Natural Development
Box 856
Concord, New Hampshire 03301

NEW JERSEY

Commissioner, Department of Environmental Protection
Box 1420
Trenton, New Jersey 08625

NEW MEXICO
State Planning Officer, State Capitol
403 Capitol Building
Santa Fe, New Mexico 87501

NEW YORK
Commissioner, Parks and Recreation
Room 303, South Swan Street Building
Albany, New York 12223

NORTH CAROLINA
Director, Division of Archives and History
Department of Cultural Resources
109 East Jones Street
Raleigh, North Carolina 27611

NORTH DAKOTA
Superintendent, State Historical Society
of North Dakota
Liberty Memorial Building
Bismarck, North Dakota 58501

OHIO
State Historical Preservation Officer
Ohio Historical Society
Interstate Number 71 at 17th Avenue
Columbus, Ohio 43211

OKLAHOMA
State Historical Preservation Officer
1108 Colcord Building
Oklahoma City, Oklahoma 73102

OREGON
State Parks Superintendent
300 State Highway Building
Salem, Oregon 97310

PENNSYLVANIA
Executive Director, Pennsylvania Historical and Museum Commission
Box 1026
Harrisburg, Pennsylvania 17120

RHODE ISLAND
Director, Rhode Island Department of
Community Affairs
150 Washington Street
Providence, Rhode Island 02903

SOUTH CAROLINA
Director, State Archives Department
1430 Senate Street
Columbia, South Carolina 29211

SOUTH DAKOTA
Director, Office of Cultural Preservation
Department of Education and Cultural
Affairs
State Capitol
Pierre, South Dakota 57501

TENNESSEE
Executive Director, Tennessee Historical
Commission
170 2nd Avenue North
Suite 100
Nashville, Tennessee 37219

TEXAS
Executive Director, Texas State Historical
Survey Committee
Box 12276, Capitol Station
Austin, Texas 78711

UTAH
Director, Division of State History
603 East South Temple
Salt Like City, Utah 84102

VERMONT
Director, Vermont Division of Historic
Sites
Pavilion Building
Montpelier, Vermont 05602

VIRGINIA
Executive Director, Virginia Historic
Landmarks Commission
221 Governor Street
Richmond, Virginia 23219

WASHINGTON
Director, Washington State Parks and
Recreation Commission
Box 1128
Olympia, Washington 98504

WEST VIRGINIA

West Virginia Antiquities Commission
Old Mountainfair, West Virginia University
Morgantown, West Virginia 26506

WICONSIN

Director, State Historical Society of Wisconsin
816 State Street
Madison, Wisconsin 53706

WYOMING

Director, Wyoming Recreation Commission
604 East 25th Street, Box 309
Cheyenne, Wyoming 82001

DISTRICT OF COLUMBIA

Acting Director, Office of Housing and Community Development
Room 112A, District Building
14th and E Streets, North West
Washington, D.C. 20004

AMERICAN SAMOA

Territorial Historical Preservation Officer
Department of Public Works
Government of American Samoa 96799

PUERTO RICO

Institute of Puerto Rico Culture
Apartado 4184
San Juan, Puerto Rico 00905

GUAM

Chief, Parks and Recreation Resources Division
Department of Commerce, Government of Guam
P.O. Box 682
Agana, Guam 96910

TRUST TERRITORY

Chief, Land Resources Branch
Department of Resources and Development
Trust Territory of the Pacific Islands
Salpan, Marianas Islands 96950

VIRGIN ISLANDS

Planning Director, Virgin Islands Planning Board
Charlotte Amalie, St. Thomas
Virgin Islands 00801

NATIONAL TRUST FOR HISTORIC PRESERVATION

President, National Trust for Historic Preservation
740 Jackson Place, North West
Washington, D.C. 20006

CHAPTER 9

Present-Day Amateur Archaeologists

It is difficult to determine the total number of full-time, part-time, and occasional amateur archaeologists in the country today, much less to account for all they have accomplished in the past and are involved with in the present. We occasionally hear about some of them, but most remain anonymous. Very often they work alone or together for years, until the professional community suspects that they have uncovered an important or valuable find, at which time it suddenly becomes necessary to investigate.

Hundreds of stories could be told about the efforts and accomplishments, the scholasticism and contributions of these nonprofessional, unpaid, public-spirited researchers. Some, like Donal Buchanan of Vienna, Virginia, have spent countless hours poring over ancient inscriptions in the hope of settling once and for all the arguments regarding their authenticity. Others, like Albert Miller of Pennsylvania, have dug in caverns for years looking for signs of primitive habitation; Miller finally discovered what is referred to as "North America's first hotel," Meadowcroft, where ancient man lived in large groups.

Before discussing in more detail the work of some amateurs today, it seems both fitting and proper that I preface such accounts with a note about America's first amateur archaeologist.

AMERICA'S FIRST ARCHAEOLOGIST

He was a well-known man of his time. Born in 1743, the son of a planter, he studied law and became a delegate to Virginia's House of Burgesses at the age of twenty-six, less than a year after Johann

Winckelmann had been murdered in a hotel room in Trieste, Italy. He was a man of many talents and many directions. He was intimately familiar with half a dozen fields of scientific inquiry, he read the classics in the original Greek and Latin, he designed and built his own home. A voracious reader and prolific writer, his personal library eventually became the foundation of the world's most outstanding library, the Library of Congress; and he authored over 18,000 letters during his lifetime. He was the founder of the University of Virginia, the author of the American Declaration of Independence, and the third president of the United States. He was also the first man to undertake a scientific archaeological excavation, and he died in 1826, the year before General Pitt-Rivers was born.

His name was Thomas Jefferson.

In 1781, exactly one hundred years before Pitt-Rivers began his systematic excavation procedures, Thomas Jefferson published what was and is considered a most unusual book, *Notes on Virginia*. Chapter 11 discusses the first attempt at archaeological excavation that can be considered scientific. It is a report that any archaeologist today could read with comfort and familiarity, knowing that the author was following rules which had not yet even been thought of, much less laid down as established and required principles. Jefferson explains his excavation of "Aborigine barrows" (Indian burial mounds) on his property in Virginia, and takes into account virtually everything that a modern archaeologist would consider important and deem necessary, from the exact measurements to the geological alterations, from the positions of materials to the type of soil, from a depiction of his exact movements to an explanatory overview as he went along. His work was so remarkable that readers today still shake their head in wonderment.

This first archaeologist, this first amateur, is hardly mentioned at all in books dealing with the history of archaeology, and certainly not by European historians. Yet Thomas Jefferson was the man who coined the term *strata*, and he was the first to publicly contemplate the origins and movements of a people who had buried some of their dead in his backyard, a people so old that their culture had been established for thousands of years before the Pilgrims made their way to New England and the Colonists began moving West.

We move now from the founder of American amateur archaeology to the father of amateur archaeology today, Maurice Robbins of Massachusetts.

Born in 1899 in Mansfield, Massachusetts, Robbins first became interested in the history and archaeology of his state as a boy scout. He maintained this interest as best he could growing up in the early 1900s, and eventually decided on electrical engineering as his life's career. After forty-two years in that profession he retired, but he had begun planning how to fill his retirement years long before he faced them. He studied history and took courses in archaeology, and in 1939 was involved in the founding of the Massachusetts Archaeological Society.

He began excavating on a fairly regular basis in order to gain valuable experience, and with the society conducted research, first at Faulkner Springs in Taunton, Massachusetts, then at excavations at the Titicut Site and the Assawompsett Site, the latter of which he's been involved with for nearly twenty-five years. In 1942 he participated in forming the Bronson Museum in Attleboro, Massachusetts, and is now its director.

Upon his retirement, Robbins became much more actively involved with New England archaeology, and when the Massachusetts secretary of state decided it was necessary to have a state archaeologist, Robbins was appointed, in March 1972. The amateur archaeologist had come a long way.

In addition to his regular duties, he was president of the Eastern States Archaeological Federation—a very large organization composed of over two dozen archaeological societies—from 1973 to 1975, and has been a vocal supporter of stricter, more enforceable state antiquities legislation. The work of Robbins and many others at the Assawompsett Site has become almost legendary. Researchers determined a great deal about the Archaic period in Massachusetts by careful excavation of structures and burial sites, excavations which Robbins says were the most exciting of his career.

Well aware of the problems in archaeology today in general and of those between the professional and amateur communities in particular, Robbins feels that professionals who take the stand that only they should be allowed to dig are unrealistic about the whole situation. "There aren't enough professionals to go around, and there isn't enough money to support the ones that are around." The only answer, Robbins says, is to train amateurs to excavate, and this is precisely what he has been doing through his society. The day before I sat down to write this chapter, I was told by a friend that an archaeologist at Clark University in Worcester, Massachusetts, had told him about another archaeologist at the University of Massachusetts who was actively trying to stop, through legislation, any excavation work by amateurs. Such professionals want to control all archaeological activity, even if it means that such activity will come to a grinding halt.

Amateur archaeologist Robbins, on the other hand, has conducted programs where amateurs are properly trained and supervised in fieldwork strictly on a voluntary basis, *without* the use of public funds.

The research department of his society lists dozens of people dedicated to investigating and preserving archaeological sites. They are on call at all times, and because they are situated around the state, Robbins can find out what's going on and direct them to threatened sites regardless of location. Thanks to volunteer work by amateurs, many of the state's important sites are studiously investigated on a regular basis. Robbins believes that as a result of the work of these and other amateurs, the professional community will soon have to realize that amateurs will have to be depended upon to do most of the work, and that a majority of them are quite capable of doing so.

It is because of open-minded, active amateurs like Maurice Robbins that archaeology is not in an even worse situation in his state. In terms of who should be called professional and who should be referred to as amateur, Robbins comments that if you drew the line based on ability, knowledge, and technique, a lot of roles would be switched.

In 1964 this amateur archaeologist was awarded the citation of Master Archaeologist by the Guild of American Prehistorians.

GLORIA FARLEY

Virtually anywhere in the United States, when someone mentions Norse inscriptions or runestones, they are familiar with the work of Gloria Farley of Oklahoma. Mrs. Farley has been involved with the study of runestones for three decades and has been instrumental in opening a new page in the saga of human activity in pre-Columbian America. Her work has been both applauded and derided, and her name is well known to scholars in many countries.

It all started in 1928, when young Gloria Stewart and her girl friend were taken by the latter's father for a hike on Poteau Mountain. They stopped and looked at a massive stone with funny writing carved in it, considered by residents of the area to be Indian and known simply as Indian Rock. The two girls were impressed with the thought of an Indian carving a message in stone, and the funny-looking symbols remained on their minds for a long time.

Some years later Gloria was shown a picture of Scandinavian runes and immediately recognized the similarity between the picture and the carved stone she had seen. That moment marked the beginning of a lifelong quest to determine the origin and meaning of Indian Rock, an activity that continues today. Gloria Stewart eventually married Ray Farley, moved from Oklahoma to Ohio, and began a systematic study of Scandinavian history with particular attention to the Vikings. She contacted authorities at the Smithsonian Institution and offered information about the stone in Oklahoma, but was told that they were familiar with it and that it was probably inscribed recently—or at least not in antiquity—by Indians. Suspicious of the Indian theory, Gloria continued her study of the history, movements, and alphabets of the Vikings, and slowly began to put together a well-supported theory that Norsemen had indeed been in Oklahoma.

In 1950 Gloria returned with her husband to live in Heavener, Oklahoma, and was pleased to find that the stone hadn't been vandalized. She began interviewing longtime residents of the area and learned to her surprise of quite a few additional stones of the type in which she was interested. She was finally able to determine that there were two additional runestones, and deduced that perhaps a Viking colony or settlement had been located in the general area. At the very least, there could be no question that genuine runes were in Oklahoma. The next step was to contact the experts.

Gloria corresponded with numerous scholars throughout the world, and their response was that the whole thing was a ridiculous joke. Without ever seeing the inscriptions, without ever assuming just for a moment that the Vikings *could* have been in Oklahoma, these supposedly open-minded, self-proclaimed scientific authorities automatically invoked the well-worn judgment that it was impossible. A few were actually *afraid* to suggest that Gloria Farley might be correct for fear of opposition from their professional colleagues. Despite constant claims to the contrary, individual archaeologists often hold back their personal conclusions about a tenuous topic unless the archaeological community in general is of the same opinion. This is something that amateur archaeologists rarely have to deal with, for with them there is no tenure involved, no professional suicide to consider, no university departmental chairman to please. Gloria Farley kept corresponding, however, and eventually found that historian Frederick J. Pohl, author of *The Lost Discovery*, was intrigued enough to come and see the runestones for himself. After examination and contemplation, Pohl estimated that the runes had been inscribed between 1,000 and 1,500 years ago.

As a result of Pohl's statement and Gloria Farley's continued hard work, a few more scholars came out of the woodwork to have a look, and the truly important question arose of what the inscriptions said. One would suppose that an expert specializing in this type of inscription could fairly easily determine at least the general content of the message. But the experts could not agree on a precise translation, and when there was some kind of agreement among them, the message made no sense at all. Many experts still insist that the whole thing is a hoax, and one wonders if this is because they couldn't translate the inscriptions.

Finally, however, an unusual team consisting of an engineer and a cryptographer worked on the inscriptions and concluded that each represented a date. Dr. Ole G. Landsverk and Alf Monge determined that the inscriptions were based on a code system using the Roman Church's ecclesiastical calendar, with which Christian Norsemen were familiar. The decoded dates of the three Heavener runestones are November 11, 1012; December 25, 1015, the Norse New Year; and December 30, 1022.

In order to determine precisely how Norse travelers could have reached Oklahoma, Gloria Farley painstakingly outlined an itinerary which very convincingly brings the Vikings down the east coast, around Florida, through the Gulf of Mexico, and into the Mississippi River. From there it was only a matter of following a tributary to the continental interior towards Oklahoma. Gloria Farley's work is not to be taken lightly, for one of the major questions in any such discussion involves establishing a possible route which voyagers can be expected to have taken.

The research continued, more correspondence ensued, additional references in Scandinavian history were checked out, and the experts were polled for their opinions. Gloria Farley continued to impress upon scholars and laymen alike the immense historical importance of the runestones. Finally, in order to preserve the inscriptions from vandalism, they were placed under state supervision, and the Heavener Runestone State Park was established. To date, Gloria Farley has received reports of over seventy additional runestones, and her work continues endlessly. She has prepared a record of all Viking penetrations into the Mississippi Valley.

The professional community has hesitated either to afford Gloria the recognition due her or to work towards a more satisfying explanation of the inscriptions with her. Instead, every possible bit of so-called negative evidence is put forth as though the slightest imperfection in Gloria's research should automatically negate the entire proposition. Worse than that, the professional researchers have not double-checked their own sources and have done a sloppy and unscientific job of disproving the facts—something they accuse amateurs of regularly. For example, one archaeologist stated that some children had told him that *they* had actually carved the inscriptions, but when Mrs. Farley challenged the children, they explained that they had only cleaned the moss from the stones containing the lettering. The archaeologist left this out of his report. Another example concerns an adult who said that when he played in the area as a boy, the inscriptions were not there. The professional community took this as evidence, not bothering to consider the fact that a young boy certainly would not carefully examine three miles of ledge looking for inscriptions, or that his memory might later be just a little faulty. Mrs. Farley reacted to this type of evidence by stating "The archaeologists, all misinformed on these and other pertinent points, kept taking their cues from each other, unfortunately in print. Their original objections are continuously reprinted until they have become accepted by many who have not been given all the facts."

When the Oklahoma Science and Arts Foundation held a runestone exhibit in 1971, a man went around saying that he and a friend had in fact carved all the runestones when they were kids in 1936. The authorities thought this was great, and the popular press carried the story far and wide. But no one happened to mention that the Smithsonian Institution had been informed of the inscriptions in 1923, two years before the carver was born. Another argument concerns the fact that no artifacts relating to Norse occupation have been found. What the professional archaeologists *don't* say is that no excavations have ever been undertaken! Gloria Farley estimates that any Norse exploration party would probably have been limited to maybe thirty-five or so persons, and that tools and artifacts would probably not have been left behind—certainly in no quantity to speak of. The three Heavener runestones are now under state control, which is good, but it means that the Oklahoma state archaeologist must approve excavation work, and he has not seen fit to do this. It is a case where the amateurs cannot excavate because the state prescribes the granting of permits, and where the state itself will not excavate because there is a shortage of funds and what funding there is "will be used for things more important." And the state archaeologist does not deem this important! So the professionals have legal control through state laws, and they are doing nothing. Finally, the state archaeologist insists that he and his colleagues are "interested but not convinced" of the authenticity of the runestones, and that "archaeologists have not been prone to hide or disregard evidence out of fear of being criticized." It's interesting that he feels he must make such a statement, particularly in view of its untruth.

Gloria Farley has worked on this project for thousands of hours. She has tracked down every lead, checked out every piece of negative and positive evidence, and successfully argued against points raised by opponents of the Norse theory. When I met this outstanding woman at a symposium in 1975, she still talked about her work with shining eyes and in excited tones. She has recently been working on some Libyan inscriptions with Professor Barry Fell, who will be discussed in the next chapter, and has written about her work in *The Vikings Were Here*

(1970). When the annual Cultural Heritage Conference was held in Georgia in 1975, Gloria Farley was asked to be chairman. This wife and mother from Heavener, Oklahoma, had done her homework.

MANUEL DA SILVA

If you are a resident of Bristol, Rhode Island, and are in need of medical assistance, chances are you will visit the Bristol County Medical Center on Hope Street. Depending on your circumstance, you may require the services of a specialist in internal medicine. This medical center has four such specialists on its staff, one of whom is Dr. Manuel Luciano Da Silva, who also happens to be the world's leading authority on Portuguese Pilgrims.

Dr. Da Silva, an aggressive and determined man, has devoted a great deal of time and energy to proving that Portuguese navigators reached New England a full generation before Columbus left Europe, and that in order that future visitors would recall their passing they left behind a calling card: Dighton Rock. As I write this chapter, plans are being made to dedicate officially the Dighton Rock State Museum six weeks hence. The story of how this inscribed rock got from the middle of the Taunton River to a specially enclosed building paid for by the state of Massachusetts is the story of one man's tireless research over a period of nearly thirty years.

Dr. Da Silva's parents were born and raised in Portugal. His father came to the United States in 1911, obtained an education, and worked for commercial shipping firms in both countries. His mother's family owned the largest farm in her native village, and still does. The elder of two sons, Manuel Luciano was born in 1926 in northern Portugal near the city of Oporto. Growing up as a boy in Portugal, he was fascinated by his father's tales of sea travel. This induced in young Manuel a desire to learn all he could about the subject, and while his fellow students spent their leisure time reading detective stories for entertainment, he studied books on geography and navigation. This background, as it turned out, was to be an important factor in his later research on Portuguese navigators and Dighton Rock.

Manuel Da Silva first heard of Dighton Writing Rock in 1939 from his high school teacher in Portugal. The fact that there was a large rock with strange writing on it lying in the Taunton River in Massachusetts, and that the writing represented evidence of Portuguese navigation in North America, was pretty well known—though not universally accepted

—by 1939. The rock had been the subject of controversy since the time of the early Pilgrims. The peculiar inscription was first recorded by Reverend John Danforth in 1680; he interpreted it as illustrating Indians swimming up the river and attacking and slaying their enemies. Others thought the inscription represented a ship without masts, and still others were sure they saw the outline of a peninsula and a gulf. Copies of the inscription were made in 1788, 1790, and 1830, and the first photograph of it was taken in 1853. None of the students of Dighton Rock recognized any of the Portuguese letters or symbols, even though some had actually outlined a few of the characters. The reason for their complete lack of proper identification is simple: they never considered the possibility that the Portuguese had beat them to America.

In 1834 a copy of the inscription was sent to Professor Charles C. Rafn of Denmark. Rafn was attempting to prove that the Norse had reached New England before Columbus and was very excited about the strange writing he had heard about on a rock in Massachusetts. When he saw the inscription, he immediately stated that one series of letters produced the name Thorfin, a known Norse explorer. Unfortunately, the letters produced no such thing, but Rafn's persistence convinced a lot of people that the Norse were responsible for the writing on Dighton Rock.

No further research was done on Dighton Rock until 1913, when Professor Edmund Delabarre, a psychologist, sought to bring together all the conflicting theories and available historical data on it so that the information would be readily available for future researchers. His impartial investigation took two solid years, and the results of his work were published in three volumes by the Colonial Society of Massachusetts, in 1915, 1916, and 1919. While working on the last volume in 1918, Delabarre noticed for the first time the date 1511 from a photograph of Dighton Rock. Now that he had a precise time period with which to work, he began searching for information about European travelers to the New World. He discovered that there existed in Lisbon, Portugal, royal charters asserting to the fact that Gaspar Corte Real had reached North America in 1501 and later had made a second voyage. Gaspar had been followed by his brother, Miguel, in 1502. Neither had ever returned to their homeland. This was the first inkling that the writing on Dighton Rock might have been made by Portuguese hands. Delabarre examined Dighton Rock again and again, and to his delight was able to make out certain characters from the name Miguel Corte Real plus parts of the Portuguese national symbol and coat of arms.

Although Delabarre is credited with establishing the Corte Real theory of Dighton Rock, he made a number of errors and did not continue his research to the extent that his theory became fact. By 1927, numerous scholars had heard enough about Dighton Rock to dismiss it altogether; there were too many theories and not enough evidence. Delabarre's Corte Real theory was one among many, and none of the so-called scholars of the day thought the rock merited their attention.

This was the situation when Manuel Da Silva first heard about the Dighton Writing Rock in 1939 while attending high school in Portugal. In 1946, at the age of twenty, Manuel moved with his family to New York. Both he and his younger brother were refused admission into the armed forces of the United States because they did not speak English well enough. Manuel worked in a factory on 23rd Street in New York City doing odd jobs, and then went to work for Westinghouse Electric Company, where he was placed in the mail room because of his knowledge of geography. He began taking night courses at New York University, mastered English quickly, and became secretary to the Portuguese general consul in New York. Within seventeen months after being refused admission by the armed forces, he passed the entrance exam to New York University and attended full-time, taking his undergraduate degree in biology.

Da Silva's interest in Portuguese navigation in general and Dighton Rock in particular continued, but he did not become deeply involved in either until he happened to pick up a book on the subject by a university professor considered to be an authority. Da Silva read the book and was amazed at its lack of clarity and conclusiveness. It was "incredibly confusing and inaccurate," he said. "The author obviously knew little about either navigation or the potential meaning behind Dighton Rock." He contacted an instructor in Portuguese at New York University who was also interested in Dighton Rock, and they formed the Miguel Corte Real Memorial Society to support further study. In 1948 Manuel Da Silva went to New England to see Dighton Rock for the first time.

What he saw was a gray brown feldspathic sandstone of medium-to-coarse density lying on the left bank of the Taunton River, within the boundary of the town of Berkley, formerly a part of Dighton, Massachusetts. Shaped like an awkward parallelepiped (a geometric term meaning a solid cube with six faces), the rock is five feet high, nine and a half feet wide, and eleven feet long, and weighs approximately forty tons. One side is almost fully covered with inscribed writing.

Manuel Da Silva went back to New York and devoted all his spare time to putting together a precise account of the history of Dighton Rock. One of the principal problems was the inscriptions themselves, for the rock contained hundreds of scratches, doodlings, and carvings which covered up the original inscription. Consequently, scholars had a difficult time deciphering the characters left by the first inscribers, and concluded that the mystery of the inscriptions would never be interpreted. These scholars never considered the possibility that the inscription was of Portuguese origin.

To claim Dighton Rock to have first been inscribed by Portuguese travelers to the New World was easier said than done. Manuel Da Silva decided it was necessary to establish unequivocally that the Portuguese had indeed been capable of such a journey in the past. To do this, he had to attack the problem from all possible angles, and Dighton Rock thus became—as he describes it—his mistress. As a medical student, he realized that medicine doesn't blush in using information and facts from other sciences; that medical researchers look to as many other fields as possible for any bit of data that may be of help in answering questions and solving problems. He decided to do the same thing in his research on Dighton Rock.

Da Silva's research included the study of navigation, geography, history, archaeology, astrology, cartography, architecture, linguistics, heraldry, genetics, and veterinary medicine. He visited museums in a dozen countries; located documents, manuscripts, letters, and maps from national archives; and went through 27,000 pages on the history of armor alone! He wrote as a result of all this work *Portuguese Pilgrims and Dighton Rock*, published privately in 1971. (It may be purchased by writing to him at 1180 Hope Street, Bristol, Rhode Island 02809.) This is the definitive work on the subject.

In 1952, the Miguel Corte Real Memorial Society purchased forty-nine and a half acres of land adjacent to Dighton Rock in order to create a park. Two years later, however, the Massachusetts Legislature expropriated the land for a state park. Professional and public interest in Dighton Rock steadily increased, and by 1955 action was taken to remove the rock from the river. The move was halted when it was noticed that the rock was being damaged by the crane's cables. It was not finally relocated to the park until 1963. To accommodate the rock, the Massachusetts Department of Natural Resources appropriated $50,000 to build a cofferdam eleven feet above the rock. By then, Dr. Da Silva had completed his book, but did not release it for another ten years. He delivered 122 public lectures on the results of his research before releasing it in print. In this way he was able to create interest and debate within the professional and lay archaeological communities.

Dr. Da Silva did not merely elaborate on the Dighton Rock inscriptions or glibly offer evidence that the Portuguese had beat Columbus to the New World. Instead he recreated the entire background of Portuguese influence on the New World from half a dozen different points of view. Detailing everything from the founding of the immensely prestigious Prince Henry School of Navigation to the fact that the New England Wampanoag Indians have some fifty words in their language which have identical meanings in Portuguese, Dr. Da Silva put all the pieces together to show that Portuguese navigators reached North America two decades before Columbus, that they discovered California and colonized Canada, and that they mated with Rhode Island Indians before the Pilgrims ever arrived. Dozens of other important points are brought out in Dr. Da Silva's book, points which will eventually be included in standard history texts.

How is this information received by the professional community? I spoke with Dr. Da Silva at length about this, as well as with other scholars, and there is no question that while the experts were busy laughing about Dighton Rock the doctor from Bristol was doing his homework. The result was that he beat them all to the punch. Dr. Da Silva explains that he is considered "a black sheep among historians, archaeologists and linguists" because his credentials are in another field entirely. Yet no one has challenged a single proposition he has put forth, and no one has detected a single error in his research. Commenting that his independence means freedom from academic political biases, Dr. Da Silva believes that "the professional community is overwhelmed by the completeness of my work. There can be no argument possible against it." His book has already become part of the curriculum in a number of schools; it is also a reference utilized by astronauts-in-training for its information on navigation techniques, and is a standard text at the Woods Hole Oceanographic Institute in Massachusetts.

Dr. Da Silva remains unimpressed with the experts who have not taken advantage of the results of all his work, saying that he is "bothered when professors place themselves in a university ivory tower and expect the public to assume they know everything. They allow the walls to close in on them and they become authoritarian." Strongly in favor of serious amateurs conducting research, Dr. Da Silva advises that they "be unconcerned with having no title or professorship. The key is to work hard and conscientiously and contribute what you can with vigor."

Dr. Da Silva came into direct contact with one scholar, Professor Rodgers of Harvard University, who claimed that "his domain was being invaded." Professor Rodgers teaches Portuguese literature. When it became obvious that Dr. Da Silva was on the right track and that both the public and the state were determined to preserve Dighton Rock and house it in a state park and museum, numerous professionals suddenly came out of the woodwork. Massachusetts had acquired a hundred acres of land for the Dighton Rock project and had spent approximately $600,000 on a park, cofferdam, roads, and buildings.

Professor Rodgers suggested to the Commission of Natural Resources that a committee of twelve persons be formed to direct the project. This committee included Dr. Da Silva, the president of the Dighton Rock Museum, the former Portuguese ambassador to the United Nations (now in Fall River, Massachusetts, working to establish a Portuguese museum), and nine other persons who were friends of Professor Rodgers (and associated either directly or indirectly with Harvard University).

It became obvious to Dr. Da Silva that these nine friends of Professor Rodgers were not particularly interested in Dighton Rock and what it represented, for none of them ever visited the park to see the rock! This led Dr. Da Silva to ask: "What are we dealing with here? These people call themselves authorities on a subject? These official members of the committee never even saw the object under discussion!"

Dr. Da Silva's book, first released in 1971, was reprinted in 1975 in Portuguese, and is now being prepared for editions in German and Spanish. After 500 years, the mystery of the Portuguese Pilgrims is solved, thanks to a medical doctor who studied navigation as a boy.

Many amateurs make tremendous contributions through years of dedicated work even though they don't become involved in single projects as Gloria Farley and Dr. Da Silva did. The names of people like Paul Holmes of New Hampshire, Harold Gladwyn of Florida, Wesley Gordon of Illinois, Charles Boland of Connecticut, Watson Smith of Arizona, Albert Wheeler of Massachusetts, and Rachel Kenny of New Mexico—to list only a few—may not be household words, but their contributions can in no way be underrated.

In addition to individual efforts, we sometimes hear of the collective efforts of an archaeological organization. One organization composed of amateur archaeologists which has profoundly affected the archaeology of the northeastern United States is the New England Antiquities Research Association, or NEARA.

CHAPTER 10

An Organization Called NEARA

Most anthropologists and archaeologists in the United States specialize in one aspect or another of Indian or Colonial (historical) archaeology. There is plenty for all them to do, of course, because there are tens of thousands of archaeological sites awaiting investigation. But there is another field of inquiry that a majority of American anthropologists tend to ignore: pre-Columbian archaeology.

We know that Indians (so named inaccurately by Columbus) crossed the Bering Strait from Asia in prehistoric times and developed as America's aborigines (from the Latin *ab* 'from,' and *origo* 'origin,' meaning the first inhabitants of a country). We are also told that Columbus "discovered" America (a popular misconception begun by Washington Irving in 1828 and carried on by Italian-Americans) in 1492, and that Columbus was eventually followed by the Pilgrims, the Colonists, and finally the immigrants.

That is the basic account by a majority of anthropologists on infiltration into North America by foreigners. The only problem with such an account, however, is that it ignores the undeniable certainty that North America was visited and inhabited by a number of European and Asian peoples between 4000 B.C. and A.D. 1000. That is, there were contacts between the old and new worlds before the time of Christ and most certainly before Columbus. Pre-Columbian archaeology has comparatively few active professional researchers in the United States, for a number of reasons. First, the idea that America was visited by Europeans and others—Phoenicians, Egyptians, Africans—has been floating around since the seventeenth century. There has always been a kind of idle fascination with strange ancient peoples wandering around the Americas when Abraham had not yet left his homeland, when Moses was on his way out of Egypt, and when Christ was altering the course of human history. This idle fascination, however, has rarely produced any evidence, and modern archaeologists hesitate to get involved with what has always been considered the province of unprofessional daydreamers speculating about events which they have no facts to substantiate. Second, archaeology in America is an anthropological discipline, and researchers thus are prone to study peoples whose origin and development is fairly well recognized. The Amerindians are, of course, an excellent group for this kind of research. Third, the Pilgrims and Colonists who followed Columbus to the New World are considered America's first modern inhabitants; their arrival represents the beginning of history here, and there is plenty of archaeological evidence for their existence. In other words, it is comparatively easy to investigate a group, culture, or people whose presence is blatantly obvious. Finally, there is not a great deal of archaeological data regarding the movements of pre-Columbian travelers to the New World. This, added to the fact that most American archaeologists are not trained to recognize the data that *are* here, results in a situation whereby such data are explained away as being of Indian or Colonial origin, or, perhaps worse, are ignored altogether as irrelevant.

Those American researchers—and they include anthropologists, archaeologists, geographers, botanists, zoologists, and others—who do suspect that North America was visited by foreign travelers before and after the time of Christ must work slowly and carefully in what is really a new field of inquiry, for they cannot afford to endanger their professional standing or reap the scorn of their professional colleagues, who are less imaginative and who prefer to play it safe by studying Indian customs. The problem is that many important sites which could have offered partial evidence—if not definitive proof—of pre-Columbian contact have been ignored or destroyed.

This is not the place for a lengthy discussion on pre-Columbian contacts in the New World, but it is certainly the place to describe one of the most outstanding amateur archaeological organizations in the world today. The New England Antiquities Research Association (NEARA) has uncovered what may very well be considered incontrovertible evidence of Europeans crossing the Atlantic and settling in North America a thousand years before Christ was born.

NEARA was founded in 1964 by six amateur archaeologists who were concerned about the possible importance of a number of rather unusual stone structures dotting the New England landscape. The professional archaeological community in New England had credited the construction of these structures to Colonial farmers, but such pronouncements were made without benefit of research. Although the archaeologists had never even seen most of the sites in question, they nonetheless proclaimed that *all* stone structures in New England were built sometime between the pre- and post-Colonial periods, and that none of them was more than 300 years old.

The idea for founding an organization like NEARA began one day in the early 1950s, when a man by the name of Robert Stone of Derry, New Hampshire, happened to be wandering through the largest and most sophisticated series of stone structures in the United States—known then as Pattee's Caves—located in North Salem, New Hampshire. The site is comprised of twenty-two structures, drains, wells, walls, and other stone features. Robert Stone was immediately impressed by the unusual architecture of the structures and vowed on that day to do all he could to preserve the site. Stone is a mechanical engineer at the Western Electric Company and a student of American history. He could find no evidence in his researches that American Colonists had ever designed or built anything resembling the massive site in North Salem. After checking with many archaeologists, he began to realize that their opinions were based on the assumptions of others who had not bothered to study the site's numerous features carefully.

The first known modern occupant of the site was Jonathan Pattee—hence Pattee's Caves—who lived in a house there with his family from 1826 to 1848. The name Pattee's Caves is unfortunate and inaccurate, for the structures are not caves at all and Pattee certainly did not build them. Many archaeologists and laymen still believe that Pattee *did* build the structures, and they give as reasons the fact that he was a bootlegger, a bank robber, and a moonshiner who needed a place to store his loot. Pattee was in fact none of these things; he was a respected member of the community, a town treasurer, and a keeper of the poor. As for storing his loot at the site, the idea is ridiculous; it would be like trying to hide something on the front lawn of the White House, the site is so conspicuous.

Jonathan Pattee inherited the land and the structures from his father, and there can be no question today that no member of the Pattee family had anything to do with building the structures. They made use of them —as any enterprising New Englander would—but, as Mrs. George Woodbury, a great-grandniece of Jonathan Pattee, said in 1959, "The structures were there a long time before the Pattees." The Pattee family historian says there is no indication in the family letters or papers that any Pattee ever built any structure of stone. The site at North Salem is so massive and so sophisticated that the building of it could hardly be considered a normal pastime for a New England farmer.

As a result of the Pattees' long occupation of the site, however, rumors persisted that the family had actually built the structures on it. These rumors persist even today among a few old-timers in North Salem. Modern archaeologists have for some reason considered these rumors to be acceptable evidence, and have looked upon subsequent research by amateurs with impassioned neglect.

Robert Stone bought the site in 1957 and renamed it Mystery Hill. This move undoubtedly saved the site from certain destruction. Stone opened the site to the public and began to put together a research program. A number of excavations were undertaken over the next few years by both professionals and amateurs, without remarkable results. The professionals kept looking for—and found—Colonial artifacts, which to them meant not only that Colonists used the site but that they built it. Their inability to determine the difference between building a site and using a site was due to their minds being made up before they had ever seen the site. The Mystery Hill site stands out as an example of arrogance and authoritarianism on the part of the professional archaeological community, but also as an example of what an amateur can accomplish if he doesn't mind being laughed at.

Some of the comments made by professionals are indeed astounding. Dr. Bruce Bourque, an archaeologist with the Maine State Museum, wrote in a letter to a teacher that although he does "not normally make an effort to keep abreast of developments at Mystery Hill," he still claims that the site is unimportant. In the same paragraph of his letter, he says first that he is not up to date with respect to research being conducted at Mystery Hill, yet he does not hesitate to say that the site is unworthy of one's serious attention. If he is unfamiliar with the research, how can he make such a statement?

In his book *New Grange*, British archaeologist and editor of the prestigious journal *Antiquity* Glyn Daniel describes the Mystery Hill site as a myth in terms of its being truly megalithic in character and designed and built by Europeans. Daniel had not seen the site before he wrote the book, and he makes a number of factual errors, such as that the site is in North Salem, *Connecticut*, and that Jonathan Pattee built it in the *eighteenth* century. Daniel finally did visit Mystery Hill (in *New Hampshire*) some years later, and wrote about the experience in the March 1972 issue of *Antiquity*. He gives the distinct impression that he happened to be in the area (while visiting friends at Harvard) and thought he'd stop by. Actually, everyone knew *exactly* when he was coming for many months, for although he had nothing but ridicule for Mystery Hill and its proponents, he was there in order to be filmed for a BBC television documentary! In his rather lengthy and sarcastic discussion of the site in *Antiquity*, he is guilty of a number of errors, quite a few inaccuracies, and a great many omissions. Dr. Richard A. Waldron, a British scientist, reacted to Daniel's editorial by writing that Daniel "has a number of pet prejudices which he takes advantage of his position to air, and he frequently attacks in this unpleasant manner various people ranging from the crackpot fringe to quite eminent professional archaeologists who happen to hold different views from his own."

An American anthropologist, Howard Sargent, also takes advantage of his position to write in an editorial in *Man in the Northeast* that Daniel's remarks represent "a well-considered opinion." Sargent fails, however, to explain the basis for such an appraisal. Glyn Daniel, I'm afraid, is not exactly an open-minded observer—despite his reputation in England: his familiarity with the site in North Salem is minimal; he knows nothing about American archaeology; he did not bother to analyze the evidence that Robert Stone and others had accumulated over the years; his description of the site in *Antiquity* was less than accurate in that he failed to mention a number of points which would have caused readers to question his opinion; he has no faith in the amateur archaeological community; and he does not hesitate to discredit anyone who disagrees with him. Howard Sargent obviously does not want to cross swords with the editor of *Antiquity*.

Despite slighting remarks by professionals over the years—or perhaps because of them—Robert Stone moved to establish a research organization to investigate sites like Mystery Hill. Although the focal point of all megalithic research in New England, Mystery Hill is by no means the only megalithic site. When Stone began to hear of other stone structures, he felt it necessary and important that they be accounted for. When he founded NEARA in 1964 with five associates, there were a couple dozen known sites in New England. By 1976 NEARA had located and catalogued 300. NEARA investigates, correlates, and maintains files on many different types of unresolved human involvement in stone or earth work, including stone huts, underground structures, cairns, menhirs, standing stones, grooved stones, carved stones, and various earthworks that appear to be pre-Columbian.

NEARA has attracted over 400 members since its founding, but the general membership remains fairly steady at between 150 and 200 persons. Many of them have devoted countless hours to searching for any unusual sites which have escaped the attention of others, photographing them, recording them, and sending the information to NEARA headquarters in Derry, New Hampshire, for site comparison, distribution to interested persons, and eventual research.

Robert Stone was NEARA's president the first eleven years and is now president emeritus and research director. As the owner of the largest megalithic site in the country, Stone has almost caused a revolution in New England archaeology. He has been responsible for the development of archaeological and archaeoastronomical research at Mystery Hill, with amazing results. A number of excavations have been conducted at Mystery Hill, and one carbon-testing date established the site as being at least 3,000 years old. Standing stones surrounding the site have been determined to be markers for astronomical alignments, thus making the site an extremely sophisticated calendrical construction. Over the years, Stone had located a number of inscribed stones which no one could identify. He held on to them, however, and they were eventually deciphered and translated by Barry Fell of Arlington, Massachusetts. Fell determined that the inscriptions were in Iberian Punic and Ogham—both utilized by the ancient Celts from the Iberian Peninsula (modern Spain and Portugal), and that Mystery Hill was probably inhabited by these people for about 500 years in the first century B.C. Barry Fell is a professor of marine biology at Harvard University; but he is also one of the world's outstanding epigraphers (a decipherer and translator of ancient inscriptions). He worked closely for a short time with Robert Stone and NEARA on the inscriptions they had located in New Hampshire and Vermont, but this association has not continued.

The archaeoastronomical work at Mystery Hill has been conducted by Osborn Stone, an engineer, who is the site manager. He is also an assistant director of research at NEARA and vice-president of the New Hampshire Archaeological Society. His careful and precise research has arrived at numerous correlations between movements of celestial bodies and terrestrial features—both standing and fallen stones and prehistoric walls (see Fig. 1).

In Vermont, a number of sites found over the past five years by Mrs. Betty Sincerbeaux have been studiously investigated by Byron Dix. Dix is an amateur astronomer and engineer, and has already shown that much of central Vermont is composed of large calendar sites. In addition, he has found many inscriptions in Iberian Punic and Ogham there, which makes the area the most important in New England after Mystery Hill. As an assistant research director of NEARA, Byron Dix has worked unceasingly to establish astronomical correlations at the various sites in Vermont. Thanks to support by the remarkable Betty Sincerbeaux and the Eva Gebhard-Gourgaud Foundation, which has donated funds for archaeoastronomical research, Dix has gathered valuable evidence to show that Celts from the Iberian Peninsula inhabited Vermont at least 2,000 years ago (see Fig. 2).

Another outstanding member of NEARA is Andrew Rothovius, one

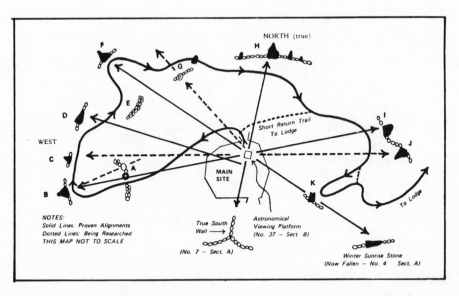

FIG. 1. Layout of astronomical alignments and their correlation with standing and fallen stones at the Mystery Hill site in North Salem, New Hampshire. (*Courtesy of Mystery Hill Corp.*)

A. Moon Standstill-Alignment Wall
B. Winter Solstice Sunset Monolith (December 21)
C. November 1 Stone (an ancient Celtic holiday)
D. Equinox Alignment Stone
E. North Pointing Wall
F. Summer Solstice Sunset Monolith (June 21)
G. Eye Stone for Lunar Alignment
H. North Stone for the Pole Star Thuban, between 1500 and 2000 B.C.
I. Summer Solstice Sunrise Stone (June 21)
J. May Day Monolith (the ancient Celtic holiday of Beltine—May Day)
K. Sighting Stone (for viewing the Winter Solstice Sunrise)

of the six original founders and currently corresponding secretary and editor of the organization's prestigious *Journal*. An interesting thing about Andrew Rothovius is that he has had no formal education. He contracted pulmonary tuberculosis as a child in the 1920s, and in those days such afflictions precluded attending any school. So Andy taught himself how to read. In addition to fluency in English and Finnish, he also has a working knowledge of French and Spanish. He is regarded today as one of the country's outstanding amateur archaeologists, he is

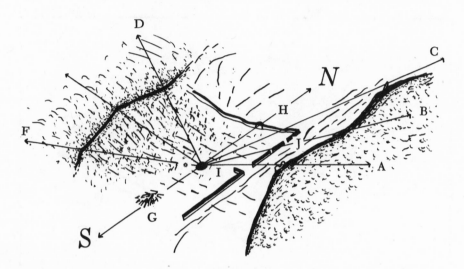

FIG. 2. Ancient calendar site in central Vermont. (*Courtesy of Byron Dix and New England Antiquities Research Association*)

* Center of Site
A. Midwinter Sunrise (December 21)
B. Equinox Sunrise (March 21, September 21)
C. Midsummer Sunrise (June 21)
D. Midsummer Sunset (June 21)
E. Equinox Sunset (March 21, September 21)
F. Midwinter Sunset (December 21)
G. Ruined Structure
H,I,J. Intermediate Features

an expert on New England history, and in 1975 he received an award from the United States Weather Service for his contributions as a weather observer. The award was presented by the governor of New Hampshire. Rothovius is a prolific writer, having published hundreds of articles in the past thirty years, and is considered NEARA's most indispensable member.

NEARA has many other highly qualified and professional people. Edward Lenik, the organization's archaeological chairman, has broad experience in excavation work. He is an instructor in historical archaeology at Rockland Community College in New York, vice-president of the New Jersey Highlands Historical Society, and vice-chairman of the Council for Northeast Historical Archaeology. His specialty is the excavation of historical sites. Another important NEARA member, Mrs. Marjorie Chandler, is a specialist in excavation recording. She has taken a number of graduate courses in anthropology and archaeology and has been involved in many excavation projects. She is an expert in writing reports, cataloguing and accounting for artifacts, and keeping records. She is currently a member of NEARA's executive board, and is among those longtime members who remain continually active.

NEARA has accomplished quite a bit in the last twelve years. In addition to locating and cataloguing some 300 sites previously ignored in New England, it has also researched a number of sites elsewhere in the country which archaeologists chose to leave to someone else. It now has the most extensive files on stone structures in the United States, perhaps in the world. It is in contact with professionals and amateurs in a variety of fields from many countries and is constantly updating its research records.

No one can now deny that NEARA has succeeded in developing convincing archaeological, astronomical, cultural, and epigraphic evidence of European travelers in America before the time of Christ. Some professional researchers, responding to NEARA's accomplishments, have offered nothing but praise, while others still cling to the belief that American Colonists were responsible for any and all unusual archaeological features. Norman Totten, professor of history at Bentley College in Waltham, Massachusetts, recently commented, "The attribution of these structures and calendar stones to colonial construction is patently absurd." Dr. George Carter, professor of geology at Texas A & M University, observed that "we cannot expect today's 'experts' to suddenly admit that they have been wrong all these years, and to begin rewriting all their notes, papers, and books." Dr. Cyrus Gordon, professor of Mediterranean studies at Brandeis University, praised the researchers at Mystery Hill "for preserving what I call the key to the past of our hemisphere. Without such people we're really in danger of losing the evidence for the history of our country."

Many professionals and amateurs are beginning to pay more attention to what NEARA has done and is continuing to do today. In fact, a number of them are beginning to move in on their own and interfere with NEARA's ongoing work. Many obtain as much information from NEARA as they can only to add a few ideas of their own and then present the results as though they had been involved from the beginning. NEARA is very interested in working *with* the professional community, but some professionals have already suggested that the research can be handled adequately only by themselves. I know of a couple of members of the academic community who are investigating sites solely on the basis of

NEARA's data and research, but who have no intention of getting involved with the organization. I suspect that these professionals will eventually publish the results of their activities with only a vague mention of NEARA's having paved the way for thirteen years. As one college instructor recently commented, "This research is too important to be left in the hands of NEARA's amateur archaeologists."

It is ironic that the professional community, which for so long ignored or ridiculed NEARA, must now face an awful truth: NEARA was right. It only remains to be seen if NEARA will get the credit.

The future of NEARA depends, of course, on the efforts of its members. New sites are being reported every day in New England and elsewhere. In Rhode Island, college student Ann Garthwaite has located two and possibly three megalithic features; some farmers in Connecticut have reported that they may have unearthed stone structures in their backyards; and a couple of researchers in Europe are working on the similarities between sites there and in America.

NEARA is now attempting to establish a research center and library, which will probably be located at the Mystery Hill site on land donated by Robert Stone. The problem, of course, is funding; with the exception of the Eva Gebhard-Gourgaud Foundation's recent support, NEARA has gone it alone for thirteen years.

One can only imagine what these amateurs would have accomplished if they could have been funded in ways with which the professionals are familiar.

CHAPTER 11

Preserving the Past for Posterity

The tremendous need for the amateur in archaeology today has, I hope, become clear in the three previous chapters. There is no question that the future of archaeology remains, as it always has, in the hands of the amateur community. Additional support is required from citizen archaeologists so that archaeology will still be an active discipline by the end of this century.

It is a mistake to assume that amateur researchers like Robert Stone and Gloria Farley represent the majority of practitioners in this field. They are the exceptions rather than the rule. Behind them, of course, were many other amateurs who were involved in similar activities. Contributions are made every day by hard-working individuals about whom we hear little, if anything; yet they are the ones who are indispensable.

In dealing with the preservation of sites, I have thus far discussed the destruction caused by land leveling of various types—road construction, building construction, etc.—but have refrained from mentioning another type of destruction which is even more difficult to control.

VANDALISM AND POTHUNTING

Archaeological looting, or pothunting as some prefer to call it, is a crime that dates back to the time of the early Egyptian kings. Both professional and amateur archaeologists shudder at the possibility that a site they are examining may be vandalized and looted, thereby causing a project to end unceremoniously.

It is a problem that has reached almost epidemic proportions around the world as the underground antiquities market is constantly requested to supply more and more authentic materials to collectors. The thievery has made its way from Egypt to America over the past few years, because more and more New World antiquities are being found and they have become the latest fad among those seeking to adorn and enhance their ill-gotten collections. Nearly every country has its horror stories of vandalism and looting at valuable sites, most of which are in the process of being excavated.

The problem with such activity involves not only the fact that important artifacts are stolen either intact or broken up into pieces for easy transport, but also the fact that the site or location itself is irreparably disturbed, and this of course precludes proper archaeological examination. In Mexico a few years ago, researchers who were in the process of studying various stelae of the Mayan ruins were surprised by professional gun-toting looters. The stelae involved weighed over a ton, rose to a height of twelve to fifteen feet, and contained valuable, hitherto undeciphered inscriptions plus sculptured faces. The looters were forced to break the slabs into smaller pieces for smuggling across borders. Any hope, therefore, of translating the remaining pieces of the stelae was gone.

Even if an entire slab were stolen intact and then found and returned to investigators, it would nevertheless be out of context, for the Mayans placed their stelae in highly symbolic locations. The specific location of a stela in relation to other objects and other stelae is an important factor in decipherment and translation.

This example represents the worst that looters can do. Even those vandals who carry no guns, however, obliterate finds to such an extent that they cause just as much damage and bring a halt to serious excavation and research. In the United States, looting usually falls into two categories. Either the looters are hastily looking for artifacts to collect, sell, or trade as other people do with butterflies, stamps, or books, or else a self-proclaimed researcher is seeking to advance a theory and needs certain artifacts to use as evidence. In either case, destruction is irreparable.

In Arizona, a ranger assigned to the Keams Canyon area and the Hopi Indian reservation missed looters by only a day or two. A wall of an ancient Hopi village had been hacked down to expose an underground chamber. The looters had stolen various pots, dishes, and bowls. Burial mounds are favorite targets of vandals and pothunters, and it is estimated that there are over 100,000 such mounds in the United States, many of which are concentrated in mid-America from Ohio to Louisiana and west of the Mississippi. Where an experienced excavator would slowly remove a section of a mound at a time, layer by layer, a pothunter will start at the top and quickly tunnel his way to the center in search of artifacts that are easily removed.

Even if the looters give up before they reach the inner sanctum of these mounds and leave empty-handed, untold damage has been done. The excavator will have difficulty determining the quality of each layer of original soil, and his examination for microscopic fossil pollen and other remains will be severely hampered. Again, artifacts which have been stolen and then recovered offer little in the way of precise archaeological data, for the specific mound in which such materials are found is important, and the looter can hardly be expected to remember or have recorded such information. In addition, the location of the artifacts in the mound—how deep down below the surface, how they were situated in relation to one another—is information that the researcher must have, but which the looter obviously cannot supply with any acceptable degree of sophistication.

The first known pothunters in America were the Pilgrims, who when looking for an acceptable site to set up a settlement dug up Indian burial mounds and collected artifacts as souvenirs. In Iowa, during a large excavation project, researchers noticed that while they were busy digging in one area, a group of pothunters were busy with shovels trying to find whatever they could in *another* part of the project before the archaeologists reached it. In Mississippi, a landowner was bulldozing "his" temple mounds when archaeologists explained the importance of what he was destroying. The landowner was uninterested. The archaeologists then asked permission to undertake at least a partial excavation, but again the landowner would have none of it and promptly proceeded to level all the mounds. As it was private property, nothing could be done. In Wyoming, amateur archaeologists caught a group of young men digging haphazardly in an area thought to contain small Indian burial sites. They chased the intruders away and went home, but the vandals simply returned and finished their indiscriminate digging. The next day the area was empty of everything except gaping holes.

In addition to the careless and carefree looter, a second type of vandal is common in the United States. He is the enthusiastic but untrained researcher, the so-called volunteer archaeologist going out on his own to excavate a site he deems important. Those familiar with the subject of archaeology in general and excavation techniques in particular can easily spot such an excavator. If you see someone in the process of excavating who is also alone, taking no notes, keeping no records, refraining from carefully separating the layers of earth, not marking each and every artifact found, and taking no photographs, you should immediately be suspicious and automatically assume that the digger does not know what he's doing, has no right to dig in such a manner, and has no archaeological credentials.

If such an individual is noticed on public land, authorities should be notified immediately and the digger should somehow be stopped until police arrive. If he is on private land, the owner should be told of the seriousness of the problem. In the event the owner isn't really interested or concerned, or he "lets his brother dig around the property 'cause he's always liked that sort of thing," then it should be diplomatically suggested that a proper excavation could be undertaken by experienced researchers who would be most pleased to include the brother in the process. If none of this does any good, then there's little left to do but inform the local archaeological community—society, museum, university archaeologist—of what has transpired. They will either attempt to persuade the owner to reconsider or assume that too much damage has already been done and that a general site report is probably the best they can expect to obtain.

Amateur or citizen archaeologists who remain alert to this type of destruction, and in the process inform their elected officials that they will not stand for it, represent a formidable bloc of voters who can influence legislation and then insist that the legislation be *enforced*.

ANTIQUITIES LAWS

As mentioned in the first chapter of this section, citizens anxious to preserve archaeological and historic sites have the law behind them. The law is on their side. The fundamental antiquities laws in the United States were enacted first on the federal level, and they serve two principal functions. The first is of a regulatory nature whereby historical sites and data will be protected and preserved. The second function is to assist funding in states and communities that would otherwise probably be forced to refrain from preserving and restoring some of their features.

It is important that public archaeologists be aware of at least the general scope of the fundamental federal laws dealing with antiquities. Following is a short explanatory overview of these laws, the full contents of which are included in Appendix IV.

The first federal legislation affecting archaeology was the Antiquities Act of 1906, in which the federal government recognized the need to protect archaeological sites and allowed for grants to assist in this task. This act also declared vandalism of such sites to be a crime.

Archaeological sites on government land may be considered for excavation and active research only by qualified individuals seeking to enlarge the scope of scientific knowledge who agree that the results of such research will be deposited with a public museum. Permits for research are controlled by the chief archaeologist of the National Park Service, though some government land of this type falls under the jurisdiction of the Forest Service.

The 1906 act was followed by the Historic Sites Act of 1935, which expressly proclaimed that archaeological and historic sites belong to the people and that all efforts regarding preservation are to be undertaken for the public good. The National Park Service was specifically directed to invite scientific research in order to accumulate data for proper historical study.

This act differs slightly from the act of 1906 in that it more actively impresses upon the National Park Service the need and desire to have active research undertaken on a regular basis, and declares it a national policy that the public be made aware of its important historical monuments.

The Reservoir Salvage Act of 1960 is a more specific elaboration of the 1935 act regarding the recovery of archaeological materials. It declares that federal construction of dams, for example, must be halted if there is evidence that an archaeological site is threatened. An attempt to recover archaeological or historical data is to be undertaken before construction may continue. This is the principal federal legislation by which many states have enacted their own statutes regarding salvage archaeology, and should be implemented fully.

The Salvage Act was followed in 1966 by the Historic Preservation Act, which is considered the single most important piece of federal legislation of its kind. Through this act the National Register (those monuments and sites recognized by the government as being of national significance) was allowed to include many of the less outstanding historic sites in the country. The act also establishes the concept of grants-in-aid to states—usually a matching funds arrangement. This act has profoundly influenced the writing of local statutes and should be familiar to all interested in or involved with archaeology.

The National Environmental Policy Act of 1969 is a broad statute with several connotations. It is in general directed towards the realization of a national policy to determine the need for actively pursuing programs which will add to the historic, cultural, and natural aspects of our national heritage. All federal programs are, according to this act, implemented by the National Park Service, which determines the extent of federal participation.

The U.S. Department of the Interior, through the National Park Service, has had overall authority for a majority of the aspects contained in the federal legislation above. The only exceptions involve those public lands under the control of either the Forest Service or the Bureau of Indian Affairs, the former of which is part of the U.S. Department of Agriculture. A list of the regional offices of the Forest Service is given in Appendix 3.

The principal complaint archaeologists have regarding the National Park Service concerns its slow-moving bureaucratic attitude. It seems to take much too long for projects to receive the required approval to get off the ground. This is undoubtedly due to the fact that while the authority, scope, and duties of the National Park Service have increased immensely, the operating budget has not. There are also organizational problems within the department, but these are gradually being brought under control.

When I contacted the National Park Service about these problems, it was in the process of publishing a new statement regarding the implementation of their assigned tasks. They were kind enough to send me a draft, however, from which part of the following is taken.

THE FEDERAL GOVERNMENT'S INTERAGENCY ARCHAEOLOGICAL PROGRAM

In 1945, at the end of World War II, Congress began appropriating funds for the construction of a system of multipurpose dams in river basins throughout the United States. American archaeologists realized that construction activities, particularly the resultant reservoir impoundments, would obliterate untold cultural resources unless surveys and excavations were started immediately. An advisory group known as the Recovery of Archaeological Remains, representing the community of scientists concerned, was formed to counsel federal agencies participating in these water resource development programs. Thus was launched the interagency Archaeological Salvage Program, the original participants being the National Park Service, the Smithsonian Institution, the Bureau of Reclamation, and the Corps of Engineers.

From the beginning the National Park Service was the coordinating agency of the Interagency Archaeological Salvage Program. As time passed the service drew upon the personnel, facilities, and resources of more than fifty universities, colleges, and museums, as well as the Smithsonian Institution, in pursuing archaeological salvage operations in many water control projects.

Park Service participation in this program was based on the Antiquities Act of 1906 (Public Law 59-209) and the Historic Sites Act of 1935. The Antiquities Act gave the secretary of interior responsibility for protecting prehistoric and historic ruins, monuments, and objects situated on most *federal* lands. This responsibility the secretary has delegated to the director of the National Park Service.

In the Historic Sites Act of 1935 (Public Law 74-292), Congress declared that "it is a national policy to preserve for public use historic sites, buildings and objects of national significance. . . ." The act empowers "the Secretary of the Interior through the National Park Service" to carry out this policy and authorizes the Service to conduct surveys, publish studies, and otherwise encourage the preservation of historic properties not federally owned.

Later, the Reservoir Salvage Act of 1960 (Public Law 86-523) gave the Department of the Interior, and through it the National Park Service, major responsibility for the preservation of archaeological data that might be lost *specifically* through dam construction.

To preserve or recover as much as possible of the Nation's prehistoric and historic heritage that would be destroyed by Federal action, the Archeological and Historic Preservation Act (Public Law 93-291) was signed into law by the President in 1974. The new law amends the Reservoir Salvage Act of 1960 and places responsibility upon the Secretary of the Interior for coordinating and administering a nationwide program for the recovery, protection, and preservation of scientific, prehistoric, and historic data which otherwise would be damaged or destroyed as a result of Federal or federally related land modification activities. Such activities include, in addition to the dam construction cited in the R.S.A., pipeline and sewer construction, power transmission facility development, airport construction, and so forth.

Further measures have also been taken to preserve our cultural heritage. For example, responsibilities of the National Park Service were expanded by the National Historic Preservation Act of 1966, which pledged Federal assistance to preservation efforts undertaken by State and local governments and by the private sector. The Act created the National Register of Historic Places and established the Advisory Council on Historic Preservation to advise the President and Congress on programs calculated to enhance the Nation's efforts in historic preservation. In addition, the Advisory Council is given the opportunity to comment on the effect that Federal undertakings might have on National Register properties.

On January 1, 1970, the Congress passed the National Environmental Policy Act of 1969 (Public Law 91-190). Its principal purpose was to establish a national policy regarding the environment and to provide for the establishment of a Council on Environmental Quality. Title I, Section 101(b) states, "In order to carry out the policy set forth in this Act, it is the continuing responsibility of the Federal Government to use all practicable means, consistent with other considerations of national policy to improve and coordinate Federal plans, functions, programs, and resources to the end that the Nation may . . . preserve important historic, cultural, and national aspects of our national heritage. . . ." Federal agencies were further directed by Title I, Section 102(2)(c) to prepare environmental impact statements for each major Federal action having an effect on the environment.

As a complement to the National Environmental Policy Act, Executive Order 11593 was issued in May 1971. Among other things it requires the Secretary of the Interior to advise other Federal agencies in matters pertaining to the identification and evaluation of historic properties located on lands under their jurisdictions. Morever, the Secretary is charged with developing and disseminating to Federal, State, and local governmental units information concerning methods and techniques for preservation, restoration, and maintenance of historic properties.

Centralized in Washington, D.C., with field offices in Atlanta, Denver, and San Francisco, the Interagency Archeological Services programs are today under the direction of the Departmental Consulting Archeologist, Department of the Interior. Principal activities include the administration of the following programs:

THE ARCHEOLOGICAL INVESTIGATIONS PROGRAM

Enters into contracts and cooperative agreements with Federal and State agencies and with qualified scientific and educational institutions for the purpose of implementing data recovery investigations. It monitors and coordinates all archaeological efforts relating to Federal and federally licensed or assisted construction projects and reports on them annually to the Congress. The program is funded by annual appropriations and through the transfer of funds from Federal agencies whose activities come under the purview of the Archeological and Historic Preservation Act of 1974.

THE ANTIQUITIES ACT PROGRAM

National Park Service responsibilities under the Antiquities Act of 1906 have been redelegated to the Departmental Consulting Archeologist, who grants permits for archeological and paleontological explorations on most federally owned or controlled lands. He reviews applications, coordinates them with all appropriate Federal agencies, and provides professional overview of all archeological research undertaken under Antiquities Act permits.

THE EXECUTIVE ORDER 11593 PROGRAM

Executive Order 11593 directs the Secretary of the Interior to provide general procedural and technical advice and assistance to Federal and State agencies and to local groups regarding identification, evaluation, and preservation of cultural resources. To implement the Executive Order, the National Park Service has appointed three full-time consultants to carry out the archeological responsibilities of the Department of the Interior.

These consultants are authorized to initiate contracts with Federal, State, and local agencies; to respond to requests for advice, and to serve as historic preservation policy and procedure generalists. They explain the Federal historic preservation mandate, discuss and aid in the analysis of agency problems, and, as needed, notify appropriate technical experts and services within other elements of the Office of Archeology and Historic Preservation.

National Park Service architects and architectural historians are also available to provide advice to Federal, State, and local agencies on specific technical preservation problems.

According to its own statements, therefore, the National Park Service is aware of its responsibility under federal law and is attempting to meet such responsibility. Most of the efforts of the service's archaeologists are devoted to sites on the National Register, but although the scope of the National Register has been expanded, it does not of course include hundreds and hundreds of sites which collectively represent enormously important features of archaeological and historical interest.

The professional archaeological community will not work on sites unless funding is provided. We have, therefore, a situation in which neither federally employed nor professionally employed archaeologists are actively engaged in locating, examining, and preserving important sites. The amateur or public archaeologist must fill this void, for we obviously cannot wait until federal funding is obtained.

None of this applies at all, of course, to sites located on privately owned land. The federal laws speak for federally owned land and the state laws are almost entirely devoted to state-owned property, though it is hoped—quite unrealistically—that the spirit of the law will extend beyond the boundaries of publicly owned lands. The amateur archaeological community, with the support of various involved organizations, has historically been responsible for bringing important sites to the attention of the government and the public, and this work must not only continue it must improve. There is simply no other way to express the need for actively involved public archaeologists than to say *if you don't do it, nobody will*. It's as simple as that.

The reader may be impressed with the quantity and quality of federal laws involving antiquities, but he shouldn't be, for the United States is far behind many other countries in this regard. John Cole of Columbia University is one member of the academic community who is astounded. "Incredibly," he comments, "the United States is one of the few countries in the world which does not carefully regulate archaeology (or at least try)." As far as Cole knows, the 1906 act providing for fines of $500 for excavating without permission on federal property "has never been successfully enforced."

Mr. Cole has touched on one of the major problems in antiquities legislation—enforcement. When looters were caught in the act of shoveling artifacts into their car trunk in Mesa Verde National Park, a local judge dismissed their case. Some archaeologists regard the antiquities laws as unenforceable, allowing virtually anyone with a shovel to dig. Others are so relieved that there is at least *some* legislation to fall back on that they feel it best to say nothing. While a maximum effort on the part of the professionals and amateurs may enact new legislation, it cannot guarantee enforcement. Moreover, if the amateur community follows the lead of the professionals and continually cries about funding and legislation, no one will be left to perform the principal task of archaeology. Those amateurs who are competent and want to work in the field should do so, while those more inclined to conduct research elsewhere should by all means undertake such endeavors. And those who feel strongly about the need for legislation and who feel they can contribute should move in that direction.

A recent incident in California brings to mind the absolute necessity for active public archaeologists. Most of the California desert is managed by the federal government, but the government does nothing to *protect* the land. Thus some concerned citizens formed a group known as the Desert Watch, and took it upon themselves to patrol the desert land. Why? Because it was known that primitive travelers in the area a thousand years before Christ had left massive drawings and sketches behind them in the sand and on the rocks, and it was important that these remain undisturbed. It is a case of vigilantes having to protect petroglyphs because the government assigns only one ranger for every million acres. And one ranger apparently did not notice the continuous series of motorcycle races held in his area of responsibility, races which were destroying the primitive art. But the Desert Watch group noticed it, and have built fences around the drawings so that drivers are forced to go around. The Bureau of Land Management, the federal agency immediately responsible for the southwest desert, they ingloriously described as "a toothless watchdog." Considering that the California desert is twice the size of West Virginia, the Desert Watch people can accomplish only so much; but if it hadn't been for these volunteer archaeologists, the desert would have been wiped clean of art left by travelers long before our culture was established.

STATE ANTIQUITIES LAWS

The federal government and its antiquities laws are somewhat removed from both professional and amateur archaeologists. Fortunately, however, the majority of the states have followed the federal government's lead and have enacted statutes of their own aimed mainly at the protection of state-owned lands. This at least brings the situation a bit closer to home, for all the individuals involved in controlling archaeology reside and work in the state, either for the state government or a university system.

The two principal problems with state programs are that the state is interested in public property only and that nothing is done without state funding. Hence the professional archaeological community usually does little more than advise on the status of sites located on state land, and the amateur archaeological community has once again to fill the void with regard to all other sites.

The difference in the laws, the funding, and the activities in the various states is enormous. Where a few states have absolutely no antiquities legislation, others have instituted precise and enforceable laws; where some states assign funding for archaeological work at less than $1,000 annually, others have a budget of $40,000 or more each year; and where some states seem to initiate no new programs at all, others sponsor field schools, research, and excavations on a regular basis. Because the professional archaeologists in the state university systems desire to have complete control over archaeological activity, they have in effect bureaucratized the whole situation. In New Jersey, university archaeologists somehow convinced the state to expend public funds to move the state museum into a new building and to spend a massive amount of money equipping it. That's fine, except the subsequent research coming out of that museum has hardly been significant. The opposite is true of Arkansas—a professional's dream—where there exists a certification program for amateurs who wish to become effective assistants on excavations.

Legislation is needed in every state and funding is needed to take care of public property. Regardless of the amount that is made available each year, however, the professional community will continue to ask for more, and I have noticed that a doubling of a state's funding effort for archaeological work does not double the amount of work performed in turn by the professionals. It is a matter of what is desired versus what is needed. That is, every archaeologist—professional or amateur—would like an open-ended budget, but one is not *needed* to begin a systematic appraisal, accounting, and evaluation of each state's sites. The difference between the professional community and the amateur community is that the latter realizes now that what is desired will not occur, so they go ahead and conduct the necessary work that *needs* to be done anyway. If they don't do it, nobody will.

In order that every amateur or public archaeologist may become familiar with the basic state-supported and state-funded programs, I have compiled a list of each state's statutes, a short explanation of what they comprise, the state agencies involved in archaeological and historical work, the annual funding for such work, and a synopsis of the activity in which the state—through its agencies—is involved. Most of the statutes are fashioned after the federal laws (and have about as much chance of active and meaningful enforcement), and the funding can change drastically from year to year depending on upcoming projects or the whims of the legislature. The information was compiled from numerous references—books, magazines, and journals; from the states themselves; from published reports; from the federal government; and from individuals familiar with various activities around the country. The list is meant to serve as a guideline to amateur and public archaeologists.

PUBLICLY FUNDED ARCHAEOLOGY IN
THE FIFTY STATES

ALABAMA

Regulations: Alabama Code, Title 55, Section 272 through 277; Alabama Act 168.
Comments: State agency only may sponsor archaeological excavation, and only residents of the state living in the state may actually excavate. The state owns all antiquities, and none may be removed except for temporary display.
State Agencies: The Museum of Natural History and the University of Alabama, University, Alabama 35436.
Funding: Approximately $3,000 is funded annually for research.
Activity: The state maintains archaeological collections and its Museum of Natural History. Researchers from the University of Alabama's Department of Sociology and Anthropology conduct projects on their own time assuming there is adequate funding from federal, state, and private organizations.

ALASKA

Regulations: Alaska Comp. Laws Ann., Section 38.12.010 through 38.12.050.
Comments: The Commissioner of Natural Resources is responsible for all archaeological excavation on state-owned land. Only recognized qualified individuals may excavate.
State Agencies: Alaska Division of Parks, under the supervision of its Historic Preservation and Archaeology Department, Anchorage, Alaska 99501.
Funding: Approximately $5,000 annually.
Activity: Archaeologists with state institutions are encouraged to determine the existence and value of any site in the state, particularly those on state land. Important new sites may be established as historically beneficial to the public and treated as such actively by the Department of Natural Resources.

ARIZONA

Regulations: Arizona Revised State Ann., Section 41.771 through 41.776.
Comments: Excavating on all state-owned land must be approved directly by the Director of the Arizona State Museum, Tucson, Arizona. All artifacts and other materials must be turned over to the museum in the condition in which they were found.
State Agencies: University of Arizona and the Arizona State Museum, Tucson, Arizona 85721, and Arizona State University, Temple, Arizona 85281.
Funding: Approximately $75,000 annually.
Activity: All state-supported archaeological research is directed or controlled by the Arizona State Museum, which is a despository for all files and data on sites. Professional archaeologists employed by the state carry out state research and personal research, and devote as much time as possible to training students.

ARKANSAS

Regulations: Arkansas Statute Ann., Section 8-801 through 8-808, Section 9-1001 through 9-1007.
Comments: Statutes were enacted principally to protect state-owned lands from vandalism and excavation by unprofessional persons. The idea of the law is meant

to extend to private lands also, with the hope that a more professional attitude will prevail regarding the digging for and subsequent disposal of important material artifacts.

State Agencies: University of Arkansas Museum, Fayetteville, Arkansas 72701.

Funding: Approximately $95,000 annually.

Activity: Under the Arkansas Archaeological Survey, directed by the University of Arkansas Museum, the state has a completely coordinated research and development program. In addition to teaching, state archaeologists conduct both funded and private research, maintain the museum, provide the scientific community with information about sites, inform the public about the state's antiquity, preserve archaeological resources, institute salvage recovery programs, and conduct training sessions. (Arkansas has the most advanced and organized system of any state in the country.)

CALIFORNIA

Regulations: California Department of Parks and Recreation Administration Code, Title 14, Chapter 5, Section 1307 through 1309; California Penal Code, Section 622½; California Water Code, Section 234; California Public Res. Code, Section 5097 through 5097.6.

Comments: Under the auspices of the Director, Division of Beaches and Parks, archaeological excavation may be conducted by experienced individuals only if it has been established that such excavation is beneficial to the state. It is a crime to deface or destroy any objects of archaeological or historical value whether on public or private lands. Various counties in the state have their own archaeological legislation.

State Agencies: Department of Parks and Recreation, Sacramento, California 95811; University of California, Berkeley, California 94720; University of California, Los Angeles, California 90023; various state colleges.

Funding: Approximately $100,00 annually.

Activity: Most of the funding is channeled through the State Department of Parks and Recreation. With advice from the Archaeological Research Facility at the University of California at Berkeley and other state educational institutions, the DPR directs salvage operations, maintenance of archaeological data, research in the state, and the location of important sites. The DPR also moves to protect the many existing sites which are in danger of being destroyed by development of the land. Input is sought and received from various quarters in the state concerned with historical and archaeological matters.

COLORADO

Regulations: Colorado Revised Statute Ann., Section 131-12-1 through 131-12-6.

Comments: The state has complete control over all archaeological activity on state land, under the auspices of the State Historical Society. Only experienced individuals may conduct archaeological research after a permit has been issued. An inventory of antiquities, sites, and objects must be maintained. Owners of private land may request that the statute apply to them also in order to defer unwanted excavation.

State Agencies: University of Colorado Museum, Boulder, Colorado 80302, and the Colorado State Museum, Denver, Colorado 80203.

Funding: Approximately $10,000 annually.

Activity: The University of Colorado Museum maintains records and data of historical sites in the state. The State Historical Society, part of the Colorado State Museum, determines those areas potentailly important for excavation purposes and offers suggestions regarding classification of a site as a state monument.

CONNECTICUT

Regulations: Connecticut General Statute Ann., Section 10-132-A and Section 10-321-A and B.

Comments: Research is conducted on any potentially important site by the state archaeologist only, or under his direction, as determined by the Historical Commission. The commission is charged with preserving sites and materials of historical value.

State Agencies: University of Connecticut, Storrs, Connecticut 06260.

Funding: Approximately $1,000 annually.

Activity: The state archaeologist, a staff member of the University of Connecticut, attempts to locate and excavate potential sites. Funding is limited, however, on the state level. A program was recently inaugurated by the state archaeologist to train volunteer field assistants in Connecticut.

DELAWARE

Regulations: Delaware Code Ann., Title 7, Section 5301 through 5306; Title 7, Section 5403 through 5405; and Title 29, Section 8705.

Comments: The state controls all excavation work on state lands, is the recipient of all materials and objects of an historical nature found on state lands, and may issue permits only to those qualified. Private excavation is actively discouraged, particularly by unqualified persons, and all sites public or private are to be reported to the state archaeologist.

State Agencies: Hall of Records, Dover, Delaware 19901.

Funding: Approximately $40,000 annually.

Activity: Delaware employs a full-time state archaeologist, who works out of the Hall of Records under the aegis of the Division of Archives and Cultural Affairs. All interested in archaeological research may become involved in state-controlled and supervised excavation work. The state archaeologist keeps an active file of ongoing research and informs the public of the state's historical benefits regularly.

FLORIDA

Regulations: Florida Statute Ann., Section 267.

Comments: The secretary of state is responsible for all historical sites on state property and actively enforces their protection. The Bureau of Historic Sites and Properties is the functioning organization responsible for antiquities, the director of which must be, by law, an archaeologist. Underwater exploration in Florida is by law controlled by the state.

State Agencies: Department of State, Tallahassee, Florida 32300; Florida State Museum at the University of Florida, Gainseville, Florida 32601; and other state educational institutions.

Funding: Approximately $200,000 annually.

Activity: Florida has divided its programs into four main categories: general archaeological research, underwater archaeological research, historic research and preservation, and laboratory research. Much activity is devoted to salvage archaeology, student training is implemented, and numerous programs are conducted. The location and preservation of historic sites and materials is very well handled in Florida.

GEORGIA

Regulations: Georgia Code Ann., Section 40-802-A through 40-814-A.

Comments: The secretary of state's office promotes interest in the preservation of historical sites and encourages public support. The state owns all archaeological finds on state land and tideland and directs excavation by qualified individuals only. The law strongly suggests that private landowners inform the state of potentially important historical sites or data and allow only recognized persons to excavate.

State Agencies: University of Georgia, Athens, Georgia 30601; Georgia State College, Atlanta, Georgia 30303; and the Georgia Historical Commission, Atlanta, Georgia 30303.

Funding: Approximately $10,000 annually.

Activity: Under the secretary of state's office, the Georgia Historical Commission oversees all archaeology-related functions in the state, for which it employs a state archaeologist. Activity includes the active preservation of sites and display of antiquities, plus publishing of information for public perusal.

HAWAII

Regulations: Hawaii Revised Laws, Section 734-1; Section 6-1 through 6-15; Act 216; and Act 236.

Comments: A very strict set of laws in the state of Hawaii demands specific conditions under which, among other things, human burial remains may be excavated. Only qualified individuals recognized by the state may excavate, reports must be filed, and improvement of state-owned historical sites must continue regularly. These laws represent the strictest of their kind in the country.

State Agencies: Department of Land and Natural Resources, Honolulu, Hawaii 96809.

Funding: Over $100,000 annually for activities.

Activity: The state employs both full-time and part-time researchers for studying and preserving historical sites and data, under the direction of the Division of State Parks. The location of sites is actively pursued, and the state is always interested in hearing about new research proposals.

IDAHO

Regulations: Idaho Code Ann., Section 67-4114 through 67-4118, and Section 67-4119 through 67-4122.

Comments: The laws in Idaho are implemented by the Board of Trustees of the State Historical Society, and govern both sites on state-owned land and on private land designated as of public importance and value. Excavators on public land must be qualified and apply for permits, and must leave all materials *in situ* unless and until authorized to do otherwise. Damaging or defacing of antiquities is strictly forbidden.

State Agencies: Idaho State University, Pocatello, Idaho 83201; Idaho State Historical Society, Boise, Idaho 83706; and University of Idaho, Moscow, Idaho 83843.

Funding: Less than $5,000 annually.

Activity: Excavations are invited by properly trained persons under the aegis of the State Historical Society, which both preserves and is responsible for actively assessing and interpreting data. Salvage archaeology is pursued when deemed absolutely necessary.

ILLINOIS

Regulations: Illinois Statute Ann., Section 133-C-1 through 133-C-6.

Comments: Excavation, preservation, and purchase of historical sites are demanded. Permission to excavate on state land must be obtained in writing with the consent of the Illinois State Museum.

State Agencies: University of Illinois, Urbana, Illinois 61801; Southern Illinois University Museum, Carbondale, Illinois 62901; and the Illinois State Museum, Springfield, Illinois 62706.

Funding: Approximately $50,000 annually.

Activity: Most of the activity in Illinois is conducted by the State Archaeological Survey at the University of Illinois. The survey assesses site reports and maintains antiquities records, suggests needed salvage work, and publishes important excavation and research results.

INDIANA

Regulations: Indiana Statute Ann., Section 48-9001 through 48-9011.
Comments: The laws in Indiana are currently under revision, as no specific statutes exist which govern archaeological activity *per se.*
State Agencies: Indiana University, Bloomington, Indiana 47401; Indiana State Museum, Indianapolis, Indiana 46304; and Ball State University.
Funding: Approximately $5,000 or more annually.
Activity: Programs are developed and conducted by the laboratory of Archaeology at Indiana University, the State Historical Society, and the State Museum mainly for survey work and the training of students in summer field schools.

IOWA

Regulations: Iowa Code Ann., Title 12, Section 303.6 and 304.1 through 304.7; Title 5, Section 111.2, 111.35, 111.41, and 111.57, plus Section 111-A-1, 111-A-7, and 305-A-1 through 305-A-6.
Comments: State law in Iowa is directed to location, excavation, and preservation of sites on state-owned land, under direction of the Curator of the State Department of History and Archives. Archaeological materials must be maintained and exhibited, and antiquities may not be damaged or removed from state land.
State Agencies: State University of Iowa, Iowa City, Iowa 52240; State Department of Archives and History, Des Moines, Iowa 50300; and Iowa State University, Ames, Iowa 50010.
Funding: Nearly $50,000 annually.
Activity: Iowa has a state archaeologist, who is on the staff of the State University of Iowa and who is responsible for preparing programs to locate and maintain historical sites along with the State Department of History and Archives, which is under the aegis of the State Museum. Programs include salvage, research, education, inspection of collections, and coordinating of various state programs.

KANSAS

Regulations: Kansas General Statute Ann., Section 74-5401 through 74-5408.
Comments: These laws apply only to state-owned lands under the direction of the Secretary, Kansas Antiquities Commission. Excavation is unlawful in the state unless approved by the commission, as is defacing or removing of archaeological materials. Research proposals are approved only for qualified individuals. All sites must be recorded with the state, and the state automatically owns all antiquities.
State Agencies: Kansas Antiquities Commission, composed of various other agencies (Kansas State Historical Society, Topeka, Kansas 66612, and the University of Kansas, Lawrence, Kansas 66044).
Funding: Approximately $20,000 annually.
Activity: A lot of activity in Kansas is directed towards active research and museum work; student training is encouraged; and historical studies are promoted.

KENTUCKY

Regulations: Kentucky Revised Statute Ann., Section 164-705 through 164.735.
Comments: These laws apply to and affect state-owned land only, and instruct the Chairman of the Department of Anthropology at the University of Kentucky to determine who is qualified to excavate and to issue subsequent permits.

State Agencies: University of Kentucky, Lexington, Kentucky 40506; University of Louisville, Louisville, Kentucky 40208; and University of Western Kentucky, Bowling Green, Kentucky 42101.
Funding: Over $10,000 annually.
Activity: Salvage archaeology is active in Kentucky and may be implemented under the direction of the Kentucky Archaeological Survey or the University of Kentucky Museum, the former of which is principally involved with all projects involving excavation.

LOUISIANA

Regulations: Louisiana Revised Statutes, Chapter 8, Section 521 through 527.
Comments: The purpose of these statutes is to ensure that important historical sites and buildings are managed and preserved.
State Agencies: Louisiana State University, Baton Rouge, Louisiana 70803.
Funding: Approximately $5,000 annually.
Activity: The archaeologist at the State University's Department of Geography and Anthropology is responsible for research and any salvage projects which may require his attention. The Historical Preservation and Cultural Commission is not specifically involved with research and archaeology, hence most of the historically related activities in Louisiana are devoted to preserving historical (as opposed to prehistoric) monuments.

MAINE

Regulations: Maine Revised Statute Ann., Title 27, Chapter 13, Section 371 through 374.
Comments: Statutes affect only state-owned land, all materials from which are automatically the property of the state, including antiquities obtained in coastal waters. Permits for excavation are allowed, but the state is beneficiary of all finds. Various agencies in Maine control different portions of land.
State Agencies: University of Maine, Orono, Maine 04473; Maine State Museum, Augusta, Maine 04430; and Maine State Park and Recreation Commission, Augusta, Maine 04330.
Funding: A fluctuating budget of $1,000 and up.
Activity: The state's Division of Historic Sites is active in maintaining existing sites, and the Department of Sociology and Anthropology at the University of Maine employs an archaeologist to determine necessary projects in salvage archaeology. The state museum owns and controls all antiquities. Amateur researchers in Maine are quite active.

MARYLAND

Regulations: Maryland Ann. Code, Article 66c, Section 110B through 110L inclusive.
Comments: Laws were enacted to protect state-owned lands. All excavation work must be approved by the state, all antiquities are immediately owned by the state, all antiquities must be displayed in a museum or similar institution, and owners of private property are encouraged—through the intent of the law—to allow excavation only by reputable persons whose function and reasons for excavating are clear.
State Agencies: Maryland Geological Survey, Baltimore, Maryland 21218; University of Maryland, College Park, Maryland 20742; and the Maryland Historical Trust, Annapolis, Maryland 10404.
Funding: Over $10,000 annually.
Activity: The Archaeological Division of the State Geological Survey at Johns Hopkins University actively coordinates research by both professional and amateur research archaeologists. Studies are conducted in all manner of archaeological

fields. Restoration is pursued, and all interested in contributing are encouraged to participate.

MASSACHUSETTS

Regulations: Massachusetts General Laws Ann., Chapter 9, Section 26–27, and Chapter 40, Section 8-D, plus Chapter 79, Section 5A.

Comments: The law establishes a Massachusetts Historical Commission composed of various other organizations in the state involved in historical and archaeological work. A state archaeologist is appointed to oversee excavation work and to direct the state museum. Various assistants to the state archaeologist are allowed. A portion of the law is very strict regarding improper use of state antiquities, and state landmarks may *never* be altered unless permitted by the *legislature*.

State Agencies: Bronson Museum, Attleboro, Massachusetts 02703.

Funding: The state is now enlarging its scope with regard to funding of archaeological activity.

Activity: Massachusetts is particularly interested in preventing the destruction of potentially valuable historic sites, and works closely with a number of agencies in this regard. The state archaeologist and director of the Bronson Museum is an amateur archaeologist who controls all excavation, directly or indirectly. There is presently a move by at least one professional archaeologist to deny excavation by amateur researchers.

MICHIGAN

Regulations: Michigan Comp. Laws, Section 399.4 and Section 299.51 through 299.55.

Comments: Laws were established to protect all state-owned land. Excavation must be approved by the director of the Department of Natural Resources, and a permit granted to qualified individuals. The state owns all materials from excavation. Underwater research requires a permit also. The Michigan Historical Commission is directed to obtain and preserve antiquities.

State Agencies: The State Museum of the Mackinac Island State Park Commission, East Lansing, Michigan 48823; Museum of Anthropology at the University of Michigan, Ann Arbor, Michigan 48104; and the State University Museum, East Lansing, Michigan 48823.

Funding: From $25,000 to $50,000, depending on planned projects.

Activity: Various educational institutions conduct research activities, but there is no widespread coordinated effort. Amateur researchers attempt to contribute.

MINNESOTA

Regulations: Minnesota Statute Ann., Section 138.31 through 138.41, and 138.51 through 138.64.

Comments: Laws affect only state-owned land, under the Field Archaeology Act. Permits must be obtained from the director of the Minnesota Historical Society for excavation on state land. The state archaeologist decides disposition of archaeological materials. No historical sites may be altered in any way. Research must be reported and/or published on a regular basis.

State Agencies: Minnesota Historical Society, St. Paul, Minnesota 55101, and the University of Minnesota, Minneapolis, Minnesota 55455.

Funding: Over $25,000 annually for research.

Activities: Activities are divided into two areas: those involving historical research and preservation of monuments; and those dealing with archaeological efforts, which are under control of the state archaeologist. A special tax (on cigarettes) exists in Minnesota for this kind of research. Salvage archaeology is undertaken whenever necessary.

MISSISSIPPI

Regulations: Mississippi Code, Section 6192-101 through 6192-123.
Comments: Laws apply to both state-owned lands and those privately owned properties designated by the state as historically valuable and beneficial to the public at large. The state, under the trustees of the Department of Archives and History, must actively locate, preserve, maintain, and account for sites and antiquities in Mississippi, including those in coastal waters. The state automatically owns all materials. Permits may be granted to qualified persons whose aims agree with the state's intentions. Active participation, under the law, is requested by the state, which encourages citizens to act when violations occur.
State Agencies: State Department of Archives and History, Jackson, Mississippi 39533, plus various educational institutions.
Funding: At least $5,000 annually, depending on scheduled projects.
Activity: Salvage archaeology is recognized as an important function, as is regular maintenance of existing sites. Citizens, professional and amateur, are empowered to personally protect and preserve anything of historical value which may be threatened.

MISSOURI

Regulations: Missouri Statute Ann., Section 560.473.
Comments: This statute affects only state land designated state park areas, and not other state-owned property. All antiquities on state park land is protected from either destruction or removal.
State Agencies: University of Missouri, Columbia, Missouri 65201.
Funding: Between $50,000 and $100,000 annually, depending on projects.
Activity: A great deal of archaeological activity goes on in Missouri, under the direction of the director of American archaeology at the University of Missouri, the Archaeological Research Center, and the State Archaeological Survey. Salvage archaeology is well coordinated, and much research is conducted regularly. A field school for students is permanently set up.

MONTANA

Regulations: Montana Revised Codes Ann., Section 75-1202 through 75-1206.
Comments: Laws refer to public land, but the situation with regard to private land is unspecified. Enforcement is difficult. The Commissioner of Public Lands is to determine importance of sites and antiquities, and to enforce state supremacy when necessary with regard to establishing historic monuments. Permits for excavation are required from the state and will be issued only to qualified individuals if and when the interests of the state are primary.
State Agencies: University of Montana, Missoula, Montana 59801, and Montana State University, Bozeman, Montana 59715.
Funding: Approximately $1,000 annually.
Activity: Archaeologists at the state universities are not actively involved in very much research and blame the problem on funding. The State Historical Society is supposed to oversee excavation and preservation of antiquities.

NEBRASKA

Regulations: Nebraska Revised Statute, Section 39-1363.
Comments: The Conservation and Survey Division controls excavation work on public land. Antiquities may not leave the state. Salvage archaeology is to be coordinated among relevant state agencies.
State Agencies: Nebraska State Historical Society, Lincoln, Nebraska 68505; University of Nebraska State Museum, Lincoln, Nebraska 68505.

Funding: At least $25,000 annually, depending on projects.
Activity: The State Historical Society regularly conducts research programs, salvage archaeology is constantly under assessment, at least one field school operates, and the state museum supports excavation projects.

NEVADA

Regulations: Nebraska Revised Statute, Section 381-200 through 381-260.
Comments: Statute meant to protect state-owned land, under control of the director of the Nevada State Museum with regard to excavation, for which permit must be obtained.
State Agencies: Nevada State Museum, Reno, Nevada 89507; Nevada Archaeological Survey, Reno, Nevada 89507; University of Nevada at Reno and Las Vegas.
Funding: At least $1,000 annually depending on projects.
Activity: The Nevada Archaeological Survey at the University of Nevada, Reno, conducts occasional research. Archaeologists refrain from continuous activity, which they blame on lack of funding. The state museum attempts to procure and preserve antiquities.

NEW HAMPSHIRE

Regulations: None at the time of this writing, though plans are under way for enactment of state laws.
Comments: The New Hampshire Preservation Office is currently gathering material and data to use in establishing a broad set of regulations. Organizations involved in this attempt include the New Hampshire Archaeological Society and the New England Antiquities Research Association.
State Agencies: The state has no archaeologist, though this is under advisement; the anthropologist at the University of New Hampshire currently fills the role when needed.
Activity: Much activity is generated by two organizations, noted above, in encouraging citizens to become involved in research. The state is filled with important Indian, Colonial, and pre-Columbian sites that require examination. Salvage archaeology is occasionally undertaken, though funding is a problem. Amateur researchers and organizations account for most of the archaeological research in this state.

NEW JERSEY

Regulations: None at the time of this writing.
Comments: The understanding, despite a lack of formal laws to the effect, is that the State Museum fill the role of principal overseer with regard to state-owned lands.
State Agencies: New Jersey State Museum, Trenton, New Jersey 08625.
Funding: Approximately $10,000 or more, depending on projects.
Activity: The Bureau of Research in Archaeology at the State Museum is prepared to undertake a number of archaeological projects, and actively seeks funding.

NEW MEXICO

Regulations: New Mexico Statute Ann., Section 4-27-4 through 4-27-16.
Comments: Laws are in effect only with regard to state-owned land. Permits must be obtained for excavation, and the state owns all antiquities for deposit and maintenance with the state museum. The Cultural Properties Review Committee must identify and preserve all historic sites.
State Agencies: Museum of New Mexico, Santa Fe, New Mexico 87501, and other educational institutions.
Funding: At least $25,000 annually.

Activity: Salvage archaeology is very active and important in this state, and input is received regularly from the University of New Mexico and the Eastern New Mexico University. There are a state archaeologist and a state historian involved with location, identification, and preservation of historical sites and antiquities, of which there are many. Restoration of antiquities sites is actively encouraged.

NEW YORK

Regulations: New York Education Law, Section 233, and New York Conservation Law, Section 831-4.
Comments: Law designed to protect state-owned land *and* any Indian cemeteries. All antiquities must be registered with the state museum. A salvage archaeology program is active. Permits required to excavate.
State Agencies: State Museum, Albany, New York 12210.
Funding: Approximately $25,000 annually, though subject to change.
Activity: The commissioner of education in New York State is in charge of all archaeological activity, and relegates his authority to a state archaeologist and director of the State Historic Trust. Archaeological research is fairly active through the university system; a central data file of antiquities is maintained; and salvage archaeology is undertaken whenever necessary.

NORTH CAROLINA

Regulations: North Carolina General Statute, Section 70-1 through 70-4 and Section 121-1 through 121-13.1.
Comments: Laws enacted to protect state-owned land, though private landowners are encouraged to respect historical sites on their property. Enforcement of laws regarding protection of sites is active. Permits required for excavation from the State Department of Archives and History.
State Agencies: State Department of Archives and History, Raleigh, North Carolina 27202.
Funding: At least $25,000 annually.
Activity: Historical research and preservation of historical sites are controlled by the Division of Historic Sites; archaeological excavation research is conducted under the aegis of the Research Laboratory of Anthropology at the University of North Carolina. Full-time research is conducted actively, and student training programs are implemented regularly.

NORTH DAKOTA

Regulations: North Dakota Revised Code, Section 55-02-07; North Dakota Cent. Code, Section 55-03-1 through 55-03-07; and North Carolina Cent. Code, Section 55-10-01 through 55-10-10.
Comments: License is required for excavation on stand land; qualified persons need only apply. A full report of such activity must be reported to the State Historical Society. State monuments may be designated on any piece of land, private or public.
State Agencies: State Historical Society, Bismarck, North Dakota 58501.
Funding: Various amounts, depending on projects involved, but usually limited to a few thousand dollars.
Activity: Salvage archaeology is occasionally conducted, and university personnel do research when possible. Much research is conducted on private land by non-professional individuals; hence, there is not a particularly active program under state supervision on a regular basis.

OHIO

Regulations: Ohio Revised Code Ann., Section 149.30 through 149.301.
Comments: The Ohio Historical Society is empowered to obtain historical sites, and must maintain and account for them. (Antiquities laws, as such, are not included in the Ohio Code.)
State Agencies: Ohio Historical Society, Columbus, Ohio 43210.
Funding: Approximately $15,000 annually.
Activity: As there is no official law regarding antiquities, the state historical society procures and deposits all archaeological materials as it can.

OKLAHOMA

Regulations: Oklahoma Statute Ann., Title 70, Chapter 50, Section 3309, and Title 74, Chapter 9-A, Section 241.
Comments: A license must be obtained for excavation. Materials must be shown to the state museum for observation and assessment.
State Agencies: University of Oklahoma, Norman, Oklahoma 73069.
Funding: Approximately $5,000 to $7,000 annually.
Activity: The state archaeologist directs all archaeological work. The River Basin Survey conducts salvage archaeological activity when necessary.

OREGON

Regulations: Oregon Revised Statute Section 273-705, Section 273-711, Section 352-090, and Section 273-715.
Comments: These laws affect only property owned by the state. Permits to excavate must be obtained from the Division of Public Lands. A report of all excavation must be filed with the state museum. The museum is the official repository of all state-owned antiquities.
State Agencies: Oregon State Museum, Eugene, Oregon 97403; Oregon State University, Corvallis, Oregon 97330.
Funding: Varies depending on projects.
Activity: Members of university staffs occasionally devote time to research, and a field school is usually active. There is no continuous program for archaeological or historical excavation or research.

PENNSYLVANIA

Regulations: Pennsylvania Statute Ann., Title 71, Section 716; Title 18, Section 4863.
Comments: All antiquities belong to the state. Historic and archaeological research is under the direction of the State Historical and Museum Commission. The public must be informed of research results, and reports must be filed for public availability.
State Agencies: Pennsylvania Historical and Museum Commission, Box 232, Harrisburg, Pennsylvania 17108.
Funding: At least $25,000 annually.
Activity: Excavations are conducted whenever possible; procuring and preserving of historical monuments is actively pursued; university personnel conduct research; and funding is continuously sought from the federal government to assist in additional projects.

RHODE ISLAND

Regulations: None at the time of this writing.
Activity: A small amount of research is occasionally conducted on a personal,

part-time basis by University of Rhode Island personnel. A small amount also is conducted by amateur archaeologists, one of whom recently convinced the state to establish a monument known as Dighton Rock plus a museum.

SOUTH CAROLINA

Regulations: South Carolina Code, Section 9-331 and Section 54-321 through 54-328.
Comments: Law allows the establishing of an Institute of Archaeology, directed by a state archaeologist on the staff of the University of South Carolina. State holds right to demand artifacts obtained through underwater archaeological research. A specialist marine archaeology advises the state on such matters.
State Agencies: Institute of Archaeology and Anthropology, University of South Carolina, Columbia, South Carolina 29208.
Funding: Between $30,000 and $40,000 annually.
Activity: Underwater archaeology receives a good deal of attention.

SOUTH DAKOTA

Regulations: South Dakota Code, Section 1-20-1 through 1-20-16.
Comments: This law is in effect to protect state-owned land only. Responsibility rests with the Secretary of the State Historical Society. Only qualified individuals may excavate, though volunteers may assist.
State Agencies: State Archaeological Commission and State Historical Society, Pierre, South Dakota 57501.
Funding: Depends on projects, each one of which is evaluated separately.
Activity: Salvage projects are occasionally undertaken, but no overall archaeological program exists. The state museum occasionally sponsors research projects and is responsible for procuring and preserving materials.

TENNESSEE

Regulations: Tennessee Code Ann., Chapter 468, Section 1 through 19.
Comments: The law allows a Division of Archaeology to be created and establishes the post of state archaeologist. An Advisory Council will establish operational procedures. Historical sites are to be considered and evaluated for potentials as state monuments.
State Agencies: Division of Archaeology in the Department of Conservation, Nashville, Tennessee.
Funding: Between $5,000 and $10,000 annually.
Activity: A field school is maintained, salvage archaeology is conducted when possible, and the Tennessee Archaeological Society conducts research occasionally and attempts to maintain a general file of sites and materials. The antiquities laws in Tennessee are very liberal and do not serve their intended purpose, hence excavation is not considered a serious, professional pursuit.

TEXAS

Regulations: Texas Revised Civil Statute, Article 6145-9.
Comments: Statutes in effect to protect state-owned land only plus historic sites elsewhere in the state. All materials are to be protected as a public concern. An Antiquities Committee serves to oversee all historical activity, including underwater projects.
State Agencies: Texas Historical Survey Committee, Austin, Texas 78711; El Paso Centennial Museum, El Paso, Texas 79902; Panhandle-Plains Museum, Canyon, Texas 79015; and other state institutions.
Funding: Approximately $20,000 and up.
Activity: Only a small amount of continuous activity prevails in Texas, as archae-

ologists seem uninterested in research and are more concerned with teaching. Salvage archaeology with regard to underwater research is pursued whenever possible. Amateur researchers accomplish much on their own.

UTAH

Regulations: Utah Code Ann., Section 63-11-2.
Comments: The code is established to protect state-owned lands only. Permits are required for excavation. Antiquities are the property of the state and may not be handled or removed from public land unless permission is granted for sufficient reason.
State Agencies: Utah State Park Board, Boulder, Utah 84716, and the Anthropology Museum at the University of Utah, Salt Lake City, Utah 84112.
Funding: Occasionally as much as $5,000 annually.
Activity: Some survey work, excavation work, and publication of archaeological research are conducted, but not on a continuous basis, and only on state and, occasionally federal land.

VERMONT

Regulations: None as of this writing.
Comments: There is activity based on a 1961 statute with regard to preservation of historical sites, but archaeology itself is not included. This will soon be changed, however, for research in archaeology is advancing in Vermont.
State Agencies: University of Vermont, Burlington, Vermont 05401.
Funding: Small amounts each year for historic preservation, but none as yet for archaeology.
Activity: Most, if not all, of the archaeological activity in Vermont is conducted by amateur researchers, though none (as yet) on state-owned land. The New England Antiquities Research Association has one of its assistant directors of research in Vermont, who devotes at least two days per week to survey work.

VIRGINIA

Regulations: Virginia Code Ann., Section 10-135 through 10-145-1.
Comments: A committee was established under this law to survey and determine importance of potential sites as historical monuments.
State Agencies: Virginia State Library, Richmond, Virginia 23219, and Virginia Historic Landmarks, Richmond, Virginia 23219.
Funding: Usually less than $5,000 annually.
Activity: State-controlled archaeological research is usually devoted to Colonial work. Much of the research conducted in Virginia in general is by citizens who are amateur/volunteer workers and who do not demand or receive state funding.

WASHINGTON

Regulations: Washington Revised Code, Section 27.44.00 through 27.44.020.
Comments: The law requires that only excavation under the direction of state institutions may be undertaken with regard to burial sites. The procurement, preservation, and display of antiquities are encouraged for public benefit.
State Agencies: University of Washington, Seattle, Washington 98105.
Funding: Approximately $35,000 or more.
Activity: Preservation of historic and prehistoric sites is as active as possible; full-time research goes on regularly; and university personnel occasionally undertake projects when funding is made available, but not otherwise.

WEST VIRGINIA

Regulations: West Virginia Code Ann., Section 5-12-1 through 5-12-5.
Comments: The outstanding aspect of this law is that excavation may occur on state land and on private land only when the state decrees disinterest. The state holds the right to excavate archaeological sites without interference. An antiquities commission is authorized to procure and preserve historic sites and materials.
State Agencies: West Virginia Geological Survey, Morgantown, West Virginia 26505.
Funding: Approximately $5,000 annually, depending on nature of projects.
Activity: The Archaeology Section within the Virginia Geological Survey works hard to determine the importance of historic sites and, with other agencies, seeks to fulfill archaeological needs in the state, conducts research, and develops and maintains artifacts and materials.

WISCONSIN

Regulations: Wisconsin Statute Ann., Section 27-012.
Comments: The statute is geared principally to the protection of state-owned lands, on which the state reserves the right to excavate. The State Historical Society may issue permits to qualified individuals for excavation. The position of state archaeologist shall be filled.
State Agencies: State Historical Society, Madison, Wisconsin 53706.
Funding: Varies, depending on projects.
Activity: Some members of the various university staffs in the state conduct occasional research. The salvage archaeology program in the state is excellent, and excavations are conducted whenever deemed appropriate. Some amateurs conduct private excavation work, though most are fairly experienced.

WYOMING

Regulations: Wyoming Statute Ann., Section 36-11 through 36-13, and Section 36-44.6D.
Comments: The law was enacted to protect state property. Permit required to excavate on state or federal land. The state, through the Board of Land Commission, must inspect all antiquities immediately following their retrieval. No antiquities may be removed from the state without consent of the commission.
State Agencies: University of Wyoming, Laramie, Wyoming 82070, and the Wyoming Recreation Commission, Laramie, Wyoming 82070.
Funding: Varies, depending on projects.
Activity: The state archaeologist is attempting to convince the public of the importance of procuring and preserving antiquities, and of the need for a more elaborate salvage archaeology program. Professional researchers accomplish very little here.

PART IV

Opportunities for the Amateur Today

CHAPTER 12

Expeditions and Excavations

Now that we have discussed the need for the amateur archaeologist today and what some amateurs have accomplished, it is time to concentrate specifically on how the interested amateur can get involved with archaeology and how he can take advantage of opportunities.

Anyone who thinks for even a moment that there is nothing for the amateur to do is either misinformed or lazy. There is a tremendous amount of work to be done in archaeology, and any amateur who wants to contribute will have no trouble at all finding suitable outlets for his energies. There are a variety of ways in which amateurs contribute, and I have broken these down into five general categories in this section. Each amateur must decide on his own the manner in which he would like to contribute, and this decision should be based on personal preference (some people like to excavate while others like to conduct research in a museum), knowledge, experience, and availability of projects which invite amateur participation in one's area. Some communities have half a dozen museums but only one small and relatively inactive archaeological organization; others may require the services of volunteers or amateurs for excavation work but offer little in terms of follow-up research on materials found in the field. Some parts of the country are simply more archaeologically active than others and offer a host of activities for amateurs of all levels.

Similarly, the extent to which one wants to get involved depends on knowledge and experience. That is, one does not *begin* as a field supervisor on salvage archaeology projects, nor can one be expected to determine the importance of certain artifacts found during an excavation project if he has had no previous experience. As archaeology becomes more sophisticated, it is only natural that amateurs should follow the trend. But make no mistake about the need for amateurs at all levels. Regardless of one's background or experience, a sincere desire to help can be put to good use.

Some states have so many opportunities for amateur archaeologists that they even see to it that those interested are properly trained in one or more functions. In Arkansas, for example, there is a certification program for amateurs sponsored jointly by the professional Arkansas Archaeological Survey and the amateur Arkansas Archaeological Society. Completion of the program signifies a particular qualification on the part of the participant. If you have received practical field training and experience in surveying, for example, you are entitled to receive a certificate stating your competence in this area. The real purpose behind such a program is to instill responsibility, and it goes without saying that professionals tend to rely on those amateurs who have demonstrated that they are serious and responsible workers.

NATIONAL EXPEDITIONS

Each year, many national organizations direct or sponsor excavation expeditions all over the country and invite amateur participation. The principal advantages of such expeditions for the amateur are the association they provide with professionals and the chance they offer of gaining experience. Different organizations have different programs, and the expeditions have different needs and requirements. In some, the amateur will be expected to put in a twelve-hour day digging under a hot sun; in others he will be allowed to help only with the recording of artifacts collected; and in still others he will be allowed only to observe and ask questions. Some expeditions may pay all expenses for the amateur plus a small allowance for his efforts, while others will pay absolutely nothing and assume the amateur is glad to get the experience. Often costs are shared, and the amateur pays his travel expenses but is fed, housed, and perhaps offered a paying position.

Some expeditions are like tours. The Smithsonian Institution, for example, offers members a chance to become involved in a variety of travel ventures, including visits to archaeological digs. These tours provide access to archaeological sites and are conducted by members of the professional community, but they do not offer the amateur a chance to experience excavation work (and they do not claim to do so). The American Anthropological Association is important to amateurs because it tries to keep track of excavation projects throughout the country which are in need of volunteers, both paid and unpaid. The Archaeological Institute of America also puts amateurs in touch with regularly scheduled excavation projects where they are welcome.

In addition to national organizations (listed at the end of this chapter), many universities and museums direct and sponsor excavation expeditions. These are not always in the home state of the sponsoring unit, nor are they restricted to residents. Some that conduct expeditions overseas will be discussed later in this chapter. Such programs offer a tremendous opportunity to the amateur interested in professional excavation work.

Again, the requirements differ and the compensation for services rendered depends on the situation. If there is national funding, chances are there is money for amateurs; if not, the amateur may receive only free lodging, if that. Each project must be checked out by the amateur ahead of time. *The opportunities are there for anyone interested.*

Examples of Existing Opportunities. The Navajo Tribal Museum in Window Rock, Arizona, offers substantial opportunities to amateurs almost continuously throughout the year. Volunteers are *always* needed for excavation, survey, and salvage work on tribal lands. The only prerequisite is a minimum age of eighteen, and the only stipulation is that one must be able to work amicably with Indian personnel and follow directions. In addition, volunteers are free to pursue a particular or personal project of archaeological interest under the supervision of an expert.

Another year-round project that invites amateurs is the research and reconstruction program at Fort Toulouse in Alabama. Approximately twenty volunteers are needed at all times, and while practical experience is preferred, it is not mandatory. Although the volunteers must pay all expenses, there are often staff positions open for diggers paying at the rate of about $2.50 per hour. The Orendorf Site in Illinois also needs quite a number of volunteer workers during certain months, though they do not pay. The only stipulation here is that a participant remain at the site for at least three weeks in order to assure continuity of the work program.

Salvage and survey work in South Dakota's Black Hills on Palaeoindian and historic sites usually needs both experienced and inexperienced amateur archaeologists. Those who can show experience in excavation work may be offered positions as field supervisors; others with some experience may be paid as members of field crews. A similar situation exists at the McKeithen and Hawthorne sites in Florida, where a few good volunteers with previous experience may be put to work. The volunteers must assume all expenses, be at least twenty years of age, and stay at the site for ten weeks. In Kentucky, a half dozen or so volunteers are needed during the summer at the Fort Ancient and other sites. Classroom experience in archaeology is a definite plus, and workers must remain at the site for at least three weeks. Lodging for volunteers is paid for through grants.

In Michigan, a dozen volunteers who have experience in drafting or photography are usually needed at various Colonial sites. The Comanche Springs sites in New Mexico need volunteers who will remain for at least thirty days. Those with previous field experience may be offered one of a number of staff positions for which salaries are available. Excavation work at the Cuddebackville Site in New York needs a couple of dozen volunteers each summer; they must remain for at least a week. Experience is not required, but anyone skilled in surveying, photography, drafting, or sketching will certainly be welcomed. There is no pay for volunteers, but expenses are very low because workers are allowed to camp out at the site. In Texas, Colonial survey and excavation work requires a few volunteers, minimum age eighteen. Amateurs must have some experience either in the classroom or in the field and must stay for at least two weeks. There is no pay for workers, though room and board is provided as an incentive.

These are just a few of the typical projects under way each year that need and welcome the services of amateur archaeologists. As I put this chapter together, I have a file containing information on over eighty current programs seeking and utilizing volunteers in the United States and Canada. Most programs of this kind occur during the summer months, for obvious reasons, but not all. The interested amateur should contact the anthropology departments at state universities, archaeological organizations, and museums in those parts of the country where he would like to work. It is best to make contact well before the summer months—except where the climate remains warm and suitable for year-round excavation work—in order to get your name on an active list of volunteers.

Opportunities in Canada.   The amateur in Canada should have no trouble finding an outlet for his services. Archaeological activity in Canada needs all the manpower it can get, for there are many parts of the country which require serious study but for which there are not enough researchers. Interested volunteers should contact universities and museums in each of the ten provinces for current information on excavation programs.

In Quebec, research is under way at Site de la Rivière à l'Ombre. They need volunteers willing to work without pay. In addition, there are always a number of staff positions available. Those who wish to apply for a staff position should have at least three seasons' previous experience in excavation work. The sponsoring university will pay travel expenses for the staff members from Quebec to the site itself, plus a salary of approximately $120 per week plus room and board. It is advised that only the more experienced amateurs seek positions on the staff.

In Alberta, excavations are scheduled for a number of historic and other sites, for which eight volunteers will be sought. A minimum age of eighteen is required, and workers must remain for two months. Anyone with experience in either classwork or fieldwork is preferred, and those familiar with mapping and photographic techniques are welcomed. The sites are in the Boreal Forest, but transportation from Edmonton is provided without charge, as are food and lodging.

INTERNATIONAL EXPEDITIONS

Some amateurs attempt to increase their knowledge of European, Mid-Eastern, Asian, or African prehistory by going on excavation expeditions to these parts of the world. In general, it is simply not worth it. If one wishes *primarily* to gain some excavation experience, there is no reason to leave the country. If one thinks an expedition to Egyptian monuments is necessary for a true understanding of that region's prehistory or previous cultures, he is wrong.

I am not suggesting that opportunities to excavate in Europe or the Middle East should be ignored, but rather that they should not be considered of paramount importance. If one is going to travel out of the country *anyway*, and wants to include some excavation work on his trip, fine; but it is a waste of good money for the amateur to travel to another country solely for the purpose of joining an expedition. There are a number of reasons for this. First, it is terribly expensive. Second, there is much to do in one's own country, and amateurs in other countries will be busy there themselves. Third, unless the expedition involves a major university program, the time spent working in another country is relatively short. Finally, the living conditions may be unexpectedly harsh and the environment unlike any most Americans are used to. The first and last of these reasons are the most important to consider.

Nevertheless, there are quite a number of projects conducted each year overseas which include American amateur archaeologists and volunteers on all levels. However, unless one feels particularly drawn to a certain part of the world, he should stay home, save his money, guard his health, and take advantage of the numerous opportunities here.

Amateurs interested in a particular phase of archaeological research may want to join an excavation expedition which concentrates specifically on their field of interest, and which may be led by the world's authority on the subject. This would seem like a good opportunity to spend some time with the expert in the field, thus making any expense worthwhile for this once-in-a-lifetime opportunity. But it usually doesn't work that way, for the world's authority is often too busy directing the fieldwork, visiting museums, lecturing at universities, and seeing old friends to bother with one or more inquisitive volunteers. One amateur archaeologist recently told me he joined a project led by Professor Gerald Hawkins solely to discuss archaeoastronomy based on Hawkins's work at Stonehenge. The project lasted four weeks, cost the amateur all his savings, took him away from other pursuits, and he never even got a chance to tip his hat to Professor Hawkins.

If there is a particularly unusual opportunity offered an amateur for an overseas project and money is no object or problem, then it should be considered with all the above objections in mind. For many, such an opportunity will come along only once, and the lure of digging in far-off lands is certainly understandable. But the amateur should keep in mind that he may be in a community that does not welcome outsiders—particularly outsiders who make holes in the ground.

Examples of Existing Opportunities.   Excavation projects which include American volunteers may be directed or sponsored by a national organization, the host country, or a local university or museum. As with volunteer work in the United States, requirements and remuneration for services rendered differ, and the amateur must check each project for specific information. If a state university or city museum is sponsoring the project, they will be able to supply all necessary information. But if the amateur is going on his own or with an unofficial group, he should contact directly the responsible government agency or academic institution in the host country.

I shall discuss some of the opportunities available in various countries, and list at the end of this chapter agencies and institutions to contact in order to have your name placed on the active list of available volunteers.

In England, general excavations are undertaken in various parts of London throughout the year and many volunteers are always needed. Most of the work involves careful excavation of existing Roman ruins. A minimum age of eighteen is required and at least a general overview of excavation techniques is desired. All volunteers must remain at their assigned task for at least two weeks and must assume all personal expenses. Anyone with special skills or experience in surveying, drawing, and processing is always welcome. A specific project, the excavation of the Wroxeter Roman City, pays a small salary, but volunteers must take care of their own food and lodging.

A number of excavations are scheduled at the Halieis Sites in Porto Cheli, Greece, directed by Indiana University in Bloomington. They will accept eight volunteers, minimum age eighteen. Some knowledge of ancient artifacts in general and pottery in particular is required, and all involved must remain for five weeks. Those with experience in drafting or restoration are especially needed. In addition to the cost of the flight overseas, expenses will run at least $100 a week.

In Tunisia, volunteers are sought each year to survey and study a variety of prehistoric ruins. No particular experience is required, though anyone with special skills is of course invited to join. In Cyprus, volunteers are welcome on a number of excavation projects, but they must be students registered with a recognized university (anywhere in the world). Most planned excavations are scheduled to last about two months, with a total cost to the volunteer in excess of $1,500 plus travel expenses.

One country in particular with a great deal of archaeological activity that admits amateurs is Israel. One excavation project at Caesarea will include research on Roman, Byzantine, and early Arabic cultures and will need more than 200 volunteers. The project will last at least five weeks and all must remain for the duration; minimum age eighteen. Some experience in field archaeology is desired, and some staff positions may be open to amateurs skilled and trained in photography, pollen study, general artifacts analysis, and paleobotany. Another excavation project will be undertaken at Tell Jemmeh involving research of the Middle Bronze Age through the Hellenistic period. At least twenty volunteers will be needed, who must remain at least five weeks. The requirements are an intense interest in archaeology, a willingness to work hard, and the ability to remain pleasant in spite of difficult working conditions. Volunteers are not paid, although those with at least two years' experience in fieldwork may have their expenses taken care of plus a small salary if appointed to a staff position.

A major archaeological project now being scheduled at Tell Halif, north of Beersheba, in Israel, will extend over a period of about ten years. Researchers will be examining Chalcolithic and Byzantine ruins in planned stages. Volunteers will be needed for two months each summer, and must stay for at least five weeks at a time. Anyone with prior experience in fieldwork or majoring in archaeology in college is most welcome to join, though there are no requirements in general for volunteers. American volunteers should contact Lake Forest College in Illinois for information on expenses. Another project, at Tel Dan, needs a minimum of 100 volunteers, preferably with at least one year of either classroom or field training.

Volunteers are needed for excavation work in Italy six weeks each summer. Workers must assume all expenses, but there may be one or two staff positions available for those with experience and formal training. Most of the sites are in the province of Cagliari. At Castellare di Casanova in Chianti, at least ten volunteers are needed during each July for excavation work on ruins from the pre-Etruscan through the end of the Roman Republican period. No experience is necessary to join this program, and it is even preferred that volunteers come expecting to be trained at the site for minor duties. Excavations will also be conducted at Castellieri di San Fedele di Rada in Chianti, dealing with the Roman Republican, Early Medieval, and late Iron Age, for which at least half a dozen volunteers will be needed. High school graduates only, minimum of four weeks. Experience in photography and drafting would help; no remuneration.

There are many more such opportunities for amateurs who feel compelled to cross the ocean in search of excavation projects. Any experience gained in such programs is of course advantageous, but the mystery and excitement that characterize excavating is available locally.

The amateur volunteer should realize that all materials obtained from excavations and all records worked on are the property of either the sponsoring organization or institution, or the host country. With the exception of those experienced amateurs who make significant contributions during an excavation project, any published reports about the work will not mention the volunteers who did most of the work. It is usually understood before the work begins that the sponsoring organization will take charge of all records and publish all findings.

Many of the projects listed above not only need volunteers, they need them badly. A majority of the difficult and boring excavation is done, I'm afraid, by the unpaid volunteers, so satisfaction must be its own reward. Depending on the size of the project and the budget supporting it, there may be only from three to ten professional archaeologists or trained staff members at a major site, and some of the latter may not even get paid, though their expenses are usually taken care of. Without the energetic volunteer, therefore, many projects would never get off the ground.

When an amateur works on such projects, he should make a point of asking to do as many different tasks as possible; a change in his or her assignment every week or so is most helpful, for it offers the worker a broader idea of what goes into an excavation. I should mention that it is difficult to have one's assignment changed during a project, for everything is pretty much planned before any digging begins and the project director wants to be sure that all tasks are being handled continuously. The amateur should be sure to get a letter from the project director to the effect that he or she was a competent worker in this or that aspect of such and such excavation project. Such a letter can be useful in the coming years when field supervisors ask if there are any *experienced* volunteers. In some cases, those who show particular proficiency in certain areas can receive educational credits for fieldwork in the event they are attending or plan to attend a university to study archaeology.

The following organizations and institutions should be contacted for information on archaeological expeditions and excavations with professionals in the United States, Canada, and countries throughout the world.

NATIONAL ORGANIZATIONS

UNITED STATES

American Anthropological Association
1703 New Hampshire Avenue, N.W.
Washington, D.C. 20009

Archaeological Institute of America
260 West Broadway
New York, New York 10013

American Association for State and Local History
1400 Eighth Avenue, South
Nashville, Tennessee 37203

American Society for Conservation Archaeology
Museum of North Arizona
Box 1389
Flagstaff, Arizona 86001

Council on International Educational Exchange
777 United Nations Plaza
New York, New York 10017

Institute of International Education
809 United Nations Plaza
New York, New York 10017

CANADA

Anthropological Association of Canada
1575 Forlan Drive
Ottawa, Ontario, Canada

ENGLAND

Council for British Archaeology
7 Marylebone Road
London, England NW1 5HA

ISRAEL

Ministry of Education and Culture
Department of Antiquities and Museums
P.O. Box 586
Jerusalem, 9100 Israel

Excavation projects overseas may be sponsored by institutions in the United States or in the host countries. Following is a list of *a few* organizations involved with overseas expeditions.

Archaeology Abroad Service
31–34 Gordon Square
London, England WC1H OPY

Department of Anthropology
University of Pennsylvania Museum
33rd and Spruce Streets
Philadelphia, Pennsylvania 19104

Department for External Studies
Rewley House
Wellington Square
Oxford, OX1 2JA, England

Department of Urban Archaeology
The Museum of London
55 Basingham Street
London, England

Extramural Department
University of Birmingham
PO Box 363, Edgbaston
Birmingham, B15 2TT, England

Department of Anthropology
University of Alberta
Edmonton, Alberta
Canada T6G 2E1

Biocultural Anthropology Department
University of Connecticut
Storrs, Connecticut 06268

Department of Classics
Cornell University
Ithaca, New York 14853

United States Director
American Research Center in Egypt
20 Nassau Street
Princeton, New Jersey 08540

Department of Anthropology
210 Switzler Hall
University of Missouri
Columbia, Missouri 65201

Field Director
Halieis Excavations
Indiana University
Bloomington, Indiana 47401

Department of Archaeology
Douglas College
Rutgers University
New Brunswick, New Jersey 08903

Department of Classics
Brock University
St. Catharines, Ontario
Canada L2S 3A1

Archaeological Expeditions
Tel Aviv University
Ramat Aviv, Tel Aviv
Israel

Institute for Archaeological Research
Drew University
Madison, New Jersey 07940

Smithsonian Institution
Room 309
Washington, D.C. 20560

Lahav Research Project
Lake Forest College
Lake Forest, Illinois 60045

Department of Anthropology
University of Utah
Salt Lake City, Utah 84112

Centre d'Etudes Nordiques
Laval University
Quebec, Canada

CHAPTER 13

Archaeological Organizations

The amateur archaeologist who wants to become actively involved with what is going on in his particular area and who wishes to work with others toward common goals will almost certainly have to associate him or herself with an archaeological organization. This is the best way—some say the *only* productive way—for the amateur to be in a position to take advantage of ongoing archaeological activity.

Every state in the United States has at least one such organization or society; some counties and cities also have one. Most of them were formed specifically for the purpose of inviting sincere amateurs to share in the archaeological activity of the town, region, or state. A majority were founded by amateurs for reasons which are almost always the same: there was no other group around that concerned itself with local archaeology. Whenever it became obvious to individuals interested in preserving historical features that there was no group of citizens to inform officials of potential dangers to important sites, a society was formed. Some societies began through the interest of high school students who wanted to continue studying the archaeology of their region after leaving school. New societies are formed every year.

Most of the societies are involved with archaeology in general; that is, any activity in their region or state that involves any type of historical research interests them. Some organizations have been formed, on the other hand, *specifically* to study Indian remains in a certain town or to excavate early Colonial structures in a particular city.

By the same token, some organizations are devoted to preserving existing sites while others spend a lot of time pinpointing the location of suspected or unknown sites. Some devote their efforts to recording information and publishing the results, while others are principally interested in assisting in salvage operations. But again I should stress that many, if not most, societies are involved directly or indirectly with all such efforts, assuming the collective membership is competent and aggressive.

As with any organization, everything depends on the leadership and the number of members willing and able to contribute. Most organizations seem to have a central core of people who do most of the work, though they may simply be in a position to offer more time to projects. Those who join archaeological societies, pay their dues, attend the monthly meetings, and contribute nothing else are still making some kind of an effort to keep the organization going, if only by offering moral (and a little financial) support. Many members are unable for personal reasons to become active, yet they at least are willing to stand up and be counted among citizens concerned about local archaeology. Everyone contributes in his or her own way.

It is desirable, if not mandatory, for success that every archaeological society run by amateurs satisfy at least three criteria. First, the organization should be registered under a state charter and its bylaws should be examined by an attorney (in order to insure that the scope and purpose of the organization does not interfere with municipal or state law). Second, a member of the professional community should be brought in as an advisor—*not* as an officer or director. The advisor need not even attend mettings; his principal function will be to offer advice when asked by the directors of the organization. A substitute for this—and one which many societies prefer—is to have a direct link with the anthropology department at a university, the state archaeologist, the city museum, or any other group of persons representing the professional archaeological community in the area. It is important that the professional community be informed of what the amateurs are doing, and vice versa, for only through continuous dialogue can there be satisfying results. The third criterion involves the leadership of the society, and here very often we find that personalities cloud the issue. The most experienced and knowledgeable amateur researcher in the group may not be a good choice for president. The one who holds this office should have administrative abilities and be the type who can deal effectively with the public. The importance of proper leadership cannot be overemphasized.

I should make it clear that the composition of the archaeological societies can differ tremendously. Some are composed of twenty or thirty persons all of whom are amateurs, whereas others may have a membership of three hundred of whom ten percent are from the professional community. In some organizations the professionals are in charge, though this is rare because they usually don't have the time. A majority of the archaeological societies in this country are run almost completely by amateurs.

A beginner to this field anxious to join a society in his area but unsure as to the competence of the leadership or the true purpose of the organization should make an attempt to find out before becoming involved. Let's face it, there are good and bad, active and lazy, professionally minded and sloppy groups in every field. Every society should make an attempt to effectively channel the energies of any amateur offering his time, and should always insist that members conduct themselves in the most professional manner. There are a number of ways in which an archaeological organization may be judged, and the beginner may want to consider some of the following.

A good cross section of the community should be encouraged to attend meetings and become actively involved if possible. The organization should make every effort to inform the public of its existence and to make the public aware that persons of all ages and from all backgrounds are welcome. Guest speakers at meetings should be responsible and, if possible, accomplished researchers. The organization should make a point of holding its meetings in a central location. Known pothunters should not be turned away; if they are invited to join or at least attend meetings they may be impressed with what they see and decide to adopt a more professional attitude. An informative newsletter or journal should be published and sent to all members on a regular basis. Accurate records of the collecting and dispersing of funds should be maintained at all times. Whoever wants to accept responsibility should be allowed to involve himself in the organization's business.

The amateur archaeological societies have collectively been responsible for more positive archaeological activity than any other segment or group in the country, and deserve the credit for pressuring Congress to enact the various federal antiquities acts. In that the activities of the various societies differ, depending to a great extent on the number of active members and the scope of the organization, their relative accomplishments also differ. What is important, however, is that archaeological societies maintain a *professional attitude* about this field and that their efforts in this regard remain *constant*.

Some organizations devote their efforts toward a single project, while others—such as NEARA—constantly evaluate sites over an area involving over half a dozen states. When the Massachusetts Archaeological Society became aware that citizens did not know of the many Indian sites in their midst, they took it upon themselves to erect town and state markers designating Indian cemeteries, battle scenes, and other historically important features.

The Montana Archaeological Society constantly works on improving excavation techniques, and anyone involved in an excavation project without supervision is immediately dismissed from the society. Members are particularly concerned with preservation of sites and have accomplished a great deal in this regard without much assistance from the professional community.

The Upper Mississippi Valley Archaeological Research Foundation, with headquarters in Chicago, is devoted to education and exploration. Concerned about the lack of archaeological education in the secondary schools, this organization is attempting to bring the idea of public archaeology out into the open. Members are also involved with salvage operations in quite a few locations.

The Albuquerque Archaeological Society works closely with the State Parks Commission and the various local chambers of commerce in setting aside lands of historical value for inclusion as part of state parks. In addition, the society has an arrangement with the City Museum whereby work space is allotted in exchange for all artifacts recovered through excavation. This society has been responsible for saving a number of petroglyph features from the bulldozer.

The Oklahoma Anthropological Association concentrates on locating sites, informing professional excavators about them, sponsoring digs, recording information, and publishing the results for the benefit of both the professional and lay communities. They are particularly involved with keeping a constant record of the status of existing sites.

In Texas, the South Plains Archaeological Society has an impressive record of protecting historic and prehistoric sites from destruction. Members have conducted surveys for various stage agencies and committees and have been instrumental in getting sites excavated before construction began. The Lower Plains Archaeological Society has conducted excavation projects and published results in a very professional manner.

The Florida Archaeological Society has attempted to gain the interest of the public by asking people to watch for valuable artifacts of the sort that began turning up near Miami a couple of years ago. Due to the efforts of society members, a Toquesta Indian campground became a state park—just barely in time to save it from becoming a used car lot. The recording of over 1,500 artifacts was undertaken in addition to excavation work, and the number of important sites has increased.

In Washington, membership activity in the Mid-Columbian Archaeological Society is devoted principally to excavation work. This organization was instrumental in starting a course on the prehistory of the region at a local college. Diggers have located and recorded thousands of artifacts, both historic and prehistoric.

These few examples will give the reader some idea of various societies' activities. The extent to which any individual in a society is involved in excavation or any number of research projects depends mainly on two things: the individual's level of competence and/or ability to follow directions, and the amount of time he or she is able to devote.

There are no prerequisites for joining any amateur archaeological organization save a sincere desire to act in a professional manner and promote the cause of good archaeology—as opposed to pothunting. No one need hesitate, therefore, because he has no experience or particular skill to offer. Some people prefer to take a few courses in archaeology, study for a while on their own, or join an expedition party as an observer before joining a society. This would certainly be of use to the society, but it is by no means necessary. Most people join *in order to learn* from more experienced persons the various procedures and principles involved in archaeological excavation and research. Any newcomer should inform those in charge of research that he would like to become an *active* member, and that he is in a position to join excavations or expeditions.

Usually there is a nominal membership fee for joining any organization (the average is $10 annually), which allows the member to vote, to be informed of all activities, to attend all meetings without charge, to receive all publications, to hold office, and to engage in research in the name of the society (when applicable). Amateur societies occasionally are recipients of excavation or research grants, though this is rare. When a project is to be undertaken and there are no outside funds appropriated, the society itself is responsible for all expenses. Depending on the size of the organization's treasury, it may underwrite all expenses; if not, each member of the expedition may be expected to take care of his own expenses, with the organization paying for equipment. All of this is of course clearly spelled out before any major projects are undertaken, but members need not be concerned about any out-of-pocket expenses with the possible exception of travel, food, and perhaps lodging.

When an excavation is undertaken by an amateur society, the results of the project—artifacts collected, photographs, records—are the property of the association, not of any individuals involved. Sometimes arrangements are made with a university or museum for deposit of all artifacts and records with proper credit going to the organization, and this should be done whenever possible. Other than that, the materials should be safely stored in a member's home with the stipulation that any other member may view them or study them. The materials and their accompanying records should *never* be separated from one another and never relocated without the knowledge and consent of the society's directors. Obviously, the individual designated keeper of materials should be a trustworthy person who intends to remain active in the organization.

In addition to the activities that a society itself generates, opportunities for members to work often come from outside sources. When a university needs volunteers to help out on an emergency excavation or salvage expedition, the amateur societies are usually the first to know, because the professionals need them and want them for their experience in such matters. This type of project is almost always on a completely voluntary basis, and it is up to the individual to decide if he or she can afford the time. There is no question that the professional community depends on the corps of amateurs who belong to and run amateur organizations, and they are rarely disappointed with the amateur's work.

The extent to which any amateur organization is involved with the professionals in the state depends solely on the quality of the work done by the amateurs. Any organization that does not have a professional attitude about archaeology is no good for anyone and serves no useful purpose for archaeology.

The following is a list of amateur archaeological societies in the United States and Canada. I have listed those organizations which openly invite new members. New societies are formed in various parts of the country every year, hence this list is only relatively complete. The addresses are as up to date as possible, based on previous communication with the organizations. If there is any question about archaeological organizations in your area, be sure to contact the anthropology department at your state university or a state museum.

ARCHAEOLOGICAL SOCIETIES

ALABAMA

Alabama Archaeological Society
1414 5th Avenue, S.E., Decatur, Alabama
35601
Chapters in Albertville, Auburn, Birmingham, Gadsden, Huntsville, Mauvilla, Mobile, Montgomery, Moundville, Muscle Shoals, Noccalulu, Selma, Sheffield, Tuscaloosa.

ALASKA

Alaska Archaeological Society
c/o University of Alaska, Fairbanks, Alaska

ARIZONA

Arizona Archaeological and Historical Society
c/o University of Arizona Museum, Tucson, Arizona

ARKANSAS

Arkansas Archaeological Society
c/o University of Southern California, Fayetteville, Arkansas 72701

North West Archaeological Society
P.O. Box 1154, Fayetteville, Arkansas 72701

CALIFORNIA

Archaeological Research Associates
c/o University of Southern Califonria, Los Angeles, California

Archaeological Survey Associates of Southern California
c/o Southwest Museum, Los Angeles, California

Pacific Coast Archaeological Society
Box 926, Costa Mesa, California, 92627

San Diego County Archaeological Society
Box 187, Encinitas, California 92024

Society for California Archaeology
725 Jacon Way, Pacific Palisades, California 90272

COLORADO

Colorado Archaeological Society
c/o University of Colorado, Boulder, Colorado

State Historical Society of Colorado
East 14th Avenue and Sherman Street, Denver, Colorado

CONNECTICUT

American Indian Archaeological Institute
Box 85, Washington, Connecticut 06793

Archaeological Society of Connecticut
Box 1916, Yale Station, New Haven, Connecticut 06520
Chapters in Hartford, Bridgeport, Norwalk

Connecticut Historical Society
1 Elizabeth Street, Hartford, Connecticut 06105

Historical Society of East Hartford
102 Connecticut Boulevard, East Hartford, Connecticut 06108

Middlesex County Historical Society
51 Main Street, Middlesex, Connecticut 06457

North Haven Historical Society
5 Quinnipiac Avenue, North Haven, Connecticut 06473

DELAWARE

Archaeological Society of Delaware
RD 2, Box 166A, Dover, Delaware 19901

Sussex Society of Archaeology and History
RD 2, Timihaw Road, Seaford, Delaware 19973

DISTRICT OF COLUMBIA (WASH-INGTON)

Anthropological Society of Washington
c/o Smithsonian Institution, Washington, D.C. 20560

FLORIDA

Florida Archaeological Society and Florida Anthropological Society
c/o Florida State University, Tallahassee, Florida
Chapters in Hollywood, Fort Walton Beach, Cocoa, Miami, Tampa.

Pensacola Historical Society
405 S. Adams Street, Pensacola, Florida 32501

Suncoast Archaeological Society
1021 4th Street, N., St. Petersburg, Florida 33701

Tallahassee Historical Society
Florida State University, Tallahassee, Florida 32306

GEORGIA

Augusta Archaeology Society
540 Telfair Street, Augusta, Georgia 30901

Northwest Georgia Archaeological Society
c/o Shorter College, Rome, Georgia

Society for the Preservation of Early Georgia History
Department of Archaeology and Anthropology
University of Georgia, Athens, Georgia

IDAHO

Idaho Historical Society
610 Parkway Drive, Boise, Idaho

Society for Historical Archaeology
Department of Sociology and Anthropology
University of Idaho, Moscow, Idaho 83843

ILLINOIS

Cairo Historical Association
508 23rd Street, Cairo, Illinois 62914

Illinois State Archaeological Society
c/o Southern Illinois University Museum, Carbondale, Illinois

Upper Mississippi Valley Archaeological Foundation
2216 West 112 Street, Chicago, Illinois 60643

INDIANA

Indiana Historical Society
140 North Senate Avenue, Indianapolis, Indiana

Indiana Society of Archeology
590 N. Washington Street, Scottsburg, Indiana 47170

IOWA

Iowa Archaeological Society
c/o State University of Iowa, Iowa City, Iowa

Quad City Archaeological Society
4106 El Rancho Drive, Davenport, Iowa 52806

KANSAS

AASCK
2328 McAdams, Wichita, Kansas 67218

Kansas Anthropological Society and Kansas State Historical Society
10th and Jackson Streets, Topeka, Kansas

KENTUCKY

Archaeological Research
c/o Department of Anthropology
University of Kentucky, Lexington, Kentucky

Green River Archaeological Society
3443 Flintridge Drive, Lexington, Kentucky 40502

LOUISIANA

Anthropological Research
Department of Anthropology
Louisiana State University, Baton Rouge, Louisiana

MAINE

Maine Archaeological Society
Museum of Stone Age Antiquities, Bar Harbor, Maine

MARYLAND

Archaeological Society of Maryland, Inc.
17 East Branch Lane, Baltimore, Maryland 21202

MASSACHUSETTS

Early Sites Research Society
10 Commercial Wharf, Boston, Massachusetts

Massachusetts Archaeological Society, Inc.
Bronson Museum, 8 North Main Street, Attleboro, Massachusetts
Chapters in Cohasset, Haverhill, Manamooskeagin, and elsewhere.

MICHIGAN

Aboriginal Research Club
828 Clay Street, Algonac, Michigan

Michigan Archaeological Society
c/o University of Michigan Museum, Ann Arbor, Michigan
Chapters in Lansing, Waterford, Fenton, Midland, Roseville, Benton Harbor, Grand Rapids.

MINNESOTA

Minnesota Archaeological Society
2303 Third Avenue South, Minneapolis, Minnesota

MISSISSIPPI

Mississippi Archaeological Association
115 Wiltshire Boulevard, Biloxi, Mississippi 39531

Mississippi Department of Archives and History
P.O. Box 571, Jackson, Mississippi

MISSOURI

Central States Archaeological Societies
1228 West Essex, St. Louis, Missouri 63122

Missouri Archaeology Club
S.E. Missouri State University
900 Normal, Cape Girardeau, Missouri 63701

Missouri Archaeological Society
15 Switzler, Hall, University of Missouri, Columbia, Missouri

St. Louis Society of Archeology
8792 E. Pine, St. Louis, Missouri 63144

MONTANA

Montana Archaeological Society
c/o Montana State University, Missoula, Montana

NEBRASKA

Nebraska State Historical Society
1500 'R' Street, Lincoln, Nebraska

University of Nebraska State Museum
101 Merrill Hall, 14th and 'U' Streets, Lincoln, Nebraska

NEVADA

Nevada Archeological Society
1650 N. Virginia Street, Reno, Nevada 89503

Nevada State Museum Associates
Carson City, Nevada

NEW HAMPSHIRE

New Hampshire Archaeological Society
Paul Holmes, Secretary, Box 522, Rt#1, Plaistow, New Hampshire 03865

New England Antiquities Research Association
Andrew Rothovius, Secretary, 4 Smith St., Milford, New Hampshire 03055

NEW JERSEY

Archaeological Society of New Jersey
Fairleigh Dickinson University, Madison, New Jersey

NEW MEXICO

Archaeological Society of New Mexico
P.O. Box 3485, Albuquerque, New Mexico 87110
Chapters in Farmington, Hobbs, Portales, and elsewhere.

Albuquerque Archaeological Society
P.O. Box 4029, Albuquerque, New Mexico 87106

NEW YORK

Archaeological Society of Central New York
Cayuga Museum of History & Art, Auburn, New York 13021

Middletown Archaeological Research Center
26 North Street, Floor 5, Middletown, New York 10940

New York Archaeological Association
State Educational Building, Albany, New York
(Membership is in local chapters: Glens Falls, Sherburne, Buffalo, Long Island, New York City, Poughkeepsie, Rochester, Middletown, Claverack.)

NORTH CAROLINA

North Carolina Archaeological Society
Box 301, Chapel Hill, North Carolina
Chapters in Wilmington, Smithfield, Pikeville, Durham, Dunn.

NORTH DAKOTA

North Dakota Historical Society
Liberty Memorial Building, Bismarck, North Dakota 58501

North Dakota State Archaeological Society
Bismarck, North Dakota

OHIO

Archaeological Society of Ohio
199 Converse Drive, Plain City, Ohio 43064

Ohio Historical Society
Columbus, Ohio

OKLAHOMA

Oklahoma Anthropological Society
1335 S. Asp Avenue, Norman, Oklahoma 73069

OREGON

Oregon Archaeological Society
c/o University of Oregon, Eugene, Oregon

PENNSYLVANIA

Society for Pennsylvania Archaeology
c/o University of Pennsylvania, Philadelphia, Pennsylvania
Chapters in Hookstown, Towanda, Sharpesville, Lancaster, Johnstown, Williamsport, Hanover, Dauphin, Meadville, Erie, Easton, and elsewhere.

RHODE ISLAND

Narragansett Archaeological Society of Rhode Island
277 Brook Street, Providence, Rhode Island

SOUTH CAROLINA

South Carolina Archaeological Society
Columbia, South Carolina

SOUTH DAKOTA

South Dakota Archaeological Commission
c/o State University Museum, Vermillion, South Dakota

TENNESSEE

Tennessee Archaeological Society
c/o The F. McClung Museum, Knoxville, Tennessee 37916
Chapters in Wartrace, Chattanooga, Johnson Ctiy, Huntington, Morristown.

TEXAS

Dallas Archaeological Society
Dallas, Texas

Texas Archaeological Society
c/o University of Texas, Austin, Texas

El Paso Archaeological Society
El Paso, Texas

UTAH

Utah Archaeological Society
c/o University of Utah Museum, Salt
Lake City, Utah

VERMONT

Vermont Archaeological Society
9 Driftwood Lane, Burlington, Vermont
05401

Vermont Historical Society
State Administration Building, Montpelier, Vermont

VIRGINIA

Archaeological Society of Virginia
Ninth Street Office Building, Richmond,
Virginia 25219
Chapters in Petersburg, Richmond,
Eclipse, Strassburg, Fairfax, Courtland,
Williamsburg, Clarkesville, Fredericks-
burg.

Chesopiean Archaeological Association
7507 Pennington Road, Norfolk, Virginia 23505

WASHINGTON

Washington Archaeological Society
Box 84, University Station, Seattle, Wash-
ington
Mid-Columbia Archaeological Society
c/o University of Washington, Seattle,
Washington

WEST VIRGINIA

West Virginia Archaeological Society
c/o Wheeling College, Wheeling, West
Virginia
Chapters in South Charleston, Mingo
Junction, Dallas.

WISCONSIN

Wisconsin Archaeological Society
Wauwatosa, Wisconsin

WYOMING

Wyoming Archaeological Society
Rt 1, Box 171, Cody, Wyoming 82414

CANADA

Ontario Archaeological Society
Box 241, Station P, Toronto, Ontario,
Canada

U.S. VIRGIN ISLANDS

Virgin Islands Archaeological Society
Box 4986, St. Thomas, U.S. Virgin Island,
00801

CHAPTER 14

Archaeological Sites

Amateur archaeologists who belong to active societies will be familiar with opportunities at archaeological and historic sites in their area. Most organizations have a list of existing sites, having no doubt been responsible for the location of many of them, and are usually involved with any activities requiring the services of nonprofessional workers. Indeed, when excavations are undertaken—particularly large ones— amateur societies are usually informed by the professional community and asked to contribute time and effort.

In this chapter I discuss opportunities for amateurs at *existing* sites; known, recorded, recognized sites which may occasionally or frequently be slated for excavation projects. Some large sites, like the Koster Site in Illinois, are worked on continuously each summer by professionals and amateurs. Another large site, Mystery Hill in New Hampshire, however, conducts infrequent excavation work owing to a lack of funding and the inability to find a professional archaeologist to direct proper research.

Archaeological sites usually fall into five categories, which can determine not only the possibility of excavation work by amateurs but also the availability of funding from federal, institutional, and foundation sources. The five categories are federal, state, municipal (city, town, county), controlled, and private.

Federal Sites. Archaeological sites in this category are simply those located on federal land, which includes national parks, wildlife reserves, open forestland protected from abuse or use by timber companies, etc. These sites may or may not be classified as national historic monuments, but they are all under the control of the National Park Service by authority of the U.S. Department of Interior. Any excavation work done at such sites must be approved by the federal agency involved, and this approval is only given to recognized professional archaeologists associated with a university system, a museum, or a research organization. This does not mean that amateurs may never work at such sites, but rather that the professional community must direct and *be responsible* for all undertakings.

Compared to sites in the other categories, there is not much excavation activity at sites on federal land. The federal government is prone to *preserve as is* those sites under its control, and after an initial investigation or two to determine the meaning and importance of a particular site, there is usually little additional work on a scale that might include a number of volunteers. When there is excavation activity, however, it is always funded by the federal government, and the funding is always very generous—much more than is usually required to get the job done, but nobody complains. The funding is always channeled through either the anthropology department of a university or the research department of a museum, and professional archaeologists are always inclined to get as involved as possible, for obvious reasons. Such projects may include room for amateurs and may even offer a stipend for services rendered, but don't count on it.

State Sites.   All archaeological sites on state land are directly controlled by the state. These sites usually receive much more attention than federal sites, because the professional community in the state can deal directly with the officials involved. The state archaeologist is almost always the ranking staff member in the anthropology department of the state university system, so the professional community is really expected to determine what's best for state-owned sites. The principal problem here is funding; most states do not have enough money to locate and preserve sites, much less to sponsor what may be considered by legislators to be arbitrary excavation projects. Nevertheless, there is always funding available for emergency excavation work on state-owned sites, and here the amateur—particularly one experienced in fieldwork—can find opportunities. In that the state university usually directs such projects, enrolled students stand the best chance of working as volunteers. The states seem to follow the lead of the federal government with regard to sites, and hesitate to undertake major excavation projects unless they are convinced that a wealth of information can be obtained.

In general, working with any federal or state agency is a bureaucratic mess. Amateurs should attempt to work through a local or statewide archaeological association when seeking assignments on state property.

Municipal Sites.   Municipal sites are those located on lands owned by the city, town, county, province, parish, or whatever, and they offer more opportunities for amateurs than federal or state sites. Very often, sites on city land just sit there; that is, either the city will not really be aware of the importance of the sites or the officials will not deem them important enough for the expenditure of city funds. Much depends on how sophisticated a city or town is in terms of the public and political realization of what archaeological sites represent. The amateur archaeological community can, of course, impress upon the town citizens and officials the fact that an archaeological site must be preserved and studied. They can also often conduct excavation work if they arrange for permission from the city to do so. Usually such an arrangement involves a promise that all materials and reports will be turned over to the city or town for display, and this is how it should be.

A number of cities and towns in the United States employ amateur archaeologists, often without pay, to advise on historic sites. In addition, some small city-owned museums are run completely by amateurs. Small cities that do not have a college in them do not have a representative of the professional archaeological community to advise them either (unless special arrangements have been made with the state). Few of the smaller cities and certainly very few townships can afford a professional advisor anyway, and are forced to depend on amateur archaeologists for a number of archaeological activities. Once again, however, I should stress the desirability of working through an archaeological organization when seeking to conduct excavation or other work at a city-owned site.

Controlled Sites.   This category involves those sites which may be on federal, state, city, or private land, but which are—for any one of a number of reasons—the responsibility of a particular institution. The institution is usually a university, a professional archaeological survey organization, or a museum which has been given direct and absolute control (short of actual ownership) over all activities at the site by the legal owners. Such a situation rarely involves sites on federal land, occasionally involves sites on state land, and frequently involves sites on municipal and private properties. The reasons for controlled sites situations are basic. Either the institution convinces the owner to allow archaeological research for an extended period of time (usually a number of years), or the owner requests that an institution be responsible for preserving the site and obtaining information through excavation work, if necessary.

Archaeological societies run by amateurs are often involved with this kind of situation, and it is of course an excellent opportunity to excavate and study a site at leisure. In Massachusetts, for example, there are thousands of sites not on federal or state land which local societies keep track of on a regular basis, and which experienced amateurs excavate when they feel valuable information may be obtained. In Arkansas, it is said that one need only pick up a handful of dirt anywhere and chances are he'll find something of importance. In Arizona, there are so many sites requiring at least minimal excavation that archaeologists don't even expect to get to all of them before the end of the century— even if by some miracle they are saved from destruction.

Private Sites.   An untold number of sites exist on private property, and owners are often either unaware or uninterested. Here an energetic amateur can excavate with a group on a regular basis, assuming the property owner has no objections. No landowner is required to permit excavation work; state laws allow him to destroy anything he wants on his property. If amateurs act fast, however, they can at least perform a basic excavation with the hope of obtaining something of value.

Many amateurs have been responsible not only for saving sites on private land, but also for effecting superb excavations and obtaining valuable and important materials. In New Hampshire, Vermont, Massachusetts, and Maine, the New England Antiquities Research Association has located and convinced owners to preserve numerous sites on their property. In New Mexico, three amateur organizations spend every weekend directing excavation projects at a number of sites. At the very least, the amateur can record the existence of sites on private land.

With the exception of sites on private land, it is usually common knowledge what sites are being worked on. The only way for the amateur to proceed is simply to approach those working at or responsible for a site and offer his or her services. One can usually determine those sites which are not meant to be tampered with. Some sites are fenced in, some are tourist attractions, and some just sit there almost unnoticed. At every excavation site, however, the problem is usually in finding enough funding to get a professional archaeologist to direct the project, not in getting a sufficient number of volunteers.

Following is a list of some of the well-known sites in the United States and Canada which may offer opportunities for amateurs.

ARCHAEOLOGICAL SITES

ALABAMA

Bridgeport
Russell Cave National Monument: on US 72; occupied from about 6000 B.C. to A.D. 1650.

Kinlock Knob
Bankhead National Forest: ½ mile west; petroglyphs.

Moundville
Mound State Monument: on State 69; 40 mounds.

Mount Hope
Bankhead National Forest: 4 miles south; petroglyphs.

ARIZONA

Camp Verde
Montezuma Castle National Monument: off State 79; five-story cliff dwelling.

Chinle
Canyon de Chelly National Monument: on Navajo Indian Reservation; state 68; pit houses and cliff dwelling representing four periods of Indian culture from A.D. 348 to 1300.

Clarkdale
Tuzigoot National Monument: US 89; Pueblo ruins dating from A.D. 1100 to 1450.

Coolidge
Casa Grande National Monument: State 87; Hohokam tower, ruins.

Flagstaff
Walnut Canyon National Monument: US 66; over 300 cliff dwellings dating from A.D. 1100 to 1275.

Wupatki National Monument: US. 89; over 800 ruins, ancient ball court.

Gila Bend
Painted Rocks State Historical Site: petroglyphs.

Globe
Besh-ba-Gowah: on Pinal Mountain Road; Pueblo ruins inhabited by Salado Indians from A.D. 1225 thru 1400.

Grand Canyon National Park
Tusayan Ruin: Grand Canyon Village; small pueblo.

Holbrook
Petrified Forest National Park: US 180; Puerco Ruins, Indian village; Newspaper Rock, 1 mile south of Puerco River; petroglyphs.

Kayenta
Navajo National Monument: State 464, on Navajo Indian reservation; Betatkin and Keet Seel cliff dwellings.

Lupton
Pueblo ruins: between Lupton and Houk; Basket Maker dwellings dating from A.D. 797 or earlier.

Phoenix
Pueblo Grande City Park: Hohokam ruin, continuing periodic excavations.

Roosevelt
Tonto National Monument: on State 88; Hohokam cliff dwellings.

Whiteriver
Kinishba Pueblo: on Whiteriver Apache Indian Reservation; partially restored ruins dating from A.D. 1050–1350.

ARKANSAS

Arkadelphia
Powell Site: south side of Caddo River; temple mounds.

Eureka Springs
Blue Spring: US 62, 1 mile north on gravel road; pictographs.

CALIFORNIA

Bishop
Chalfont Valley petroglyphs: Fish Slough Road.

Fort Ross
Fort Ross State Historic Park; early 19th-century Russian fur-trading post and fort.

Indio
Travertine Rock: State 86; petroglyphs.

Santa Barbara
Mission Santa Barbara: Los Olivas and Laguna Sts.

Sequoia and Kings Canyon National Parks
Hospital Rock: Ash Mountain; pictographs.

Tulelake
Lava Beds Monument: petroglyphs.

COLORADO

Cortez
Mesa Verde National Park: on US 160; pit houses and pueblo ruins and cliff dwellings.

FLORIDA

Crystal River
Crystal River State Park: temple and burial mounds, shell heaps.

Jacksonville
Fort Carolina National Memorial: off State 10; 16th-century French fort.

St. Augustine
Castillo de San Marcos National Monument: 17th-century Spanish fortress.

Fort Matanzas National Monument: off State A1A; 18th-century Spanish fort.

GEORGIA

Blakely
Kolomoki Mounds State Park: US 27; temple and burial mounds.

Cartersville
Etowah Mounds: temple and burial mounds.

Macon
Ocmulgee National Monument: on US 80 and 129; temple mounds; earth lodge.

St. Simons Island
Fort Frederica: 18th-century British fort.

ILLINOIS

East St. Louis
Cahokia Mounds State Park: on US 40 and 66; temple mounds.

Havana
Dickson Mounds State Memorial: off State 78 and 97; skeletons in burial mound.

Utica
Starved Rock State Park: on State 178; Hopewellian burial mounds.

INDIANA

Andersón
Mounds State Park: on State 32; mounds.

Evansville
Angel Mounds: State 266 and 662; mounds; excavations during July and August.

Mitchell
Spring Mill State Park: on State 60; early 19th-century frontier trading post.

IOWA

McGregor
Effigy Mounds National Monument: off US 18; mounds in bird and animal shapes.

KENTUCKY

Ashland
Central Park: burial mounds.

Lexington
Adena Park: off US 27 and 68; mound (for permission to visit, apply to University of Kentucky).

Wickliffe
Ancient Burial City (or King Mounds): northwest on US 51, 60, and 62; council houses, burial and temple mounds.

LOUISIANA

Epps
Poverty Point: on Bayou Macon; geometric mounds (private property, no admission fee).

Marksville
Marksville Prehistoric Indian Park.

MAINE

Augusta
Fort Western: Bowman and Cony Sts.; 18th-century fort.

Kittery
Fort McClary Memorial: 19th-century fort.

Wiscasset
Fort Edgecomb Memorial: Davis Island; early 19th-century wooden blockhouse.

MASSACHUSETTS

Pittsfield
Hancock Shaker Village: on US 20; 18th-century community.

Saugus
The Ironworks: 17th-century blast furnace, forge, and rolling and slitting mill.

MICHIGAN

Houghton
Isle Royale National Park: prehistoric camp sites.

MINNESOTA

Pipestone
Pipestone National Monument: on US 75; ancient quarries of red stones for ceremonial pipes.

MISSISSIPPI

Natchez
Emerald Mound: Natchez Trace Parkway; temple mound.

MISSOURI

De Soto
Washington State Park: on State 21; pictographs.

Marshall
Van Meter State Park: on State 122; Hopewellian mounds.

MONTANA

Kalispell
Pictographs: on US 2.

NEBRASKA

Gering
Scotts Bluff National Monument: extinct bison remains with stone artifacts.

NEVADA

Moapa
Valley of Fire State Park: on State 40; petroglyphs.

NEW HAMPSHIRE

North Salem
Mystery Hill: Route 111; stone structures, astronomical alignments, inscriptions, special collection.

NEW JERSEY

Batsto
Batsto Area of the Wharton Forest: County 52; Revolutionary War ironworks.

NEW MEXICO

Alamogordo
The Petroglyphs: on US 54, 5 miles east of Three Rivers.

Aztec
Aztec Ruins National Monument: off US 550; ancient pueblo and kivas.

Bernalillo
Coronado State Monument: on State 44; ancient pueblo and kivas.

Espanola
Puye Cliff Dweller and Communal House Ruins: on State 30, then 9 miles west on State 5.

Folsom
Folsom State Monument: off US 64; ancient pueblo and Franciscan mission.

Jemez Springs
Jemez State Monument: on State 4; ancient pueblo and Franciscan mission.

Mountainair
Abo State Mounment: on US 60; ruins of ancient pueblo and mission.

Gran Quivira National Monument: on State 10; ruins of Franciscan missions.

Quarai State Monument: off State 10; ruins of mission church.

Pecos
Pecos State Monument: US 85; ruins of ancient pueblo and mission.

Santa Fe
Bandelier National Monument: off State 4; ancient pueblo and caves.

Silver City
Cila Cliff Dwelling National Monument: no auto road; write Superintendent, Box 1320; cliff dwellings.

Thoreau
Chaco Canyon National Monument: on US 66; Pueblo Bonito and ruins of smaller sites.

NEW YORK

Fort Ticonderoga
Fort Ticonderoga: 18th-century fort.

Rensselaer
Fort Crailo: 17th-century Dutch fort.

NORTH CAROLINA

Mt. Gilead
Town Creek Indian Mound State Historic Site: off State 731; restored temple mound.

Roanoke Island
Fort Raleigh National Historic Site: 16th-century British fort.

Winston-Salem
Old Salem: Reception Center, 614 Main Street; long-range restoration of 18th-century Moravian village.

NORTH DAKOTA

Hebron
Crowley Flint Quarry: off US 10; sources of flint for artifacts.

OHIO

Bainbridge
Slip Mound State Memorial: US 50; large central mound of Slip group.

Chillicothe
Mound City Group National Monument: on State 104; 24 Hopewellian burial mounds (500 B.C.–A.D. 500).

Story Mound: Deano Avenue; conical Adena mound.

Fort Recovery
Fort Recovery State Memorial: on State 49; 18th-century blockhouse with connecting stockade wall.

Jackson
Leo Petroglyph: many petroglyphs.

Kelly's Island
Inscription Rock: in Lake Erie, reached by ferry; fine examples of pictograph rock.

Lebanon
Fort Ancient: on State 350; earthworks, burial mounds, cemeteries, remains of village sites.

Locust Grove
Serpent Mound State Memorial: on State 73; large effigy mounds.

Marietta
Mound Cemetery: "Conus" burial mound of chief.

Miamisburg
Miamisburg Mound State Memorial: on US 25; largest conical mound in state.

Newark
The Newark Earthworks: Wright Earthworks (James and Waldo Sts.); Moundbuilders State Memorial (Southwest on State 79); and Octagon State Memorial (west on State 16); geometric earthworks and effigy mound.

New Philadelphia
Schoenbrunn Village State Memorial; on US 250; pioneer 18th-century Moravian village.

Rochester
Warren County Serpent Mound: on US 22; effigy mound.

Sinking Spring
Fort Hill Memorial: near State 41; Hopewellian earthworks.

Tarlton
Tarlton Cross Mound State Memorial: near State 159; effigy mound in form of cross.

OKLAHOMA

Boise City
Black Mesa State Park: cave with ancient pictographs.

PENNSYLVANIA

Chester
Caleb Pusey House: oldest millhouse in state; inhabited almost continuously since 17th century; under restoration; will become state park.

Cornwall
Cornwall Charcoal Furnace: 18th-century iron-casting furnace.

Ligonier
Fort Ligonier: on State 711; 18-century fortification.

Uniontown
Necessity National Battlefield: on US 40; 18th-century fort and earthworks.

SOUTH CAROLINA

Charleston
Francis Marion National Forest: on State 41; preliminary excavation of Sewee Indian mound.

Summerville
Old Dorchester Historical State Park: on State 642; ruins of Revolutionary fort and settlement.

TENNESSEE

Memphis
Chucalissa Indian Town: on Mitchell Road; temple and burial mounds.

Vonore
Fort Loudoun: off US 411; 18th-century French fort.

UTAH

Blanding
National Bridges National Monument: ancient cliff dwellings.

Monticello
Indian Creek Historic State Park: off US 160; Newspaper Rock, large cliff mural of petroglyphs and pictographs.

Torrey
Capitol Reef National Monument: on State 24; petroglyphs in Fremont River Canyon.

VIRGINIA

Jamestown
Colonial National Historical Park: remains of early English settlement.

Williamsburg
Colonial Williamsburg: 18th-century state capitol.

WASHINGTON

Walla Walla
Whitman Mission National Historic Site: portion of early earthworks and buildings have been excavated.

Yakima
Indian petroglyphs: on US 410.

WEST VIRGINIA

Moundsville
Mammoth Mound: Tomlinson Avenue, between 9th and 10th Streets; large conical Adena mound.

WISCONSIN

Baraboo
Devil's Lake State Park: on State 123; effigy mounds.

Black Lion Falls
Gullickson's Glen: County Roads C and X; artifacts and petroglyphs.

Fort Atkinson
Mounds.

Lake Mills
Aztalan State Park: on County Road B; mounds.

Prairie du Chien
Wyalusing State Park: US 18 and State 35, then, 5 miles west on County Road C; mounds.

West Bend
Lizard Mound State Park: on County Road A; 31 effigy mounds.

WYOMING

Fort Laramie
Fort Laramie National Historic Site: remains of trading center and military post.

CANADA

BRITISH COLUMBIA
Nanaimo (Vancouver Island)
Petroglyph Park: on highway 1; ancient rock carvings.

NEW BRUNSWICK
Sackville
Fort Beauséjour National Historic Park: on highway 2; 18th-century French fort.

NOVA SCOTIA
Annapolis Royal
Port Royal National Historic Park: on north shore of Annapolis River; 17th-century French settlement.

Cape Breton Island
Fortress of Louisburg National Historic Park: 18th-cenutry French fortification.

ONTARIO
Amherstburg
Fort Malden National Historic Park: on highway 18; War of 1812 fortification.

Fort Erie
Old Fort Erie: in Government Park; fort used in War of 1812.

Kingston
Old Fort Henry: completely restored 19th-century fort.

Prescott
Fort Wellington National Historic Park: War of 1812 fortification.

QUEBEC
Chambly
Fort Chambly National Historic Park: 17th-century French fort.

St. John
Fort Lennox National Historic Park: 12 miles south on Ile-Aux-Noix; 17th-century fort, used by British during Revolution and War of 1812.

CHAPTER 15

Archaeological Museums

When people hear the word *archaeology*, many immediately think of excavation work, when in fact some archaeologists spend a very small part of their careers in the field.

The same can be said of amateurs. Many amateur archaeologists prefer not to be involved with excavations or with fieldwork of any kind. They are more interested in the material results of digging, in the artifacts themselves. Such individuals would probably feel right at home in a museum, and museums offer yet another opportunity for the amateur.

There are many different kinds of museums serving different functions, from city, privately endowed, and commercial museums to company, university, and federally supported museums, but not all of them offer opportunities for the amateur. Each museum has to be checked out individually by the interested amateur.

Many archaeological societies deal directly with local and university museums, hence it is advantageous for the amateur to join an organization. The societies are able in many cases to make use of museum equipment and know they have a secure depository for materials recovered through excavation. This situation is advantageous for the museums also, for they are prone to support those organizations which intend to turn materials over to them for study and public display. We are dealing here obviously with archaeological or historical museums as opposed to industrial museums or those which specialize only in, say, art, botany, or astronomy. Some large museums, such as federally supported science museums, cover a whole range of subjects, from anthropology to zoology.

There are over 3,000 museums in the United States, and their size, budget, and number of employees differ enormously. In Kansas, the Butler County Museum is run by one woman, while in Pennsylvania, the Carnegie Museum employs dozens of professional scientists and researchers. A small science museum in Wyoming accommodates about

2,000 visitors a year, while the Boston Museum of Science is host to that many in a single weekend during the summer.

Many museums have some kind of program to accommodate interested amateurs. The smaller ones really have no program at all and can usually be persuaded to take on an enthusiastic volunteer who is willing to perform a number of tasks for free. These museums have an extremely limited budget and are usually forced to depend on visitor fees for support. In contrast with the commercial museums, however, the smaller ones are often more devoted to the general public. A number of curators of small museums have complained that the commercial enterprises are interested only in serving the elite of a city and keeping the money rolling in.

Most of the noncommercial museums need all the help they can get, but this help should be both positive and qualitative. A knowledgeable amateur can assist needy museums in a great number of ways, but again, this is usually done on a voluntary basis. Many museums may have a dozen people on the staff, but only one—the director or curator—may receive a salary.

Amateur archaeologists can arrange with museums to serve as collectors for them. This is not to say that amateurs should randomly begin picking up artifacts or taking over collections for inclusion in museum property. On the contrary, a properly run museum will choose very carefully what it collects and displays, and will accept only those artifacts gathered professionally and ethically. The museum will also require all relevant records and reports on who located the artifacts, where they were found, and how they were acounted for.

All museums have a special file or catalogue system to account for incoming materials, and very often a volunteer worker can handle this task easily. It is more involved than merely making a list of what comes through the door, however, and the quality of the cataloguing is what separates the good museums from the bad. The artifacts must be carefully described, weighed, measured, cleaned, and placed on the proper list in the catalogue system. In addition, a separate file should be maintained which includes all the known history of the artifact to date, and this file must be updated as new information is obtained.

Another duty of major importance in any museum involves conducting research on incoming materials, and a knowledgeable amateur can be of immense assistance in this regard. Few museums can afford full-time researchers, and the small ones do not have the necessary funds to hire a university anthropologist or historian even on an advisory basis. The few staff members of such museums may not have the time to conduct research, hence it may simply go undone. An amateur who is particularly proficient in a certain period in history or who has had some experience with artifacts may be assigned the job of preparing a report on a collection of Indian utensils or on Colonial picture-framing. This will aid the museum in explaining to visitors the meaning of various collections.

The most obvious function of a museum is to present displays. If the workers at a museum are unaware of the meaning or importance of the various materials, the displays are probably not in any type of acceptable order. Further, many museums have back rooms full of stuff which is never displayed because no one knows just where it fits. An informed amateur can offer his services to a museum by arranging collections in proper chronological sequence. Displays must also be presented in an informative and dignified manner. In Wichita, for example, the Friends University Museum has an arrowhead display in the form of an airplane. This is *not* an example of a dignified presentation. If a small museum has more material than it can easily display—and most do—no problem, for displays should be changed on a regular basis.

It is important that museums be aware of the latest research on materials they house, and here the informed amateur can serve as sort of an outside advisor. In addition, all known stories, legends, or tales about an historic event or place should be written down before the oral history is lost through the death of elderly people. Here again the amateur researcher can take it upon himself to obtain such information for museum files or perhaps publication.

Some enterprising amateurs have brought museums to the public in addition to letting the public come to them. In Oklahoma, it was noticed that few young schoolchildren ever attended museums, so the museum was brought to them. An amateur archaeologist approached a museum and asked if they would consider putting aside certain original artifacts plus copies of others for a suitcase display to be taken around to local schools. The museum agreed, if the amateur would present and discuss the materials in public, and this is now done on a weekly basis. If it weren't for the amateur offering his time, the museum could never have afforded to undertake this kind of a project. Other museums around the country now offer similar programs by arranging for schoolteachers to take suitcase displays for presentation during history classes. The "stuff in the back room" is there no more.

An excellent example of amateur activity at a prominent museum can be found in the Schenectady Museum in Schenectady, New York. Founded in 1934, the museum was chartered by New York State in 1939 and is fully accredited by the American Association of Museums. Although a private, nonprofit operation which relies on local citizens and businesses for its main support, the museum is large and impressive. It includes a planetarium; a variety of exhibitions on art, science, and technology; an education division devoted to sponsoring special activities for children; and classes in painting, fossil identification, astronomy, and many other subjects. It is an excellent example of what a public-oriented museum should be.

Archaeological activities at the museum are handled by Laura Lee Linder, an amateur archaeologist, who is honorary curator of archaeology. Mrs. Linder graduated from college with a degree in psychology, but decided that her main field of interest was archaeology. She attended seminars and field trips in the United States and England, has been involved with numerous archaeological organizations for the past ten years, and began working as a volunteer at the Schenectady Museum two and a half years ago. She assumed her present position after about a year and a half, and began creating programs to educate interested citizens on the importance of archaeological research. She teaches classes on the principles of archaeology, for which she is paid, but Mrs. Linder receives no remuneration for her numerous other efforts. The directors are extremely pleased with what she is doing, and her programs have been well received by the public. If it were not for dedicated amateur archaeologists like Laura Lee Linder, many museums would not be able to accommodate classes and other programs dealing with archaeology.

Thus far in this chapter I have dealt with the more general and obvious duties that an amateur might undertake at smaller museums. The larger museums, particularly those run by scientists or university systems, do much more than collect, record, and display materials for the public—although this is the *primary* function of *all* museums. The more sophisticated, noncommercial museums—and this includes those devoted to archaeological and historical research—are intensely involved with laboratory work. The public rarely if ever sees this facet of the museum, but it goes on all the time and its importance is increasing.

The reason for this increase has to do with the fact that a knowledge revolution is now under way in the field of archaeology, and professionals are beginning to suggest that the future of this revolution may depend on the amateur community. Archaeology—or the focus of the archaeologist—is slowly undergoing a change, and this change will not really be fully recognized for another generation. However, what we do today will affect the quality of archaeological research tomorrow. Let me first offer some background information before bringing the amateur into the picture.

The limits of knowledge in science today are expanding with great rapidity, and the same is true in archaeology. Prior to the carbon-14 and dendrochronology systems of dating, archaeology was quite limited in its ability to satisfactorily establish absolute dating. We are still limited today; there are still many things that archaeology cannot do. It can be stated without hesitation that we have not even begun to reach the potentials of archaeology, and that the limits of the information obtainable from archaeological data are not even suspected. There are at least six hours of research and lab work required for every hour of field excavation, and there is no question that this ratio will continue to increase in the future. The increase is already noticeable because of the vastly expanding information potential of archaeological data.

There are many unanswered questions, many problems, in archaeological research today. There are also many new techniques being planned, developed, and established. The professional archaeologists are swamped with both new problems and new techniques, and they cannot keep up with the knowledge revolution. There is, in effect, an information gap and a technique lag, and farsighted members of the professional community are beginning to work out ways to cope with the problem. This is where the amateur comes in.

Museums that sponsor and direct laboratory research in archaeology are beginning to establish a new role in the world of archaeology, known as the archaeological technician. Such a technician would be trained in specific areas of research and analysis—pollen, ceramics, lithcal, etc. The only drawback at the moment is the funding necessary for the implementation of this new position within archaeology. Many professional archaeologists have suggested that the only way to handle the problem is to train and use amateur archaeologists.

This would not only be less expensive, obviously, but in the words of professionals it would be "a potentially more efficient approach." The idea is to train and use amateur volunteers to handle the tremendous amount of laboratory work which museums (and other institutions) conduct. As the need for more lab work increases, amateurs should become involved with this changing situation within archaeology today. For those interested in indoor archaeology or laboratory work, there is no reason to hesitate in taking advantage of this new and rapidly evolving function.

Laboratory work is one area where most professional archaeologists have little experience. Any intelligent amateur could make a major contribution to archaeology by learning the new techniques being developed in laboratories. Museums offering such opportunities to amateurs should be taken advantage of.

On the following pages I have listed the major museums in the United

States and Canada devoted to archaeology and history. Listed also are special collections of individuals or groups which do not qualify—or wish to be known—as museums as such. Most of the museums listed are large enough to support some kind of amateur activity, though many do not for a variety of reasons. Each must be checked individually by the amateur who is more interested in experience and the work itself than in remuneration.

ARCHAEOLOGICAL MUSEUMS AND
SPECIAL COLLECTIONS

ALABAMA

Alabama Museum of Natural History, University of Alabama, Montgomery.
Museum, Mound State Monument, Moundville.

ALASKA

Alaska Historical Library and Museum (2nd floor, Capitol Building), Juneau.
Sitka National Museum, Sitka.
University Museum, Fairbanks.

ARIZONA

Amerind Foundation, Dragoon.
Arizona Museum, 10th Avenue, at Van Buren, Phoenix.
Arizona-Sonora Desert Museum, Tucson.
Arizona State Museum, University of Arizona, Tucson.
Heard Museum of Anthropology and Primitive Art, 22 East Monte Vista Road, Phoenix.
Museum at Grand Canyon National Park.
Museum of Northern Arizona, Fort Valley Road, Flagstaff.
Museums at these National Monuments: Casa Grande, near Coolidge; Chiricahau, Dos Cabezas; Camp Verde; Navajo, southwest of Kayenta: Petrified Forest, near Holbrook; Tonto, near Roosevelt; Tuzigoot, Clarkdale; Walnut Canyon, Flagstaff; Wupatki, Flagstaff.
Pueblo Grande City Park Museum, 4619 East Washington, Phoenix.

ARKANSAS

Little Rock Museum of Natural History, McArthur Park, Little Rock.
University of Arkansas Museum, Fayetteville.

CALIFORNIA

Antelope Valley Indian Research Museum, Wilsona Route, Lancaster
Indian Museum, Lakeport.
Los Angeles County Museum, Exposition Park, Los Angeles.
Robert H. Lowie Museum of Anthropology, University of California, Berkeley.
Municipal Museum, Riverside.
Museum of Natural History, Santa Barbara.
Oakland Public Museum, Oakland.
San Diego Museum of Man, Balboa Park, San Diego.

Southwest Museum, 10 Highland Park, Los Angeles.
State Indian Museum, 2618 K Street, Sacramento.

COLORADO

Colorado State Museum, East 14th Avenue and Sherman Street, Denver.
Denver Museum of Natural History, City Park, Denver.
Durango Public Library Museum, Durango.
Museum at Mesa Verde National Park.
Trinidad State Junior College Museum, Trinidad.
University of Colorado Museum, Boulder.
Western State College Museum, Gunnison.

CONNECTICUT

Connecticut State Library Museum, 231 Capitol Avenue, Hartford.
Fort Hill Indian Memorial Association, Gallup Hill, Old Mystic.
Gunn Memorial Library and Museum, Washington.
Mattatuck Historical Society, 119 West Main Street, Waterbury.
Peabody Museum of Natural History, Yale University, 170 Whitney Avenue, New Haven.
Somers Mountain Indian Museum, Somers.

DELAWARE

Delaware State Museum, 316 Governors Avenue, Dover.
Hagley Museum, Wilmington.
Zwaanendael Museum, Lewes.

DISTRICT OF COLUMBIA

Natural History Building, Smithsonian Institution.

FLORIDA

Florida State Museum, University of Florida, Seagle Building, Gainesville.
Fort Pierce Museum, Fort Pierce.
Museum of Science and Natural History, 3280 South Miami Avenue, Miami.
Museums at these National Monuments: Castillo de San Marcos, St. Augustine; Fort Caroline, Jacksonville; Fort Matanzas, St. Augustine; and these State Parks: Crystal River; Fort Clinch.
Southeast Museum of the North American Indian, US 1, Marathon.
South Florida Museum, Bradenton.
Temple Mound Museum, Fort Walton Beach.
University Museum, Florida State University, Tallahassee.

GEORGIA

Emory University Museum, Bishop's Hall, Atlanta.

Museums at these National Monuments: Fort Frederica, St. Simons Island; Ocmulgee, Macon; and State Parks: Etowah Mounds, Cartersville; Kolomoki Mounds near Blakely.

IDAHO

Idaho State College Museum, Pocatello.

ILLINOIS

Chicago Academy of Science, 2001 North Clark Street, Chicago.

Chicago Natural History Museum, Roosevelt Road and Lake Shore Drive, Chicago.

Illinois State Museum of Natural History and Art, Springfield.

University of Illinois Museum of Natural History, Natural History Building, Springfield.

INDIANA

Indiana Historical Society, 140 North Senate Street, Indianapolis.

Indiana State Museum, 311 West Washington Street, Indianapolis.

Indiana University Museum of Anthropology, Bloomington.

IOWA

Museum of Natural History, State University, Iowa City.

Museums at Effigy Mounds National Monument, off US 18, McGregor; and Maquoketa Cave State Park, off US 61, south of Dubuque.

Sanford Museum and Planetarium, 117 East Willow Street, Cherokee.

KANSAS

Fort Hayes Kansas State College Museum, Hayes.

Kansas State Historical Society, Memorial Building, 10th and Jackson Streets, Topeka.

Museum of Natural History, University of Kansas, Lawrence.

KENTUCKY

Behringer Museum of Natural History, Devow Park, Covington.

Museum of Anthropology and Archaeology, University of Kentucky, Lexington.

Museum at Mammoth Cave National Park, near Cave City.

LOUISIANA

Louisiana State Exhibit Museum, Shreveport.

Louisiana State Museum, New Orelans.

Middle American Research Institute Museum, Tulane University, New Orleans.

Prehistoric Indian Museum, Marksville State Monument, Marksville.

MAINE

Robert Abbe Museum of Archaeology, Acadia National Park, Bar Harbor.
Maine Historical Society, Portland.
Wilson Museum, Perkins Street, Castine.

MARYLAND

Baltimore Museum of Art, Wyman Park, Baltimore.
Maryland Academy of Sciences, 400 Cathedral Street, Baltimore.

MASSACHUSETTS

Aptucxet Trading Post, Bourne.
Berkshire Museum, South Street, Pittsfield.
Blue Hills Trailside Museum, 1904 Canton Avenue, Milton.
Bronson Museum, 8 North Main Street, Attleboro.
Haverhill Historical Society, 240 Water Street, Haverhill.
Robert S. Peabody Foundation for Archaeology, Phillips Academy, Andover.
Peabody Museum, 161 Essex Street, Salem.
Peabody Museum of Archaeology and Ethnology, Harvard University, Cambridge.
Pilgrim Hall, Plymouth.

MICHIGAN

Detroit Historical Museum, Woodward and Kirby Streets, Detroit.
Grand Rapids Public Museum, 54 Jefferson Avenue, Southeast, Grand Rapids.
Kelsey Museum of Archaeology, University of Michigan, Ann Arbor.
Marquette Park, French and Indian Museum, St. Ignace.
Michigan Historical Museum, Lansing.
Michigan State Museum, East Lansing.
Museum of Anthropology, Wayne State University, Detroit.
Muskegon County Museum, 1259 Marquette Avenue, Muskegon.

MINNESOTA

Minneapolis Public Library, Minneapolis
Museum of Anthropology, University of Minnesota, 325 Ford Hall, Minneapolis.
Runestone Museum, Alexandria.
The Science Museum, 51 University Avenue, St. Paul.

MISSISSIPPI

State Historical Museum, State Street at East Capitol, Jackson.
University of Mississippi Museum, University.

MISSOURI

Archaeological Research Center, University of Missouri, Van Meter State Park, near Marshall.

Kansas City Museum, 3218 Gladstone Boulevard, Kansas City.

Missouri State Museum, Capitol Building, Jefferson.

Museum of Anthropology, University of Missouri, 15 Switzler Hall, Columbia

Museum of Science and Natural History, 2 Oak Knoll Park, St. Louis.

MONTANA

Carter County Museum, County High School, Carter County.

McGill Museum, Montana State College, Bozeman.

Museum of the Plains Indian, Browning.

NEBRASKA

Nebraska State Historical Society, 1500 R Street, Lincoln.

University of Nebraska State Museum, 101 Merrill Hall, 14th and U Streets, Lincoln.

NEVADA

Nevada State Museum, Carson City.

NEW HAMPSHIRE

Dartmouth College Museum, Hanover.

NEW JERSEY

Museum of Natural History, Guyot Hall, Princeton University, Princeton.

Newark Museum, 49 Washington, Newark.

New Jersey State Museum, State House Annex, Trenton.

Paterson Museum, 268 Summer Street, Paterson.

NEW MEXICO

Grant County Museum, Silver City.

Isleta, State 47, south of Albuquerque (pueblo noted for its pottery).

Museum of Anthropology, University of New Mexico, Albuquerque.

Museum of Ceremonial Navajo Art, Santa Fe.

Museum of New Mexico, Palace Avenue, Santa Fe.

Museum, Pecos State Monument, Pecos.

Museums at these National Monuments: Aztec Ruins, Aztec; Bandelier, off US 64, northwest of Santa Fe; Chaco Canyon, off US 66, east of Gallup.

Roswell Museum, Roswell.

School of American Research, Santa Fe.

NEW YORK

American Museum of Natural History, Central Park West and 79th Street, New York.
Blue Mountain Lake Museum, Blue Mountain Lake.
Brooklyn Museum, Eastern Parkway, Brooklyn.
Buffalo Museum of Science, Humboldt Park, Buffalo.
Cooperstown Indian Museum, 1 Pioneer Street, Cooperstown.
Mohawk-Caughnawaga Museum, Fonda.
Museum of Primitive Art, 15 West 54th Street, New York.
Museum of the American Indian, Broadway at 155th Street, New York.
New York State Museum, Washington Avenue, Albany.
Rochester Museum of Arts and Sciences, 657 East Avenue, Rochester.
The Schenectady Museum, Nott Terrace Heights, Schenectady.

NORTH CAROLINA

Brunswick Town State Historical Museum, 255 Pine Grove, Wilmington.
Museum of the Cherokee Indian, Cherokee (west of Asheville).
Museum, Town Creek Indian Mound, State 73, Mount Gilead.
Research Laboratory of Anthropology, Person Hall, University of North Carolina, Chapel Hill.

NORTH DAKOTA

Museum, Fort Lincoln State Park near Mandan.

OHIO

Cincinnati State Museum, Cincinnati.
Cleveland Museum of National History, Cleveland.
Firelands Historical Museum, Norwalk.
Museum, Fort Ancient State Memorial, State 350, southeast of Lebanon.
Natural History Museum, Mill Creek Park, Youngstown.
Vietzen Archaeology and Pioneer Museum, Elyria.

OKLAHOMA

Black Mesa State Park, Panhandle at New Mexico line.
The Gilcrease Institute of American History and Art, 2401 Newton Street, Tulsa.
Indian Council House Museum, Ocmulgee.
Oklahoma Historical Society Museum, Oklahoma City.
Southern Plains Indian Arts and Crafts Museum, Anadarko.

OREGON

Horner Museum, Oregon State Museum, Corvallis.
Klamath County Museum, Klamath Falls.
Museum of Natural History, University of Oregon, Eugene.
Oregon State Historical Society, 235 Southwest Market Street, Portland.

PENNSYLVANIA

Carnegie Museum, Carnegie Institute, Pittsburgh.
Everhart Museum of National History, Science and Art, Nay Aug Park, Scranton.
Museum, Hopewell Village Historic Site, near Reading.
North Museum, Franklin and Marshall College, Lancaster.
Pennsylvania State Museum, Harrisburg.
University Museum, University of Pennsylvania, Philadelphia.

RHODE ISLAND

Haffenreffer Museum of the American Indian, Brown University, Providence.
Mount Hope Museum, Bristol.
Museum of Primitive Cultures, Peacedale.
Roger Williams Park Museum of Natural History, Providence.
Tomaquag Indian Memorial Museum, Burdikville Road, Ashaway.

SOUTH CAROLINA

Charleston Museum, 125 Rutledge Avenue, Charleston.

SOUTH DAKOTA

W. H. Over Museum, University of South Dakota, Vermillion.
Pettigrew Museum, 131 North Duluth Avenue, Sioux Falls.
South Dakota State Historical Museum, Memorial Building, Pierre.

TENNESSEE

Chucalissa Indian Museum, Memphis.
The Frank McClung Museum, University of Tennessee, Knoxville.
The Memphis Museum, Memphis.

TEXAS

The A.V. Lane Museum of Archaeology, Southern Methodist University, Dallas.
Museum of Anthropology, University of Texas, Austin.
Texas Western College, Centennial Museum, El Paso.
White Memorial Museum, Brackenridge Park, San Antonio.

UTAH

Moab Museum, Moab.
Museum of Anthropology and Archaeology, University of Utah, Salt Lake City.

VERMONT

Robert Hull Fleming Museum, University of Vermont, Burlington.
Vermont Historical Society Museum, Montpelier.

VIRGINIA

Colonial Williamsburg, Williamsburg.
Valentine Museum, Richmond.

WASHINGTON

Eastern Washington State Historical Society and Museum, Spokane.
Washington State Museum, University of Washington, 4037 15th Street, Northeast Seattle.
Willis Carey Historical Museum, Cashmere.
Yakima Valley Museum, 2105 Tieton Drive, Yakima.

WEST VIRGINIA

Museum, Mammoth Mound, Moundsville.

WISCONSIN

Douglas County Historical Museum, Superior.
Indian Museum, LaPointe, on Madeline Island (Apostle Islands).
Logan Museum of Anthropology, Beloit College, Beloit.
Milwaukee Public Museum, 818 Wisconsin Avenue, Milwaukee.
Neville Public Museum, 129 South Jefferson Street, Green Bay.
Oshkosh Public Museum, Oshkosh.
State Historical Society of Wisconsin Museum, Madison.

WYOMING

Wyoming State Museum, State Office Building, Cheyenne.

CANADA

Glenbow Foundation, 902 11th Avenue, Southwest Calgary, Alberta.
Historical Museum of Medicine Hat, Medicine Hat, Alberta.
Luxton Museum, Banff, Alberta.
Museum of Geology, Paleontology and Archaeology, University of Alberta, Edmonton, Alberta.
Chilliwack Museum, Chilliwack, British Columbia.
Museum of Northern British Columbia, Prince Rupert, British Columbia.
Pacific National Museum, Vancouver, British Columbia.
Provincial Museum of Natural History and Anthropology, Victoria, British Columbia.
Vancouver City Museum, 401 Main Street, Vancouver, British Columbia.
Museum, Fort Beauséjour National Historic Park, near Sackville, New Brunswick.
New Brunswick Museum, St. John, New Brunswick.
Newfoundland Museum, St. John's, Newfoundland.
Debrissay Museum, Bridgewater, Nova Scotia.
Assiginack Museum, Manitowaning, Monotulin Island, Ontario.

Museum, Fort Malden National Historic Park, Amherstburg, Ontario.

Museum, Fort Wellington National Historic Park, Prescott, Ontario.

Museum of Indian Archaeology, University of Western Ontario, London, Ontario.

The National Museum of Canada, Netcalf and McLeod Streets, Ottawa, Ontario.

Royal Ontario Museum, University of Toronto, Toronto, Ontario.

McCord Museum, McGill University, Montreal, Quebec.

Saskatchewan Museum of Natural History, Wascana Park, Regina, Saskatchewan.

University of Saskatchewan Museum, Saskatoon, Saskatchewan.

W.D. MacBride Museum, Whitehorse, Yukon.

CHAPTER 16

Salvage Archaeology

The four previous chapters have dealt with the principal ways in which amateur archaeologists can become actively involved in this field. It is not only a matter of opportunities being *available* to amateurs—through expeditions, organizations, existing sites, and museums—but also a matter of the amateur being *needed* for a variety of purposes. The amateur who sincerely wants to offer his services should not feel that he is imposing or that he may only be tolerated by the professional community. On the contrary, the accomplishments of amateur archaeologists in this country over the years amply illustrate the need for their services, and the new generation of professionals is aware of the fact that they cannot handle the work load alone.

One final, major opportunity for amateurs, and one which is extremely important, is salvage archaeology. This function, which is also referred to as emergency, or rescue, archaeology, involves the excavation of sites which are in *immediate* danger of being destroyed. Such a situation occurs when a construction project is under way, from the giant Aswan dam in Egypt to a small gas station on the edge of town. The main difference between salvage archaeology and normal excavation work is the time factor; salvage archaeology usually must be done within a certain period of time, ranging from a couple of months to a few days or even less. The amount of time available depends on three factors: the type of construction under way; where the endangered site is located and who owns the land; and the speed with which excavators can arrive at the scene.

Salvage archaeology is undertaken *specifically in reaction to* a construction project or any other activity resulting in the eventual destruction of a site. It must first be realized, however, that a site is in danger of being destroyed before adequate salvage work can begin. In other

words, if archaeologists do not investigate and then report that a pend-
ing highway or pipeline will be laid right through a suspected archaeological site, it is certainly not the fault of the construction crew for
destroying it. Construction crews are not trained to look for hints of
possible sites as they work, *nor are they inclined* to report the existence
of, say, artifacts which they may notice. There have been instances
where construction workers told of funny-looking tools they had seen
while digging trenches, and from their descriptions it was obvious to
archaeologists that they had come upon a valuable burial site. There
have also been cases where construction supervisors found the remains
of human activity, were convinced they had come upon an important
site of interest to archaeologists, but said nothing because they didn't
want their schedule to be altered as they waited for excavators to finish
their work. This sort of situation happens all too often, though there are
exceptions. When a construction company was drilling a gas well near
Rawlins, Wyoming, one of the workers noticed that the giant bones of
an unusual-looking animal had been exposed. Realizing that this might
be of some importance, the worker convinced the crew to stop while
he phoned a university in Laramie. Two researchers from the university's
anthropology department set out for the site immediately, and what
they found was well worth the trip. The digging crew had uncovered the
remains of a huge elephant which roamed North America more than
10,000 years ago. The drilling company agreed to halt work until the
archaeologists had completed excavating the site. So much work had
to be done fast, that without the help of amateurs it could not have
been accomplished. Upon hearing of the project, college and high school
students, housewives, janitors, and others offered their help.

Fortunately, the well digger acted quickly to alert authorities to the
exposed animal bones, and the company agreed to halt work until the
excavators were satisfied. But another discovery by a motel owner in
Virginia did not turn out so well. As the foundation for a new motel was
being dug, workers noticed a dozen skeletons, some weapons, and a
hearth area. Obviously, they had uncovered a burial site. The owner
was aware of the potential importance of these finds, but did not notify
anyone. He did, however, draw a sketch of the location of the various
skeletons in relation to one another and to the hearth, and saved a
couple of the weapons. Eventually, he managed to lose the weapons, but
drew an accurate sketch of them for an inquisitive archaeologist. The
archaeologist was stunned, for it was almost certain that the motel owner
had had in his grasp the long-sought-for physical evidence that a mysterious Ice Age hunting culture had indeed flourished in North America

10,000 years before the time of Christ. Except for the two lost weapons, all the evidence was firmly packed beneath the foundation of a sprawling motel.

The importance of salvage archaeology has grown tremendously over the past few decades. For not only are we continuing to build new highways, new pipelines, and new communities, but we are also well into the practice of replacing *old* buildings of various kinds. In New York City, for example, buildings are continuously being torn down to make way for new and bigger ones. When the Cadman Plaza housing project was being built in Brooklyn Heights, dozens of early and mid-nineteenth-century homes and shops had to be cleared away. Before construction began on the *new* buildings, however, three amateur archaeologists moved in and spent their evenings digging for anything important. Their only source of light was flashlights, but their efforts paid off. They found numerous artifacts—bottles, crockery, cutlery, pipes, utensils, even clothes—used in New York 100 to 150 years ago. In some places they dug frantically as construction workers laid cement two feet behind them, and they did not stop until there was no more land to be dug.

In Detroit, construction of the massive Renaissance Center signaled archaeologists to move in and excavate for remnants of that city's life at the turn of the nineteenth century. They worked right alongside construction crews and uncovered what is considered by many to be the richest early nineteenth-century urban archaeological site in the country. As the archaeologists worked, they showed the construction crews what they were doing and the importance of what they found. The construction workers became impressed and began to assist the archaeologists by pointing out finds of their own, marking features, shifting their schedules so that excavation work could continue in all parts of the site, and even by clearing only a few inches of topsoil at a time so that the excavators could immediately get to the all-important second and third levels of dirt.

The Renaissance Center excavation project is an outstanding example of cooperation between archaeologists and contractors. It is also a rare example, for archaeologists in Michigan fear that most of the state's prehistoric sites—over 10,000 of them—will be destroyed in less than thirty years because of a lack of public support.

SALVAGE ARCHAEOLOGY AND THE AMATEUR

There are numerous salvage projects undertaken each year in the United States, but they represent—according to one archaeologist at New York University—about ten percent of what should be done. Some of these projects are large-scale efforts involving half a dozen professional archaeologists and scores of amateurs; others may involve only a few amateurs or just one amateur with experience and a handful of interested citizens. There is so much construction going on all over the country that archaeologists complete one project only to find they have missed five others.

Sometimes the professional community is forced to accept the services of completely untrained persons for salvage work. At least *something* may be saved in this manner. When the California state archaeologist was informed that some women from Malibu were pothunting the Zuma Creek Site as bulldozers began clearing it, he was faced with two problems: first, the pothunters; and second, the fact that he was involved with two other major salvage efforts and could spare no personnel to work at Zuma Creek, which lay directly in the path of a new mobile home park development. The archaeologist went to the site and informed the women that they were being as destructive as the bulldozer, that they weren't trained, and that they were working against all that archaeology stands for. As it turned out, the women were only trying to salvage as much as possible, and immediately asked the archaeologist to show them precisely what to do. When they were told that there were no personnel to train them and no time to do it, they said that they could at least make an effort to follow the rules. The archaeologist quickly explained what was required and left the site thinking it was all a waste of time. But he was surprised beyond all belief, for the women kept excellent records of who worked where, what they collected, where everything was located, and how deep it was in the earth. The women were so careful, as a matter of fact, that the subsequent research allowed professionals to determine that the area had been inhabited over a period of a thousand years. The women have since moved on to other projects, and are recognized as outstanding amateur archaeologists in their city.

Amateur archaeologists are needed in salvage efforts for two main reasons. First, there are not nearly enough professionals to go around. (Some say there aren't even enough *amateurs* in this country to adequately handle all the necessary salvage work.) Second, funding for salvage projects is usually small, and only the amateur can be counted on to work for nothing. If there is no funding available, professional archaeologists will almost never get involved. Even when there is funding, a majority of the work is done by volunteers.

EXISTING OPPORTUNITIES

Certain parts of the country are more growth prone than others. Opportunities for amateurs depend on where they live, for the most part, for while there is constant construction going on in New York, San Francisco, and Chicago, there is comparatively little in northern Maine. But there is always *some* construction going on *everywhere*, and the new gas station slated for construction in a remote area may be just as important to the salvage archaeologist as a massive shopping center being built in Los Angeles.

Federal laws require that construction halt if a suspected site is about to be destroyed, and most states have their own laws for the same purpose. Any interested amateur should, in addition to checking with his local archaeological society, keep in touch with the anthropology department of his state's university system. Whenever a major construction project is announced, many amateurs immediately get in touch with professional archaeologists to find out about salvage work and to offer their services. Some states, like Arizona and Texas, have dozens of salvage projects going at the same time year-round, and amateurs are always welcome—particularly those with some experience. Nebraska and California are examples of states which often plan ahead in accordance with scheduled construction programs, and can usually determine salvage activity a year in advance. Whenever a major construction project is scheduled under the auspices, direction, or licensing of the federal government, there is always funding available for salvage archaeology if required. The same goes for state projects. But there are numerous *private* construction efforts undertaken every day, and here the amateur community can only try its best to convince the contractor to allow excavation work. Occasionally, archaeological organizations may receive emergency funding from private foundations for salvage archaeology projects, but this is rare.

During the summer months, when most construction is under way in many parts of the country, the interested amateur should have no trouble locating salvage operations. If there is no information available from the state university or state museum, amateurs may write to the Smithsonian Institution for information about salvage operations anywhere in the· country. The Smithsonian attempts to keep track of such activities, because federal funding is involved and the Smithsonian often acts as advisor with regard to the importance of certain suspected sites.

QUALIFICATIONS

The very first qualification for any amateur interested in salvage archaeology is a sincere desire to work—and work hard. As opposed to normal excavation projects, salvage archaeology requires that workers do twice as much in half the time. Anyone who is not used to physical work for hours at a time should probably stay clear of a salvage project, for volunteers will be asked to stand in the hot sun, in the rain, or in chilling winds all day. Added to this is the amount of physical work involved, much of it boring. The amateur must also be able to take orders without question, for the time factor does not allow supervisors and diggers to argue about who will do what for how long. When a job is assigned, that's it: do it or get out.

Many amateurs involved with salvage work claim it is the best way to learn about archaeology fast. Everything is in high gear; everyone works faster than normal. Hence, there is the opportunity to gain a great deal of experience in a relatively short amount of time. But salvage archaeology, by its very nature, is different from normal excavation work. Under normal conditions we would undertake an initial survey, break the area down into sections, divide the sections into subsections, and carefully begin to insert the spade into the dirt, keeping track of every move and working with others to bring about a useful overview of the entire site; but there is no time for this in salvage work. Areas are assigned, as much recording as possible takes place, and the *small*, *unusual*, or *outstanding* feature is looked for. There is no useful overview planned along the way; salvage archaeologists look for anything which can aid specifically in determining what this site could have represented.

Not all salvage projects are hurried, however. When the federal government approves the construction of a nuclear power plant, for example, the location is usually picked out years before construction actually begins. Professional archaeologists often take such an opportunity to train amateurs and interested citizens in salvage work at such sites. But even at the more relaxed salvage projects, the point is emphasized that workers must look for the small and unusual artifact, for very often such a find can drastically alter the eventual interpretation of the site's meaning and historic importance.

Anyone trained in any aspect of archaeology is always welcome at salvage sites. The professionals know they must rely on amateurs, and they will certainly be more at ease knowing that some with experience have shown up. Directors of some of the largest salvage projects will take anybody they can get, and they usually get a wide assortment of people from various backgrounds: students, lawyers, housewives, salesmen. Since the work can be grueling and there is no pay, the professionals are not about to turn anyone away.

PART V
How to Excavate

CHAPTER 17

Introduction

We come now to the final section in this book: archaeological excavation. The term *excavate* means simply to hollow out, to expose or uncover by digging (from the Latin *ex* 'out,' and *cavare* 'to make hollow'). It is a common term (engineers excavate a tunnel for a railway; animals burrow in excavations of their own forming), but in archaeology it specifically means a precise method based on scientific principles which have been developed over the years. Excavation is the primary function of archaeology; no other discipline—with the occasional exception of geology—attempts it.

In this section we will move from the general to the specific; from excavation in theory to excavation in practice. It is important that amateurs in archaeology, particularly beginners, understand the *concept*, the *purpose*, of archaeological excavation; for it is just as important to know when *not* to excavate as to know when to dig as fast as possible. Archaeological excavation is very precise and methodical, and may be compared to surgery in the operating theater. A good excavator is both a scientist and an artist. At the very least, he is a specialist, an expert, and should be recognized as such.

There are many professional archaeologists who are not good excavators, though this may be due to a desire to specialize in other areas of archaeology. As for amateurs, it is desirable for those who choose to become involved with fieldwork to gain both theoretical experience in the classroom and practical experience in the field. *The reader should not assume that a careful reading of this section suddenly qualifies him to grab a spade and begin digging at a site.* It will, however, offer an advantage as he works in the field, particularly over those who have not bothered to familiarize themselves with the principles, practice, and terminology of archaeological excavation. As with any other specialty or technically oriented function, the beginner should expect to start at the bottom. In excavation work, this means anything from doing odd jobs at the site in support of other workers to carefully sifting through endless piles of dirt looking for something unusual.

The amateur should also realize that archaeology is undergoing constant change, on two fronts. First, archaeologists are always attempting to improve their theoretical outlook on the subject, and second, new techniques are always being developed—as in any other field of science. Computers, for example, are beginning to play a more specific role as analytical tools in archaeology, and the next generation will no doubt see them playing a major role in classifying data. So the serious amateur must continue to keep abreast of changes in archaeology, and the best way to do this is simply to read current journals and books.

SURFACE EXCAVATION

There is one type of fieldwork, known as surface excavation or, more accurately, surface hunting, which many persons engage in and which requires a few words here. Surface hunting, as the name implies, is simply hunting around for artifacts lying on the surface of the ground; no excavation is involved.

Both professional and amateur archaeologists argue about the advisability of surface hunting, which usually involves the collecting of Indian artifacts. Some say it serves a useful purpose while others contend that it is pothunting under a different name. Surface hunting does conserve artifacts which might otherwise be destroyed by the plow or bulldozer, and it also helps to locate possible sites in the area. Many surface hunters have been responsible for locating previously unknown sites. The problem with most surface hunters, however, lies in their disregard for accounting for their finds. Even though some may report what they have found to a professional archaeologist, and even turn over their collections, they usually have kept no record of what they found where. Giving an archaeologist a bag full of artifacts found "all over the place from here to my Aunt Sally's" is not exactly giving him a precise account of one's finds. The problem of surface hunting is worsened by those who jealously guard what they find, telling no one in authority about it and allowing no one "except very close and discreet friends" to view their collections.

Surface hunting should be discouraged, except as a last resort, and even then a professional archaeologist or experienced amateur should be called in. Those who pursue this activity should, at the very least, photograph and sketch the area, mark on the sketch where every single artifact was found, number each artifact, and make a list of all the artifacts with corresponding numbers and as exact a description as possible (length, width, shape), including drawings. It is also important that the *exact* location of these finds be described, and that a university, museum, or archaeological organization be informed. The local newspaper should not be told of the site, for any published story about artifacts up for grabs will bring a horde of collectors swarming to the site.

Most state antiquities laws allow surface hunting simply because they do not proscribe it. Nevertheless, surface hunting should be considered analogous to pothunting unless those involved are serious students intending to report their finds to authorities. Few who are engaged in surface hunting seem inclined to go about it in a systematic way.

EXCAVATION AND THE LAW

The amateur should familiarize himself with federal, state, and local laws prior to undertaking any excavation work. Without permission from the owner, no archaeologist should even approach an area with the intent of conducting research. If one merely wants to explore an area, oral permission from the owner is adequate to avoid any charge of trespassing. But any collecting of artifacts or digging by an archaeologist should be made clear to the owner *before* he begins, and permission should be obtained *in every instance* in writing. This will protect researchers from charges of vandalism or theft. Property owners should be informed of the importance of protecting sites on their land; amateurs should not take advantage of an owner's ignorance of either antiquities laws or the value of archaeological sites.

Some states have very strict laws against disturbing any kind of burial site. A cemetery still in active use cannot be disturbed without permission from the municipality, the owner of the cemetery, and the owner of the land on which the cemetery is located. An archaeologist who proceeds to conduct excavation work at a cemetery without proper permission can be charged, under the civil code, with trespassing, grave molestation, and larceny. In the case of graveyards or burial sites which appear to be abandoned, a researcher may be exonerated from charges of grave molestation, but he may not be free from charges of trespassing or larceny. To be on the safe side of the law, researchers should go out of their way to obtain permission in writing from the proper authorities or individuals prior to conducting any exploration, survey, or excavation work.

The following permit may be used as a guide in obtaining permission in writing for conducting archaeological research on private land.

FORM 1

PERMISSION TO CONDUCT ARCHAEOLOGICAL RESEARCH

Date_____

I, the undersigned, owner of C. Small Farms, located off Page Road in the town of Litchfield, New Hampshire, hereby authorize

_____

_____

_____

to explore / survey / excavate two acres of, my land at the northern portion of my property. It is understood that, provided excavation work is undertaken, that portion of the land will be filled in and graded so as to remain substantially similar to its original condition. It is also understood that all research is being conducted in the best interests of science, and that all artifacts recovered will be turned over to an authorized repository for continued scientific research. This permit is valid until revoked in writing.

C. Small, Owner

LEVELS OF ARCHAEOLOGICAL STUDY

Before we get into the techniques of excavation, the beginner should understand how the functions of archaeology fit into the framework of modern science.

All fields of science—physics, chemistry, biology—deal with specified phenomena. Although each discipline works with different things and concentrates on different subjects, they all follow the same general principles of science. It is the adoption of these principles which separates science from pseudoscience, semiscience, and just plain common sense.

The physicist, the biologist, and the chemist all have three levels of study which they follow. These levels are observation, description, and explanation. All scientists analyze a phenomenon or study a subject by observing what it is, what it does, how it acts, and how it reacts to various suggestions or stimuli. Research is conducted, experiments are undertaken, and the scientist describes the result. As research continues, data is accumulated, and finally an attempt is made to explain what has occurred and why, based on our current level of knowledge.

The archaeologist also observes, describes, and explains, and, like other scientists, he reaches certain conclusions based on what he has seen and what he has done with the things that are the object of his study. *Observation* in archaeology is the collecting of data. The archaeologist begins by obtaining material remains of past cultures. This he does through the function known as *excavation*. Excavation is the first and primary function of archaeology; it is the first of the three levels of archaeological study. *Description* in archaeology begins when the materials collected from the excavation are analyzed. The analyzing of materials is done on two levels, the singular and the collective. Each artifact is examined individually, and an initial description is prepared. The next step is to examine *all* the artifacts, all the materials, *together*, collectively. This is known as the *integration* of the data and is the second level of archaeological study. Once the data has been analyzed and classified, conclusions are drawn, and these conclusions represent *explanation* in archaeology. The archaeologist draws certain *inferences* from the collective data, attempts to recognize some kind of pattern, and finally explains what it all means.

In terms of anthropology, the archaeologist attempts to explain things about past cultures by describing what he has found during the excavation. Each of the three levels of archaeological study has been developed and refined over the years so that a proper excavation—the first level—will ultimately result in an accurate conclusion about the culture whose remains were investigated. All archaeological study, therefore, begins with the excavation.

THE DIMENSIONS OF ARCHAEOLOGY

Once the excavation is complete and the archaeologist is prepared to bring some order to the numerous and various artifacts collected, he invokes the three dimensions of archaeology. These dimensions are *space*, *time*, and *form*, and they represent the three ways all artifacts are *described*. The second level of archaeology is where formal analysis begins, and all materials must be described based on these three dimensions. The dimension of *space* refers to geographical space, where the artifact was found. This is both general (the artifact was found in Florida where the excavation took place) and specific (the artifact was found twelve miles inland from the northeast coast of Florida, one hundred feet above sea level, at the edge of a small swamp, in very close proximity to all other similar artifacts located during this excavation). The dimension of *time* means simply the age of the artifact, and this also proceeds from the general (the artifact is pre-Columbian) to the specific (specific testing procedures conclude that the artifact was worked by Indians between A.D. 900 and 1000). The dimension of *form* refers to the physical appearance of the artifact, beginning with a general (it's an Indian arrow point) to a specific (its sides are parallel, it has a concave base, and it is fluted approximately halfway to the tip; total length is three inches: a Palaeoindian Clovis Point) description.

So the importance of the descriptive level of archaeological study based on these three dimensions is that we learn initially where the materials were found, how old they are, and what they look like. This, however, is just the beginning in the attempt to reach a set of conclusions about what these artifacts represent in terms of the culture that used them and left them behind.

ASPECTS OF ARCHAEOLOGICAL DATA

Once the archaeologist has described the artifacts as completely as possible and has exhausted all efforts in gathering information about where they were found, how old they are, and what they look like, he moves to draw inferences, to *interpret*, to explain what it all means. In order to explain the meaning and importance of material remains in terms of the culture which produced them, the archaeologist contemplates these materials—for the first time—according to four aspects of archaeological data. These aspects are context, function, structure, and behavior.

Before the archaeologist attempts to explain the meaning or purpose of an artifact, he will want to know the *context* in which it was originally found. That is, he must know not only where it was found in general (at a burial site), but also where specifically in relation to all other material remains (it was the central piece of a series of similar artifacts located in the burial chamber of a king, placed next to the king's headgear). If a piece of armor, for example, were found on the outskirts of a burial chamber, it would not be considered as important as one found on top of a king's tomb. Similarly, a clay bowl found on the altar of a temple certainly had more meaning *to the original users* than one found in a pile off some corridor. Because we are attempting to reconstruct the culture in question, we need to know what value was placed on certain things, and therefore the location of a shield or bowl is important.

The aspect of archaeological data known as *function* refers obviously to how the object was used. This is closely connected with *context*, for we attempt to deduce the use of an object by its original location. If we know, for example, that a certain culture always used a single bowl for some religious service once a year, and we find only one bowl in their temple, we can deduce the function of the bowl. The aspect of function in analyzing archaeological data is based on many other factors and inferences, for the context in which an object is found may have been left inadvertently by a tribe anxious to leave the area.

The *structure* of certain artifacts or objects is very important to the archaeologist, particularly as compared with the structure of similar objects. If, out of a hundred little boxes, only one is covered with special drawings, the researcher is inclined to assume that this particular box either had some special meaning or else belonged to a special person. It is initially a matter of comparison. Another important point regarding structure involves the idea that all artifacts represent the thoughts of the people who produced them. Why, therefore, does one tribe or one culture insist on no handles for its pitchers while others always have one, or two? Why are the bowls in one culture always round at the bottom while those in contiguous cultures are always square?

The reader can no doubt recognize that numerous factors must be taken into consideration by researchers when analyzing archaeological data, and it is for this reason that it sometimes takes years before acceptable conclusions can be reached. As research continues on the material remains of an excavation, the archaeologist continuously broadens his realm of information and knowledge. He must find out as much as he can about similar research. Do his interpretations contradict the research of others? Is there reason to believe that he is dealing with a new, previously unknown culture? As his research broadens, the archaeologist eventually begins dealing with material remains in terms of the behavior of the culture that produced them. Thus *behavior* is the fourth aspect of archaeological data. American archaeologists are well trained in this particular aspect, for they are all—with the exception of classical historians—essentially anthropologists.

The behavior of artifacts refers to the patterning of behavior which the artifact represents. All artifacts have a behavioral aspect, and in that we are unable to question the people who produced the artifact or to observe their behavior for ourselves, we therefore look to the objects they left behind for hints of just what kind of people they were. Researchers essentially look for *patterns* in material objects, though even the absence of pattern allows the archaeologist to reach certain conclusions about the culture. The social, economic, and religious aspects of a culture can be recognized to some extent based on patterns in material objects, and here the archaeologist becomes involved with how this culture fit in with the overall society of its day.

When the archaeological researcher takes all these things into consideration, analyzes them individually and collectively, and produces what can be considered acceptable conclusions, he has completed the explanation of material remains brought to him through excavation.

CHAPTER 18

The Purpose of Excavation

Excavation is a specific technique for the collecting of archaeological data. Archaeological data is the *material* culture of the past; the material objects that cultures left behind.

Societies and cultures have come and gone, and were it not for what they left behind we would never even know they existed. Archaeological excavation is devoted to obtaining material remains in order that we may learn as much as possible about a culture or group of people from the past. These material remains range from the massive pyramids in Egypt to the tiny pieces of hand-worked stone used by ancient hunters in prehistoric Europe. Without benefit of written records, we must rely on objects used by past peoples: their tools, utensils, weapons, clothing, buildings—in short, *anything* that can offer information about who they were and what they did.

The study of any society or culture by archaeologists begins with the excavation. The manner in which an excavation is conducted determines the degree to which we will eventually be able to find answers to questions about a long-dead people. As historians began to realize that there existed great gaps in modern man's knowledge of who preceded him, and that there were many cultures whose existence we only suspected, the purpose of excavation grew in importance. As it was realized that all excavation is destruction, and that the more complete the excavation the more total the destruction, it became necessary to instill in the minds of workers that the first time a site is excavated is also the last time. The excavation of a site occurs only once; there is no chance to repeat, to return and do it again. Therefore, it must be done right the first time.

The excavation does not merely result in the finding of material objects; it is also the main source of *new information* for the researcher. Even if similar types of sites are excavated in close proximity to one another, it is highly unlikely that all will contain the exact same objects;

hence, the amount and type of information will differ. Those involved in excavation work are interested in a fundamental unit of study, known as the *site*. An archaeological site is any place where an archaeologist chooses to dig. Sites are located on mountains, on the prairies, in the city, in the desert, and under the water; they can be the remains of a town or one small well, a huge temple reaching to the sky or a few little statues eight feet below the surface. Most sites represent the remains of some kind of human activity, from communities to burial holes and from hunting areas to ceremonial ones. It is incorrect to assume that archaeologists excavate only sites that were once residences. Any site where any kind of human activity once occurred is of interest to the archaeologist. Other types of sites, such as those which contain the remains of animals that perished by other than human hands, are also of great importance. The evolution of animals and where they lived always incites interest for the simple reason that there are more extinct species than there are living ones. This kind of information gives us an idea of what *Homo sapiens* and his predecessors had to contend with in the past. Animals were not only enemies of man, they were also sources of food, so the more we can learn about what animals lived where in prehistory the better.

Any archaeological site—or potential site—must be approached with respect, for two reasons. First, in a philosophical sense, a site contains all that may be left of the aspirations, goals, and ideals of a dead culture. If one feels unmoved or unimpressed with the remains of a culture that ceased to exist long before our present society was born, he should keep in mind that our present society was somehow influenced by all the cultures that preceded it; that we are today the result of all that man has ever been. Second, in a more academic sense, a site may represent a major addition to our knowledge of the past; it may contain one particular object that can answer dozens of questions. The excavator should be reminded that the researchers keep their fingers crossed and hope the excavation will be a proper one.

In the same sense, no excavation should be undertaken just for the fun of it or out of curiosity. When a site is in imminent danger of being destroyed, every effort should be made first to *save* it. If this proves impossible, *then* salvage excavation should begin. It is always better to excavate without the problem of time staring you in the face; therefore, if destruction of a site can be postponed so that a more careful excavation can be undertaken, there is a much better chance of important data being recovered and turned over to researchers for analysis. In general, no site should be excavated unless the individuals involved sincerely have reason to believe that some questions may be answered. In other words, if the consensus of opinion is that little will be learned from a particular site, then it should not be excavated; it should be left for future researchers to decide when it would be advisable to dig. This is a question which professional archaeologists should entertain, for they are usually closely involved and familiar with previous excavation work and subsequent research in their region. The obvious question at this point is, How do we know if it's an important site unless we excavate it? That question is only part of what must be considered. If the site appears to be a small Indian burial mound, and archaeologists have already devoted years to excavating dozens of larger mounds around it, they may feel that all remaining mounds should be left untouched, at least until current data is analyzed. More important than that, however, is the question of whether this is a *crucial site*. There are many, many sites which should be excavated, both for salvage and informational reasons, and there is therefore no reason to assume that every little site one comes across is important enough to spend time on. There is much to do in archaeological excavation, and everyone involved should strive to excavate the most important sites *first*—or you may never get the chance to excavate them at all.

One final point in this matter involves the number of capable people— both professionals and amateurs—around for excavation work: there are never enough trained excavators to go around, so naturally they should spend their time on those sites deemed particularly important.

Excavation expeditions, like sites, come in all sizes. A major excavation project along the Nile may involve hundreds of persons, while the excavation of a Colonial fire pit may only require three. It is important that the excavators objectively analyze their capabilities, and that they don't take on more than they can handle. A crew of three may be sufficient to excavate one fire pit, but is woefully inadequate to excavate a series of structures in a community that spreads over two miles. By the same token, a party of twenty would cause all kinds of problems in excavating a small well. Anyone who exaggerates his capabilities or experience will be found out soon enough as the excavation gets under way, and this may require the entire project to come to a standstill as workers frantically try to find a replacement.

Another consideration is the amount of time required for a proper excavation. A small burial site may take only a few days to excavate properly, but a site containing two dozen structures will take months. If the excavation party can only devote a week, then the project should never even begin. The excavation is too important to be left half-finished.

Excavators must always keep future workers in mind—the next generation of diggers. The techniques of excavation will no doubt be improved and further refined, so anyone digging today should understand that the future diggers will have no chance to do the same at this site. If an archaeologist returns to a site that was excavated five, ten, or twenty years earlier, he can only go by the records that the original diggers left behind. If those records are incomplete or represent an improper excavation, the archaeologist can do nothing about it. It's too late.

CHAPTER 19

Principles of Excavation

This chapter will give a more detailed discussion of excavation. From the moment the excavator begins his work, he continuously interprets the meaning of what he sees as he goes along. This will be made clearer as we proceed, but the point is that excavation is not merely digging holes in the ground with the hope of eventually finding an artifact. Everything the excavator does he does for a reason, from the moment he shoves a spade in the ground for the first time.

The fundamental unit of archaeological study is the site, and the fundamental unit at a site that requires digging is the soil, or more specifically, the *stratification*, or layers of soil. Stratification is a geological term used in archaeology to denote those layers of soil *plus anything else* which has been there *since man was there*. Any alteration, disturbance, or addition to the layers of soil during or since man's occupation at a site falls into the category of stratification and is of interest to the archaeologist. The levels of these layers are known as the *strata*, and strata are never regular, level units. An example of an alteration of strata occurs when normal soil below the surface has been used by man for burying; a disturbance of strata comes about when levels of soil have been added—either filled in by man or perhaps added by a windstorm; the addition of strata comes about when man has added a "floor" of garbage, wood, or anything else which is not part of the natural earth.

Stratification, or stratigraphy, is important for a number of reasons. We learn, by interpreting the strata correctly, the number of different groups at a site or the length of time any one group was at a site. If there are layers upon layers of debris at a site, then either one group remained for a long time (making this a single component site) or else a number of groups continued to add to the already existing pile of debris (a multicomponent site). If we are dealing with a multicomponent site, we can observe the differences between the occupants by examining what they left behind.

A trained excavator is able to note any changes in the strata, and this ability is of the utmost importance in excavation. There are numerous varied layers which make up the soil at a site that experienced human occupation, and every action by humans involving the soil can be determined through careful excavation. The soil is such that it reflects distinctly all types of activity in association with it. Once any such activity occurs it cannot be changed, for any attempt to change it would in itself alter the various strata. Geologists have told me that it is literally impossible to disturb the soil in any way without a trained archaeologist being able to explain what happened. The correct interpretation of the strata at a site is the beginning of the history of what happened there.

Why are these layers there at all? In order for any excavator to understand the importance of stratigraphy, he must appreciate just exactly how and why these layers exist. Prehistoric man did not have closets and cabinets for every little thing as we do today. Most of what he owned was placed on the ground at one time or another. These objects were eventually walked and trampled on by both man and animals and managed to find their way below topsoil. In addition, nature caused wind to blow and grass to grow, so the objects were further covered by dirt and vegetation. When other people moved into the site, they did pretty much the same thing, plus perhaps adding a structure or building of stone. This structure might later have been removed but tools might remain, and they would eventually be covered up. Another structure might be built and eventually destroyed or left to decay, and it, also, would over the years be covered by trampling and vegetation. The purpose of excavation is for all this activity to be recognized by the archaeologist.

Two things, therefore, are important with regard to stratigraphy. First, the different layers must be *recognized*; and second, any artifacts or objects found *must be assigned to the correct layer*. A layer is itself capable of being dated, but only in terms of the date of objects found in it. Each layer must be accounted for as it is associated with all other layers, and never on its own. If a particular layer, or stratum, is described as being "the third layer in a series of five, two feet below the surface," the information is worthless unless all the data from the first two and last two layers are available. The lower the stratum, the longer ago the occupation at a site, naturally, but we must be able to determine the relative association of all the levels. All we know from the outset is that the lower strata are older than the higher ones, although even this "first law of stratigraphy" has occasionally been challenged (an

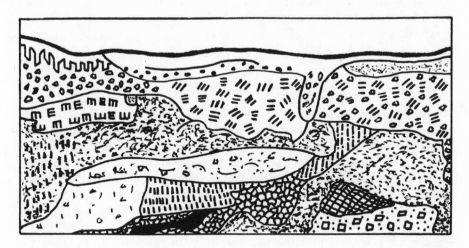

FIG. 3. Example of a profile of varied stratification at a site of human occupation.

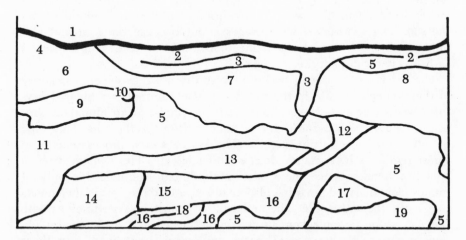

FIG. 4. Identification of various strata: (1) topsoil; (2) loam; (3) subsoil, pebbles; (4) stone wall; (5) sand; (6) gravel; (7) brick earth; (8) brick earth, gravel; (9) clay; (10) tree-pit; (11) sand and mortar; (12) brown earth; (13) prehistoric human occupation level; (14) human refuse pit; (15) mortar; (16) stone rubble; (17) ash; (18) carbon; (19) sand and gravel.

archaeologist in New Mexico found a site where the oldest artifacts were on top and the most recent on the bottom, owing to the fact that the last inhabitants had dug around the site and turned everything literally upside down).

WHAT IS SOIL?

Archaeologists around the world deal with all different types of soil. It is important that the amateur have a fundamental understanding of how soil is formed and classified, and that he become comfortable with the idea of working with soil. Research conducted by soil scientists has been of great value to the archaeologist, and every excavator will want to familiarize himself with the texture and structure of soil.

Soil is formed by the combination of four entities. They are the raw material of rock; the organic matter from vegetables and/or animals; the climate of a region; and the passage of time. These four entities, in different combinations and quantities, make up the different types of soil. The most important influence on soil is climate. Climate determines the characteristics of soil everywhere in the world, by one of three processes. These processes are *laterization, calcification,* and *podzolization.*

The laterization process occurs in those parts of the world that are hot and humid, where the movement of water in the form of rain removes all the elements (with the exception of iron and aluminum) from the soil. The term *laterization* comes about because the iron and aluminum left in the soil harden due to continuous heat. This hardened texture is known as laterite.

The *calcification* process occurs in very dry areas in which a majority of the elements remain in the soil. Grass goes through a regular decaying process due to a lack of rain, and this produces an abundant supply of humus, which forms the organic portion of the soil. This type of soil is the most fertile there is. The *podzolization* process occurs in forest regions where matter decays rather slowly. The climate itself is cool but humid, hence there is a small though continuous supply of humus from decayed grass but also an absence of those essential elements that make the soil fertile. The archaeologist must become familiar with the soil in the region where he is conducting excavation work, for obviously the decay of organic matter will occur most readily in those parts of the world where the climatic process of laterization is at work. The podzolization process also damages organic matter at a steady rate, though not as quickly.

There are three general classifications of soil: zonal, intrazonal, and azonal. Zonal soil is by far the most common and is distributed around the world; it is well developed as a result of receiving the right amount of rain. Intrazonal soil is the type found in swamps and marshes, and lacks proper drainage. Azonal soil is "new" soil, the effect of climate not yet having taken place, and is simply mud or wet sand. Soil can be more specifically broken down into types. The different types of soil depend initially on the kinds of rock from which they were formed. Soil is also affected by the nature of the plants that grow in it and by the temperature of the air around it. Some soils are made up of coarse particles. If three-fourths of their mineral content are sand, these soils are known simply as *sandy soils*. A *clay soil* is at least 25 percent clay. *Silt* contains particles larger than those of clay, but is still quite fine. *Muck* and *peat soils* contain approximately 25 percent organic matter. When sand, clay, silt, and peat or muck are mixed together, they form *loam*, of which there are in turn various types.

SOIL AND EXCAVATION

It is not difficult for the excavator to know when he has reached a new level of soil. As long as he is paying attention to what he is doing, a new level can be recognized by a change in color, texture, or consistency. As the excavator reaches a new layer, he should be sure that the previous layer is well cleared, or he will run the risk of having materials from the previous layer fall into the new one. By materials I mean anything from the soil itself to small artifacts or other objects. Once this happens the digger will find himself in a precarious situation.

The quantity of soil retrieved at each step should never be large; most excavators dig no deeper than six inches at a time. Depending on the type of soil, larger quantities taken at once may fall apart and back into the hole or elsewhere, thus causing confusion in the event it can no longer be determined which stratum the soil came from. All soil must of course be carefully examined for objects of any kind, and this may be done by hand or with a sieve.

EXCAVATION OF FEATURES

There are many different kinds of sites that excavators come in contact with, and they are referred to as *features*. Some archaeologists are particularly experienced in the excavation of one or two kinds of features, while others have chosen not to specialize and have instead sought to work at as many different kinds as possible. If someone has spent a good deal of time excavating in Egypt, he obviously is unfamiliar with Indian burial sites; but an American archaeologist may deal regularly with everything from stone walls, mounds, and pits to wooden buildings, graves, and earthworks. Amateurs who intend to become involved with excavation work should be familiar with the various kinds of features, the problems presented by each, and how to deal with those problems.

BURIALS

There are a number of kinds of burial sites, but here I mean specifically the simple grave containing one or perhaps two burials. All burials, ancient and modern, are either inhumations or cremations. The simple burial, or grave, is what archaeologists deal with most frequently. The proper excavation of a burial site offers information on the religious beliefs, physical traits, particular habits, and mortuary customs of the culture responsible.

The excavator must first locate what he believes to be a burial site, or grave. This can be initially determined by noticing any disturbance in the natural layering of the earth. If this disturbance includes the presence of charcoal or any other traces of fire, the chances that it is indeed a grave increase. If it was a cremation burial, the body was probably burnt near the final resting place, and evidence of this should be available. If the burial was an inhumation, there probably still occurred some kind of burning near or right on top of the grave itself (this was both a common religious function and an attempt to keep animal predators away from fresh graves).

Once a grave has been located, the excavator must first determine the outline of the burial hole. Digging should begin a foot or so *outside* the perimeter, going towards the center, and should be done in sections. No more than half the grave should be dug at one time, and the strata should be examined as the excavation proceeds. As the first half of the burial is being dug, objects should *not* be removed: everything should be left *in situ* (exactly where it was found), so that the placement of objects can be compared one with another. Once the fill from the first half is entirely removed *and cleared away* from the digging area, the second half of the burial can be excavated. Again, all objects are left *in situ* so that their relative positioning can be seen at once in the entire grave. A detailed account of these objects must be made—

both a written explanation and a sketch. Excavators must be sure that all dirt has been cleared away from the actual grave so that none falls back in inadvertently, thereby perhaps damaging skeletal remains. Graves are never very deeply dug; the standard "six feet under" is really about as far down as one usually must dig. It is advisable to dig a little deeper than is necessary, however, so that the center of the grave— where the remains are located—will be raised a bit when exposed, as though on a platform. The excavator should never stand inside the grave while digging; his back should never face the center of the site. He always moves *toward* the center from the perimeter.

When the skeleton has been found, it should be carefully cleaned and all the earth cut away from it so that it sits fully exposed. It is advisable that a specialist examine the skeleton *in situ*, for he can usually determine the sex, age, height, weight, build, and manner of death. The skeleton should then be described in writing *and* sketched *and* photographed. If the burial was a cremation, the ashes could have been stored in a wooden box, a leather pouch, a clay pot, or a glass urn. If the container was of organic material, such as wood, it may have thoroughly decayed. However, there may have been some kind of fittings or clamps around it of inorganic material such as iron. The excavator must keep a sharp lookout for any nails or other such subjects which suggest some kind of cremation container. Cremation burials are much easier to work with than inhumations, and the locating of such a site usually means that others are nearby.

PITS AND HEARTHS

A pit is simply a hole that was dug in the ground, but all holes were dug for a particular reason. A hearth is a specific kind of pit, one that was used for firing, as in cooking. Pits of various kinds are very common at archaeological sites; many of them were originally dug for the burying of rubbish. Locating a pit is similar to locating a grave, but the pit will usually have more "junk" visible, such as charcoal, various decayed material, broken stones, and perhaps pieces of utensils. The topsoil of a pit is usually discolored; in almost all cases the soil is somewhat different in character.

The excavation of a pit can yield a great deal of information, particularly if it contains a lot of rubbish. All kinds of artifacts may be present, items which the users threw away, and from these the researchers can learn much about a culture. Because of this, archaeology has been referred to only half-jokingly as "the science of rubbish." Stratigraphy is important in excavating a pit, for it could have been used not only by successive generations, but by successive cultures in a region. If a pit was used for just a short period—a few days, a month, or even a year— then the excavation will yield contemporary artifacts and refuse. But if used over a period of many years, a pit can literally show the growth and evolution of a culture by what it made, used, and disposed of.

A pit could also have been used for storage. Some pits that began as storage pits ended as rubbish pits. The largest kind of pit is the quarry pit, dug originally so that certain material could be extracted, like gravel or chalk. Most quarry pits will contain only those artifacts used by the diggers to extract the material; some quarry pits contain no artifacts whatsoever, and this along with what kind of material existed in the region offers the archaeologist the necessary information to determine that he has indeed found a quarry pit.

Pits, particularly large ones, should be dug in *quadrants*. The quadrant method in excavation is the removal of two alternate quarters of a feature, so that a complete transverse section is exposed. This will offer the excavator a better interpretation of the stratigraphy of the feature. A hearth is noticeable because more stones, particularly reddened or blackened ones, are found there than in other kinds of pits. As the digger proceeds towards the hearth itself, he will notice more and more stones in each successive strata. The hearth itself will usually be either a small stone structure consisting of a basin and two or three sides, or else simply a shallow basin filled with charcoal and ash. The charcoal and ash give the excavator an opportunity to obtain samples for dating by the carbon-14 method, discussed later in this section.

One will almost always find a good supply of artifacts around a hearth, the most common being cooking utensils. The excavator should make a point of digging away from the hearth, once it is exposed, so that a larger area can be checked for artifacts. It is safe to assume that the eating area was near the hearth, hence eating utensils may be evident.

MASONRY BUILDINGS AND STONE WALLS

A masonry building is one built of stone or brick, and is very common in England, Europe, and the Near East. For the purposes of excavation, the archaeologist is interested in examining the foundation of such buildings plus whatever else remains of them. One must first be aware of how such structures are built, and the first rule in constructing any substantial structure is the laying of a firm foundation. Almost without exception, foundations are sunk below the topsoil. Once they have been laid, foundations must be stabilized by the filling in of dirt *and other materials*, and these other materials are of great interest to the archaeologist. They may include the original builders' tools, rubbish, utensils, and other objects in addition to any available landfill from the immediate area.

Stone walls are a type of masonry structure, though they may not be buildings as such. The foundations of a masonry building and of a stone wall are excavated in the same manner, but the building will have an accompanying floor where the wall will not. Stone walls were held in place by their builders with all kinds of different materials, depending on what was available and what the particular culture liked using. Anything from compacted clay, timber, and gravel to mortar, garbage, and tile can be found next to the base of foundations. The excavator should make a point of studying the construction techniques of the cultures he is excavating so that he will immediately recognize materials in the ground. Masonry buildings and walls are excavated mainly to determine the purpose of the structure, but a great deal of additional information can be learned about the culture from artifacts and other objects found during the digging process.

The digging itself never begins right next to the structure. One always begins a number of feet away in order to study the strata and to find broken tools or utensils which were left in place during the construction period by the builders. Another reason involves the possibility that the structure neither begins nor ends where it appears to; that is, it may have been broken up and then continued nearby or added to in any direction. The digging is conducted at right angles to the structure in the form of trenches. The trenches must be dug carefully, neatly, and accurately; the minimum width of the trench should be at least three feet. The soil from the trench, to be safe, should be dumped clear of the trench itself, for additional excavation may be required if it is noticed that the structure is much larger than originally thought. By dumping the dirt clear of the trench, the digger is free to enlarge the size of the trench without having to stop and move dirt around. This will also ensure that artifacts from one trench will not slide into another because of an abundance of loose dirt lying around on the surface.

The excavation should be planned so that the digging occurs in phases. The first phase of digging should be to the highest level of the structure —the top of the remaining stone wall, for instance. When this has been reached, an additional trench should be dug at right angles to the first trench, and the dirt immediately surrounding the top of the structure should be cleared. The excavator will then be able to get an idea of the plan of the wall itself. Does it continue in all directions? Is the main part of the wall located to the east? This is of course just a preliminary diagnosis, and the first two trenches are just preliminary trenches. Trenches should continue to be dug at right angles to one another; eventually, the entire structure will be exposed. As each additional trench is dug, the excavator improves upon his plan for determining where the structure lies. The second stage of digging—that of proceeding downward—should not be done until the level of all trenches is equal and the dirt has been cleared away. In this way, all diggers in the various trenches will always be at the same level below the surface in relation to the structure; the absence of such a procedure leads to confusion, with one digger examining the top of a wall while another is digging out the bottom. The director of the excavation must see to it that all diggers follow this procedure.

WOODEN BUILDINGS AND POST MOLDS

Whereas the excavation of masonry buildings and stone walls is conducive to amateur archaeologists, both experienced and inexperienced, the excavation of wooden structures is not. No inexperienced amateur should become involved with excavating wooden structures; it is difficult, exacting, and even depressing, and no amateur should be *expected* to do this kind of work strictly on a voluntary basis.

At a site containing wooden features, the succession of structures is complicated, the plan is unpredictable, and the structures are always in some—often extreme—degree of decay. This makes the excavation very difficult and monotonous, and the results may hardly seem worth the effort. Indeed, often they are not worth the effort, but there is no way to tell until the entire site has been excavated.

Wooden structures are built where there is a plentiful supply of trees, which depends on the climate of the region. In some parts of the world, all organic material completely decays in less than five years; there is virtually no trace of it left, but a trained archaeologist can still determine where a wooden structure was located by careful examination of the soil. The excavation of a site composed of wooden structures is done by stripping the topsoil by hand and analyzing every handful of dirt. Artifacts should begin to appear immediately below the surface soil, and the location of these can give the archaeologist an idea of the original layout of the site. All such excavations should be large-scale; it is a waste of time to spend a week digging a few square yards here and there, for the remains of wooden structures are much more easily moved around than stone walls with foundations five feet below the surface. Once an excavation is begun, it should continue until completed; there should be no partial or occasional excavation of wooden features. As artifacts are found, their location should be plotted. It will eventually become clear that a majority of them lead or point to a specific area. This means that the excavator is approaching the center of the site, where people congregated and where work of various kinds was undertaken.

As the excavator strips a second and third level of dirt from the ground, he will notice that the dirt retains some form of record of the existence of wood. A "mold" outlining the general shape of the wood will remain for a surprisingly long period. Even if a piece of wood such as a beam is pulled up, the color of the soil will not match the soil immediately surrounding it: it will appear a bit darker and the texture will be slightly dissimilar. All wooden structures, like stone ones, need a foundation, and this foundation, too, is usually set below the surface. Wooden posts set in the ground had to be packed in in order to remain firm, and this packing could have been done with dirt from various areas at the site, other wooden timbers, stone, or various kinds of junk. Eventually, depending on the climate and hence the type of soil, the wood would begin to rot. The pit, or hole, in which the wood rested would not be affected by this decay, however; it will continue to reflect the outline of the wood it held. A wooden post or beam in a pit should *never* be removed by moving it back and forth to loosen it and then pulling it up. This will alter the profile of the pit or hole and will cause dirt to begin filling up the space. Once a post is noticed, a circle should be drawn around it and all members of the excavation should be informed of it lest someone inadvertently disturb it. Then, two procedures should be carried out. First, a series of digs should commence near the post in a square pattern. This will reveal, it is hoped, additional beams or post molds that will identify the foundation of a structure. Also, if there is indeed a building, chances are the flooring will be very close to any one of a number of posts. This procedure should continue until the director of the excavation is convinced that no other post holes exist and that the flooring, if there is any, is in another part of the site. This is an example where a great deal of work may reveal nothing, for a huge area can be excavated, by hand, after a single post or post mold is located, and the result may be nil. The second procedure involves the excavating of the post hole or mold itself, and this should be done by digging towards it and down from at least three directions. This will ensure that the hole itself is not disturbed by the digging activity, and will allow the excavator to examine the soil for evidence of what was used to pack the original post.

If a series of post holes have been located, they may outline the entire structure and should form either a square or a circle. The next step is to dig from one post to the next, and then towards the center with the hope of locating a floor. If one finds a series of post holes in a straight line, this may indicate a fence or boundary of some kind. It can be of great help to the excavator in the field if he makes a point of studying the construction habits of the culture he is working with, for some peoples (such as the Hopi Indians) used stone and wood together whenever both were available, in which case the excavator should be prepared to come into contact with some kind of stonework.

MOUNDS AND TELLS

Mounds exist in many parts of the world, and are common features excavated by archaeologists. The archaeologist is of course interested in *man-made* mounds as opposed to natural ones. Natural mounds consist internally of an orderly deposit of soil layers, while man-made mounds are built up by bringing earth to the site. The composition of man-made mounds, therefore, is usually a mixture of different kinds of soil obtained from the surrounding area, and the levels, or strata, in the mound do not in any way resemble the orderliness of nature. Mounds were usually built for four main reasons. They were used as fortifications, as effigy mounds, as burial sites, or as hills upon which to build another special structure such as the residence of a leader or the temple of a priest.

The term *tell* comes from the Arabic and means "artificial mound"; it is employed by some British archaeologists.

The excavation of a mound is a major project, and no amateur should attempt it unless an experienced excavator is directing the work. A mound can yield many different kinds of information about a culture, and sometimes about a number of cultures. In Eastern countries, for example, many of the small villages were built on top of villages that preceded them. In effect, these villages exist on top of man-made mounds. Where the first village or town was built on flat land, the succeeding villages were built on the remaining rubble, and today one can find villages fifty or a hundred feet above ground level on artificial mounds. While this process existed in Europe for only a few hundred years, it continued in the East for thousands of years. The excavation of such a mound, therefore, may yield information about a score of cultures, from the Neolithic Age to the present. We can learn the chronology of cultures of a certain region by examining each level within the mound, and we can determine to some extent the length of time each culture or village remained. The depth of deposit can be associated with the length of occupation, and this gives the archaeologist a chance to determine the movement of cultures and subcultures. A knowledge of the principles of stratigraphy is obviously important here, as is a knowledge of anthropology in general. Some peoples, for example, had the habit of digging up the villages of their predecessors in the hope of finding useful objects or materials. Needless to say, their digging procedure was less than scientific, so the archaeologist must be able to recognize the possibility of such disturbances through the years and centuries as he excavates the various levels making up the mound. There will no doubt be quite a bit of confusion in those mounds that were disturbed more than once, for the levels will be shifted around, turned upside down, and in general greatly altered by curious diggers. It is beyond the experience of most amateurs to deal effectively with this kind of situation, and they should immediately stand back and observe the experienced archaeologist at work. Analyzing a disturbed mound is something that can hardly be learned by reading books or attending classes; it must be experienced firsthand in the field.

In order to learn as much as possible from a mound, a considerable majority of it must be excavated. There are four possible excavation procedures archaeologists employ in digging mounds: the *strip* method, the *sondage* method, the *quadrant* method, and the *grid* method. The strip method entails the removing of parallel strips successively from the mound. The *sondage* method entails digging a single, deep trench from the top of a mound to the bottom. Neither of these methods is used very often today. The quadrant method is fairly common; it involves dividing the mound into quarters and digging from opposite ends toward the center. *Balks*, or walls (strips of earth), are left standing between the quadrants so that a sample of the stratigraphy remains available for study. The quadrant method allows for a complete cross section of the mound to be excavated. The grid method of excavation is very similar to the quadrant method, the only difference being that the grid method entails the digging of a series of squares. The feature is divided into a series of squares, rather than into quarters, and each square is dug leaving a *balk*. Many archaeologists prefer the grid method because it deals with smaller amounts of space at a time than the quadrant, and is easier for recording strata, features, and objects found. The

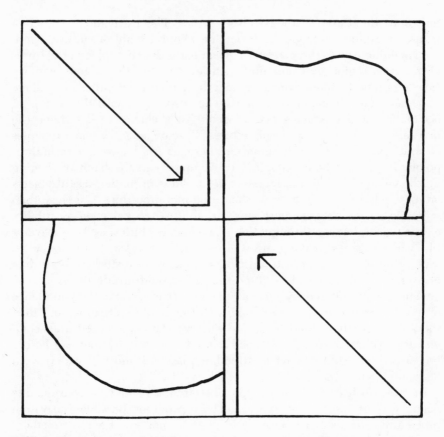

FIG. 5. Small site showing the quadrant method of excavation. The site is divided into quarters and dug from opposite ends toward the center.

size of each square depends on the length, width, and depth of the mound. The length of each square should be at least the size of the depth of the mound; otherwise the digger will find himself at the bottom of a long but small hole. The balks widen, of course, as the length of the square increases.

As the digging continues down, all objects should be removed from each level after careful recording; only in this way can the digging continue to the bottom of the mound. There are exceptions to this, however, as when one comes across a particularly important building; in such cases, the director of the excavation may decide to stop the digging and leave the lower levels undisturbed. Those experienced in excavating mounds are always anxious to get to the bottom quickly, for the top levels naturally represent the most recent occupation, and therefore are the least interesting and valuable levels in the mound. Nevertheless, each successive layer must be examined and recorded carefully, for there is always the possibility that a particular artifact or object will be found that will cause researchers to rethink their ideas about the activities of a certain relatively recent culture.

DITCHES, BANKS, AND EARTHWORKS

These three terms are pretty much synonymous in archaeology, though one or another may be employed more commonly in certain parts of the world. The term *ditch*, however, amply describes the type of feature we are dealing with here. Ditches may or may not be man-made, but they have been used or filled in by man somewhere along the line. Ditches, for the purpose of distinction in archaeology, are larger than pits and were not used as hearths; that is, they were not used for firing.

Ditches, banks, and earthworks could have been used for collecting refuse, forming boundaries around a community, or stabilizing structures. In some cases, a ditch could have served two functions: it could have been dug near a stone wall, filled in with garbage and dirt over a period of time, and finally packed with additional dirt plus stones and timber to solidify the earth around the wall. Earthworks have also been used as dividing lines between certain structures or buildings within a community.

These features at a site are not particularly difficult to excavate properly, but they are difficult to analyze and interpret. The excavator must first determine the size *and shape* of the ditch. At first glance, it may appear to be a relatively simple shape covering perhaps a few square feet. But upon closer investigation, the diggers may find that they have come upon a massive feature shaped like a half-moon. The "first law of stratigraphy"—that the oldest objects are at the bottom and the most recent are at the top—does not necessarily apply (in fact, it very often does not apply) when it comes to ditches, banks, and earthworks. This, of course, causes problems in attempting to date the feature. The effect known as *interdigitation*, or "reversed stratigraphy," occurs when material from the topsoil or from the second stratum finds its way to a much lower level either naturally or through redigging by man; in addition, old material can be found at a higher stratum than younger material. All of this occurs mainly due to vegetation "pushing up" material from the lower strata and to man "pushing down" material from the higher strata.

The primary thing to keep in mind regarding the construction of ditches, banks, and earthworks is that they are "loose" features which probably underwent more than one life cycle. When they became filled, they could have been redug and spread out to cover more area, and this accounts for some of the unusual shapes we notice today.

Assuming the original characteristics of a ditch have not been too badly altered, the date of it can be deduced from the artifacts and other objects it contains. The closer such a feature is to an occupation site, the more objects it will contain; therefore it is always advisable to excavate those ditches, banks, or earthworks which appear to be located near other kinds of features. The most important thing in excavating *any* kind of earthwork feature is a knowledge of soil. Few archaeologists receive training in soil science; hence it is advisable to have a specialist nearby when such features are being excavated. If the strata of a ditch are very confusing and the objects therefore cannot be dated with any degree of accuracy, one can only attempt to associate the ditch in time with surrounding structures. This is another reason for hesitating to excavate ditches which appear to be separated from other features that represent human occupation.

Because ditches are usually loosely constructed features, excavation must be slow and deliberate. Beginning a couple of feet away from the perimeter, small trenches should be dug at right angles to one another, *one layer at a time*, and, if possible, *balks* should be left standing. The main problem is that often the balks will not remain in place, and some kind of support must be brought in to keep them upright. This in turn prevents the excavator from viewing the strata as a whole, however, and it must be decided by the director of the project whether or not the procedure is worthwhile.

It must again be stressed that no careful reading of any instructional material is sufficent to qualify an individual as a proficient excavator. *There is no substitute for field experience.* Amateur archaeologists who desire to do fieldwork should make every attempt to become associated with an excavation expedition, even if it only involves watching others for the first few times. The principles of excavation are both general and specific; that is, there are certain rules that everyone follows in general, and there are specific techniques involved. But every archaeologist, particularly those with a great deal of field experience, has developed over the years his own way of doing things. This does not necessarily contradict the principles of excavation; it may just involve a particular technique that an excavator picked up along the way that works well for him or her.

It is difficult to describe excavation techniques to someone who has never been in the field. There is no substitute that I know of for actually seeing an excavation in progress, any more than there is a substitute for personally witnessing a major surgical operation. A knowledge of the different types of features that an archaeologist works with, of how he approaches them in excavation, and of how he deals with the problems presented by each is a major plus for any amateur who wants to do field-work. Unless a particular excavation project is part of a classroom session, the professional archaeologist usually does not bother to discuss the basic principles involved in digging a feature. Any amateur who is at least familiar with the basics, therefore, is in a position to learn more about the specifics. And this can only be done during the excavation itself.

CHAPTER 20

Where to Excavate

In order to know where to excavate in North America, the amateur archaeologist must first learn two things. First, he must learn the anthropological patterns and cultural areas into which North America is generally divided—or at least those in his region. In short, he must learn who lived where in prehistory. Second, he must learn the various procedures that an archaeologist goes through in finding a site.

Readers will recall from chapter 2 that prehistory is divided into various stages: the Paleolithic, Mesolithic, and Neolithic, followed by the Bronze and Iron Ages. These terms remain in use for determining the various developmental stages in the prehistory of the Old World, but they are not employed in the Americas. New World archaeology also employs a system which represents developmental stages, but it uses different terms for them. These stages are the *Lithic, Archaic, Formative, Classic,* and *Postclassic.* The developmental stages in North American prehistory (or "New World archaeology," as some prefer) are approximately equivalent to those of the Old World, though they occurred later in time. Keep in mind that these stages do not represent specific cultures, which will be discussed later.

The prehistory of North America begins with the *assumption* that people first arrived here by crossing the Bering Strait, a trip which remains possible today. North America was originally inhabited by Asians who were searching for more abundant lands. In this respect, no one went looking for America or migrated here. Prehistoric people followed the movements of animals, and the animals eventually found their way to the Americas. North America was first populated, therefore, almost by accident; hunters just sort of wandered on the heels of animals. The Asian influence, according to most physical anthropologists, is well-represented by the features of the Amerindians, though other strains are also evident.

FIG. 6. Major migration routes of prehistoric Asians into North America.

The movement of people into North America occurred in spite of the four major glacial periods, or Ice Ages, that began well over a million years ago. A number of points regarding the Ice Ages must be understood in order to visualize the comings and goings of man. At no time did the ice cover the entire continent and so leave inhabitants free and unhampered. At certain periods the ice drew back, but this allowed movement only toward the south, for the retreating ice caused water to rise further north, and this created a wall that precluded any return to Asia. In other words, it was a one-way trip. This whole process occurred over hundreds of thousands of years, so a dozen generations could live and die in one area before moving further into America. As man underwent necessary changes in order to survive during the Ice Ages, he altered his subsistence pattern and began a slow evolution from prehistory to history. This evolution occurred in developmental stages, beginning with the Lithic stage.

The Lithic Stage.   This first stage in prehistory is the longest, for it begins at the point in time at which man separated himself once and for all from other animals. Man began using stone for tools. Evidence of these oldest Americans can be found throughout most of the country, though a majority of the sites seem to be in the Great Plains area. There are also some Lithic sites in South America, and it is believed today that human movement had covered all of North *and* South America by 7000 B.C.

The Archaic Stage.   As the Ice Age came to a close, it signaled the beginning of this new stage of development. Man was by now distinctly superior to other animals. He had domesticated the dog, he employed the spear for hunting, and he was increasingly able to deal effectively with his environment.

The Formative Stage.   The Formative stage is principally identified as the period during which agriculture was born in America. It took a very long time for this stage of development to spread throughout North and South America. Archaeologists have determined that the earliest Formative stage developed in Mexico, Guatemala, and Peru around 1500 B.C. North America did not reach this point until around 200 B.C., in the Southeast and Southwest. Various types of "buildings" were raised, first from clay and tree branches and later from thinly split timber. In what is now British Columbia and the northwest coast of Alaska, the Formative stage also appeared, though there was no agriculture. As man continued to evolve past the Formative stage of development, civilization as we know it today began.

The Classic Stage. The Formative stage lasted for about 1,500 years. Then the Classic stage began, again first in central Mexico, Guatemala, and Peru. The differences in these two stages are dramatic, and there is no question that Western civilization began south of the border. Knowledge had taken on all new forms: mathematics, astronomy, engineering, architecture, religion, art, a central government, and a strong social order. The Classic stage developed later in the north, with continuous improvement and elaboration of the arts of metallurgy, textiles, and ceramics. Up until the end of the Classic stage, the inhabitants of the Americas were indigenous to the area; their evolution in the New World was without benefit of Old World influence.

The Postclassic Stage. This final stage in American prehistory began around A.D. 700 in the south and A.D. 900 in the north. When the Spaniards conquered the Aztec and the Inca, they were experiencing the postclassic stage of development. From that point on, the Americas received Europeans continuously. There is no question that the natural development of the first Americans was altered and influenced by the travelers from across the ocean—travelers who preached Christianity, who led terrestrial gods which they called horses, who killed for the yellow stone known as gold, and who taught the Indians what colonial rule meant.

This quick discussion of developmental stages in American prehistory is meant to serve only as background information for the following section. As noted at the beginning of this chapter, the stages are generally similar to those of the Old World, and the reader may refer to earlier sections of the book for more information.

The reader will also recall, and may refer to, the discussion of human *culture* earlier in the book. The idea of culture in anthropology applies everywhere: wherever human beings exist in distinctive groups, there is culture, and culture is distinctly human. We proceed now to an explanation of anthropological patterns, or cultures, in North America, followed by the cultural areas into which North America is generally divided for purposes of archaeological investigation. These cultures or cultural patterns represent the first societies on this continent.

ANTHROPOLOGICAL PATTERNS

American anthropologists have their hands full when it comes to depicting the various Indian cultures. The Indians did not keep written records, so their "history" begins with the arrival of the white man who did. Virtually everything we know about prior to that time comes from research by anthropologists and archaeologists.

There were thousands of different tribes, many of them cultures unto themselves. The population spoke hundreds of different languages and thousands of dialects; two tribes a mere twenty-five miles apart could not understand each other. Anthropologists have nevertheless attempted to combine various tribes and subcultural groups into major cultural patterns, and have come up with the Palaeoindians, the Desert Culture, the Archaic Culture, the Woodland Culture, and the Mogollon, Hohokam, and Anasazi cultures.

The Palaeoindians.   This name literally means "old Indians," for they are the oldest firmly dated indigenous American culture. Several sites from Nevada to Texas have been dated as far back as 12,000 B.C., and others on the East coast to about 10,000 B.C. Artifacts located in many parts of both North and South America are believed to be Palaeoindian. These artifacts include lance-shaped spear points, various fluted points, and grinding stones.

The Desert Culture.   These people lived primarily in caves, and were not particularly society-oriented; they preferred to remain scattered. They devoted a lot of time to agriculture, and excavators have found numerous tools and implements which were obviously used for gathering and harvesting various simple crops. The sites spread from Oregon straight south and from California to Colorado, and contain chopping sticks, flat milling stones, hand stones, digging tools, and mortars. They attempted to plant primitive maize, wild grain, and now extinct hybrid plants, and fashioned trays, baskets, containers, and pouches.

The Archaic Culture.   This cultural group represents many varied subcultures. They lived throughout the United States and Canada, and are particularly distinctive because they were fishermen. The idea of fishing to supplement the meat diet began in eastern Canada and spread to the northeastern and southeastern United States. They were not agriculturists at all, did not domesticate animals, and congregated in very small groups. All excavated sites are very small and show a distinct lack of a sedentary attitude on the part of the people. Archaic sites usually, though not always, produce a hearth feature, for fired clay pottery was developed by this culture around 1000 B.C.

The Woodland Culture.
The Woodland cultures were comparatively sedentary. They were agriculturists, their villages were fairly large and permanent, and they developed religious and social customs. They were mound builders and spread their influence from Mississippi to New York. Excavated sites contain a great variety of artifacts, and the Woodland culture spawned an untold number of tribes.

The Mogollon, Hohokam, and Anasazi Cultures.
There is a standing argument about which of these cultures came first. Begun in the late 1930s by Harold Gladwin and Emil Haury, the theory was that the Cochise culture produced the Mogollon, which developed to the Hohokam, with the Anasazi trailing sometime later. The argument has been temporarily halted by dividing the Mogollon into five stages, from about 200 B.C. to A.D. 1000, and by assigning the cultural development of the Hohokam to between A.D. 500 and 1200, in seven phases. This is not the place to discuss the pros and cons of the various theories. Suffice it to say that the Mogollon and Hohokam were sedentary agricultural societies. The Mogollon lived primarily in and around Mexico and Arizona and began forming a distinctive culture of their own after a break with the Desert culture. The Hohokam culture, also from Arizona, is known for its digging of large irrigation canals. This culture existed for approximately a thousand years. The Anasazi culture lived north of the Hohokam and was also known as the *Pueblo*. They built multistoried dwellings (*pueblo* is simply the Spanish word for "village"), but are also well known as basket makers. They were sophisticated agriculturally, politically, socially, and religiously. They were driven south by nomadic Indians, and settled finally in New Mexico, where their descendants live today.

CULTURES AND CULTURAL REGIONS

The above are the major anthropological *patterns*, or cultural *groups*, of the prehistoric American Indians. The amateur archaeologist should become familiar with these patterns, for they provide the necessary background, or overview, for studying the particular Indians of one's region.

We move now to a discussion of *specific* cultures, or *tribal groupings*, and their geographical location in the Americas. This will be followed by a list of some seventy *specific tribes* and their locations.

Arctic Indians. The home of these Indians is divided into two regions: the eastern and central Arctic, which extends from Greenland to the Mackenzie River, and the western Arctic, which includes the Aleutian Islands and Alaska. The principal cultures are the Aleuts and the Eskimos, and their ability to survive depended on hunting and fishing for sea mammals.

Subarctic Indians. Geographically, these Indians lived in what is now the Yukon territory, Ontario, Quebec, Manitoba, Labrador, most of the interior of Canada, and southern Alaska. The culture is referred to as Caribou Hunters because they developed rather ingenious ways of capturing and killing the animal, which they did ceaselessly. Their housing was in the form of a crude conical *tipi* (or tepee), covered with hide or bark and framed with poles. They also used a single or double lean-to, supported with a framework of poles and covered with bark, hides, or brush. Subarctic Indians did not have furnishings for their dwellings. While in the forest, each family was responsible for its own survival; on barren lands, however, families always hunted together in groups. This culture had no true religious or governmental organization, and organized warfare was unknown to them. Virtually no specialized craft came out of this culture, though one tribe, the Ingalik, did make wooden bowls for trading.

Eastern Indians. This is a vast area that generally includes Indians from southern Canada to the Gulf of Mexico and from the Atlantic Ocean to the Prairies; and New York, the six New England states, the mid-Atlantic states, and the southern states as far west as Louisiana. These cultural regions represent sedentary and sophisticated Indian tribes; they were agriculturalists, hunters, and fishermen. The two most outstanding cultures are the Mohawks and the Iroquois.

Many archaeologists prefer to break down the Eastern Indian cultures into four subcultures. The *northeast* Indians lived in the famous *longhouse*, so named because the average size was 60 feet long, 18 feet wide, and 18 feet high. The frame consisted of paired vertical poles set in the ground with horizontal poles across their tops and along the walls. A central hall ran the length of the building, flanked on each side by a series of booths for individual family occupation and for storage. The culture was a very strong one politically and socially: it was highly organized, had a representative system of government, and a "League of Nations." The basic political system was decidedly democratic. The *southeast* Indian culture included the Creek, Chickasaw, Choctaw, Cherokee, and Seminole tribes. Their dwellings were similar to the longhouse of the Iroquois, but smaller, and families usually lived alone. They were primarily farmers. There are quite a number of extant sites of the southeast Indian cultures along the Atlantic coast; the Mississippi, Tennessee, and St. Johns rivers; and the Gulf of Mexico. The system of government of this cultural region was absolutely autocratic. The two other subcultures that some researchers list in this category are the Middle West and Plains Indians, but they are separate cultures of their own.

Prairie Indians. This cultural region includes most of Oklahoma, Texas, Arkansas, Tennessee, and Kentucky, and parts of Missouri and southern Ontario (Canada). The two main tribes are the Dakotas and the Fox. Four types of housing were used: hide-covered tipis, earth lodges, grass-thatched huts, and low-domed structures, or *wigwams*. Depending on the type of dwelling, families lived alone or in groups. All of the tribes had some form of governmental and social organization, but it was generally loose; warfare among tribes was virtually nonexistent.

North Woodland Indians. This culture, dominated mainly by the Chippewa and Menominee subcultures, existed in the valley of the upper Mississippi River, along Lake Superior, and in Minnesota. Not a great deal is known about them, partly because researchers have frequently chosen to include them as subcultures within other cultural regions, from the Prairie to the subarctic Indians. They were primarily hunters and fishermen, although they occasionally attempted to raise crude crops. The North Woodland culture was extremely male-dominated; women were used almost as slaves.

Plains Indians.   This culture spread from central Canada south to the Mexican border and from the Missouri River to the Rocky Mountains. They were principally hunters of buffalo, but occasionally tried farming. They were a particularly warring culture, however, and made life difficult for all who crossed their path. They were roamers, nomads, living in portable tipis. Most of the tribes, particularly the more warring ones, achieved tribal organization and had fairly well-defined areas of occupation.

Plateau Indians.   The region inhabited by these Indians lies in the plateaus of the Columbia and Fraser rivers, now parts of British Columbia, Washington, Montana, Idaho, and Oregon. Some refer to this as the Northwest culture, though that is a separate grouping of tribes. The Plateau culture was a mixture, however, of the Plains and Northwest Coast cultures. The common dwelling of the Plateau Indians was a subterranean house consisting of a circular pit four or five feet down, over which a conical roof was laid. This culture was a familial, as opposed to a tribal, one; there was much family organization but little on the tribal or subcultural level. Each subculture more or less managed its own affairs, with only a general recognition of and association with the Plateau culture.

Northwest Indians.   Also referred to as Northwest Coast Indians, their culture thrived from the regions of southeastern Alaska southward through British Columbia, Washington, Oregon, and the northern portion of California. The earliest sites in this region seem to be Archaic, though some archaeologists believe that Palaeoindian specimens are now submerged along the coastal waters of the Pacific Ocean. This culture is mainly known for its woodworking. Their dwellings were built of solid planks, usually carved, and with gabled roofs. The hearth was located in the center, and several families occupied a single dwelling. They developed a strong social order and political organization. The social system was a hierarchy of noblemen, common people, and slaves; they were among the first cultures to have definitive classes based on both birth and wealth—upper, middle, and lower.

Oasis Indians.   The region of this culture included most of Arizona, New Mexico, and Mexico. The name Oasis Indians was applied because most of the land where they lived was desert, and hence they tended to gather around streams or oases. Some of the more outstanding tribes and subcultural groups include the Pueblo, Apaches, Navahos, and Yumans. There is a tremendous amount of archaeological activity in this region, with hundreds of sites located. The Oasis culture was responsible for developing six different types of housing: pueblos and stone and mud structures of various designs for various uses. Each clan —which might consist of more than one family—within a tribe was allotted a certain amount of space in the larger pueblos. With the exception of the Apache subculture, the Oasis Indians were a peaceful culture. The Pueblo subculture was the first in North America to wear garments made of cloth instead of skins. Social and political organization within the Oasis culture ranged from small, weak subcultural groups to large, strong ones. The Yuman subculture was the most organized, followed by the Pueblo.

Great Basin Indians.   This culture was located in parts of California, Idaho, Wyoming, Oregon, and Colorado, and all of Utah and Nevada. Theirs was a difficult existence, and there was little social or political organization. The Indians subsisted on wild plants and small game. The typical dwelling was the tipi, covered with thatch rather than skins. Their culture was eventually influenced by the Plains Indians. The most important site in this region is the Danger Cave site, near Wendover, Utah, dating back to about 10,000 B.C.

California Indians.   This culture represents the subcultural groups in central and southern California, and for the purpose of clarification I will divide it into these two geographical entities. The Central Cali-

FIG. 7. Major cultures and cultural regions of prehistoric peoples in the United States and Canada.

1a. Eastern and Central Arctic Indians
1b. Western Arctic Indians
2. Subarctic Indians
3. Eastern Indians
4. Prairie Indians
5. North Woodland Indians
6. Plains Indians
7. Plateau Indians
8. Northwest Indians
9. Oasis Indians
10. Great Basin Indians
11. California Indians

fornia Indians are known as the Acorn Gatherers, since acorns formed a major part of their diet. To the acorns they added fish, various wild plants, rodents, birds, worms, and insects. Their common dwelling was made of poles to which leaves were tied, the tipi was also used occasionally. This culture also built subterranean, earth-covered structures for religious ceremonies only. The largest subcultural group was the Yokuts, which divided itself into tribes and subtribes for organizational purposes. The smaller subcultures had their own land areas, but they were loosely organized and often consisted of no more than six families. The Southern California Indians formed what many have referred to as a lazy culture, though the circumstances of their existence allowed them few advantages. Most of this cultural area was and is desert, though there is some rainfall in the lower region. In the dryer regions, desert plants formed the major portion of the diet; along the coast, seafoods were the staple. Because of the warm climate, housing was of little need. There was virtually no social or political organization or cultural ceremony, and warfare was unknown. This culture is occasionally referred to as the Baja (Lower) People.

CULTURES AND CULTURAL REGIONS IN LATIN AMERICA

The Indians of Latin America can be divided into two major cultural *groups*, and from these into five specific cultures and cultural regions. The first of the two major groups, or anthropological patterns, includes those cultures that reached a comparatively high degree of civilization very quickly, like the Aztecs, Mayas, and Incas. The second cultural group is comprised of those Indian tribes that remained rather primitive for thousands of years, which even today have refused to partake of modern technological advances, and of those tribes that became extinct. The Cuna culture of Cape San Blas in Panama is an example of a continuous primitive existence.

The Middle American Indians. This culture descended chiefly from the anthropological patterns of the Aztecs and Mayas in Mexico and Central America. The subcultural groups lived in villages of clay or stone huts surrounding a great temple. They were mainly farmers.

The Andean Indians.   This culture can be divided into two main subcultural groups: those of the central Andean plateau of Ecuador, Peru, and Bolivia, who descended from the major cultural pattern of the Incas; and those of the northern Andes of Colombia. The most important tribe in the northern Andes was the Chibcha. This second subcultural group was not as sophisticated or as "civilized" as the first, which descended from the Incas, but they adopted a number of ways, habits, and functions of both the Incas and the Aztecs. The difference between the two groups was a matter of degree, hence they are placed in the same cultural grouping.

The remaining three cultural groups represent the most primitive in Latin America and cover three broad regions.

The Caribbean Indians.   This culture was distributed in sort of a semicircle that included northern Venezuela and the West Indian islands from Cuba down to the Windward Islands. They were farmers, maintained large villages of thatched houses, were warlike, and were often cannibalistic. They are almost extinct as a culture.

The Tropical Forest Indians.   This culture occupied most of South America around the Orinoco, the Amazon, and the Parana-Paraguay rivers. The Indians here were both farmers and hunters, the chief subcultural group among them being the Jivaros.

The Marginal Indians.   This culture existed in the southern grasslands, savannas, and treeless plains. They also were both hunters and farmers, though not very successful at either because the climate discourages continuously active life patterns.

SUBCULTURES AND TRIBAL REGIONS

As the first Americans moved through the developmental stages and anthropological patterns to form specific cultures in certain regions, they continued to become less similar, developing different tribal traits. This was represented by the founding of tribes, or subcultures. In some cases, subcultures and tribes came together to make up a culture and cultural region; in other instances, the prevailing culture subdivided into subcultures. Some of these prehistoric groups are represented today by modern tribal names and some are extinct.

The reader has no doubt noticed that we cannot point to a map and say such-and-such group lived from here to here and that group from there to there. There is a lot of geographical mixing of cultures. In addition, not all subcultures were contiguous; they did not all live in the same region at the same time. Some subcultures are much older than others; some were sedentary and some moved around a lot. For a listing of important archaeological sites that have been excavated in the United States and Canada, see chapter 14. Following is a list of major subcultures, or tribes, and their geographical locations in antiquity.

1. ALGONQUIAN. Woodland Indians living north of the St. Lawrence River near Ottawa.
2. APACHE. Left western Canada about A.D. 1000 and settled, with the Navaho, in Arizona and New Mexico.
3. ARAPAHO. Migrated to the Great Plains from Minnesota, settling in Colorado and Arkansas.
4. ASSINIBOIN. Migrated from the headwaters of the Mississippi River to North Dakota, Montana, and Saskatchewan.
5. ATHAPASCAN. Roamed the interior of Alaska and Canada.
6. AZTECS. Settled on the high plateau of central Mexico.
7. BLACKFOOT. Settled in northern Montana and nearby parts of Canada.
8. CHEROKEE. Settled in the southern part of the Appalachian Mountains.
9. CHEYENNE. Settled as farmers in Minnesota.
10. CHICKASAW. Settled in northern Mississippi and in Tennessee.
11. CHINOOK. Settled as fishermen along the shores of the Columbia River.
12. CHIPPEWA. Woodland Indians (also known as Ojibway or Ojibwa) who lived on both sides of Lake Huron and Lake Superior.
13. CHOCTAW. First settled in southern Mississippi and Alabama.
14. COMANCHE. Settled throughout the Plains region.
15. CREE. First settled in central Canada and roamed as far north as Hudson Bay.
16. CREEKS. Also known as Muskogee, they "lined the creeks" of Georgia and Alabama.
17. CROW. Original territory was in the valley of the Big Horn River, in Montana.
18. DELAWARE. Also known as *Leni-Lenape* (literally "real men"), they occupied large portions of Pennsylvania, New Jersey, and New York.
19. ESKIMOS. Occupy the land in and around the Arctic Zone, and have for over 4,000 years.

20. FIVE CIVILIZED TRIBES. The Cherokee, Chickasaw, Choctaw, Creek, and Seminole (see elsewhere in this list).

21. FLATHEAD. Settled in western Montana.

22. FOX. A Woodland tribe that lived originally in Wisconsin.

23. HAIDA. Settled in the Queen Charlotte Island of British Columbia.

24. HOPI. A tribe within the Pueblo subculture settling around northeastern Arizona and a few other points south.

25. HURON. Part of the Northeast Indian Cultural Region, their territory was originally along the St. Lawrence River and bordered Lake Ontario and Georgian Bay of Lake Huron.

26. ILLINOIS. A group of Woodland Indians who originally occupied southern Wisconsin, northern Illinois, and parts of Iowa and Missouri.

27. INCA. Also called Quechuas, they originally settled in the mountain valley of Cuzco in southern Peru.

28. IOWA. Originally settled in and around the Mississippi Valley.

29. IROQUOIS. A major subculture composed of five tribes: the Cayuga, Mohawk, Onondaga, Oneida, and Seneca, who settled in upper New York State.

30. KAW. Also known as Kansa, they roamed through the Mississippi Valley and settled in Kansas.

31. KICKAPOO. Settled in scattered groups through central Illinois and Indiana.

32. KIOWA. Originally settled in Montana.

33. KLAMATH. Roamed over a wide territory around Klamath Lake in Oregon.

34. KOOTENAY. Settled on the borderland between Montana and British Columbia (also spelled Kutenai, Kootenai).

35. MAHICAN. Originally settled in New York along the Hudson River.

36. MANDAN. Originally settled along the upper Missouri River.

37. MAYA. Settled in northeastern Guatemala, the peninsula of Yucatan, and parts of the adjoining Mexican states in Central America.

38. MENOMINEE. Originally settled in northern Wisconsin.

39. MIAMI. Settled in parts of Wisconsin, Illinois, and Indiana.

40. MICMAC. Originally settled in eastern Canada: Newfoundland, Nova Scotia, Prince Edward Island, and New Brunswick.

41. MODOC. Settled originally in northern California.

42. MOHAVE. Originally settled in the valley of the lower Colorado River on the Arizona-California border (also spelled Mojave).

43. MOHAWK. The main tribe, and most easterly of the Iroquoian subculture (see no. 29), they lived in eastern New York along the Mohawk River.

44. MOHEGAN. Settled originally in southern Connecticut along the Thames River and in New York along the Hudson River (also spelled Mohican).

45. MUSKHOGEAN. Those Indians who were members of the Five Civilized Tribes, excluding the Cherokee (see no. 20), held together by a common language, and settling for the most part in the southeastern United States.

46. NARRAGANSET. Originally occupied part of Long Island and much of Rhode Island.

47. NAVAHO. Formed originally with other subcultures in Alaska and northwestern Canada, they moved southward and settled in and around Arizona and New Mexico (also spelled Navajo).

48. NEZ PERCÉ. Settled originally in central Idaho.

49. OMAHA. Part of the Plains Indian cultural group, settling originally in Nevada.

50. OSAGE. Originally roamed through Oklahoma, Arkansas, and Missouri.

51. OTTAWA. Settled originally along the Ottawa River in Canada.

52. PAPAGO. Settled in southern Arizona and across the border in Mexico.

53. PAWNEE. Part of the Plains Indian cultural group, they lived originally along the Platte River in Nebraska. The name, Pawnee, literally means "horn."

54. PEQUOT. A large subculture that spawned the Mohegan tribe (see no. 44), they inhabited eastern Connecticut and parts of Rhode Island.

55. PIMA. Settled along the Gila and Salt rivers in southwestern Arizona; they are culturally tied to the Papago (see no. 52).

56. POTAWATOMI. A tribe of Woodland Indians, they first lived on the mid-Atlantic coast, but moved to Lake Michigan and into Illinois, northwestern Indiana, southwestern Michigan, and finally Wisconsin.

57. PUEBLO. Originally scattered throughout southern Colorado, Utah, Nevada, Arizona, and New Mexico, the Pueblo was a major subcultural group in the Oasis Indian culture. They spawned the Hopi, Shoshone, and the Zuni tribes.

58. QUAPAW. Once referred to as the Arkansas tribe, they were part of the Plains Indian culture and lived originally in the Mississippi Valley.

59. SAC. Settled originally along the Mississippi Valley, mostly in southern Wisconsin (also spelled Sauk).

60. SEMINOLE. Settled originally in Georgia and then in Florida (the name literally means "separatists" or "runaways").

61. SENECA. The largest tribe making up the Iroquois subculture (see no. 29), they settled originally in the western part of New York State.

62. SHAWNEE. Part of the Woodland Indian culture, they lived originally in Tennessee.

63. SHOSHONE. Part of the Pueblo subculture (see no. 57), they lived mainly around the Sierra Nevada, Cascade Range, and the Rockies.

64. SIOUX. A large subcultural group within the Woodland Indian culture, they originally lived in Minnesota, and spawned the Dakota, Lakota, Nakota, Teton, Santee, Yankton, and Yanktonai tribes.

65. TOLTEC. A very old group that preceded and subsequently influenced the Aztecs and Mayas. They originally inhabited the valley of Mexico near what is today Mexico City.

66. TSIMSHIAN. Settled originally along the coast of British Columbia (also spelled Tsimpsian).

67. TUSCARORA. Settled originally in North Carolina, but migrated
    eventually to New York State. They are considered part of the Iroquois
    subculture.
68. UTE. Originally occupied western Colorado, Utah, and parts of New
    Mexico.
69. WINNEBAGO. Settled originally in Wisconsin, south of what is now
    Green Bay and east of Lake Winnebago.
70. YAKIMA. Settled originally in western Washington.
71. YAQUI. Settled originally in northern Mexico.
72. YUMANS. A peaceful tribe of the Oasis group that settled in parts
    of Arizona, New Mexico, and Mexico.
73. ZUNI. Part of the Pueblo subculture, they originally lived in west-
    ern New Mexico.

This concludes our discussion of the developmental stages, anthropological patterns, cultural regions, and subcultural groups in American
prehistory. The amateur archaeologist who decides to do excavation
work should study the prehistory of his particular region for more detailed information than could be included here. The terms applied to
name and describe the various Indian cultures and tribes were devised
by the white man, hence they are sometimes too general and even arbitrary. But the Indians kept no written records, and the white man was
forced to bring some order of his own to the vast expanse of time during
which these cultures developed. The lack of written records means that
we must rely on the testimony of the spade, on the excavation, to find
out about the first Americans.

Many amateur archaeologists have contributed in no small way to
putting together a picture of early man on this continent. While some
are particularly interested in the developmental stages and cultural
beginnings of early man, many prefer to study the peoples who represent pre-Columbian contacts, and still others concentrate on the Pilgrims,
Colonists, and others who began pouring in during the sixteenth century.
Whether one decides to specialize in palaeoanthropology, pre-Columbian
archaeology, or historical archaeology, it is imperative that a study be
made of one's region from archaeological literature. Only in this way
can the amateur be aware of what has already occurred and what
archaeologists are now concentrating on.

FINDING THE ARCHAEOLOGICAL SITE

Once one has made a study of the cultural history of a region, he can
move on to the next step in determining where to excavate. This next
step has two phases: the initial research and the physical survey.

Before getting into specifics, however, the amateur should understand that an excavation is undertaken in order to collect *important* information. There are thousands of archaeological sites all over the world waiting to be excavated, but archaeologists do not have the time to work at all of them; therefore, the most important must be excavated first. The location of important sites is determined through the initial research and then is double-checked by the physical survey. Through excavation, archaeologists attempt to establish a sequence of cultures in a region. Many parts of the world have gaps in their cultural sequence, so archaeologists are especially anxious to find important sites in those regions. Very rarely does an archaeologist go into the field merely out of curiosity. The amateur should take the same attitude by carefully determining where excavation work would be most useful in a particular region. By familiarizing himself with previous archaeological research, he can deduce what areas the professionals consider to be in need of additional work.

Although there are thousands of archaeological sites all over the world, most of them are hardly obvious. Archaeological sites fall into two categories, those which are completely or partially visible above ground and those which are below ground level and no longer visible. The second category represents a majority of sites today.

How did these sites get to be the way they are when the archaeologist finds them? Most features long in disuse are only vaguely similar to their original design. Such features go through a change because of one or more of three things. First, many sites are simply abandoned by those who either built or used them. Depending on the type of features at a site, they deteriorate in varying degrees of rapidity. Those composed of wood will decay first, while stone structures will remain pretty much the same for a considerable amount of time. The main decaying agents are wind, water, vegetation, below-ground chemical and bacterial processes, and vandals, robbers, and pothunters. These last—people who disturb or destroy sites for various reasons—are the most active and destructive agents, for once a structure begins to fall apart it becomes more susceptible to the other decaying processes. Vandals and robbers can do in one day what would take the natural elements a thousand years to accomplish.

Human destruction of sites is so rampant that it represents the second way they undergo a change. It is a form of demolition, of altering the original structure. Many robbers look not only for valuables and artifacts to sell to collectors, but for *anything* that can possibly be sold or reused. This includes the structure itself—wood, stone, masonry work of any kind. By stealing such items to reuse as building materials, they reduce structures to little more than their original foundations.

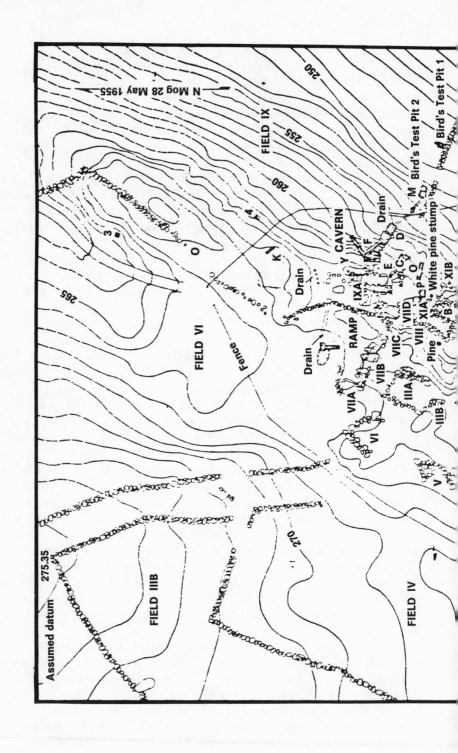

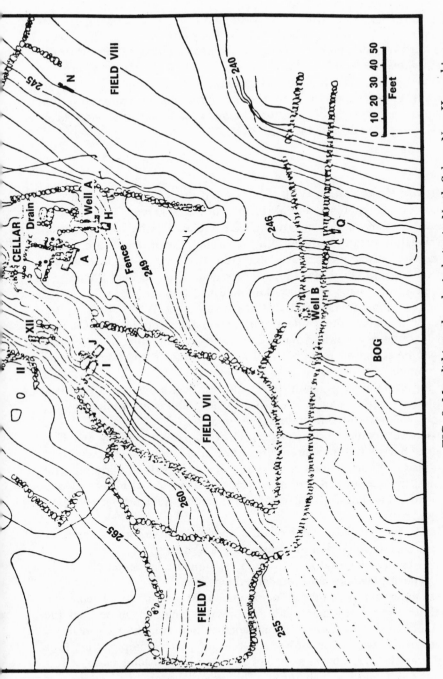

FIG. 8. Megalithic archaeological site in North Salem, New Hampshire, on a topographical map. (*Courtesy of Mystery Hill Corp.*)

The third way in which a structure undergoes a change is also through human-related destruction. This can be either accidental, by fire, or deliberate, by an enemy attack. Regardless of the cause, however, all features eventually succumb to the geomorphological processes. For this reason a majority of sites are below ground level, having been buried through soil development.

The Initial Research.   With that in mind, we move to the first step in locating a site, known as initial research or initial survey. This research is mainly a study of the geography of a region by the use of special maps which indicate surface form, or relief. Such maps are called topographical maps and are available from the U.S. Geological Survey. There are topographical maps for every region of the United States.

Topographical maps are important because they show by means of color and symbols the natural features of an area. When studying the culture of a region, the student will notice that certain peoples preferred to settle near various natural features—water, forests, hills—and these can be found on topographical maps. Certain natural features are more common than others in terms of importance to cultures. Drinking water, for example, is common to all cultures. People who utilized wood attempted to settle near forests; those who were stone builders were naturally more interested in finding stone quarries.

The natural features on a topographical map published by the U.S. Geological Survey fall into three categories: man-made, relief, and water.

Man-made features include cities, villages, roads, buildings, cliff dwellings, trails, roadworks, tunnels, bridges, dams, canal locks, reservations, land grant lines, parks, cemeteries, mines, quarries, shafts, coke ovens, and wells.

Relief features include the elevation above mean sea level, contours, depressions, cliffs, mine dumps, debris, and sand dunes.

Water features include streams, rapids, tunnels, lakes, ponds, wells, glacier deposits, marshes, and submerged marshes.

In scanning a topographical map, one must use a lot of common sense. Both natural and man-made features are included, so one has the opportunity to decide if there is any conflict between the two in terms of a successful excavation project. Let us say, for example, that in a certain area the map shows a fresh-water stream, a fishing pond, a few substantial hills, and a lush forest. This would be an ideal settlement area—and it still is, for it is covered with modern houses! An excavation in this area might, therefore, be a problem for a number of reasons. Due to substantial buildup, many sites have probably been destroyed or are now firmly locked beneath foundations. In addition, the excavation might have to take place in somebody's front yard. For these reasons, an archaeologist may choose to refrain from attempting to excavate in so popular a locale.

Based on the knowledge of what various cultures in prehistory seemed to prefer for settlement locations, the amateur should be able to select potential sites. If an area has continuous abrupt and unlevel spots with no water nearby, chances are that few peoples would have wanted to live there. Abrupt relief *with* water is a more likely possibility. A spot that is fairly level and includes a lot of water sources—though not *too much* water, for fear of flooding—would be an ideal location. A highly elevated spot with water nearby but few trees would discourage cultures that needed wood for building purposes. Those cultures that built with stone but used firewood—as opposed to heating rocks—would also tend to seek an area with at least a small forest nearby. Hunting cultures would of course settle, at least temporarily, in an area that could support game, while fishing cultures would look for a well-stocked lake or swamp.

All of these things must be considered when ·contemplating the features on a topographical map. The student should also make a point of checking general maps, both old and recent. Modern maps may actually reveal some kind of ancient site—perhaps a· road or even settlement—by the way natural features are arranged or by the patterns of areas. Older maps, even those that are two hundred years old, may reveal features on them which are today no longer visible. If a structure was in its last throes of decay or destruction in the 1700s, for example, it may still have been partially visible aboveground at that time, and may therefore have been included on a general map of the area.

Before going on to the next step in finding an archaeological site, the physical survey, some archaeologists take advantage of a procedure that is considered today to be the most valuable part of initial research—aerial photography. Obviously, few amateurs can run out and hire a plane equipped and manned for this purpose; even professional archaeologists usually employ aerial photography through foundation, university, or museum funding. It is an expensive process.

The advantages in using aerial photography cannot, however, be overemphasized. Photographs can reveal anything from a huge buried city to a small grave. Two factors play an important part in aerial photography: shadows and vegetation. At certain times of the day and on certain days of the year, particularly low features will be caught on film because of a shadow effect. Generally, however, everything de-

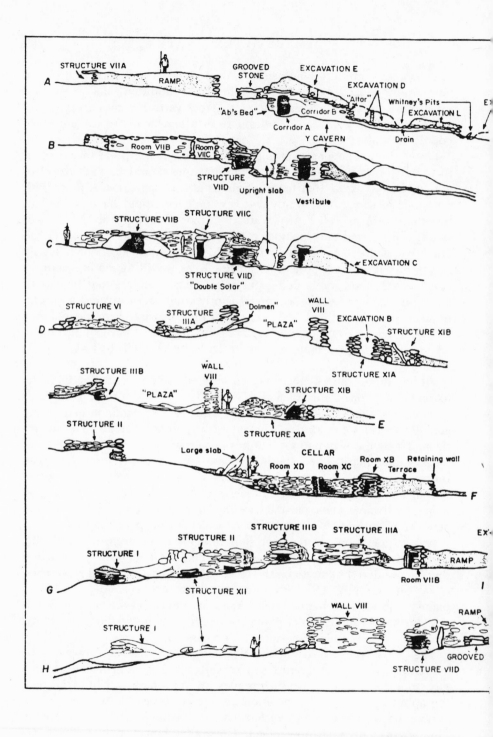

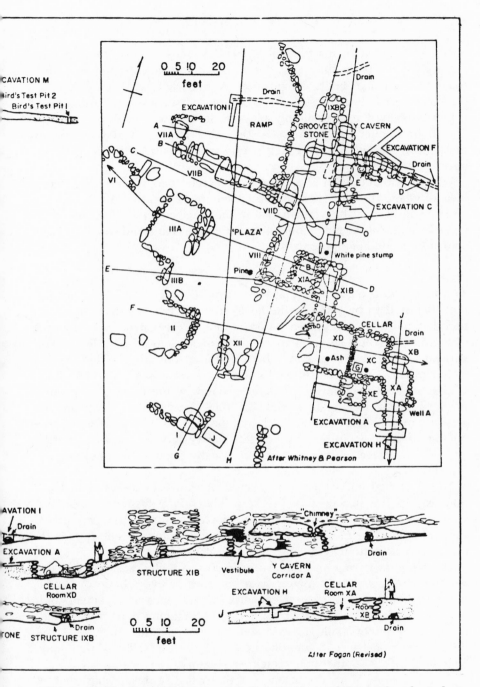

FIG. 9. Profile map and layout plan (inset) of megalithic archaeological site in North Salem, New Hampshire. (*Courtesy of Mystery Hill Corp.*)

pends on vegetation, for the soil reflects all activity and alterations it has undergone. It's mainly a matter of being able to interpret *how* the soil reflects change in its composition. A wall that has been buried a couple of feet below the surface, for example, will cause the soil above it to sink below the surrounding soil. This in turn will cause the vegetation to be thinner and lighter. On the other hand, soil above a ditch that has been filled in over a long period will be noticeable for its dark, lush vegetation.,

With or without aerial photography, the archaeologist now has a good idea of where the best sites are most likely to be located. All the initial research must now be verified before any excavation begins, and this verification involves going out and seeing the spots indicated on the map or in the photographs.

The Physical Survey.   This preexcavation procedure is very important. Referred to by some as the field, or ground survey, it is the final test that must be undertaken before a site is excavated. The absence of a proper physical survey may result in digging in an area for weeks without finding anything, simply because there is nothing to find.

The physical survey involves locating and recording potential sites. Choose an area that can be properly covered by the number of people involved in an acceptable amount of time. Large survey expeditions are rare, for it is felt that too much may be overlooked regardless of the number of members in the party. A satisfactory survey is best conducted on foot, and three or four persons are usually enough for most survey expeditions.

Topographical and other maps should of course be referred to continuously as the survey is in progress. The survey team will look for three things: any unusual patterns of color or texture in the soil, or of vegetation growth; rises or dips in the ground which do not appear to conform to the natural landscape; and artifacts.

The equipment required for a proper survey includes small shovels, pointing trowels, hoes, knives, axes, brushes, gloves, bags or small pouches, identification tags, a compass, a tape measure, camera and film, pencils, notebooks, and sketch pads. The digging equipment listed should be brought along in case some sample digging should be required; the pouches and identification tags are for artifacts that may be found; use of the other items is self-explanatory.

It is extremely important that careful notes be taken and that a legible recording of the survey be completed in a manner which others will find easy to understand. The recording sheet should include the following information: the geographical location of sites or suspected sites; the name of sites (any reference will do, such as the closest road or farm); the geological environment of the site, including the soil and vegetation type, natural drainage systems, and all natural features; man-made features, like roads, houses, and bridges; and all notes of the survey from all persons involved (some people are more observant than others).

A particularly helpful reference in finding what may be important sites is the people who live nearby. Old-timers may remember when "the ground looked kind of funny." In addition, nearby residents may know of an existing feature which the survey team overlooked, or where pieces of artifacts were found when they were children. Local historical and archaeological societies may also know of sites or suspected sites the locations of which have not yet been published or released, and which they have not yet had time to investigate. All of these sources of information should be considered.

I have noticed that many amateurs who prefer not to get involved with actual excavation work nevertheless devote a great deal of time to helping on field surveys. Professional archaeologists usually welcome amateurs, even raw beginners, if only because there is little damage they can do to sites. Amateurs who go along on professionally run surveys may be asked to record everything that is said by following the archaeologist wherever he goes; those with experience should not hesitate to make this clear and offer their help. One does not need a Ph.D. in anthropology to conduct, much less assist on, a field survey.

Thanks to modern technology, a number of mechanical devices have been developed for use by archaeologists. These instruments may be used during both the survey and the excavation. Amateur archaeologists rarely use them, because they are rather expensive and because some of them require a great deal of training on the part of the user. Professionals use them whenever they are available, though few archaeologists really depend on them. They should be used as an adjunct to the procedures already discussed in this chapter.

The most common of these instruments are the metal detector, the proton magnetometer, and the resistivity meter. British archaeologists today seem to prefer them more than their American counterparts do, though they do not rely on them to the exclusion of traditional survey techniques in the field.

Assuming the survey team has done its work well, and has concluded that there is ample evidence indicating the existence of an archaeological site, the next step is to prepare for the excavation. There is still a great deal to do before the first digger goes to work.

CHAPTER 21

Planning the Excavation

Proper planning before the excavation begins is extremely important. Without it, scores of things can go wrong. In this chapter I will discuss the three most important things in planning an excavation: personnel, equipment, and preparation of the site.

The very first thing to do, however, is obtain permission to excavate from the owner of the land. Once this has been accomplished, it is advisable to inform both a professional and an amateur organization of your intended project. The professional organization will usually be the anthropology department of the nearest university or the research department of a museum. The amateur organization will be the nearest group of amateur archaeologists or amateur archaeological society. There are two reasons for informing both professionals and amateurs. First, both may be able to offer information on what you may expect to find at sites in a particular area, and they may also offer the use of materials or equipment. Second, they may serve as a backup unit in the event that anything goes wrong, or any questions have to be answered, or someone gets sick. It is always helpful to know that there are people who are aware of what you are doing and where you are located, and who will come to your aid if necessary.

PERSONNEL

An excavation is only as good as the people who conduct it. Owing to the numerous types and sizes of sites around the world, there is no uniform standard for staffing excavation expeditions. The number of persons necessary is based on the considered opinion of the director of the project, who should of course be the one with the most experience.

Expeditions in the United States usually employ fewer people than expeditions elsewhere in the world, because the sites are generally smaller.

All excavation projects are run by the director, who not only should be more experienced than his associates but should be considered an experienced excavator—professional or amateur—in his own right. The director is responsible for the entire project, from deciding who is to dig in what area to finding lodging for the workers, and from obtaining permission to excavate to publishing the results at a later time. In choosing people to join the project, the director should of course attempt to attract as many experienced people as possible. In addition to himself, there should be one or two others who have had some experience in the field. The ratio of experienced to inexperienced workers is difficult to determine for a successful excavation, however. Some of the larger expeditions, like those common in the Near East, have employed over three hundred untrained workers who were guided by only five archaeologists. A small site in the United States, on the other hand, may require only four members on the team—but they should all be experienced. The best way to handle this problem is to decide first how many parts of the site may be dug at once. If two, then there should be at least two persons along who have had some experience.

In addition to the director, there should be a field supervisor to direct the actual digging. He *must* be experienced, for he is responsible for seeing that the soil is checked for artifacts and that proper recording procedures are followed. Each digger should have at least one person assisting him in checking for artifacts. Each digger should also have someone recording what is going on. Some projects assign two or three workers to each digger, while others have one assistant for every two diggers. At a small site, it is suggested that digging occur at no more than two spots at once, and that the following personnel be involved:

1. Director
2. Field Supervisor-Digger
3. Digger
4. Assistant
5. Recorder
6. Digger
7. Assistant
8. Recorder
9. Photographer-Artist

If all involved are experienced, then a larger excavation can be undertaken or fewer people can be used. With inexperienced workers, however, the director and field supervisor must keep a watchful eye on what transpires. Nothing should be dug, removed from the ground, sifted, or recorded without the director first being aware of it. If he misses something important, it's too late to go back and do it again. Many excavations conducted by amateurs are more liberal and less hierarchical than what I have outlined here, but if carried to extremes they can become nothing more than glorified pothunting. Archaeological excavation is serious business, and discipline must be established.

The above list of nine personnel, based on digging at two spots at a site, is specifically meant to encourage *no more* than that number. Some archaeologists say it is better to have too few people than too many. When there are four or five people more than are really needed, they tend to get in the way, complain because there's so little to do, demand more responsibility, or just wander around taking pictures. Having too few people means at worst that the project will take a bit longer and that those involved will have to work a bit harder. I tend to agree with those who say that too many people means too many problems.

EQUIPMENT

Two types of equipment must accompany the excavators. The first type is that which is used in the digging process, and the second type is for recording the excavation.

As with choosing personnel, much depends on the type and size of site involved. Some sites require three bulldozers; others require water pumps, cranes, and a dozen buckets. Some sites should be fenced in during the excavation. All such sites should not be excavated under the direction of amateurs; as such, amateurs will not be responsible for supplying the equipment. Most sites in the United States require certain basic tools, the quantity of which depends of course on the number of persons on the project. Following is a list of the basic tools that should be brought along for excavating an archaeological site.

1. Shovels with both rounded and pointed ends and long and short handles
2. Hoes with both short and long handles
3. Trowels (single-piece blade and shank)
4. Shears (standard pruning shears or root cutters)
5. Axes, small and large
6. Knives (medium-sized jackknives)
7. Brushes (standard paint brushes for cleaning)
8. Tweezers of various sizes for picking up artifacts
9. Toothbrushes for scrubbing artifacts

10. Bags or pouches (cloth or paper) for storing artifacts
11. Tags for identifying artifacts
12. Screens for sifting soil
13. Compass
14. Tape measure (steel)

The recording equipment is as important as the excavating equipment, for the record of an excavation is all that future workers have to go by. If records are not made properly and in a fairly standard manner, future workers will be left wondering just what it was the excavation accomplished. The uses of the various items for recording the excavation are discussed in the next chapter. Every archaeological society has supplies of the proper forms for keeping records, and it is important that amateurs utilize these instead of doing things their own way. Following is the most basic recording equipment used today.

1. Site Record
2. Daily Field Report
3. Feature Report
4. Stratigraphy Record
5. Field Catalogue
6. Photo Report
7. Camera
8. Film
9. Note Pads
10. Sketch Pads
11. Pencils
12. Maps

PREPARING THE SITE FOR EXCAVATION

When the personnel have been chosen and the excavating and recording equipment assembled, it is time to plan the excavation itself. The first thing to do is *account* for the site; that is, the existence and location of the site must be recorded, and this is done by drawing a large map of the site with all natural and man-made features included on or near it. This is done mainly so that the site will be recognizable to future researchers. In addition, a *marker* is placed near the site so it can be easily found, and this marker is included on the map. The marker should be of a permanent type, such as a steel rod embedded in cement. This will allow future workers to find the site even if it is eventually plowed over, or if a hotel is built on it. At least one can determine where it *was*. This marker is known at the *datum point*.

The next step is to choose a spot near, but not part of, the actual site for preliminary digging. This too should be noted on the map. Many archaeologists use the topographical map as a reference when drawing their own map of a particular site; the site map then becomes an enlargement of a small point on the more general topographical map. The purpose for digging at a spot near the actual site is for comparison, and the spot itself is referred to as the *control pit*. The idea is to learn the *natural* composition of the strata in order to show what it was like *before* man entered the scene. Later, when the actual site is excavated, one can see the extent to which man altered the natural soil deposit. A control pit need not be more than five feet deep.

Before the site is excavated, it must be *qualified*. This is done by laying out a *grid*. The grid establishes the boundaries of a site by means of four markers around the site in the form of a square. The site is then broken down into internal squares, and each square is numbered. This procedure effectively ensures that each portion of the site will be recorded separately, and that sections will not get mixed up. The mathematical center of the site is located, and the numbering of the squares usually begins there. Some archaeologists like to tie string to the four stakes outlining the site so that diggers will not accidentally venture outside the prescribed area. This process is known as establishing a *base line*, and is arbitrary.

If the site is on unlevel land, the contour should also be accounted for; this is known as determining the *profile*. One need only measure the height of any feature above what is determined to be the ground-level spot and record the information on the map.

Finally, a drawing should be made of the grid plan of the site, and a sheet should be numbered for each square. As the excavation proceeds, all relevant data regarding each square should be recorded on the proper sheet. The size of each square depends, of course, on the size of the site itself, but the average is five feet.

The excavation may finally begin.

CHAPTER 22

Excavating, Recording, and Preserving

EXCAVATING

There are a number of excavation techniques in use today. Which one is used at any given archaeological site depends mainly on what the director of the excavation considers the most practical. Some excavators prefer a single method, while others alternate, depending on the type of site. The more experienced diggers may even switch from one technique to another as the excavation proceeds. They do this when the character of a site changes; that is, it may turn out to be a multicomponent instead of a single-component site, or it may be much larger than originally perceived. The director must base his decision on which technique will serve the function of obtaining the maximum amount of information from the site, and this he can only do according to his own experience in the field.

The excavator concentrates, as he works, on the stratigraphy of the site and on looking for artifacts. The importance of stratigraphy has already been stressed at the beginning of this section. A discussion on the excavating of artifacts will immediately follow an overview of excavation techniques.

Techniques. The decision as to which technique to employ should never be made by the amateur unless he or she has had a number of seasons' experience with each. The beginning amateur, whether he digs or not, will want to become familiar with the various techniques and the reasons for employing them.

HOW TO EXCAVATE

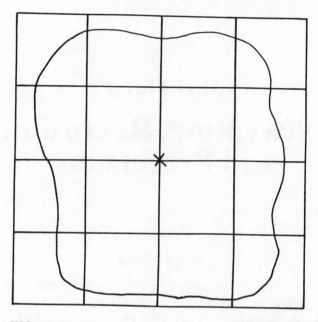

FIG. 10. A small site squared off and laid out by the grid method.

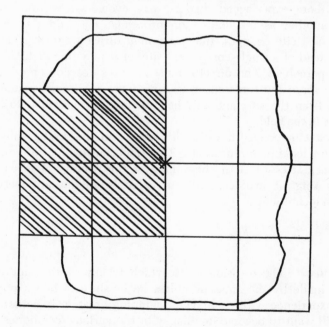

FIG. 11. Same site with four squares (shaded area) excavated.

The *gridding* technique is one of the two major excavation methods, though it is becoming less and less popular among modern archaeologists. The main reason for using this method is control. The excavator can dig in any direction, following the base line and grid plan, without disrupting the layout of the site. If the excavator decides to change the direction in which he is digging or to follow what appears to be the beginning of a feature, he need only move to another square. Everything is still accounted for in terms of where a feature or artifact was located, because the grid plan of squares was established for that very purpose. As a square is dug, it is not always dug to the same level all at once. Some excavators will dig a small hole in one corner of the square *ahead* of the rest of the square, in order to get an idea of any important changes in stratification, such as the beginning of a feature. The principle of the gridding technique is that all excavation should be done first vertically and then horizontally. The gridding technique allows the digger to proceed straight down *first* and then, if a feature is located, to proceed *across* to another square.

The *vertical-face* method is done in a horizontal direction. The idea is to choose a section of the site, say the length or width, and excavate the entire section *across* all at once. Each layer is therefore made visible over a larger area than in the gridding method, which allows only for the strata in one square to be revealed at a time. The advantage in using the vertical-face method comes through when excavating those sites whose features are spread out horizontally rather than situated deep in the dirt vertically. An excavator may switch from the gridding to the vertical-face method if, for example, he locates a broad floor of a structure. He will have located an edge of the flooring through the gridding method, and then switched to vertical-facing in order to expose the entire flooring at once for more practical viewing.

Another technique, called *stripping* or *level-stripping*, is a sort of combination of the above two techniques. It involves digging vertically, as in gridding, but not maintaining the same level throughout the site. Each square, section, or arbitrary area within the site is excavated vertically to any level in which a feature or artifacts are located. The excavation may then discontinue at that spot and move to the next square or another section. The result is a number of different and arbitrary levels throughout the site (digging may stop in one square at any time if no artifacts have been found or if the strata seem unimportant), which some archaeologists prefer. Another level-stripping technique involves digging a trench either the length or width of the site to a certain prescribed level, *and then* proceeding horizontally *across* the entire site.

A final important excavation technique is the *feature-level*, or *unit-*

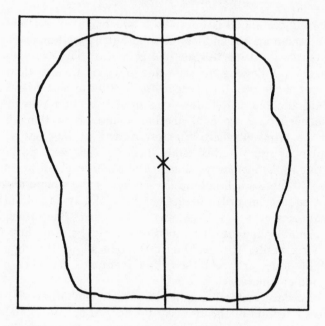

FIG. 12. A small site squared off and laid out for the vertical-face or stripping method of excavation.

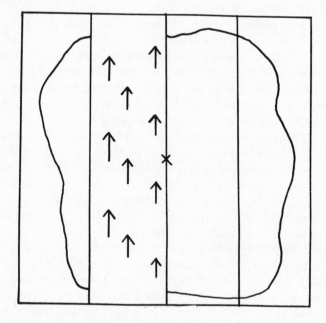

FIG. 13. Same site, with one section excavated.

level, method. This is similar to level-stripping, but where the level-stripping method continues across the site, gathering material as it goes, the unit-level method allows for everything to stop and everyone to concentrate on each feature or artifact as it is located. Once an object is located, all the general techniques are abandoned for the moment and the object is excavated in a manner depending on its size, shape, and context, as discussed in chapter 19.

Artifacts. All digging must be conducted with great care. Those who try to hurry should be thrown off the site, for they will undoubtedly disturb the strata and dislocate, damage, or just plain overlook artifacts. Each stratum should be excavated with a trowel or short-handled hoe, and no more than a half-inch of soil should be removed at a time. This will allow the digger to notice, hopefully, even the smallest artifacts. The careful digger will soon get the feel of the soil; he or she will notice any change in the soil's structure, and this is an initial indication that some kind of artifact has been reached. Once this occurs, *no metal tool* should be used. The digger should proceed to clear the dirt with a brush, looking for even the most minute artifact, such as a micro-lith (hand-worked stone less than an inch long).

Once the artifact is located, leave it alone. Using a small brush, attempt to clean the exposed part of it of any dirt. Then look around slowly to see if any other artifacts are in the immediate area, particularly if the first artifact appears to be a piece broken off from a larger object. If the artifact is a *sherd* (a piece of broken pottery), for example, there is a possibility that the rest of the item is nearby.

All objects found in the ground fall into two categories: *artifacts*, which are man-made, and *natural objects*, which are not. Artifacts can be anything from the pyramids to a clay bowl, from Stonehenge to a stone tool. Artifacts themselves are of two types. They are either *additive* artifacts or *subtractive* artifacts. An additive artifact is one which was formed from other, more basic materials which bear no resemblance to the finished product, such as pottery. A subtractive artifact is one which was formed by removing or altering pieces or parts of the original material, such as a stone tool.

Needless to say, there are numerous kinds and types of artifacts that an excavator may find as he digs. Stone artifacts alone comprise a huge list, as do the different types of pottery, and some researchers devote their whole careers to analyzing all the different types and establishing from them certain cultural traits.

A *Sandia* projectile point of the Palaeoindian Culture. Average length 3 inches.

A *Clovis* projectile point of the Palaeoindian Culture. Average length 3 inches.

A *Folsom* projectile point of the Palaeoindian Culture. Average length 2 inches.

A *Plainview* projectile point of the Palaeoindian Culture. Average length 4 inches.

A *Gypsum Cave* projectile point of the Desert Culture. Average length 2 inches.

A *Corner-removed* projectile point of the Early Archaic Culture. Average length 2 inches.

A *Tapered-stem* projectile point of the Archaic Culture. Varying lengths.

A *Corner-notched* projectile point of the Woodland Culture. Varying lengths and widths.

A *Leaf* projectile point of the Woodland Culture. Average length 4 inches.

A *Ceremonial* knife of the Early Archaic Culture. Average length 6 inches.

A *Flake* knife of the Palaeoindian, Desert, Archaic, and Woodland cultures. Average length 1½ inches.

A *Celt* axe of the Archaic and Woodland cultures. Average length 8 inches.

A *Whetstone* grinding stone of the Archaic and Woodland cultures. Average length 7 inches.

A *Stem* scraper stone of the Palaeoindian, Desert, Archaic, and Woodland cultures. Average length 2 inches.

A *Stem spade* agricultural tool of the Woodland Culture. Average length 12 inches.

FIG. 14. Some stone artifacts of prehistoric cultures in America.

The three most common types of sites in the United States and Canada are the prehistoric, Indian, and Colonial. With the exception of Colonial sites, where artifacts are relatively modern, the majority of artifacts will be in the form of stone products and fired clay, followed by artifacts made of antlers, teeth, shells, wood, iron, copper, and bone. Products of these materials are usually classified as belonging in one of the following categories: Projectile Points (15 types); Knives (5 types); Notchers (2 types); Blades (5 types); Sinkers (4 types); Weights (3 types); Rubbers (3 types); Scrapers (4 types); Agricultural (5 types); Vessels (numerous types); and Pipes (numerous types). Part of one's basic study of the prehistory of his particular region should be a study of those types of artifacts which seem to be the most common there. The student should learn how to recognize the various artifacts assigned to the Palaeoindian, Desert, Archaic, Woodland, and other cultures, as well as to the numerous subcultural groups.

RECORDING

All excavations must be scrupulously recorded. Regardless of the quality of the excavation itself, a lack of good records means that no one but the actual diggers can know what transpired, and eventually none of them will remember the numerous details involved. As far as the archaeological community is concerned, an excavation without proper records is no excavation at all. Amateurs are strongly advised to adopt this view. Even if the site under excavation is a small one and of no particular importance as far as can be determined, it *may* be of immense importance to researchers in the future. A friend of mine recently told me he had just come from observing an amateur archaeologist in the process of excavating a rather small site. The amateur archaeologist is known to me, and there is no question that he may be properly considered a professional amateur. But I was told that he was not bothering to keep any record of what he was doing, though the excavation itself was certainly commendable. There are two things wrong with this kind of situation: first, the amateur archaeologist was alone; second, he was keeping no records. As a result, he can no longer be considered a competent excavator.

In addition to the initial map and sketch of the site outlined in the previous chapter as part of the preparation for excavating, there are a number of necessary forms and records to keep during the excavation itself. It is advisable to use standard forms which may be obtained from any institution or organization involved with archaeology.

Site Record.   The first form to fill out is the Site Record, or Site Report. This is meant only to contain general information about the site *before* the excavation begins. The information on the Site Record should reflect principally the name, type, location, and owner of the site.

Daily Field Report.   As the name implies, the Daily Field Report accounts for each day's activity. What part of the site was excavated, how long it took, who did the digging, what features were found—all should be included in this report. In addition, any general comments or observations should be noted, such as weather conditions, difficulties with a particular feature, and thoughts on the progress of the expedition.

Feature Report.   The Feature Report is very important. Included here are *specific* descriptions of all features and artifacts located. Each artifact must be numbered, tagged, and placed in a safe container (an envelope, pouch, box, bag), and the Feature Report must specify (a) where *exactly* the artifact was found; (b) its description; (c) its assigned number; and (d) where it was deposited. All features, all artifacts, plus anything else that may be considered a bit out of the ordinary are to be listed and discussed in detail on the Feature Report.

Stratigraphy Record.   This report must give a precise description of all strata excavated, and is no job for the beginner. Each level of strata, beginning with the topsoil, is to be both described and measured. The description should include both the type of material (loam, gravel, sand) and the texture of it (fine, coarse, pebbles, thick). The measurement of each stratum must be from the surface of the land, and is to include the depth of the layer. For example, "The gravel represents the third stratum and is 12 inches from the surface. The stratum itself is 10 inches thick."

Field Catalogue.   The Field Catalogue is really a duplicate of just about all the other reports. Its main function is to put everything together on a daily basis. It is usually written at the end of the day after the ex-

FORM 2

SITE RECORD

Issue No._____

Site No._____

_____ Town

_____ State

1. Type of Site_____

2. Name of Site_____

3. Location (Directions from the nearest town)_____

_____

_____

_____

4. Location (Measurements from U.S. Geological Survey
   [Topographical] Map)_____

_____

   Date of Map_____

5. Site Owner_____

6. Address_____

7. Description of Site_____

_____

_____

8. References of Site_____

_____

9. Site Reported to (Individuals/Organization)_____

_____

_____

10. Initial Comments_____

_____

_____

11. Reported By_____ _____

_____ _____

Date_____

FORM 3

DAILY FIELD RECORD

Site Name/No._____Recorder_____

Date_____Excavation Day No._____

Section Excavated_____

Size_____Depth _____

Excavated by_____ _____

Assisted by_____ _____

Time Began (Hour)_____Ended _____

Features Located_____

Description_____

_____

_____

Comments on Features_____

_____

Artifacts/Objects_____

_____

_____

Description_____

_____

_____

_____

Comments_____

_____

Weather Conditions_____

Notes_____

_____

_____

_____

FORM 4

FEATURE REPORT

Site Name/No._____Recorder_____

Feature Name_____No._____

Date Found_____Exc. Day No._____

Location of Feature:

    a. From Center of Site_____

    b. From NE Corner_____

    c. From NW Corner_____

    d. From SE Corner_____

    e. From SW Corner_____

    f. Grid Squares_____

Depth from Surface_____

Strata Layer_____Material_____

Size of Feature_____Shape_____

Definition_____

Description_____

Disposition_____

Associated Objects_____ _____

_____ _____

Artifact Name_____No._____

Date Found_____Exc. Day No._____

Location of Artifact:

    a. From Center of Site_____

    b. From Any Two Corners_____

Depth from Surface_____

Strata Layer_____Material_____

Size of Artifact_____Shape_____

Definition_____Description_____

_____Disposition_____

Associated Objects_____

Observations/Comments_____

_____ _____

FORM 5

STRATIGRAPHY RECORD

Site Name/No._____Date_____Recorder_____

Stratigraphy Record No._____Stratrum _____to_____

Layer # - Definition - Description - Depth - Thickness -

1. _____ _____ _____ _____

2. _____ _____ _____ _____

3. _____ _____ _____ _____

4. _____ _____ _____ _____

5. _____ _____ _____ _____

Section Excavated_____

Natural Features_____

Artifacts_____

Conclusions #1 _____

#2 _____

#3 _____

#4 _____

#5 _____

#6 _____

Notes

cavation has ceased. The recorder can use this report to show the day-to-day progress of the excavation on all fronts. Comments made by other members of the team may be included as part of the daily summary.

Photo Report. In addition to all the note taking and filling out of forms, sketches and photographs should be part of the Field Catalogue. Whenever something occurs during the digging that may be difficult to explain in words on paper, a sketch and/or photograph should be made. A Photo Report should include all relevant information so that when the

FORM 6

FIELD CATALOGUE

Site Name/No. _____ Date _____

Catalogue No. _____ Recorder _____

Sections Excavated _____

Features Excavated _____

Artifact Catalogue:

#	Name	Description	Location	Association	Remarks

Progress/Comments:

Director _____

Supervisor _____

Others _____

FORM 7

PHOTO REPORT

Site Name/No._____Date_____Photographer_____

Camera_____Type Film_____ASA_____

Exc. Day No._____

Roll #-Exposure #-Subject-   Location-Direction Toward

___ _____ _____ _____ _____

___ _____ _____ _____ _____

___ _____ _____ _____ _____

___ _____ _____ _____ _____

___ _____ _____ _____ _____

___ _____ _____ _____ _____

___ _____ _____ _____ _____

___ _____ _____ _____ _____

Notes

---

film is processed there can be no question as to precisely what the pictures represent. The Photo Report should include the date, day number of the excavation, roll (of film) number, exposure number, and an explanation of each exposure. In addition, the *direction* toward which the camera is pointing (north, south, east, west) should be noted.

At the end of the excavation project, the final report must be written. There is no standard form for this, nor should there be. The final report is an accounting of the entire excavation, usually written by the director with input from every single member of the project. All the above-noted reports comprise the appendixes of the final report. In some cases, each member of the expedition writes his or her own final report, and these are then combined. I have one such final report that is six inches thick.

When the final report is completed, a number of things may be done with it. These will be discussed in the last chapter.

PRESERVING

Care must be taken during the excavation to preserve and conserve artifacts for subsequent study and dating. As noted at the beginning of this
section, the excavation is the first step in the three levels of archaeological
study. Many hours of laboratory work and research follow the excavation's conclusion, so it is imperative that all artifacts be handled by
those experienced in this matter. Even if the results of an excavation are
not going to be sent to a research facility, it is nonetheless just as
important that artifacts be treated correctly so that they may remain
intact.

Once an artifact is removed from the ground, it must be decided first,
whether or not to clean it, and second, how to go about it. The clean-or-
not-to-clean argument is almost always won in favor of "clean." The
reasons for not cleaning an artifact *at the site* are (a) conditions are
better at a laboratory or even at home; (b) materials may not be available at or near the site; and (c) the appropriate expert may not be part
of the excavation expedition. I personally do not like to clean materials
at the site, for *all* of the above reasons. Most people, however, are anxious
to see just what it is they have found, and proceed to clean the item
immediately. There is no harm in this, really, *assuming* there is somebody along who knows what he's doing. Cleaning an artifact is not
always a simple matter of scraping off some dirt. Unless one knows
what to expect from various kinds of materials, he should not clean
artifacts. I have heard too many stories of people scraping off dirt that
turned out to be paint, and of people using steel brushes on an artifact
that promptly crumbled into a million pieces.

You must realize that when an artifact is removed from the ground
it changes environment, and this can cause a number of reactions. When
an airtight cave in Spain was found a number of years ago to contain
prehistoric art sketches, it was opened to the public. Within weeks a
fungus began to grow on the cave walls and damage the original art-
work. The growth has been retarded, but experts visit the site once a
week to control it. If a bone is pulled out of a wet soil environment
where it has remained for hundreds of years, and left to dry under a hot
sun after being washed in water, it will crack and split. It must be dried
slowly, out of the sun, at a temperature of about 60 degrees. Antlers
should be cleaned twice, because they have a tendency to retain salt.
Iron should be dried as quickly as possible by artificial means (oven,
electric heater) after washing. Following is a list and explanation of how
various materials are best preserved.

STONE: should be cleaned with soap and warm water in order to remove salt, which might otherwise recrystallize, thereby causing flaking.

GOLD: should be cleaned carefully with soap and warm water; never scrape with anything hard, for gold is very soft and easily scratched.

SILVER: should be cleaned only by careful brushing, for silver is very fragile.

BRONZE: should be cleaned only by careful brushing; if dry, it should be stored in a dry place; if wet, it should be dried slowly.

IRON: if badly rusted, iron should be cleaned by soaking in water with carbonate of soda and dried by artificial means; if slightly rusted, it may be cleaned with a hard brush but should not be washed.

LEAD, TIN, AND COPPER: should *not* be handled in the field at all.

WOOD: if wet, it must be *kept* wet in a solution of equal parts of water and alcohol until it may be studied, and should then be allowed to dry away from the sun at a temperature of approximately 60 degrees; if dry, it must be kept dry, preferably in an enclosed, nonhumid atmosphere; if the wood is going to be analyzed, it should be left in the same condition as found and *immediately* brought to the laboratory.

BONE: if sturdy, it may be cleaned with a brush, washed in warm water and soap, and left to dry at a temperature of approximately 60 degrees; if fragile, it should be kept in a dry place or, preferably, rushed to a laboratory.

IVORY: should never be washed; may be cleaned with a wooden tool and then a brush; if wet, it should be left to dry *in situ* before removal.

ANTLERS: should be cleaned twice, but quickly, in warm water after brushing, and placed in the shade to dry.

POTTERY: to be safe, it should not be washed at all, but cleaned carefully with a brush.

LEATHER: should be cleaned in liquid lanolin and then rubbed with same; must be handled very carefully.

CHAPTER 23

Dating Methods in Archaeology

When the excavation and all it entails is finished, everyone wants to know the "when" of what was found. The "when" is determined in archaeology by two methods of dating, *relative* and *absolute*. As the terms themselves suggest, relative dating is based on comparisons, while absolute dating is precise. Similarly, relative dating is an initial and general procedure, and absolute dating is a final and specific one.

RELATIVE DATING

This procedure involves comparing the age of an artifact found at a site with that of other artifacts found at the same site. It is *strictly* a comparative procedure, and in that sense is not really a dating system at all. Relative dating is important, however, and is accomplished through *general stratigraphy, seriation,* and *geomorphic stratigraphy*.

Stratigraphy, which has already been discussed, is the prime method in obtaining relative dating. The first law of stratigraphy is that the lower the strata, the older the strata. Therefore, an artifact found ten layers down from the surface is naturally older than an artifact located in the third layer. The archaeologist can determine a *dating sequence* by comparing the various layers and what's in them. From there he will initially conclude, say, that artifact K is older than artifact J but not as old as artifact L. The artifact is older in the sense that it was used, and subsequently left behind by the user, *sooner*. If one is excavating a site that accommodated five groups over a period of five hundred years, then the lower strata will contain artifacts that are much older than those in the upper strata. However, if a site was of the single-component type that accommodated a few families for three or four years, the artifacts in the lower strata will simply represent those that were discarded first but are comparatively the same age as all the others. The excavating of large mounds affords the classic example of the importance of stratigraphy in relative dating, because in mounds there are many layers representing many years of occupation.

Seriation is another method of relative dating, though not as impressive as stratigraphy. The seriation method is based on the *development* of more sophisticated artifacts by early man and on their *popularity*. When a new tool or utensil was first invented, it went through a phase—as everything new does today—of acceptance. If it was immediately accepted, many copies were made and put into use. As this new tool or utensil made the rounds, it became popular among various contiguous groups or cultures. When it was first invented, there may only have been a few copies spread out over a particular area. *In time*, however, it became more plentiful and could be found everywhere. Therefore, when an excavator finds a particular tool that he knows first came into use at a certain point in time, he immediately looks for additional copies. If he doesn't find any, and if similar neighboring sites also contain only an occasional tool of the same type, he may initially conclude that the site is *no older* than the point in time at which the artifact was first introduced. By the same reasoning, he knows the site is older than those other sites which contain the same artifact in plentiful numbers. The archaeologist must obviously take many things into consideration when contemplating seriation. It provides a means for determining the comparative age of two or more sites, but is no more than a *relative method*.

The final method of relative dating, *geomorphic stratigraphy*, is based on geological processes. Archaeologists make a point of being aware of the geohistory (geological changes the earth has undergone) of a region they are excavating. They may learn, for example, that certain geomorphological features such as a river or a volcano have undergone change since human occupation is known to have existed in a certain area. The river may have receded and the volcano may have erupted; therefore, careful examination of the strata on an excavation may reveal this. If a stratum is lined with volcanic deposits *below* the layers containing artifacts, then it can be deduced that the human occupation occurred *after* the volcanic activity. If layers containing volcanic deposits are above those containing artifacts, then obviously man was in the area before the volcano erupted. The next step is to revert to the relative dating method of stratigraphy, and if the date the volcano erupted is known, then relative dating of a site is based on that time. This method can be useful only if there indeed was a noted geological event whose occurrence can be dated.

ABSOLUTE DATING

Fortunately, there are more precise methods for dating archaeological materials. Some of these methods were introduced in chapter 7. All represent major achievements in terms of the archaeologist's ability to bring chronological order to the chaos of time.

The most outstanding of these methods is *radiocarbon* dating, which can be applied to the entire range of *organic* remains. Also known as the *carbon-14* method, it is the basis of prehistoric chronology. Radiocarbon (C-14) is a radioactive isotope of carbon received into the earth's atmosphere in the form of cosmic rays. When it combines with oxygen, C-14 forms carbon dioxide, and is therefore taken in by all living things in the same ratio that ordinary carbon, or C-12, is taken in. Ordinary carbon has an atomic weight of 12, hence C-12. This means that the nucleus of the carbon atom contains twelve particles of protons and neutrons. The radioactive isotope, however, has an additional pair of neutrons in the nucleus, or a total of fourteen, hence C-14. When an organism dies, it no longer takes in carbon-14. The C-14 already in the organism begins to change to C-12, and the rate of this change can be measured by determining how much C-14 is in the organism at any given time. The important thing is that C-14 changes to C-12 at a regular, constant rate. Having determined the half-life of C-14 (the point at which half of the C-14 in the organism has changed to C-12) at right around 5,600 years after the organism died, a physical chemist gave archaeology a method which can date organic remains to as far back as 50,000 years. The procedure for dating an organic remain is very technical and quite costly. The average cost for a single dating is at least $100 in the United States. All anthropology departments at universities either own the necessary equipment or deal with a firm which does, as do museums and archaeological organizations. The amateur should be aware of those materials suitable for carbon dating in order to be sure that he saves a large enough piece to be analyzed.

Charcoal, of course, has a high carbon content. A piece of charcoal weighing about 10 grams is desirable.

Bone is low in carbon, and to be safe the laboratory should be sent two pieces, each weighing between 150 and 250 grams.

Wood is very good material, and a piece weighing 40 grams is usually adequate.

Peat is also quite good, and 30 grams of it should be enough.

Shells should weigh at least 100 grams.

A comparatively large amount of skin or parchment from animals is required for suitable dating. The laboratory one intends to send it to should be asked how much they prefer to receive.

When a carbon date is given, it is usually followed with the letters *B.P.* This stands for "Before Present," "Present" being the year 1950. Thus, 1250 B.P. means 1,250 years prior to A.D. 1950.

Another important method of absolute dating is *dendrochronology*, or tree-ring dating. This method is based on the fact that a tree accounts for its annual growth by producing an internal ring. The width of each ring depends on the amount of rain each year: the wider the ring the more rain. Scientists have catalogues, or *master charts*, of climatic activity going back hundreds of years, and these charts can be compared with the chart of a particular tree to determine its age. The age of the tree is determined from the year it died. Dendrochronology is at this time in use principally in the southwestern United States. Humid areas like the East Coast are not conducive to wood preservation, hence there is little wood there of sufficient antiquity. Master charts have not been developed for most parts of the country for this reason, and all tree-ring dating must be based on scientific master charts. When trees are cut and beams from them are used in housing, for example, the tree rings are retained. The researcher, by obtaining a piece of the beam, can determine when the tree was cut, and from this the dating of the structure is deduced. The only problem with this method is that the wood from a tree may not have been used—though it may have been preserved—for any number of years after the tree was felled. In addition, beams are sometimes procured from existing older structures to use in the building of newer ones. To date a tree or beam, a piece should be cut measuring about three inches thick. If the sample from a beam is hard to read, it should be waxed in order to bring out the details of the rings. In those areas of the country where this method is in use, any university or museum has copies of the appropriate master charts.

Archaeologists are also interested in the vegetation of an area for dating purposes, and the method used for this is known as *pollen analysis*. Plants and trees that flower produce, in various quantities, amounts of pollen. When the pollen accumulates on wet features like ponds, swamps, lakes, or bogs, they are in effect preserved, and this preservation allows the researcher to determine a continuous record of the plant life in an area. Those species which produce an abundance of pollen include hazel, birch, alder, and pine; those producing limited quantities are willow, oak, elm, lime, and beech. Pollens that do not survive well include poplar, ash, and juniper. Pollen analysis is a difficult method requiring a botanist specializing in paleobotany. Various species must be recognized in the field so that a proper collection of grains can be undertaken.

A particularly interesting method of absolute dating used at appropriate Colonial archaeological sites is *pipe stem* dating. This system is based on the fact that pipes of white clay, manufactured in England and traded to America, can be dated according to the width of their bore and stem. The older the pipe, the larger the bore diameter of the stem. The measuring of the diameter must be very precise to be meaningful and is usually given in sixty-fourths of an inch. A diameter measuring 9/64, for example, was manufactured around 1600; 6/64 around 1700; and 4/64 around 1800. This system allows the archaeologist to date Colonial structures to within approximately thirty years, or at least to number the years since the pipe was manufactured.

A final popular dating system is *spectrography*, for dating metallic objects. The materials from which a metal object was made can be exposed by burning a piece of it (and thus destroying it) in order to analyze its composition. This method, also known as spectroanalysis, reveals a pattern of lines by means of which an expert can deduce not only what materials were used but where they came from.

All these methods of dating should be conducted only by experts. The amateur who has acquired artifacts and objects through excavation should first seek advice from an archaeologist on what items are suitable for dating before sending them off to a museum or company.

CHAPTER 24

Analyzing the Excavation

The project that began with a study of topographical maps and ended with the scientific dating of artifacts is complete. Almost. It is now time to analyze what has occurred. This should be done together by all who were involved in the project, and should be recorded by the director of the excavation.

What was the purpose of the project? Based on a study of existing research, it is assumed that the excavation was undertaken to solve a problem or to answer—at least in part—a properly posed question. Perhaps there was reason to believe that the site subsequently excavated would offer evidence of Palaeoindian occupation or of early Colonial settlers.

Was the excavation done well? Can all involved conclude that it was conducted in a professional manner? Although the team members may have had a particular purpose in mind when the project was being organized, this should not have precluded the possibility that their premise was completely off base; that the site they dug was of a different type entirely. Too many archaeologists begin an excavation in order to find evidence to support their own theories and end up ignoring *all other* kinds of evidence. If one is hoping to find the remains of early Colonial occupation at a site that turns out to have been used by an Archaic culture, he should immediately react to the testimony of the spade by considering the importance of the evidence at hand. A site occupied by an Archaic culture is a bit more important than one used by early Colonial settlers. If it is concluded by even one member of the team that the excavation was not conducted properly in its entirety, it's already too late to do anything about it: you can't go back and try again. All you can do is carefully analyze all the field reports in the hope of determining what went wrong where, and thus perhaps recreate the situation and offer comments in the final excavation report to explain and correct any errors.

What was accomplished? Assuming the excavation was performed in a correct manner, something is always accomplished. Even if the original premise was disproved, at least you know the site *is not* Indian or Colonial or whatever. The degree to which a site is important depends on conclusions from the excavation. Many sites are excavated today which can be properly deemed unimportant. Nevertheless, this information will at least inform others about similar sites in the area which may also be left undisturbed in favor of potentially more important sites.

What can be concluded? The information obtained from the excavation should be compared with the results of other excavations and with the general theories about the culture and history of a region. The conclusions may or may not confirm existing theories. Analyzing the excavation can take weeks, months, or even years, depending on one's background and ability to compare the research of others. Also, many people can offer only a few hours each week to this kind of work, and it may drag on, therefore, for many months.

The final excavation report is meant to serve as a complete record of the entire excavation, and may or may not include subsequent research in conclusions. A number of copies should be made of this final report for distribution. First, each member of the project should have one, and a number of extra copies should be kept in a safe place. Second, the archaeological community in one's local area and state should be informed. A copy should be sent to the amateur archaeological societies, the anthropology departments of universities, archaeological museums, research institutions, and even to individual archaeologists who are known to be interested in particular kinds of sites. Depending on how important the site turned out to be, copies may also be sent to national organizations like the Smithsonian Institution, the American Anthropological Association, and the Society for American Archaeology. The point is, don't keep the project a secret! The final excavation report may contain something that you don't consider very important, but a professional or amateur archaeologist may have been studying this very thing for years, and your report may provide the answer to an important question or supply evidence to support a particular theory.

If the amateurs involved with the excavation are associated with an archaeological society, the society may want to send copies of the report to all its members as well as to other societies for distribution to their members. In the case of a particularly lengthy report, the director of the excavation or the editor of the society's journal or newsletter may be asked to abridge it.

The next thing to consider is whether the report should be formally published in an archaeological or popular magazine. There are three general types of publications which may decide to publish such a report. The scientific publications, like *Science* or *American Antiquity*, are almost exclusively reserved for professionals. If an excavation were of immense importance in the information it produced, it would probably still be necessary for a professional archaeologist to publish the report. Scientific publications are jealously guarded, and amateurs are all but ignored. There are, however, archaeological publications, such as *The Amateur Archaeologist* and *Popular Archaeology*, which are more receptive to the work of amateurs. Make no mistake about it, though, these publications are often edited by professionals and have high standards. One must have something very important to say to both the amateur and professional archaeological communities in order to be published in these magazines, as they are read by both segments. Finally, there are a number of general publications, from *National Geographic* to *Argosy*, which carry articles about excavation work. Each of these should be contacted individually with a short explanation of the project.

If the excavation was conducted on private land, it is considered appropriate to give a copy of the final report to the landowner, with a note of appreciation contained in the report. The landowner should also be consulted before you attempt to publish your report, for there is a possibility—particularly if the site turned out to be an important one— that the word will get out and cause curiosity seekers to begin trampling all over the site and the owner's property.

In conclusion, if the project was conducted from beginning to end in a professional manner, you can take satisfaction in the fact that you have contributed to a better understanding of man's development through time.

Appendixes

Appendixes

APPENDIX I

Glossary of Archaeological Terms

This glossary was put together with the amateur archaeologist in mind. It contains more archaeological terms than are actually used in the preceding pages. Many of the terms are general and used by archaeologists everywhere; others, however, may be important only to those involved in archaeological research. Beginning or amateur archaeologists should make a point of familiarizing themselves with these terms.

A

acculturation: the adoption of a trait by one society from another.

A.D.: used as a prefix to a date, it denotes the number of years since the beginning of the Christian calendar (literally *Anno Domini*, 'In the year of our Lord').

adobe: a house or temple built out of sun-dried mudbrick.

adze: a cutting tool of stone or metal, similar to an axe.

aerial (air) photography: photography from an airplane, based on the principle that a high viewpoint gives a clearer distinction between details or features on the ground.

alloy: a mixture of metals having properties superior to those of the individual ingredients.

Altithermal: a warm climatic period in the western United States approximately five to six thousand years ago; also referred to as the climatic optimum, thermal maximum, and long drought period.

amber: fossilized pine resin, popular in Bronze Age Europe.

amphora: a large plump storage jar with a narrow mouth and two handles.

Anathermal: a cool climate period in the United States approximately 8,000 years ago.

archaeoastronomy: the study of mathematical correlations between archaeological features and the movements of celestial bodies; also known as *astroarchaeology*.

archaeology: the study of man's past based on his material remains; a technique of studying man's past through the excavation.

Archaic Period: an early stage in the development of civilization; specifically, a cultural stage in the Americas before the introduction of agriculture and pottery.

archaistic: imitating an older style or form.

ard: a plow or tool for cultivating earth.

arrowhead: a small object of stone, bone, or metal used for penetrating; there are numerous varieties.

arsenic: a metal found with copper in some ore deposits.

articulated: in physical anthropology, the term indicates that the bones of a mammal have all stayed in their original position since the mammal died.

artifact: any object manufactured or shaped by the hand of man.

aryballus: a large pottery jar of the Inca.

askos: an asymmetric vessel with a single handle.

aspect: one of the components that make up traits of a culture.

assemblage: different kinds of objects found in association with one another.

association: two or more objects deposited or built at the same time approximately.

auger: an archaeologist's tool used for digging a very small hole.

awl: the point of a sharp object used for piercing holes.

Aztec: the last Indian cultural group to enter Mexico after the demise of the Toltec subculture.

B

balk: a strip or wall of earth left standing between trenches; also spelled baulk.

barbotine: the practice of decorating pots with certain kinds of substances.

barrow: a burial mound.

basal grinding: the grounding of projectile points, common in Palaeoindian culture.

basketry: the practice of weaving containers from fibres, twigs, or leaves; it was known in Mexico before 7000 B.C. and in Oregon before 8000 B.C.

batter: the slope of a structure built specifically to increase the stability of a wall; usually subterranean.

B.C.: used as a suffix to a date to denote the number of years before the Christian calendar; 'Before Christ.'

berm: the area between the center of a mound and the ditch surrounding the mound at its base.

blade: a sharp-edged tool; a piece of stone removed from a larger piece.

bosing: an unsophisticated though occasionally effective way of searching for earthworks, by striking the topsoil with a wooden beam hoping to hear a dull thud caused by the presence of a ditch or bank.

breccia: a series of small rocks held together by natural adhesives, like sap.

bronze: an alloy of copper and tin.

Bronze Age: the second period in the Three Age System, before the use of iron; bronze was utilized throughout the world at different points in prehistory and history.

burin: a pointed tool of chipped flint or stone used to engrave other tools and utensils.

burnish: the polishing of the surface of an artifact both to improve its appearance and, as with clay, to compact it.

C

cairn: a stone structure covering a burial; in America, a structure of rounded stones.

capstone: a stone slab placed horizontally over a series of other stones, as a roof.

Carbon-14 dating: the process of measuring the amount of carbon-14 in an organism after it has died, thereby determining the number of years since the organism ceased taking in the isotope; also called radiocarbon dating.

carnelian: a red semiprecious stone used for decoration by the Indus and other cultures; also spelled *cornelian*.

celt: the name applied to an axe, adze, or hoe made of stone or bronze.

cephalic index: the measurement of the skull, an important anthropological criterion.

chalcedony: a hard stone, like agate and carnelian, used in decoration, occasionally replacing flint.

channeled: decorated by incisions or grooves.

chert: a flint of poor quality.

chopper: a large tool with a single cutting edge.

chronology: the order in which events occurred.

cinerary urn: a cremation urn.

Clovis point: a Palaeoindian stone projectile point found in most parts of North America, in use between eight and thirteen thousand years ago.

Cochise: an American Indian tribal group within the Desert Culture.

Codex: religious documents painted on deerskin or bark paper in Mexico before the Spanish conquest.

contour fort: a fort on a hill which is completely enclosed by a ditch or bank.

copper: a pure metal, like gold, that requires no smelting.

Copper Age: in a strict sense, the period when copper was the principal metal used by man, between the Neolithic and Bronze ages.

coprolite: fossilized dung, of interest to American archaeologists in order to determine early diets.

corded ware: pottery decorated by winding cords around it.

core: the piece of stone from which other pieces, or flakes, have been removed.

crannog: an artificial island made of various materials, like stones, logs, and peat.

cross-dating: the relative dating of two cultural groups based on the discovery of links or similarities in artifacts between them.

cultivation: the raising of plants by man for his use.

culture: a group of people whose total activities define what they represent and are transmitted to others in the group by social—as opposed to genetic —means.

cyclopean masonry: a type of architecture that calls for large, close-fitting, irregularly shaped stones.

D

daub: clay smeared over a surface to cover it completely.

delta: the buildup of silt at the mouth of a river.

demography: an estimation of the population of a region.

dendrochronology: a method of absolute dating based on the number and condition of tree rings.

diffusion: the spread of cultural traits.

distribution: on a topographical map, the comparative location of archaeological features.

dog: the first animal domesticated by man.

dolmen: generally the term applied to certain megalithic (stone) structures based on their architecture and design.

Dorset: a prehistoric Eskimo culture that settled in the eastern Canadian Arctic and Greenland around 800 B.C.

dun: a structure that serves as a fort as well as a house.

E

effigy mound: a low but very long burial mound constructed by a group of the Woodland culture in the Mississippi Valley. A number of them have been found in the shape of animals and birds, built around A.D. 700, perhaps sooner.

einkorn: a type of wheat used in primitive times.

electrum: a decorative alloy of gold and silver.

El Jobo: a series of forty-five preagricultural hunting sites in northwest Venezuela.

emmer: a type of wheat used in primitive times, similar to einkorn.

Eneolithic: referring to the Copper Age.

eolian: referring to layers of sand or silt which have been deposited over a number of years by wind action.

epi-Paleolithic cultures: those Paleolithic cultures that survived longer than most.

erosion: the wearing away of soil or rock by water action; weathering.

Eskimo: the cultural group of the Arctic, having developed and remained there for well over 2,000 years; in certain cultural traits they resemble the Alaskan Eskimos from Siberian subcultures.

eustasy: an alteration in the sea level caused by the melting of ice, on a world-wide scale.

excavation: the archaeological technique of obtaining material remains of people based on sound principles.

F

fabricator: a tool used to make other tools, usually of stone.

fibula: a small ornament of various designs, but usually shaped like a modern safety pin.

field archaeology: referring to archaeology work in the field, as in survey work or excavating.

flake: a piece of stone removed from a large piece, or core.

flint: a hard stone, chemically similar to quartz stone, found in chalk or limestone and easy to fashion.

flute: the groove or channel running up the center of a projectile point made of stone. The length of the flute helps determine the culture that produced the projectile point.

Folsom: the name of a famous site in New Mexico excavated in 1926; also the name of a projectile point found mainly along the Rocky Mountains, dated to approximately 11,000 years old.

Formative Period: the developmental stage of man in the Americas before the Classic Period; also known as the Preclassic Period.

G

geochronology: the term applied to all methods of dating that involve the earth's physical changes, like radiocarbon dating and dendrochronology.

geophysics: the discipline that studies the physical properties of the earth; of assistance to archaeology in establishing various dating methods in geochronology.

glaciation: a period during which there was an increase in the amount of ice covering the earth's surface; several glaciations are required to make up an Ice Age.

glass: a material produced artificially by fusing sand with an alkali; first developed about 4,000 years ago in the Near East.

gourd: a plant of the melon family developed and cultivated in both prehistoric America and Europe.

grid layout: division of an archaeological site into squares for easy control and recording during the excavation.

H

hearth: a pit dug and used specifically for firing, usually outlined with stones.

hematite: a deep red iron oxide used by the Indians as decorative paint.

hieroglyphs: originally referring to the Egyptian scripts of 3000 B.C., the term is now used to label inscriptions of symbols.

hillfort: a well-fortified structure located on a hilltop and enclosed by at least one wall of stone and earth.

hoard: any collection of materials.

Hohokam: a cultural unit within the Cochise subculture that first settled around southern Arizona before 100 B.C.

Holocene: the period from about 8300 B.C. to the present, or from the end of the Pleistocene Ice Age to the present.

Homo: the genus of the human species that includes modern man, Neanderthal Man, and *Homo erectus*.

Homo erectus: an extinct form of *Homo sapiens* who lived about half a million years ago, just before Neanderthal Man.

Homo habilis: a very early form of man in the line of descent leading to *Homo erectus*.

Homo sapiens: modern man, evolving out of Neanderthal Man, a little over 35,000 years ago.

homostadial: in archaeology, those cultures that represent similar levels of technological advance with other cultures, regardless of a difference derived in absolute dating methods.

Hopewell: an agricultural subculture of the Woodland culture settling in Ohio and Illinois around 100 B.C.

horizon: in archaeology, the spread of similar or identical artifacts over a certain region; in anthropology, the spread of certain levels of cultural development; in geology, the layers of natural features in a region.

huaca: a term referring to any number or kinds of ancient mounds, ruins, or tombs in Latin America; also spelled *guaca*, the term denotes sanctity.

Huaca Prieta: the first preceramic village excavated and dated in north Peru (along the desert coast), established to be nearly 5,000 years old.

hypogeum: an underground chamber; in European archaeology, an underground vault used for burial.

I

ideogram: any single written symbol that conveys the meaning of a whole word.

in situ: the archaeological term for an object that was "in place"—in its original position—when first located, as during an excavation.

intaglio: a design, or seal, cut into hard stone or metal.

Integration Period: the term employed by palaeoanthropologists to denote the last stage of prehistory in Ecuador, from about A.D. 500 to the emergence of the Inca influence.

interglacial: a warm period between two glaciations during which the ice diminished, allowing for some growth of vegetation.

interstadial: similar to an interglacial period, although too cold or too short to allow for growth of vegetation.

Ipiutak: the largest Eskimo village, in Alaska, ever discovered, built and utilized prior to A.D. 200.

Iron Age: the period during which iron was utilized by early man; in Europe, the Iron Age began around 1100 B.C.; in America, iron was introduced by the arrival of Europeans; in Africa, it began before the earlier metal ages; in Asia, iron was introduced during the historic era. The Iron Age, as an age, is today considered very arbitrary, anomalous, and general.

isostasy: the raising of a land surface based solely on the action of the ocean.

Izapa: a ceremonial site in Chiapas, Mexico, built about 3,500 years ago, between the Olmec and Mayan influences.

J

Java man: a now obsolete name for *Homo erectus*.

K

Kaminaljuyu: a large and important archaeological site near Guatemala City that originally contained over 200 mounds. The history of the site goes back nearly 4,000 years.

kitchen midden: any pile of domestic garbage or food refuse.

kiva: an underground chamber found in Pueblo villages, used for various ceremonies.

L

lancehead: a handcrafted projectile point which is larger than an arrowhead but smaller than a spearhead.

La Venta: the most important Olmec ceremonial center, located in Tabasco, Mexico, and built around 1000 B.C.

levigation: a process of producing fine clay for high-quality pottery by water purification.

linear earthwork: an earthwork, dike, ditch, or bank that continues in a straight line.

longevity: the expectation of the life span of a person, culture, etc.

lynchet: the pile of earth at the bottom of a hill, field, or mound which has accumulated by the soil on the incline falling because of gravity.

M

mace: a small weapon, usually of stone, crafted to fit fairly snuggly in the hand, for pounding.

Machu Picchu: an Inca town discovered in 1911, ingeniously situated on a hillcrest in the Andes overlooking a drop of 1,500 feet on either side.

magnetometer: a mechanical device that measures the intensity of the earth's magnetic field.

maize: a staple food originating in Mexico about 9,000 years ago; corn.

mano: the name of the stone tool used for grinding maize.

Mazapan ware: pottery decorated by straight or wavy parallel lines made by the Toltecs of Mexico.

megalithic: a structure built of large stones; anything to do with cultures that built large structures of stone.

menhir: a standing stone; a large vertical standing stone, usually by itself.

metate: the slab of stone on which grain was ground.

microburin: a small piece of stone snapped off of a microlith.

microlith: a small stone less than an inch in length.

midden: any pile or heap of refuse or junk left by man.

Middle Mississippi culture: part of the Woodland culture in the central Mississippi valley.

milpa: a maize field.

Mixtec: a subcultural group of skilled craftsmen living in southern Mexico from about A.D. 700.

Monte Alban: a major ceremonial site of the Zapotec people in Oaxaca, Mexico, built around 600 B.C.

mudbrick: unbaked brick.

N

Nahuatl: the language spoken by the Aztecs, and others.

Neanderthal man: an extinct ancestor of *Homo sapiens.*

negative painting: a method of pottery decoration used in many parts of the Americas. The technique is also known as resist dyeing, using wax as an agent on a vessel or on cloth.

neo: a prefix literally meaning "new," but used to describe the reemergence of a culture following a decline.

O

obsidian: a natural glass.

Old Bering Sea Culture: an Eskimo subculture that settled in northern Alaska and northeast Siberia between 1,500 and 2,000 years ago.

Old Copper Culture: a subcultural group of hunters and fishermen that settled along the Great Lakes region of Canada and the United States approximately 5,000 years ago.

Old Cordilleran Culture: an obsolete name for hunters who settled in Oregon and Washington around 10,000 years ago.

Olmec: a subcultural group that settled along the Mexican Gulf Coast during the Formative Stage.

Onion Portage: a very important site in northwest Alaska containing one of the continent's longest stratigraphies; occupied from 13,000 to 6000 B.C. by a number of Eskimo-Siberian-Indian subcultures.

orthostat: a vertical stone slab used to form a wall on megalithic structures.

P

palaeo or *paleo*: a prefix meaning "old."

paleobotany: the study of the remains of ancient or extinct plants.

paleontology: the study of animal fossil remains.

paleopathology: the study of man's ills, diseases, etc., by examination of human remains; paleophysioanthropology.

paleoserology: the study of ancient man by blood groups.

Peking man: an obsolete name for *Homo erectus.*

petroglyph: an inscription or painting on rock.

petrological identification: a study of the strains of stone in order to determine their original location in a region.

phosphate analysis: the examination of phosphates from decayed organic matter.

pithos: a large pottery jar used specifically as a storage container.

polypod bowl: in Middle American archaeology, a bowl that stands on two, three, or four small legs.

population estimation: the determination by archaeologists of the suspected population of an ancient culture.

prehistory: before history; that period in a given region before the onset of written records.

primary silt: the initial silt from the top and sides of a ditch that falls naturally to the bottom.

Q

quadrant method: a procedure for excavating a mound and other features by laying out trenches.

R

rabotage: the process of carefully scraping a horizontal surface.

raised beach: an ancient or previous shoreline from a period when the land level was lower than it is today in relation to the sea level.

revetment: a wall built to hold the sides of a bank in place.

rocker pattern: a pottery decoration design employed by various pre-Classic cultures in North and South America.

runes: inscriptions in stone by pre-Columbian travelers to America.

S

Sandia Cave: an archaeological site in New Mexico in which have been found projectile points dating from 12,000 to 20,000 B.C. The age of these points is still debatable.

San Lorenzo Tenochtitlan: a series of archaeological sites in Veracruz, Mexico, revealing information on Olmec origins; built around 1500 B.C.

Santa Isabel Iztapan: two sites in Mexico revealing human occupation around 9,000 years ago.

section: in excavation, exposing a deposit vertically to reveal the stratigraphy.

sherd: a broken piece of pottery; also *shard*.

site: in archaeology, wherever an archaeologist decides to excavate after determining occupation or use by man; any specific portion of an area where excavation is undertaken.

slash and burn: the phrase used to describe a primitive but widespread form of agriculture, where the forest was cleared by chopping and burning small trees.

slip: a thin, final layer of clay spread over pottery.

sondage: a single deep trench at a site dug solely to observe the stratigraphy; an initial trench dug at a site to determine if excavation is advisable.

stadial: a period during glaciation when the temperature was at its lowest.

stele: a stone slab or column; also *stela*.

strip method: a method of excavating whereby a large horizontal area is dug instead of a deep vertical one.

T

Tehuacan Valley: an archaeological site in Puebla, Mexico, revealing human occupation from about 9000 B.C.

tell: a mound.

Teotihuacan: an important site north of Mexico City inhabited a few centuries B.C.

Tepexpan: a site in the valley of Mexico where a human skeleton was dated to around 9000 B.C. in 1949.

Thule: a subculture of the Eskimos who settled throughout the northern Arctic from Siberia to Greenland around A.D. 500.

Tikal: an important site of the Maya people in Preten, Guatemala, dating to 600 B.C.

Tlapacoya: a site in central Mexico containing human remains dated to 21,000 B.C.

Tlatilco: a site right next to Mexico City dated to 1000 B.C. or older.

tradition: a sequence of styles or traits which develop continuously, thus forming an easily accounted-for series of advancements from one culture to another.

trait: any element of human culture.

trilithon: a stone structure consisting of two standing stones with a third placed across the top of them, forming the shape of an upside-down U.

Tule Springs: a site in Nevada near Las Vegas containing traces of human occupation going back 9,000 years.

tumbaga: an alloy of gold and copper common in Central America during the first millennium A.D.

tumulus: a mound built over a burial.

type fossil: an artifact employed over a large geographic area but for a limited length of time.

typology: the study of classifying objects by shape, type, etc.

U

urn: any pottery vessel without handles used for storage (the term may be more loosely employed).

urnfields: a group of cremation graves in which the ashes of the dead were placed in similar or identical vessels.

V

Valders Advance: the final advance of the ice during the Wisconsin glaciation in North America, beginning about 12,000 years ago.

Valdivia: a cultural group settling along the central coast of Ecuador around 3000 B.C.

Ventana Cave: a site in Arizona containing remains of many extinct animal species.

vitrified fort: any fort where the external walls of stone have become smooth by the heat of the sun.

W

wheel: a simple but important device first used in Mexico in the Americas, but only on children's toys; its full use was not employed until after Columbus.

Wisconsin glaciation: the final glaciation in North America, beginning some 70,000 years ago.

X

X-ray fluorescence: a procedure for analyzing chemical elements in various materials, replaced recently by spectrographic analysis.

Z

Zapotec: a pre-Christian tribe in the valley of Oaxaca, Mexico, whose origins cannot be determined.

APPENDIX II

Magazines

Following is a list of magazines which the amateur archaeologist will find useful and interesting. Those marked with an asterisk (*) are highly recommended.

Amateur Archaeologist (Box 8012, Wichita, Kansas 67208). This is by far the best publication on archaeology for amateurs. Edited by Dan Vap, each issue contains reports on the latest scientific research, articles on important activities within the archaeological community, information on organizations, interviews with outstanding amateur archaeologists, updates on excavation work at various sites, and book reviews. Material is written by both amateurs and professionals; correspondents are located around the country to keep track of developments. With an open-minded and well-constructed editorial format, this magazine is produced by experienced people with the amateur in mind. Recent articles include "The Computer and Archaeology," "A Pictorial Essay of a First Dig," "Working in the Archaeology Lab," "Basic Geology for the Amateur Archaeologist," and "What China Has to Offer."

American Anthropologist (1703 New Hampshire Avenue, N.W., Washington, D.C. 20009). Written mostly by and for professionals, this magazine is full of important theoretical and practical information on anthropology today. The beginning amateur archaeologist should gain some experience, however, before subscribing. Although it is not available at newsstands, most public and all university libraries subscribe. Published by the American Anthropological Association.

American Antiquity (1703 New Hampshire Avenue, N.W., Washington, D.C. 20009). A very well-written publication for professionals and amateurs. Each issue contains a section on current research and lists the various salvage projects scheduled around the country. The publication deals only with New World archaeology, however, and consequently does not include a lot of important information on research and activities which do not fall into this category. Published by the Society for American Archaeology.

Archaeology (260 West Broadway, New York, New York 10013). A very good magazine, well written and well produced. Articles are informative without being too technical for the amateur, and the editors are interested in both amateur and professional activities. Although it is a conservative publication, the material relates to archaeological developments all over the world. Published by the Archaeological Institute of America.

Man in the Northeast (c/o Franklin Pierce College, Rindge, New Hampshire 03461). A good publication for the experienced or advanced amateur who is particularly interested and involved with Indian and historical archaeology in the northeastern United States. All of the material is written by professionals according to the standards of other professional publications. Occasional articles and reports deal with the amateur archaeological community, but the editor hesitates to give credit to amateurs. The editorial scope is very limited and conservative.

National Geographic (17th and M Streets N.W., Washington, D.C. 20036). All of the material published in this magazine is very carefully edited in order to offer general information. Each issue usually contains an article of interest to archaeologists and historians, though nothing technical. The photography is outstanding. Published by the National Geographic Society.

Natural History (Museum of Natural History, Central Park West at 79th Street, New York, New York 10024). An outstanding magazine for professional historians, with articles of interest to amateur and professional archaeologists. The magazine is very conservative, however, and rarely publishes controversial material. Nevertheless, it is highly articulate and represents very thorough research. Those amateur archaeologists particularly interested in natural history will find this magazine to be one of the best of its kind. Published by the American Museum of Natural History.

NEARA Journal (4 Smith Street, Milford, New Hampshire 03055). This is an organizational publication dealing with all aspects of American and European archaeology. It is the only publication in the United States that specializes, however, in pre-Columbian archaeology. Much of the material deals with megalithic studies; material is written by both professionals and amateurs, and edited by Andrew Rothovius. Book reviews. A highly regarded, open-minded journal for amateurs and professionals. Published by the New England Antiquities Research Association.

Science (1515 Massachusetts Ave., N.W., Washington, D.C. 20005). An immensely prestigious publication for professional scientists in all fields. Occasionally an issue will contain an article or report on American anthropology, archaeology, or ethnology. Recent issues have dealt with public archaeology, the crisis in archaeology today, site destruction, etc. Recommended only for the advanced amateur archaeologist and/or individuals with formal backgrounds in a field of science. Not available at newsstands. Published by the American Association for the Advancement of Science.

Science Digest (224 West 57th Street, New York, New York 10019). This is the best magazine on science today for the layman. The editors deal with all fields of science and attempt to include either an article or report on some aspect of anthropology or archaeology in each issue. All material is well written, nontechnical, and carefully edited; contributors are both professionals and amateurs. Contributing editor Barbara Ford is their best writer on archaeology. Book reviews. The "Short Takes" section often includes current research notes in anthropology.

Science News (1719 N Street N.W., Washington, D.C. 20036). As the name implies, this is strictly a news publication on science. The latest research in all fields of science, from anthropology to zoology, is reported in condensed form. As a weekly, however, this magazine is able to release information long before other science magazines. All material is staff-written. Recommended only for those amateurs who are interested in new developments in all fields of science.

Scientific American (415 Madison Avenue, New York, New York 10017). An excellent and popular magazine. Few articles, however, deal with archaeology. Perhaps four issues in a year will contain an article on anthropology or archaeology, all of which are written by professionals. The standards of this magazine are very high, and the amateur should look through an issue whenever possible for information on new research. All fields and aspects of archaeology are included in the scope of the material published.

Smithsonian (900 Jefferson Drive, Washington, D.C. 20560). An excellent publication containing occasional articles relating to anthropology and history. Very little on archaeology *per se*. The amateur should look through an issue whenever the opportunity presents itself. Published by the Smithsonian Institution.

There are also a number of popular magazines which occasionally carry articles on archaeology, though they are mainly meant to entertain rather than to educate.

APPENDIX III
Field Offices of the Forest Service

The following is a list of Forest Service Regional Offices and addresses, followed by National Forests and their headquarters locations, Research unit, and State and Private Forestry area headquarters.

NORTHERN REGION
Federal Building
Missoula, Montana 59801

IDAHO

Clearwater	Orofino
Nezperce	Grangeville
Panhandle National Forests	Coeur d'Alene

MONTANA

Beaverhead	Dillon
Bitterroot	Hamilton
Custer	Billings
Deerlodge	Butte
Flathead	Kalispell
Gallatin	Bozeman
Helena	Helena
Kootenai	Libby
Lewis and Clark	Great Falls
Lolo	Missoula

ROCKY MOUNTAIN REGION
11177 West 8th Avenue, Box 25127
Lakewood, Colorado 80225

COLORADO

Arapaho-Roosevelt	Ft. Collins
Grand Mesa-Uncompahgre*	Delta
Gunnison	Delta
Pike-San Isabel	Pueblo
Rio Grande	Monte Vista
Routt	Steamboat Springs
San Juan	Durango
White River	Glenwood Springs

NEBRASKA

Nebraska   Chadron

SOUTH DAKOTA

Black-Hills   Custer

WYOMING

Bighorn	Sheridan
Medicine Bow	Laramie
Shoshone	Cody

SOUTHWESTERN REGION
517 Gold Avenue, South West,
Albuquerque, New Mexico 87102

ARIZONA

Apache-Sitgreaves	Springerville
Coconino	Flagstaff
Coronado	Tucson
Kaibab	Williams
Prescott	Prescott
Tonto	Phoenix

NEW MEXICO

Carson	Taos
Cibola	Albuquerque
Gila	Silver City
Lincoln	Alamogordo
Santa Fe	Santa Fe

* Two separately proclaimed National Forests under one supervisor.

APPENDIX III

INTERMOUNTAIN REGION
324 25th Street
Ogden, Utah 84401

IDAHO

Boise	Boise
Caribou	Pocatello
Challis	Challis
Payette	McCall
Salmon	Salmon
Sawtooth	Twin Falls
Targhee	St. Anthony

NEVADA

Humboldt	Elko
Toiyabe	Reno

UTAH

Ashley	Vernal
Dixie	Cedar City
Fishlake	Richfield
Manti-La Sal	Price
Uinta	Provo
Wasatch	Salt Lake City

WYOMING

Bridger-Teton	Jackson

CALIFORNIA REGION
630 Sansome Street
San Francisco, California 94111

CALIFORNIA

Angles	Pasadena
Cleveland	San Diego
Eldorado	Placerville
Inyo	Bishop
Klamath	Yreka
Lassen	Susanville
Los Padres	Goleta
Mendocino	Willows
Modoc	Alturas
Plumas	Quincy
San Bernardino	San Bernardino
Sequoia	Porterville

Shasta-Trinity*	Redding
Sierra	Fresno
Six Rivers	Eureka
Stanislaus	Sonora
Tahoe	Nevada City

PACIFIC NORTHWEST REGION
319 South West Pine Street, P.O. Box 3623
Portland, Oregon 97208

OREGON

Deschutes	Bend
Freemont	Lakeview
Malheur	John Day
Mt. Hood	Portland
Ochoco	Prineville
Rogue River	Medford
Siskiyou	Grants Pass
Siuslaw	Corvallis
Umatilla	Pendleton
Umpqua	Roseburg
Wallowa-Whitman*	Baker
Willamette	Eugene
Winema	Klamath Falls

WASHINGTON

Colville	Colville
Gifford Pinchot	Vancouver
Mt. Baker-Snoqualime	Seattle
Okanogan	Okanogan
Olympic	Olympia
Wenatchee	Wenatchee

EASTERN REGION
633 West Wisconsin Avenue
Milwaukee, Wisconsin 53203

ILLINOIS

Shawnee   Harrisburg

INDIANA

Wayne-Hoosier   Bedford

* Two separately proclaimed National Forests under one supervisor.

MICHIGAN

Hiawatha	Escanaba
Huron-Manistee	Cadillac
Ottawa	Ironwood

MINNESOTA

Chippewa	Cass Lake
Superior	Duluth

MISSOURI

National Forests in Missouri
Clark-Mark Twain
Rolla, Missouri 65401

NEW HAMPSHIRE

White Mountain   Laconia

PENNSYLVANIA

Allegheny   Warren

VERMONT

Green Mountain   Rutland

WEST VIRGINIA

Monongahela   Elkins

WISCONSIN

Chequamegon	Park Falls
Nicolet	Rhinelander

SOUTHERN REGION
1720 Peachtree Road
North West Atlanta, Georgia 30309

ALABAMA

National Forests in Alabama
William B. Bankhead   Talladega
Coneuch   Tuskegee
1765 Highland Avenue, P.O. Box 40
Montgomery, Alabama 36101

ARKANSAS

Ouachita	Hot Springs
Ozark	Russellville
St. Francis	Russellville

FLORIDA

National Forests in Florida
Apalachicola   Osceola
Ocala
214 South Bronough Street
P.O. Box 1050
Tallahassee, Florida 32302

GEORGIA

Chattahooche   Oconee
322 Oak Street, North West
Gainesville, Georgia 30501

KENTUCKY

Daniel Boone   Winchester

LOUISIANA

Kisatchie   Pineville

MISSISSIPPI

National Forests in Mississippi
Bienville   Holly Springs
Delta   Homochitto
DeSoto   Tombigbee
350 Milner Building, P.O. Box 1291
Jackson, Mississippi 39205

NORTH CAROLINA

National Forests in North Carolina
Croatan   Pisgah
Nantahala   Uwharrie
B-level Plateau Building,
    50 South French Broad, P.O. Box 2750
Asheville, North Carolina 28802

SOUTH CAROLINA

Francis Marion   Sumter
Room 350, 1801 Assumbly Street
Columbia, South Carolina 29201

TENNESSEE

Cherokee   Cleveland

TEXAS

National Forests in Texas
   Angelina   Sabine
   Davy Crockett   Sam Houston
Federal Building, P.O. Box 969m
   Lufkin, Texas 75901

VIRGINIA

George Washington   Harrisonburg
Jefferson   Roanoke

ALASKA REGION
Federal Office Building, P.O. Box 1628
Juneau, Alaska 99502

ALASKA

Chugach   Anchorage
Tongass-Stikine Area   Petersburg
Tongass-Ketchikan Area Ketchikan
Tongass-Chatham Area   Sitka

RESEARCH HEADQUARTERS

LABORATORY

Forest Products Laboratory, North Walnut Street, P.O. Box 5130
Madison, Wisconsin 53705

INSTITUTES

Institute of Tropical Forestry, P.O. Box 577-AQ,
Rio Piedras, Puerto Rico 00928

Institute of Northern Forestry
Fairbanks, Alaska 99701

FOREST AND RANGE EXPERIMENT STATIONS

Pacific Northwest—809 North East Sixth Avenue,
P.O. Box 3141
Portland, Oregon 97208

Pacific Southwest—1960 Addison Street
Berkeley, California 94701

Intermountain—507 25th Street
Ogden, Utah 84401

Rocky Mountain—240 West Prospect Street
Fort Collins, Colorado 80521

North Central—Folwell Avenue
St. Paul, Minnesota 55101

Northeastern—6816 Market Street
Upper Darby, Pennsylvania 19082

Southern—Headquarter T-10210 Federal Building,
701 Loyola Avenue
New Orleans, Louisiana

Southeastern—Post Office Building, P.O. Box 2750
Asheville, North Carolina 28802

APPENDIX IV

Federal Antiquities Acts

ANTIQUITIES ACT OF 1906

AN ACT For the Preservation of American Antiquities, Approved June 8, 1906 (Public Law 59-209; 34 STAT. 225; 16 USC 431–433)

Be it enacted by the Senate and House of Representatives of the United States of America in Congress assembled, That any person who shall appropriate, excavate, injure or destroy any historic or prehistoric ruin or monument, or any object of antiquity, situated on lands owned or controlled by the Government of the United States, without the permission of the Secretary of the Department of the Government having jurisdiction over the lands on which said antiquities are situated, shall upon conviction, be fined in a sum of not more than five hundred dollars or be imprisoned for a period of not more than ninety days, or shall suffer both fine and imprisonment, in the discretion of the court.

SECTION 2. That the President of the United States is hereby authorized, in his discretion, to declare by public proclamation historic landmarks, historic and prehistoric structures, and other objects of historic or scientific interest that are situated upon the lands owned or controlled by the Government of the United States to be national monuments, and may reserve as a part thereof parcels of land, the limits of which in all cases shall be confined to the smallest area compatible with the proper care and management of the objects to be protected: *Provided,* That when such objects are situated upon a tract covered by a bona fide unperfected claim or held in private ownership, the tract, or so much thereof as may be necessary for the proper care and management of the object, may be relinquished to the Government, and the Secretary of the Interior is hereby authorized to accept the relinquishment of such tracts in behalf of the Government of the United States.

SECTION 3. That permits for the examination of ruins, the excavation of archaeological sites, and the gathering of objects of antiquity upon the lands under their respective jurisdictions may be granted by the Secretaries of the Interior, Agriculture, and War to institutions which they may deem properly qualified to conduct such examinations, excavation, or gathering, subject to such rules and regulations as they may prescribe: *Provided,* That the examinations, excavations, and gatherings are undertaken for the benefit of reputable museums, universities, colleges, or other recognized scientific or educational institutions, with a view to increasing the knowledge of such objects, and that the gatherings shall be made for permanent preservation in public museums.

SECTION 4. That the Secretaries of the Departments aforesaid shall make and publish from time to time uniform rules and regulations for the purpose of carrying out the provisions of this Act.

Uniform Rules and Regulations Prescribed by the Secretaries of the Interior, Agriculture, and War To Carry Out the Provisions of the "Act for the Preservation of American Antiquities,"

1. Jurisdiction over ruins, archaeological sites, historic, and prehistoric monuments and structures, objects of antiquity, historic landmarks, and other objects of historic or scientific interest, shall be exercised under the act by the respective Departments as follows:

By the Secretary of Agriculture over lands within the exterior limits of forest reserves, by the Secretary of War over lands within the exterior limits of military reservations, by the Secretary of the Interior over all lands owned or controlled by the Government of the United States, provided the Secretaries of War and Agriculture may by agreement cooperate with the Secretary of the Interior in the supervision of such monuments and objects covered by the act of June 8, 1906, as may be located on lands near or adjacent to forest reserves and military reservations, respectively.

2. No permit for the removal of any ancient monument or structure which can be permanently preserved under the control of the United States *in situ*, and remain an object of interest, shall be granted.

3. Permits for the examination of ruins, the excavation of archaeological sites, and the gathering of objects of antiquity will be granted, by the respective Secretaries having jurisdiction, to reputable museums, universities, colleges, or other recognized scientific or educational institutions, or to their duly authorized agents.

4. No exclusive permits shall be granted for a larger area than the applicant can reasonably be expected to explore fully and systematically within the time limit named in the permit.

5. Each application for a permit should be filed with the Secretary having jurisdiction, and must be accompanied by a definite outline of the proposed work indicating the name of the institution making the request, the date proposed for the beginning of the field work, the length of time proposed to be devoted to it, and the person who will have immediate charge of the work. The application must also contain an exact statement of the character of the work, whether examination, excavation, or gathering, and the public museum in which the collections made under the permit are to be permanently preserved. The application must be accompanied by a sketch plan or description of the particular site or area to be examined, excavated, or searched, so definite that it can be located on the map with reasonable accuracy.

6. No permit will be granted for a period of more than three years, but if the work has been diligently prosecuted under the permit, the time may be extended for proper cause upon application.

7. Failure to begin work under a permit within six months after it is granted, or failure to diligently prosecute such work after it has been begun, shall make the permit void without any order or proceeding by the Secretary having jurisdiction.

8. Applications for permits shall be referred to the Smithsonian Institution for recommendation.

9. Every permit shall be in writing and copies shall be transmitted to the Smithsonian Institution and the field officer in charge of the land involved. The permittee will be furnished with a copy of rules and regulations.

10. At the close of each season's field work the permittee shall report in duplicate to the Smithsonian Institution, in such form as its secretary may prescribe, and shall prepare in duplicate a catalogue of the collections and the photographs made during the season, indicating therein such material, if any, as may be available for exchange.

11. Institutions and persons receiving permits for excavation shall, after the completion of the work, restore the lands upon which they have worked to their customary condition, to the satisfaction of the field officer in charge.

12. All permits shall be terminable at the discretion of the Secretary having jurisdiction.

13. The field officer in charge of land owned or controlled by the Government of the United States shall, from time to time, inquire and report as to the existence, on or near such lands, of ruins and archaeological sites, historic or prehistoric ruins or monuments, objects or antiquity, historic landmarks, historic and prehistoric structures, and other objects of historic or scientific interest.

14. The field officer in charge may at all times examine the permit of any person or institution claiming privileges granted in accordance with the act and these rules and regulations, and may fully examine all work done under such permit.

15. All persons duly authorized by the Secretaries of Agriculture, War, and Interior may apprehend or cause to be arrested, as provided in the act of February 6, 1905 (33 Stat. 700), any person or persons who appropriate, excavate, injure, or destroy any historic or prehistoric ruin or monument, or any object of antiquity on lands under the supervision of the Secretaries of Agriculture, War, and Interior, respectively.

16. Any object of antiquity taken, or collection made, on the lands owned or controlled by the United States, without a permit, as prescribed by the act and these rules and regulations, or there taken or made, contrary to the terms of permit, or contrary to the act and these rules and regulations, may be seized whenever found and at any time, by the proper field officer or by any person duly authorized by the Secretary having jurisdiction, and disposed of as the Secretary shall determine, by deposit in the proper national depository or otherwise.

17. Every collection made under the authority of the act and of these rules and regulations shall be preserved in the public museum designated in the permit and shall be accessible to the public. No such collection shall be removed from such public museum without the written authority of the Secretary of the Smithsonian Institution, and then only to another public museum, where it shall be accessible to the public; and when any public museum, which is a depository of any collection made under the provisions of the act and these rules and regulations, shall cease to exist, every such collection in such public museum shall thereupon revert to the national collections and be placed in the proper national depository.

Washington, D.C., *December 8, 1906*

The foregoing rules and regulations are hereby approved in triplicate and, under authority conferred by law on the Secretaries of the Interior, Agriculture, and War, are hereby made and established, to take effect immediately. *E.A. Hitchcock, Secretary of the Interior. James Wilson, Secretary of Agriculture. William H. Taft, Secretary of War.*

HISTORIC SITES ACT OF 1935

AN ACT To Provide for the Preservation of Historic American Sites, Buildings, Objects, and Antiquities of National Significance, and for Other Purposes, Approved August 21, 1935 (Public Law 74-292; 49 STAT. 666; 16 U.S.C. 461–467)

Be it enacted by the Senate and House of Representatives of the United States of America in Congress assembled, That it is a national policy to preserve for public use historic sites, buildings and objects of national significance for the inspiration and benefit of the people of the United States. (16 U.S.C. sec. 461)

SECTION 2. The Secretary of the Interior (hereinafter referred to as the Secretary), through the National Park Service, for the purpose of effectuating the policy expressed in section 1 hereof, shall have the following powers and perform the following duties and functions:

(a) Secure, collate, and preserve drawings, plans, photographs, and other data of historic and archaeologic sites, buildings and objects.

(b) Make a survey of historic and archaeologic sites, buildings, and objects for the purpose of determining which possess exceptional value as commemorating or illustrating the history of the United States.

(c) Make necessary investigations and researches in the United States relating to particular sites, buildings, or objects to obtain and accurate historical and archaeological facts and information concerning the same.

(d) For the purpose of this Act, acquire in the name of the United States by gift, purchase, or otherwise any property, personal or real, or any interest or estate therein, title to any real property to be satisfactory to the Secretary: *Provided,* That no such property which is owned by any religious or educational institution, or which is owned or administered for the benefit of the public shall be so acquired without the consent of the owner: *Provided further,* That no such property shall be acquired or contract or agreement for the acquisition thereof made which will obligate the general fund of the Treasury for the payment of such property, unless or until Congress has appropriated money which is available for that purpose.

(e) Contract and make cooperative agreements with States, municipal subdivisions, corporations, associations, or individuals, with proper bond where deemed advisable, to protect, preserve, maintain, or operate any historic or archaeologic building, site, object, or property used in connection therewith for public use, regardless as to whether the title thereto is in the United States: *Provided,* That no contract or cooperative agreement shall be made or entered into which will obligate the general fund of the Treasury unless or until Congress has appropriated money for such purpose.

(f) Restore, reconstruct, rehabilitate, preserve, and maintain historic or pre-

historic sites, buildings, objects, and properties of national historical or
archaeological significance and where deemed desirable establish and maintain museums in connection therewith.

(g) Erect and maintain tablets to mark or commemorate historic or prehistoric places and events of national historical or archaeological significance.

(h) Operate and manage historic and archaeologic sites, buildings, and
properties acquired under the provisions of this Act together with lands and
subordinate buildings for the benefit of the public, such authority to include
the power to charge reasonable visitation fees and grant concessions, leases,
or permits for the use of land, building space, roads, or trails when necessary
or desirable either to accommodate the public or to facilitate administration:
Provided, That such concessions, leases, or permits, shall be let at competitive
bidding, to the person making the highest and best bid.

(i) When the Secretary determines that it would be administratively bur-
densome to restore, reconstruct, operate, or maintain any particular historic
or archaeologic site, building, or property donated to the United States
through the National Park Service, he may cause the same to be done by
organizing a corporation for that purpose under the laws of the District of
Columbia or any State.

(j) Develop an education program and service for the purpose of making
available to the public facts and information pertaining to American historic
and archaeologic sites, buildings, and properties of national significance.
Reasonable charges may be made for the dissemination of any such facts or
information.

(k) Perform any and all acts, and make such rules and regulations not
inconsistent with this Act as may be necessary and proper to carry out the
provisions thereof. Any person violating any of the rules and regulations
authorized by this Act shall be punished by a fine of not more than $500 and
be adjudged to pay all cost of the proceedings (16 U.S.C. sec 462.)

SECTION 3. A general advisory board to be known as the "Advisory Board on
National Parks, Historic Sites, Buildings, and Monuments" is hereby established, to be composed of not to exceed eleven persons, citizens of the United
States, to include representatives competent in the fields of history, archaeology, architecture, and human geography, who shall be appointed by the
Secretary and serve at his pleasure. The members of such board shall receive
no salary but may be paid expenses incidental to travel engaged in discharging
their duties as members.

It shall be the duty of such board to advise on any matters relating to
national parks and to the administration of this Act submitted to it for consideration by the Secretary. It may also recommend policies to the Secretary
from time to time pertaining to national parks and to the restoration, reconstruction, conservation, and general administration of historic and archaeologic
sites, buildings, and properties. (16 U.S.C. sec. 463)

SECTION 4. The Secretary, in administering this Act, is authorized to cooperate with and may seek and accept the assistance of any Federal, State, or
municipal department or agency, or any educational or scientific institution,
or any patriotic association, or any individual.

(b) When deemed necessary, technical advisory committees may be established to act in an advisory capacity in connection with the restoration or
reconstruction of any historic or prehistoric building or structure.

(c) Such professional and technical assistance may be employed without regard to the civil-service laws, and such service may be established as may be required to accomplish the purposes of this Act and for which money may be appropriated by Congress or made available by gifts for such purpose. (16 U.S.C. sec. 464)

SECTION 5. Nothing in this Act shall be held to deprive any State, or political subdivision thereof, of its civil and criminal jurisdiction in and over lands acquired by the United States under this Act. (16 U.S.C. sec. 465)

SECTION 6. There is authorized to be appropriated for carrying out the purposes of this Act such sums as the Congress may from time to time determine. (16 U.S.C. sec. 466)

SECTION 7. The provisions of this Act shall control if any of them are in conflict with any other Act or Acts relating to the same subject matter. (16 U.S.C. sec. 467)

RESERVOIR SALVAGE ACT OF 1960

AN ACT to Provide for the Preservation of Historical and Archaeological Data (including Relics and Specimens) which Might Otherwise be Lost as the Result of the Construction of a Dam, Approved June 27, 1960 (Public Law 860523; 74 STAT. 220; 16 U.S.C. 469–469c)

Be it enacted by the Senate and House of Representatives of the United States of America in Congress assembled, That it is the purpose of this Act to further the policy set forth in the Act entitled "An Act to provide for the preservation of historic American sites, buildings, objects, and antiquities of national significance, and for other purposes," approved August 21, 1935 (16 U.S.C. 461–467) by specifically providing for the preservation of historical and archaeological data (including relics and specimens) which might otherwise be irreparably lost or destroyed as the result of flooding, the building of access roads, the erection of workmen's communities, the relocation of railroads and highways, and other alterations of the terrain caused by the construction of a dam by an agency of the United States, or by any private person or corporation holding a license issued by any such agency.

SECTION 2

(a) Before any agency of the United States shall undertake the construction of a dam, or issue a license to any private individual or corporation for the construction of a dam, it shall give written notice to the Secretary of the Interior setting forth the site of the proposed dam and the approximate area to be flooded, and otherwise changed if such construction is undertaken; *Provided,* with respect to any floodwater retarding dam which provides less than five thousand acre-feet of detention capacity and with respect to any other type of dam which creates a reservoir of less than forty surface acres the provisions of this section shall apply only when the constructing agency, in his preliminary surveys, finds, or is presented with evidence that historical or archaeological materials exist or may be present in the proposed reservoir area.

(b) Upon receipt of any notice, as provided in subsection (a), the Secretary of the Interior (hereinafter referred to as the "Secretary"), shall cause a survey to be made of the area proposed to be flooded to ascertain whether such area contains historical and archaeological data (including relics and specimens) which should be preserved in the public interest. Any such survey shall be conducted as expeditiously as possible. If as a result of any such survey, the Secretary shall determine (1) that such data exists in such area, (2) that such data has exceptional historical or archaeological significance, and should be collected and preserved in the public interest, and (3) that it is feasible to collect and preserve such data, he shall cause the necessary work to be performed in such area to collect and preserve such data. All such work shall be performed as expeditiously as possible.

(c) The Secretary shall keep the instigating agency notified at all times of the progress of any survey made under this Act, or of any work undertaken as a result of such survey, in order that there will be as little disruption or delay as possible in the carrying out of the functions of such agency.

(d) A survey similar to that provided for by section (b) of this section and the work required to be performed as a result thereof shall so far as practicable also be undertaken in connection with any dam the construction of which has been heretofore authorized by any agency of the United States, or by any such private person or corporation holding a license issued by any such agency.

(e) The Secretary shall consult with any interested Federal and State agencies, educational and scientific organizations, and private institutions and qualified individuals, with a view to determining the ownership of and the most appropriate repository for any relics and specimens recovered as a result of any work performed as provided for in this section.

SECTION 3

In the administration of this Act, the Secretary may—

(1) enter into contracts or make cooperative agreements with any Federal or State agency, any educational or scientific organization, or any institution, corporation, association, or qualified individual; and

(2) procure the temporary or intermittent services of experts or consultants or organizations thereof as provided in Section 15 of the Act of August 2, 1946 (5 U.S.C. 55a); and

(3) accept and utilize funds made available for salvage archaeological purposes by any private person or corporations holding a license issued by an agency of the United States for the construction of a dam or other type of water or power control project.

SECTION 4

There are hereby authorized to be appropriated such sums as may be necessary to carry out the purposes of this Act.

HISTORIC PRESERVATION ACT OF 1966

AN' ACT To Establish a Program for the Preservation of Additional Historic Properties Throughout the Nation, and for Other Purposes, Approved October 15, 1966 (Public Law 89-655; 80 STAT. 915; 16 U.S.C. 470)

Be it enacted by the Senate and House of Representatives of the United States of America in Congress assembled, That Congress finds and declares—

(a) That the spirit and direction of the Nation are founded upon and reflected in its historic past;

(b) That the historical and cultural foundations of the Nation should be preserved as a living part of our community life and development in order to give a sense of orientation to the American people;

(c) That, in the fact of ever-increasing extensions of urban centers, high-ways, and residential, commercial, and industrial developments, the present governmental and non-governmental historic preservation programs and activities are inadequate to insure future generations a genuine opportunity to appreciate and enjoy the rich heritage of our Nation; and

(d) That, although the major burdens of historic preservation have been borne and major efforts initiated by private agencies and individuals, and both should continue to play a vital role, it is nevertheless necessary and appropriate for the Federal Government to accelerate its historic preservation programs and activities, to give maximum encouragement to agencies and individuals undertaking preservation by private means, and to assist State and local governments and the National Trust for Historic Preservation in the United States to expand and accelerate their historic preservation programs and activities.

TITLE I

SECTION 101

(a) The Secretary of the Interior is authorized—

(1) to expand and maintain a national register of districts, sites, buildings, structures, and objects significant in American history, architecture, archeology, and culture, hereinafter referred to as the National Register, and to grant funds to States for the purpose of preparing comprehensive statewide historic surveys and plans, in accordance with criteria established by the Secretary, for the preservation, acquisition, and development of such properties;

(2) to establish a program of matching grants-in-aid to States for projects having as their purpose the preservation for public benefit of properties that are significant in American history, architecture, archeology, and culture; and

(3) to establish a program of matching grants-in-aid to the National Trust for Historic Preservation in the United States, chartered by act of Congress approved October 26, 1949 (63 Stat. 927), as amended, for the purpose of carrying out the responsibilities of the National Trust.

(b) As used in this Act—

(1) The term "State" includes, in addition to the several States of the Union, the District of Columbia, the Commonwealth of Puerto Rico, the Virgin Islands, Guam, and American Samoa.

(2) The term "project" means programs of State and local governments and other public bodies and private organizations and individuals for the acquisition of title or interests in, and for the development of, any district, site, building, structure, or object that is significant in American history, architecture, archeology, and culture, or property used in connection therewith, and for its development in order to assure the preservation for public benefit of any such historical properties.

(3) The term "historic preservation" includes the protection, rehabilitation, restoration, and reconstruction of districts, sites, buildings, structures, and objects significant in American history, architecture, archeology, or culture.

(4) The term "Secretary" means the Secretary of the Interior.

SECTION 102

(a) No grant may be made under this Act—

(1) unless application therefore is submitted to the Secretary in accordance with regulations and procedures prescribed by him;

(2) unless the application is in accordance with the comprehensive statewide historic preservation plan which has been approved by the Secretary after considering its relationship to the comprehensive statewide outdoor recreation plan prepared pursuant to the Land and Water Conservation Fund Act of 1965 (78 Stat. 897)

(3) for more than 50 per centum of the total cost involved, as determined by the Secretary and his determination shall be final;

(4) unless the grantee has agreed to make such reports, in such form and containing such information as the Secretary may from time to time require;

(5) unless the grantee has agreed to assume, after completion of the project, the total cost of the continued maintenance, repair, and administration of the property in a manner satisfactory to the Secretary; and

(6) until the grantee has complied with such further terms and conditions as the Secretary may deem necessary or advisable.

(b) The Secretary may in his discretion waive the requirements of subsection (a), paragraphs (2) and (5) of this section for any grant under this Act to the National Trust for Historic Preservation in the United States, in which case a grant to the National Trust may include funds for the maintenance, repair, and administration of the property in a manner satisfactory to the Secretary.

(c) No State shall be permitted to utilize the value of real property obtained before the date of approval of this Act in meeting the remaining cost of a project for which a grant is made under this Act.

SECTION 103

(a) The amounts appropriated and made available for grants to the State for comprehensive statewide historic surveys and plans under this Act shall be apportioned among the States by the Secretary on the basis of needs as determined by him: *Provided, however,* That the amount granted to any one State shall not exceed 50 per centum of the total cost of the comprehensive statewide historic survey and plan for that State as determined by the Secretary.

(b) The amounts appropriated and made available for grants to the States for projects under this Act for each fiscal year shall be apportioned among the States by the Secretary in accordance with needs as disclosed in approved statewide historic preservation plans.

The Secretary shall notify each State of its appointment, and the amounts thereof shall be available thereafter for payment to such State for projects in accordance with the provisions of this Act. Any amount of any apportionment that has not been paid or obligated by the Secretary during the fiscal year in which such notification is given, and for two fiscal years thereafter, shall be reapportioned by the Secretary in accordance with this subsection.

SECTION 104

(a) No grant may be made by the Secretary for or on account of any survey or project under this Act with respect to which financial assistance has been given or promised under any other Federal program or activity, and no financial assistance may be given under any other Federal program or activity for or on account of any survey or project with respect to which assistance has been given or promised under this Act.

(b) In order to assure consistency in policies and actions under this Act with other related Federal programs and activities, and to assure coordination of the planning, acquisition, and development assistance to States under this Act with other related Federal programs and activities, the President may issue such regulations with respect thereto as he deems desirable, and such assistance may be provided only in accordance with such regulations.

SECTION 105

The beneficiary of assistance under this Act shall keep such records as the Secretary shall prescribe, including records which fully disclose the disposition by the beneficiary of the proceeds of such assistance, the total cost of the project or undertaking in connection with which such assistance is given or used, and the amount and nature of that portion of the cost of the project or undertaking supplied by other sources, and such other records as will facilitate an effective audit.

SECTION 106

The head of any Federal Agency having direct or indirect jurisdiction over a proposed Federal or federally assisted undertaking in any State and the head of any Federal department or independent agency having authority to license any undertaking shall prior to the approval of the expenditure of any Federal funds on the undertaking or prior to the issuance of any license, as the case may be, take into account the effect of the undertaking on any district, site building structure, or object that is included in the National Register. The head of any such Federal agency shall afford the Advisory Council on Historic Preservation established under title II of this Act a reasonable opportunity to comment with regard to such undertaking.

SECTION 107

Nothing in this Act shall be construed to be applicable to the White House and its grounds, the Supreme Court building and its grounds, or the United States Capitol and its related buildings and grounds.

SECTION 108
There are authorized to be appropriated not to exceed $2,000,000 to carry
out the provisions of this Act for the fiscal year 1967, and not more than
$10,000,000 for each of the three succeeding fiscal years. Such appropriations
shall be available for the financial assistance authorized by this title and for
the administrative expenses of the Secretary in connection therewith, and shall
remain available until expended.

TITLE II

SECTION 201
(a) There is established an Advisory Council on Historic Preservation (hereinafter referred to as the "Council") which shall be composed of seventeen
members as follows:
  (1) The Secretary of the Interior.
  (2) The Secretary of Housing and Urban Development.
  (3) The Secretary of Commerce.
  (4) The Administrator of the General Services Administration.
  (5) The Secretary of the Treasury.
  (6) The Attorney General.
  (7) The Chairman of the National Trust for Historic Preservation.
  (8) Ten appointed by the President from outside the Federal Government.
In making these appointments, the President shall give due consideration
to the selection of officers of State and local governments and individuals who
are significantly interested and experienced in the matters to be considered by
the Council.
  (b) Each member of the Council specified in paragraphs (1) through (6)
of subsection (a) may designate another officer of his department or agency
to serve on the Council in his stead.
  (c) Each member of the Council appointed under paragraph (8) of
subsection (a) shall serve for a term of five years from the expiration of his
predecessor's term; except that the members first appointed under that paragraph shall serve for terms of from one to five years, as designated by the
President at the time of appointment, in such manner as to insure that the
terms of not less than one nor more than two of them will expire in any one
year.
  (d) A vacancy in the Council shall not affect its powers, but shall be filled
in the same manner as the original appointment (and for the balance of the
unexpired term).
  (e) The Chairman of the Council shall be designated by the President.
  (f) Eight members of the Council shall constitute a quorum.

SECTION 202
(a) The Council shall—
  (1) Advise the President and the Congress on matters relating to historic
preservation; recommend measures to coordinate activities of Federal, State,
and local agencies and private institutions and individuals relating to historic

preservation; and advise on the dissemination of information pertaining to such activities;

(2) encourage, in cooperation with the National Trust for Historic Preservation and appropriate private agencies, public interest and participation in historic preservation;

(3) recommend the conduct of studies in such areas as the adequacy of legislative and administrative statutes and regulations pertaining to historic preservation activities of State and local governments and the effects of tax policies at all levels of government on historic preservation;

(4) advise as to guidelines for the assistance of State and local governments in drafting legislation relating to historic preservation; and

(5) encourage, in cooperation with appropriate public and private agencies and institutions, training and education in the field of historic preservation.

(b) The council shall submit annually a comprehensive report of its activities and the results of its studies to the President and the Congress and shall from time to time submit such additional and special reports as it deems advisable. Each report shall propose such legislative enactments and other actions as, in the judgment of the Council, are necessary and appropriate to carry out its recommendations.

SECTION 203

The Council is authorized to secure directly from any department, bureau, agency, board, commission, office, independent establishment or instrumentality of the executive branch of the Federal Government information, suggestions, estimates and statistics for the purpose of this title; and each such department, bureau, agency, board, commission, office, independent establishment or instrumentality is authorized to furnish such information, suggestions, estimates, and statistics to the extent permitted by law and within available funds.

SECTION 204

The members of the Council specified in paragraphs (1) through (7) of section 201 (a) shall serve without additional compensation. The members of the Council appointed under paragraph (8) of section 201 (a) shall receive $100 per diem when engaged in the performances of the duties of the Council. All members of the Council shall receive reimbursement for necessary traveling and subsistence expenses incurred by them in the performance of the duties of the Council.

SECTION 205

(a) The Director of the National Park Service or his designee shall be the Executive Director of the Council. Financial and administrative services (including those related to budgeting, accounting, financial reporting, personnel and procurement) shall be provided the Council by the Department of the Interior, for which payments shall be made in advance, or by reimbursement, from funds of the Council in such amounts as may be agreed upon by the Chairman of the Council and the Secretary of the Interior: *Provided,* That the regulations of the Department of the Interior for the collection of indebtedness of personnel resulting from erroneous payments (5 U.S.C. 46e) shall apply to the collection of erroneous payments made to or on behalf of a Council employee, and regulations of said Secretary for the administrative control of funds (31 U.S.C. 665.(g)) shall apply to appropriations of the Council: *And provided further,* That the Council shall not be required to prescribe such regulations.

(b) The Council shall have power to appoint and fix the compensation of such additional personnel as may be necessary to carry out its duties, without regard to the provisions of the civil service laws and the Classification Act of 1949.

(c) The Council may also procure, without regard to the civil service laws and the Classification Act of 1949, temporary and intermittent services to the same extent as is authorized for the executive departments by section 15 of the Administrative Expenses Act of 1946 (5 U.S.C. 55a), but at rates not to exceed $50 per diem for individuals.

(d) The members of the Council specified in paragraphs (1) through (6) of section 210 (a) shall provide the Council, on a reimbursable basis, with such facilities and services under their jurisdiction and control as may be needed by the Council to carry out its duties, to the extent that such facilities and services are requested by the Council and are otherwise available for that purpose. To the extent of available appropriations, the Council may obtain, by purchase, rental, donation, or otherwise, such additional property, facilities, and services as may be needed to carry out its duties.

NATIONAL ENVIRONMENTAL POLICY ACT OF 1969

AN ACT To establish a National policy for the environment, to provide for the establishment of a Council on Environmental Quality, and for other purposes, Approved January 1, 1970 (Public Law 91-190; 91 STAT. 852; 42 U.S.C. 4321–4347)

Be it enacted by the Senate and House of Representatives of the United States of America in Congress assembled, That this Act may be cited as the "National Environmental Policy Act of 1969".

PURPOSE

SECTION 2. The purposes of this Act are: to declare a national policy which will encourage production and enjoyable harmony between man and his environment; to promote efforts which will prevent or eliminate damage to the environment and biosphere and stimulate the health and welfare of man; to enrich the understanding of the ecological systems and natural resources important to the Nation; and to establish a Council on Environmental Quality.

TITLE I

Declaration of National Environmental Policy

SECTION 101. (a) The Congress, recognizing the profound impact of man's activity on the interrelations of all components of the natural environment, particularly the profound influences of population growth, high-density urbanization, industrial expansion, resource exploitation, and new expanding technological advances and recognizing further the critical importance of restoring and maintaining environmental quality to the overall welfare and development of man, declares that it is the continuing policy of the Federal Government, in cooperation with State and local governments, and other concerned public and private organizations, to use all practicable means and measures, including financial and technical assistance, in a manner calculated to foster and promote the general welfare, to create and maintain conditions under which man and nature can exist in productive harmony, and fulfill the social, economic, and other requirements of present and future generations of Americans.

(b) In order to carry out the policy set forth in this Act, it is the continuing responsibility of the Federal Government to use all practicable means, consistent with other essential considerations of national policy, to improve and coordinate Federal plans, functions, programs, and resources to the end that the Nation may—

(1) fulfill the responsibilities of each generation as trustee of the environment for suceeding generations;

(2) assure for all Americans safe, healthful, productive, and esthetically and culturally pleasing surroundings;

(3) attain the widest range of beneficial uses of the environment without degradation, risk to health or safety, or other undesirable and unintended consequences;

(4) preserve important historic, cultural, and natural aspects of our national heritage, and maintain, wherever possible, an environment which supports diversity and variety of individual choice;

(5) achieve a balance between population and resource use which will permit high standards of living and a wide sharing of life's amenities; and

(6) enhance the quality of renewable resources and approach the maximum attainable recycling of depletable resources.

(c) The Congress recognizes that each person should enjoy a healthful environment and that each person has a responsibility to contribute to the preservation and enhancement of the environment.

SECTION 102. The Congress authorizes and directs that, to the fullest extent possible: (1) the policies, regulations, and public laws of the United States shall be interpreted and administered in accordance with the policies set forth in this Act, and (2) all agencies of the Federal Government shall—

(A) utilize a systematic, interdisciplinary approach which will insure the integrated use of the natural and social sciences and the environmental design arts in planning and in decisionmaking which may have an impact on man's environment;

(B) identify and develop methods and procedures, in consultations with the Council on Environmental Quality established by title II of this Act, which will insure that presently unquantified environmental amenities and values may be given appropriate consideration in decisionmaking along with economic and technical considerations;

(C) include in every recommendation or report on proposals for legislation and other major Federal actions significantly affecting the quality of the human environment, a detailed statement by the responsible official on—

(i) the environmental impact of the proposed action,

(ii) any adverse environmental effects which cannot be avoided should the proposal be implemented,

(iii) alternatives to the proposed action,

(iv) the relationship between local short-term uses of man's environment and the maintenance and enhancement of long-term productivity and

(v) any irreversible and irretrievable commitments of resources which would be involved in the proposed action should it be implemented. Prior to making any detailed statement, the responsible Federal official shall consult with and obtain the comments of any Federal agency which has jurisdiction by law or special expertise with respect to any environmental impact involved. Copies of such statement and the comments and views of the appropriate Federal, State, and local agencies, which are authorized to develop and enforce environmental standards, shall be made available to the President, the Council on Environmental Quality and to the public as provided by section 552 of title 5, United States Code, and shall accompany the proposal through the existing agency review processes;

(D) study, develop, and describe appropriate alternatives to recommend courses of action in any proposal which involves unresolved conflicts concerning alternative uses of available resources;

(E) recognize the worldwide and long-range character of environmental problems and, where consistent with the foreign policy of the United States, lend appropriate support to initiatives, resolutions, and programs designed to maximize international cooperation in anticipating and preventing a decline in the quality of mankind's world environment;

(F) make available to States, counties, municipalities, institutions, and individuals, advice and information useful in restoring, maintaining, and enhancing the quality of the environment;

(G) initiate and utilize ecological information in the planning and development of resource-oriented projects; and

(H) assist the Council on Environmental Quality established by title II of this Act.

SECTION 103. All agencies of the Federal Government shall review their present statutory authority, administrative regulations, and current policies and procedures for the purpose of determining whether there are any deficiencies or inconsistencies therein which prohibit full compliance with the purposes and provisions of this Act and shall propose to the President not later than July 1, 1971, such measures as may be necessary to bring their authority and policies into conformity with the intent, purposes, and procedures set forth in this Act.

SECTION 104. Nothing in Section 102 or 103 shall in any way affect the specific statutory obligations of any Federal agency (1) to comply with criteria or standards of environmental quality, (2) to coordinate or consult with any other Federal or State agency, or (3) to act, or refrain from acting contingent upon the recommendations or certification of any other Federal or State agency.

SECTION 105. The policies and goals set forth in this Act are supplementary to those set forth in existing authorization of Federal agencies.

TITLE II

Council On Environmental Quality

SECTION 201. The President shall transmit to the Congress annually beginning July 1, 1970, an Environmental Quality Report (hereinafter referred to as the "report") which shall set forth (1) the status and condition of the major natural, manmade, or altered environmental classes of the Nation, including, but not limited to, the air, the aquatic, including marine, estuarine, and fresh water, and the terrestrial environment, including, but not limited to, the forest, dryland, wetland, range, urban, suburban, and rural environment;

(2) current and foreseeable trends in the quality, management and utilization of such environments and the effects of those trends on the social, economic, and other requirements of the Nation; (3) the adequacy of available natural resources for fulfilling human and economic requirements of the Nation in the light of expected population pressures; (4) a review of the programs and activities (including regulatory activities) of the Federal Government, the State and local governments, and nongovernmental entities or individuals, with particular reference to their effect on the environment and on the conservation, development and utilization of natural resources; and (5) a program for remedying the deficiencies of existing programs and activities, together with recommendations for legislation.

SECTION 202. There is created in the Executive Office of the President a Council on Environmental Quality (hereinafter referred to as the "Council"). The Council shall be composed of three members who shall be appointed by the President to serve at his pleasure, by and with the advice and consent of the Senate. The President shall designate one of the members of the Council to serve as Chairman. Each member shall be a person who, as a result of his training, experience, and attainments, is exceptionally well qualified to analyze and interpret environmental trends and information of all kinds; to appraise programs and activities of the Federal Government in the light of the policy set forth in title I of this Act; to be conscious of and responsive to the scientific, economic, social, esthetic, and cultural needs and interests of the Nation; and to formulate and recommend national policies to promote the improvement of the quality of the environment.

SECTION 203. The Council may employ such officers and employees as may be necessary for the carrying out of its functions under this Act, in accordance may employ and fix the compensation of such experts and consultants as may be necessary for the carrying out of its functions under this Act, in accordance with section 3109 of title 5, United States Code (but without regard to the last sentence thereof).

SECTION 204. It shall be the duty and function of the Council—
(1) to assist and advise the President in the preparation of the Environmental Quality Report required by section 201;
(2) to gather timely and authoritative information concerning the conditions and trends in the quality of the environment both current and prospective, to analyze and interpret such information for the purpose of determining whether such conditions and trends are interfering, or are likely to interfere, with the achievement of the policy set forth in title I of this Act, and to compile and submit to the President studies relating to such conditions and trends;
(3) to review and appraise the various programs and activities of the Federal Government in the light of the policy set forth in title I of this Act for the purpose of determining the extent to which such programs and activities are contributing to the achievement of such policy, and to make recommendations to the President with respect thereto;
(4) to develop and recommend to the President national policies to foster and promote the improvement of environmental quality to meet the conservation, social, economic, health, and other requirements and goals of the Nation;
(5) to conduct investigations, studies, surveys, research, and analysis relating to ecological systems and environmental quality;
(6) to document and define changes in the natural environment, including the plant and animal systems, and to accumulate necessary data and other information for a continuing analysis of these changes or trends and an interpretation of their underlying causes;
(7) to report at least once each year to the President on the state and condition of the environment; and
(8) to make and furnish such studies, reports thereon, and recommendations with respect to matters of policy and legislation as the President may request.

SECTION 205. In exercising its powers, functions, and duties under this Act, the Council shall
(1) consult with the Citizens' Advisory Committee on Environmental Quality established by Executive Order numbered 11472, dated May 29, 1969, and with such representatives of science, industry, agriculture, labor, conservation organizations, State and local governments and other groups, as it deems advisable; and
(2) utilize, to the fullest extent possible, the services, facilities, and information (including statistical information) of public and private agencies and organizations, and individuals, in order that duplication of effort and expense may be avoided, thus assuring that the Council's activities will not unnecessarily overlap or conflict with similar activities authorized by law and performed by established agencies.

SECTION 206. Members of the Council shall serve full time and the Chairman of the Council shall be compensated at the rate provided for Level II of the Executive Schedule Pay Rates (5 U.S.C. 5313). The other members of the Council shall be compensated at the rate provided for Level IV of the Executive Schedule Pay Rates (5 U.S.C. 5315).

SECTION 207. There are authorized to be appropriated to carry out the provisions of this Act not to exceed $300,000 for fiscal year 1970, $700,000 for fiscal 1971, and $1,000,000 for each fiscal year thereafter.

AMENDMENT TO THE
RESERVOIR SALVAGE ACT OF 1960
(1974)

Be it enacted by the Senate and House of Representatives of the United States of America in Congress assembled, "That it is the purpose of this Act to further the policy set forth in the Act entitled 'An Act to provide for the preservation of historic American sites, buildings, objects, and antiquities of national significance, and for other purposes,' approved August 21, 1935 (16 U.S.C. 461-467), and the Act entitled 'An Act to establish a program for the preservation of additional historic properties throughout the Nation, and for other purposes,' approved October 15, 1966 (80 Stat. 915), by specifically providing for the preservation of scientific, prehistorical, historical, and archaeological data (including relics and specimens) which might otherwise be irreparably lost or destroyed as the result of (1) flooding, the building of access roads, the erection of workmen's communities, the relocation of railroads and highways, and other alterations of the terrain caused by the construction of a dam by any agency of the United States, or by any private person or corporation holding a license issued by any such agency; or (2) any alteration of the terrain caused as a result of any Federal, federally assisted, or federally licensed activity or program.

SECTION 2. Before any agency of the United States shall undertake the construction of a dam or issue a license to any private individual or corporation for the construction of a dam it shall give written notice to the Secretary of the Interior (hereinafter referred to as the 'secretary') setting forth the site of the proposed dam and the approximate area to be flooded and otherwise changed if such construction is undertaken: *Provided,* That with respect to any floodwater retarding dam which provides less than five thousand acre-feet of detention capacity and with respect to any other type of dam which creates a reservoir of less than forty surface acres the provision of this section shall apply only when the construction agency, in its preliminary surveys, finds, or is presented with evidence that scientific, prehistorical, historical, or archeological data exist or may be present in the proposed reservoir area.

SECTION 3. (a) When any Federal agency finds, or is made aware by an appropriate historical or archeological authority, that its operation in connection with any Federal, federally assisted, or federally licensed project, activity, or program adversely affects or may adversely affect significant scientific, prehistorical, historical, or archeological data, such agency shall notify the Secretary, in writing, and shall provide the Secretary with appropriate information concerning the project, program, or activity. Such agency (1) may request the Secretary to undertake the recovery, protection, and preservation of such data (including preliminary survey, or other investigation as needed, and analysis and publication of the reports resulting from such investigation), or (2) may, with funds appropriated for such project, program, or activity, undertake the activities referred to in clause (1). Copies of reports of any investigations made pursuant to clause (2) shall be made available to the Secretary.

(b) The Secretary, upon notification by any such agency or by any other Federal or State agency or appropriate historical or archeological authority that scientific prehistorical, historical, or archeological data is or may be adversely affected by any Federal, federally assisted, or federally licensed project, activity, or program, shall, if he determines that such data is being or may be adversely affected, and after reasonable notice, to the agency responsible for such project, activity, or program, conduct or cause to be conducted a survey and other investigation of the areas which are or may be affected and recover and preserve such data (including analysis and publication) which, in his opinion are not being but should be recovered and preserved in the public interest. The Secretary shall initiate action within sixty days of notification to him by an agency pursuant to subsection (a), and within such time as may be agreed upon with the head of the responsible agency in all other cases. The responsible agency upon request of the Secretary is hereby authorized to assist the Secretary and to transfer to the Secretary such funds as may be necessary, in an amount not to exceed one per centum of the total amount appropriated for such project, activity, or program, to enable the Secretary to conduct such survey or other investigation and recover and preserve such data (including analysis and publication) or, in the case of small projects which cause extensive scientific, prehistorical, historical, or archeological damage, such larger amount as may be mutually agreed upon by the Secretary and the responsible Federal agency as being necessary to effect adequate protection and recovery; *Provided*, That the costs of such survey, recovery, analysis and publication shall be considered project costs allocated to the several project purposes. An appropriate share, as determined by the responsible Federal agency, of the costs of survey, analysis, and publication shall be borne by the grantee in the case of projects, activities, or programs funded under Federal grant-in-aid programs.

(c) The Secretary shall keep the responsible agency notified at all times of the progress of any survey or other investigation made under this Act, or of any work undertaken as a result of such survey, in order that there will be as little disruption or delay as possible in the carrying out of the functions of such agency.

(d) A survey or other investigation similar to that provided for by subsection (b) of this section and the work required to be performed as a result thereof shall so far as practicable also be undertaken in connection with any dam, project, activity, or program which has been heretofore authorized by any agency of the United States, by any private person or corporation holding a license issued by any such agency, or by Federal law.

(e) The Secretary shall consult with any interested Federal and State agencies, educational and scientific organizations, and private institutions and qualified individuals, with a view to determining the ownership of and the most appropriate repository for any relics and specimens recovered as a result of any work performed as provided for in this section.

SECTION 4. In the administration of this Act, the Secretary may—

(1) accept and utilize funds transferred to him by any Federal agency pursuant to this Act;

(2) enter into contracts or make cooperative agreements with any Federal or State agency, any educational or scientific organization, or any institution, corporation, association, or qualified individual;

(3) obtain the services of experts and consultants or organizations thereof in accordance with section 3109 of title 5, United States Code; and

(4) accept and utilize funds made available for salvage archeological purposes by any private person or corporation.

SECTION 5. There are hereby authorized to be appropriated such sums as may be necessary to carry out the purposes of this Act.

Bibliography
and References

Aitken, M. 1974. *Physics and Archaeology*. New York: Interscience Publications.

Alexander, J. 1970. *The Directing of Archaeological Excavations*. London: John Baker.

Ascher, R. "Teaching Archaeology in the University," *Archaeology*, October, 1968.

Atkinson, R. 1953. *Field Archaeology*. London: Methuen.

Baldwin, G. 1962. *America's Buried Past: The Story of North American Archaeology*. New York: Putnam's.

Barnouw, V. 1963. *Culture and Personality*. Homewood, Ill.: Dorsey Press.

Bascom, W. 1976. *Deep Water, Ancient Ships*. New York: Doubleday.

Bass, G. "Trials of an Underwater Archaeologist," *Science Digest*, March, 1973.

Benfer, R. "A Design for the Study of Archaeological Characteristics," *American Anthropology*, December, 1967.

*Bibby, G. 1956. *The Testimony of the Spade*. New York: New American Library.

Bick, L. 1963. *Archaeology and the Microscope: The Scientific Examination of Archaeological Evidence*. New York: Praeger.

Binford, L. 1972. *An Archaeological Perspective*. New York: Seminar Press.

———. "Archaeological Systematics and the Study of Culture Process," *American Antiquity*, October, 1965.

Boas, F. 1928. *Anthropology in Modern Life*. New York: W.W. Norton.

*———. 1970. *General Anthropology*. New York: Johnson Reprint Corporation.

Boland, C. 1961. *They All Discovered America*. New York: Doubleday.

Braidwood, R. 1960. *Archaeologists and What They Do*. New York: Franklin Watts.

Bredemeier, H. 1962. *The Analysis of Social Systems*. New York: Holt, Rinehart, and Winston.

*Breed, C. 1957. *Surveying*. New York: John Wiley.

Brennan, L. 1970. *American Dawn*. New York: Macmillan.

Brew, J. (Ed.). 1968. *100 Years of Anthropology*. Cambridge: Harvard University Press.

* Recommended for amateurs.

Brew, O. "Emergency Archaeology," *Proceedings* of the American Philosophical Society, February, 1961.

Brill, R. 1971. *Science and Archaeology*. Cambridge: Massachusetts Institute of Technology.

Brinton, C. *et al.* 1967. *A History of Civilization*. Englewood Cliffs: Prentice-Hall.

Brodick, A. 1964. *Man and His Ancestry*. New York: Fawcett.

Browne, D. 1975. *Principles and Practice in Modern Archaeology*. London: Hodder & Stoughton.

Burckhardt, J. 1958. *Judgements on History and Historians*. Boston: Beacon Press.

Campbell, B. 1966. *Human Evolution*. Chicago: Aldine.

Cantril, H. 1965. *The Pattern of Human Concerns*. New Brunswick, N.J.: Rutgers University Press.

*Ceram, C. 1972. *Gods, Graves, and Scholars*. New York: Bantam.

*————. 1971. *The First American*. New York: New American Library.

Childe, V. 1956. *Piecing Together the Past*. London: Routledge.

————. 1946. *What Happened in History*. New York: Penguin.

Christensen, R. "Did the Phoenicians Cross the Atlantic?" Society for Early Historic Archaeology, Brigham Young University, Provo, Utah, January, 1970.

Clark, D. 1968. *Analytical Archaeology*. London: Methuen.

Clark, J. 1960. *Archaeology and Society: Reconstructing the Prehistoric Past*. London: Methuen.

Clewlow, C. *et al.* "A Crisis in Archaeology," *American Antiquity*, 36, 1971.

Colligan, D. "Brawl Over a 2000-Year-Old Archaeological Site," *Science Digest*, January, 1973.

Coon, C. 1965. *The Story of Man*. New York: Knopf.

Cornwall, I. 1964. *The World of Ancient Man*. New York: John Day.

Cotter, J. 1958. *Archaeological Excavations at Jamestown Virginia*. Washington, D.C.: National Park Service.

Cuneo, E. 1963. *Science and History*. New York: Duell, Sloan and Pearce.

Daniel, G. 1968. *The Origins and Growth of Archaeology*. New York: T.Y. Crowell.

————. Editorial, *Antiquity*, March, 1972.

Darwin, C. 1960. *Origin of Species by Means of Natural Selection*. New York: Doubleday.

Da Silva, M. "The Meaning of the Dighton Rock," NEARA *Newsletter*, June, 1967.

————. 1971. *Portuguese Pilgrims and Dighton Rock*. Bristol, R.I.

Deetz, J. "Archaeology as a Social Science," *Current Directions in Anthropology*, September, 1970.

————. 1967. *Invitation to Archaeology*. Garden City, New York: Natural History Press.

Dekin, A. "Forever Lost? Some Practical Responses to the Present Emergency in Archaeology," *Man in the Northeast*, Fall, 1972.

Deuel, G. 1967. *The Story of Aerial Archaeology*. New York: St. Martin's Press.

*Dimbley, G. 1970. *Plants and Archaeology*. London: John Baker.

* Recommended for amateurs.

Dix, B. "An Early Calendar Site in Central Vermont," NEARA *Journal*, Spring, 1976.

Driver, H. 1961. *Indians of North America*. Chicago: University of Chicago Press.

Ehrich, R. (Ed.). 1954. *Relative Chronologies in Old World Archaeology*. Chicago: University of Chicago Press.

Fagan, B. "The Ancient Art of Tomb Robbing," *Science Digest*, May, 1975.

Feldman, M. "Ancient Inscriptions Found at Mystery Hill," *Granite State Vacationer*, November 28, 1975.

————. "Anthropology and History," *Journal* of the Social Research Institute, Fall, 1974.

————. "Archaeological Research Goes On," *Salem* (N.H.) *Observer*, April 21, 1976.

————. "Evidence of Ancient Man in America," *Beyond Reality*, May, 1975.

————. "Evidence of Ancient Man in New Hampshire," *New Hampshire Reader*, November, 1974.

————. "Mystery Hill May Be More Than 3,000 Years Old," *New Hampshire Sunday News*, September 7, 1975.

————. 1976. *The Mystery Hill Story*. North Salem, N.H.: Mystery Hill Press.

————. "Redefining Cultural Anthropology," *Journal* of the Social Research Institute, Spring, 1974.

————. "Towards a Public Archaeology," NEARA *Journal*, Winter, 1976.

Fell, H. "Celtic Iberian Inscriptions of New England," *Occasional Publications* of the Epigraphic Society, August, 1975.

*Flint, R. 1957. *Glacial and Pleistocene Geology*. New York: John Wiley.

Ford, B. "Archaeological Looters Even Murder for Pre-Columbian Treasures," *Science Digest*, December, 1972.

Ford, J. 1962. *A Quantitative Method for Deriving Cultural Chronology*. Washington: Pan American Union.

Ford, J. et al. 1972. *Site Destruction Due to Agricultural Practices in Southeast and Northern Arkansas*. Fayetteville: Arkansas Archaeological Survey.

Friendly, J. "High Schools Giving Lower Priority to Teaching U.S. History," *New York Times*, May 3, 1976.

Gardou, C. 1971: *Before Columbus*. New York: Crown.

Giddings, J. 1967. *Ancient Man of the Arctic*. New York: Knopf.

Gladwin, H., E. Haury, E. Sayles, and N. Gladwin. 1965. *Excavations at Snaketown: Material Culture*. Tucson: University of Arizona Press.

Gombrich, E. 1966. *The Story of Art*. London: Phaidon.

Goodwin, W. 1946. *The Ruins of Great Ireland in New England*. Boston: Meador.

Gorenstein, S. 1965. *Introduction to Archaeology*. New York: Basic Books.

Gould, R. "Chipping Stones in the Outback," *Natural History*, February, 1968.

Gwynne, P. et al. "The Oldest Man," *Newsweek*, March 22, 1976.

Hamblin, D. 1970. *Pots and Robbers*. New York: Simon and Schuster.

Harris, M. 1968. *The Rise of Anthropological Theory: A History of Theories of Cultures*. New York: T.Y. Crowell.

* Recommended for amateurs.

Haviland, W. and L. Basa. "Anthropology and the Academy," *Man in the Northeast*, Fall, 1974.

Hawkins, G. 1965. *Stonehenge Decoded*. New York: Doubleday.

Haynes, C. "Elephant Hunting in North America," *Scientific American*, June 1966.

*Heizer, R. (Ed.). 1958. *A Guide to Archaeological Field Methods*. Millbrae, Calif.: National Press.

Henry, J. 1963. *Culture Against Man*. New York: Random House.

Hibben, F. 1960. *Digging Up America*. New York: Hill and Wang.

Hill, E. "The North Salem Mystery," *Saturday Evening Post*, August, 1959.

Hopkins, D. (Ed.). 1967. *The Bering Land Bridge*. Stanford: Stanford University Press.

Hough, J. 1958, *Geology of the Great Lakes*. Urbana: University of Illinois Press.

*Hume, I. 1969. *Historical Archaeology*. New York: Knopf.

Ingersoll, D. "Problems of Urban Historical Archaeology," *Man in the Northeast*, November, 1971.

Irwin, C. and H., and G. Agogino. "Ice Age Man vs. Mammoth in Wyoming," *National Geographic*, June, 1962.

Jaeger, G. and P. Selznick. "A Normative Theory of Culture," *American Sociological Review*, 29, 1964.

Jennings, J. and E. Norbeck (Eds.). 1964. *Prehistoric Man in the New World*. Chicago: University of Chicago Press.

Jensen, E. and H. Ellis. "Pipelines," *Scientific American*, January, 1967.

Johnson, F. "Archaeology in an Emergency," *Science*, June 17, 1966.

Jones, E. " 'Dig-It-Yourself' Archaeologists," *The New York Times Magazine*, February 16, 1958.

Juleus, N. "What's an American Indian Language Doing in Africa?" *Science Digest*, December, 1973.

King, T. "The Last Days of Zuma Creek," *Popular Archaeology*, March, 1973.

Knight, H. (Ed.). 1938. *Soils and Men*. Washington: U.S. Department of Agriculture.

Kroeber, A. 1948. *Anthropology*. New York: Harcourt Brace Jovanovich.

Kroeber, A. and C. Kluckhohn. "Culture: A Critical Review of Concepts and Definitions," *Papers* of the Peabody Museum of American Archaeology and Ethnology, 47, 1952. Cambridge: Harvard University.

Kyselka, W. and R. Lanterman. 1976. *North Star to Southern Cross*. Honolulu: University Press of Hawaii.

Lanning, E. and T. Patterson. "Early Man in South America," *Scientific American*, November, 1967.

Leakey, L. "Finding the World's Earliest Man," *National Geographic*, September, 1960.

Levi-Strauss, C. 1967. *Structural Anthropology*. New York: Doubleday.

*Libby, W. 1952. *Radiocarbon Dating*. Chicago: University of Chicago Press.

Linton, R. 1955. *The Tree of Culture*. New York: Knopf.

Lorimer, F. 1929. *The Growth of Reason*. New York: Harcourt Brace.

Malin, E. and N. Feder. 1962. *Indian Art of the Northwest Coast*. Denver: Denver Art Museum.

* Recommended for amateurs.

Marx, R. "America's 12,000 Year Old Man," *Argosy*, March, 1974.

———. "Sunken Treasures of Lebanon," *Argosy*, June, 1973.

Mason, R. "The Paleo-Indian in the Eastern United States," *Current Anthropology*, Volume 3, 1962.

Mathis, M. "Amateur Archaeologists Praised," *Christian Science Monitor*, April 3, 1970.

McGimsey, C. 1972. *Public Archaeology*. New York: Seminar Press.

Mead, M. and R. Bunzel (Eds.). 1960. *The Golden Age of American Archaeology*. New York: G. Braziller.

Mead, R. (Gen. Ed.). 1975. *Europe Reborn*. New York: New American Library.

Meredith, G. "The Museum Professional," *Popular Archaeology*, July, 1973.

*Moore, R. 1953. *Man, Time and Fossils*. New York: Knopf.

Muller, H. 1954. *The Uses of the Past*. New York: New American Library.

Müller-Beck, H. "Paleohunters in America: Origin and Diffusion," *Science*, May 27, 1966.

*Oakley, K. 1964. *Man the Tool-Maker*. Chicago: University of Chicago Press.

O'Neil, T. "Archaeological Looting and Site Destruction," *Science*, 176, 1972.

ÓRíordáin, S. and G. Daniel. 1964. *New Grange*. New York: Praeger.

Oxenstierna, E. "The Vikings," *Scientific American*, May, 1967.

Padover, S. 1943. *The Complete Jefferson*. New York: Books for Libraries.

Perino, G. "Surface Hunting," *Popular Archaeology*, May, 1973.

Plenderleith, H. 1956. *The Conservation of Antiquities and Works of Art: Treatment, Repair and Restoration*. London: Oxford University Press.

Quam, A. (Trans.). 1972. *The Zunis: Self-Portrayals*. New York: New American Library.

Riley, C. *et al.* (Eds.). 1971. *Man Across the Sea*. Austin: University of Texas Press.

Rothovius, A. "The Celt-Iberian Culture of New England," *NEARA Journal*, Summer, 1975.

Rubin, H. "History Is a Many-Layered Cake," *Science Digest*, May, 1974.

Ruppe, R. "The Archaeological Survey: A Defense," *American Antiquity*, January, 1966.

Sargent, H. Editorial, *Man in the Northeast*, Fall, 1972.

Scholte, B. "Some Problems in Cross-Cultural Research on Social Anthropological History and Theory," *American Anthropologist*, October, 1969.

Schulz, W. "The Great Research Boondoggle," *Reader's Digest*, March, 1967.

Silverberg, R. 1967. *Men against Time*. New York: Macmillan.

———. 1963. *Sunken History: The Story of Underwater Archaeology*. Philadelphia: Chilton.

Stallings, W. 1960. *Dating Prehistoric Ruins by Tree Rings*. Tucson: University of Arizona Press.

Stone, R. and A. Rothovius. "Searching for Answers, Not Opinions," *Man in the Northeast*, Spring, 1973.

Suess, H. "U.S. Geological Survey Radiocarbon Dates I," *Science*, 120, 1954.

Thomas, W. and A. Pikelis (Eds.). 1953. *International Directory of Anthropological Institutions*. Wenner-Gren Foundation for Anthropological Research, Inc.

* Recommended for amateurs.

Totten, N. "The First European Colonists in New England," *Occasional Publications* of the Epigraphic Society, August, 1975.

Toynbee, A. 1957. *A Study of History.* New York: Oxford University Press.

Waldron, R. Letter to R. E. Stone, President, New England Antiquities Research Association, March 13, 1972.

————. Letter to G. Daniel, Editor, *Antiquity,* March 13, 1972.

Wedel, W. 1961. *Prehistoric Man on the Great Plains.* Norman: University of Oklahoma Press.

Wendorf, F. 1962. *A Guide for Salvage Archaeology.* Santa Fe: Museum of New Mexico Press.

Wheeler, R. 1956. *Archaeology from the Earth.* Baltimore: Pelican.

Willey, G. and P. Phillips. 1958. *Method and Theory in American Archaeology.* Chicago: University of Chicago Press.

Wormington, H. 1957. *Ancient Man in North America.* Denver: Denver Museum of Natural History.

Wyckoff, D. "No Stones Unturned," *Popular Archaeology,* August, 1973.

Young, G. 1970. *Miguel Corte-Real and the Dighton Writing Rock.* Taunton, Mass.: Old Colony Historical Society.

Zeuner, F. 1950. *Dating the Past.* London: Methuen.

Unsigned articles:

"Emperor in the Dust," *Time,* August 18, 1975.

"Stone Age Discovery in U.K." *The Globe and Mail,* Toronto, September 10, 1975.

"Connecticut Site Yields 5000 Artifacts," *Boston Sunday Globe,* September 21, 1975.

"Rocks May Be Ancient Anchors," *Lawrence Eagle-Tribune,* January 15, 1976.

"Archaeologists Delve into Historic Past," *The Nashville* (N.C.) *Graphic,* January 29, 1976.

"Early Human Clues Hunted in Maine," *Boston Globe,* February 12, 1976.

"Turning the Clock Back," *Time,* May 31, 1976.

* Recommended for amateurs.

Index

A

absolute dating, 298-300
Académie des Sciences (France), 62
Acorn Gatherers, 259
additive artifacts, 283
aerial photography, 78, 269, 272
agriculture, 15, 30, 250
agronomy, 30
Alaska, 254
Albuquerque Archaeological Society, 177
Aleutian Islands, 254
Aleuts, 254
Algonquian, 261
alignments (*see* astronomical alignments)
amateur archaeology
    contributions of, 82-86, 88
    definition of, 26-28, 102-104
    and excavating, 274, 279, 286, 302
    and field experience, 246
    first amateur, 112
    history of, 65, 72
    importance of, 91-92, 98-100, 135
    laws for, 138-146
    in North America, 35-36
    opportunities for, 163-216
    organization for (NEARA), 126-134

in professional community, 73, 80, 90
    salvage archaeology and, 213-216
    as a tradition, 55, 58
American Anthropological Association, 77, 164, 302
American Antiquity magazine, 98, 303
American Association of Museums, 197
American History Knowledge and Attitude Survey, 104
American Institute of Nautical Archaeology, 79
Amerindian, 36, 82, 126, 251-264
Anasazi Culture, 253
Andean Indians, 260
Andes, 260
animals, 7, 15
antehistory, 12
Anthropological Institute of England, 70
anthropological patterns, 252-253
anthropology, 11, 15, 21, 24, 86, 126, 223, 248
antiquarians, 55-58, 64, 71, 72
antiquities laws, 99, 101, 107, 138-160
Antiquity magazine, 128, 129
Antiquity of Man (Lyell), 53
Apaches, 257, 261
Arapaho, 261
archaeoastronomy, 79-80, 130